Transnational Crime

This volume offers a diverse set of perspectives on transnational crime. Providing a wide-ranging overview of the legal and policy issues that arise in connection with various forms of transnational crime, the authors outline the criminal justice responses adopted across different jurisdictions. Including contributions from high profile Chinese and European academics and practitioners across a variety of disciplines and methodological backgrounds, the authors address some of the hitherto underexplored issues related to transnational crime. These range from trafficking in cultural objects derived from illicit metal-detecting and metal-detecting tourism in China to the European approaches to criminalising the denial of historical truth. The central theme of the book is that useful lessons can be drawn from each other's experiences, and that a cross-fertilisation of domestic approaches to transnational crime is essential to effective cooperation.

This book will be of use to students and academics of comparative criminal justice and anyone interested in transnational crime.

Valsamis Mitsilegas is Professor of European Criminal Law, head of the Department of Law and co-director of the Criminal Justice Centre at Queen Mary University of London.

Saskia Hufnagel is a senior lecturer in Criminal Law and co-director of the Criminal Justice Centre at Queen Mary University of London.

Anton Moiseienko is a research analyst at the Centre for Financial Crime & Security Studies of the Royal United Services Institute, UK.

Shi Yanan is a professor at the Law School of the Renmin University of China.

Liu Mingxiang is a professor at the Research Centre for Criminal Justice of the Renmin University of China.

The Queen Mary-Renmin Series on Comparative Criminal Justice Issues

Series Editors:
Valsamis Mitsilegas, *Queen Mary University of London, UK*
Saskia Hufnagel, *Queen Mary University of London, UK*
Shi Yanan, *Renmin University, China*
Liu Mingxiang, *Renmin University, China*

This series presents the results of the annual Queen Mary-Renmin Criminal Justice Conferences arising from the partnership between the Criminal Justice Centres of Queen Mary University of London (QMUL), School of Law and Renmin University of China, School of Law.

The series gathers together the different views from two systems on one common legal topic to inform in a comparative way the theory and practice in both systems. Academics and practitioners from a variety of disciplines and institutions come together to develop a practice-focused, cross-cultural dialogue on a variety of different criminal justice related topics.

Titles in the series:

Transnational Crime
European and Chinese Perspectives
Edited by Valsamis Mitsilegas, Saskia Hufnagel, Anton Moiseienko, Shi Yanan and Liu Mingxiang

For more information about this series, please visit: www.routledge.com/The-Queen-Mary-Renmin-Series-on-Comparative-Criminal-Justice-Issues-in-China-and-Europe/book-series/ASHSER1445

Transnational Crime

European and Chinese Perspectives

Edited by Valsamis Mitsilegas, Saskia Hufnagel, Anton Moiseienko, Shi Yanan and Liu Mingxiang

Routledge
Taylor & Francis Group
LONDON AND NEW YORK

First published 2019
by Routledge
2 Park Square, Milton Park, Abingdon, Oxon OX14 4RN

and by Routledge
52 Vanderbilt Avenue, New York, NY 10017, USA

First issued in paperback 2020

Routledge is an imprint of the Taylor & Francis Group, an informa business

British Library Cataloguing-in-Publication Data
A catalogue record for this book is available from the British Library

Library of Congress Cataloging-in-Publication Data
Names: Mitsilegas, Valsamis, editor. | Hufnagel, Saskia, editor. | Moiseienko, Anton, editor.
Title: Transnational crime : European and Chinese perspectives / edited by Valsamis Mitsilegas, Saskia Hufnagel and Anton Moiseienko.
Description: Abingdon, Oxon ; New York, NY : Routledge, 2019. | Series: The Queen Mary-Remin series on comparative criminal justice issues | Includes index. | "This edited collection inaugurates a book series on European and Chinese approaches to criminal justice, which was launched in partnership by the Criminal Justice Centres of Queen Mary University of London (QMUL) and the School of Law of Renmin University of China. It draws together papers from a number of conferences jointly conducted..."
Identifiers: LCCN 2018022016| ISBN 9781138494015 (hbk) | ISBN 9781351026826 (ebk)
Subjects: LCSH: Transnational crime--Law and legislation--Congresses. | Transnational crime--Congresses. | Criminal law--China--Congresses. | Criminal law--Europe--Congresses. | Crime--China--Congresses. | Crime--Europe--Congresses.
Classification: LCC K5014.8 .T734 2019 | DDC 345.4/02--dc23
LC record available at https://lccn.loc.gov/2018022016

ISBN 13: 978-0-367-58565-5 (pbk)
ISBN 13: 978-1-138-49401-5 (hbk)

Typeset in Galliard
by Swales & Willis Ltd, Exeter, UK

Contents

Contributors

Dr **Emmanouil Billis**, LLM, is a senior researcher at the Max Planck Institute for Foreign and International Criminal Law in Freiburg (Germany) and a lawyer in Athens (Greece).

Simon Bronitt is a Professor of Law in TC Beirne School of Law, The University of Queensland, where he serves as Deputy Head of School and Deputy Dean Research. Before joining UQ he was the director of the Australian Research Council Centre of Excellence in Policing and Security (2009–2014). Before moving to Queensland in 2009, he was a member of the Law School at The Australian National University (1991–2009). His research primarily focuses on criminal law and policing issues, having published widely on comparative criminal justice, with a growing interest in transnational forms of corporate crime. His key publications include two leading textbooks, *Principles of Criminal Law* (4th edn, Thomson Reuters, 2017) and *Law in Context* (4th edn, Federation Press, 2012).

Cheng Lei is an associate professor at the Law School of the Renmin University of China.

Petter Gottschalk is a professor in the Department of Leadership and Organizational Behavior at BI Norwegian Business School, Oslo, Norway. Dr Gottschalk has published extensively on knowledge management, fraud investigations, white-collar crime and criminal organisations.

Samuel Hardy is an honorary research associate at the Institute of Archaeology, University College London, and an adjunct professor at the American University of Rome. He blogs at https://conflictantiquities.wordpress.com/.

Saskia Hufnagel is a senior lecturer in Criminal Law and co-director of the Criminal Justice Centre at Queen Mary University of London.

Dr **Jade Lindley** is a criminologist at the University of Western Australia Law School and UWA Oceans Institute. Her research focuses on the intersection of transnational crimes, international law and regulation. She is particularly interested in marine-based crimes such as maritime piracy and illegal fishing.

Liu Mingxiang is a professor at the Research Centre for Criminal Justice of the Renmin University of China.

Shanna Mehlbaum is a researcher who focuses on environmental crime, in particular on waste crime. Her projects included waste trafficking (EU-project BlockWaste) and dumping of chemical waste from synthetic drugs laboratories in the Netherlands. She is currently working on her PhD at Tilburg University.

Valsamis Mitsilegas is Professor of European Criminal Law, head of the Department of Law and co-director of the Criminal Justice Centre at Queen Mary University of London.

Anton Moiseienko is a research analyst at the Centre for Financial Crime & Security Studies of the Royal United Services Institute, UK. He holds a PhD from Queen Mary University of London, where he wrote his thesis about the use of entry sanctions against individuals suspected of corruption.

Rudie Neve is a senior researcher at the Analysis and Research Department of the National Police of the Netherlands. He published reports on organised crime, terrorism and environmental crime.

Naomi Oosterman is a PhD candidate at the Department of Sociology at City, University of London and a lecturer at the Department of Arts & Culture Studies at Erasmus University, Rotterdam. She studies the criminal dynamics of art crime in a European context and is specialised in the analysis of crime data.

Shi Yanan is a professor at the Law School of the Renmin University of China.

Toine Spapens is a full professor of Criminology at Tilburg University, the Netherlands. He specialises in research on organised crime, environmental crime and cross-border enforcement cooperation.

Dr **Erika J. Techera** is a Professor of Environmental Law at the University of Western Australia Law School and UWA Oceans Institute. Her research focuses on International and comparative environmental law particularly in relation to marine governance and small island states.

Grazia Maria Vagliasindi is Associate Professor of Criminal Law at the University of Catania, Italy, Department of Law.

Clive Walker is Professor Emeritus of Criminal Justice Studies at the School of Law, University of Leeds, where he has served as the Director of the Centre for Criminal Justice Studies (1987–2000) and as Head of School (2000–2005, 2010). He has written extensively on terrorism issues, with many published papers and books not only in the UK but also in several other jurisdictions, especially the USA. In 2003, he was a special adviser to the UK Parliamentary select committee, which scrutinised what became the Civil Contingencies Act 2004, from which experience he published *The Civil Contingencies Act 2004: Risk, Resilience and the Law in the United Kingdom* (Oxford University Press, 2006). His books on terrorism are recognised and cited widely and include

Terrorism and the Law (Oxford University Press, 2011), *The Anti-Terrorism Legislation*, (3rd ed., Oxford University Press, 2014), and the *Routledge Handbook of Law and Terrorism* (Routledge, 2015). More recent works have concentrated on the financing of terrorism, including, King, C., and Walker, C. (eds), *Dirty Assets: Emerging Issues in the Regulation of Criminal and Terrorist Assets* (Ashgate, Farnham, 2014) and King, C., Walker, C. and Gurulé, J. (eds), *Handbook of Criminal and Terrorism Financing Law* (Palgrave Macmillan, London, 2018). He was appointed in 2010 by the Home Office as Senior Adviser to the Independent Reviewer of Terrorism Legislation. He became a Queen's Counsel (Hons) in 2016.

Wang Wenhua is the Vice Dean and Professor at the Law School of Beijing Foreign Studies University.

1 Introduction

Valsamis Mitsilegas, Saskia Hufnagel and Anton Moiseienko

This edited collection inaugurates a book series on European and Chinese approaches to criminal justice, which was launched in partnership by the Criminal Justice Centres of Queen Mary University of London (QMUL) and the School of Law of Renmin University of China. It draws together papers from a number of conferences jointly conducted over the course of the last five years by the two research centres. While the types of crime discussed in the chapters vary, the focus of the present volume is specifically on transnational crime. Different types of crime are reflected, under the umbrella of transnational crime, in the different parts of this volume. As the first book in a series, it aims to provide a wide-ranging – although, inevitably, not comprehensive – overview of the legal and policy issues that arise in connection with various forms of transnational crime, as well as outline the criminal justice responses adopted across different jurisdictions. It is hoped that this approach will be of use to students of comparative criminal justice and anyone interested in transnational crime.

The collaboration between QMUL and the Renmin University of China began in the form of a series of annual joint conferences that date from 2013. The first such conference was convened at Renmin University in October 2013 to discuss the legal regulation of organised crime in Europe and China. Subsequent conferences focused on financial crime (London 2014), corruption (Beijing 2015), transnational crime (London 2016) and cybercrime (Beijing 2017). Notwithstanding the particular emphasis on Chinese and European experiences, each instalment of the conference also brought together a diverse range of scholars and practitioners from elsewhere, including the US, Canada, Australia, Russia and South Africa.

The publication of a joint book series was conceived as a means of promoting the understanding of the Chinese legal system among English-speaking scholars, but also as a valuable tool of highlighting the similarities and differences in approaches to various forms of crime. In order to ensure consistent quality and the balanced representation of Chinese and European perspectives on criminal justice, the book series is co-edited by Professor Shi Yanan and Professor Liu Mingxiang (Renmin University of China) and Professor Valsamis Mitsilegas and Dr Saskia Hufnagel (QMUL).

While there is a growing body of literature on Chinese criminal law and criminal justice, few works so far have attempted the task of juxtaposing Chinese and European perspectives within a single volume focused on a specific type of criminality. With many specialised publications on Chinese criminal law only being available in Chinese, it is hoped that a series of such books will facilitate a fruitful dialogue between academics and policy-makers. The need for such dialogue is particularly evident in the area of criminal justice, with issues such as financial crime and cybercrime acquiring ever-increasing prominence as China undergoes rapid economic and technological development.

Furthermore, as the papers in this volume were presented at international and interdisciplinary conferences, their content has already undergone the scrutiny of peer assessment, or, more generally, has been subjected to the views of 'outsiders' to the jurisdictions discussed. This has enabled authors to address questions arising in relation to work in an international context, making the chapters more accessible to readers unfamiliar with the jurisdictional issues discussed.

In line with the overarching purpose of the series, this volume offers a diverse set of perspectives on transnational crime. With contributors coming from a variety of disciplines and methodological backgrounds, efforts have been taken to address, amongst other things, some of the hitherto underexplored issues related to transnational crime from different international perspectives. These range from trafficking in cultural objects derived from illicit metal-detecting and metal-detecting tourism in China to the European approaches to criminalising the denial of historical truth. For all the diversity of the contributions and issues raised by the contributors, the central theme of the book is the notion that useful lessons can be drawn from each other's experiences, and that a cross-fertilisation of domestic approaches to transnational crime is essential to effective cooperation.

The book begins with a chapter by Valsamis Mitsilegas on the global governance of transnational crime. Mitsilegas offers an account of the various types of international responses to transnational crime, ranging from international treaties to 'soft law' to the decisions of the UN Security Council, and questions whether the democratic deficit surrounding their adoption makes them unfit for purpose. The chapter sets the stage for the rest of the material in the book. By looking specifically at the informal norm-making by the Financial Action Task Force (FATF), the global standard-setter in anti-money laundering and counter-terrorist financing (AML/CTF), as well as terrorist-financing sanctions lists promulgated by the UN Security Council, Mitsilegas's chapter also serves as an appropriate introduction to the section of the book that deals with money laundering, terrorist financing and cybercrime.

It opens with Shi Yanan's chapter on the Chinese AML legal framework. Shi's comprehensive account of the evolution and functions of Chinese institutions entrusted with AML functions clearly demonstrates the policy attention that the issue of money laundering has received in China in recent years. As such, it is a welcome contribution to the predominantly Western-centric literature on AML laws and regulations.

The following chapter by Clive Walker focuses on the use of UK charities for terrorist financing and the evolution of regulatory responses to the phenomenon. By zooming in on one specific sector, Walker's contribution highlights the importance of political will and practical resources in the fight against money laundering and terrorist financing. It shows how a reform of one particular agency – Charity Commission – has dramatically expanded its capacity to tackle terrorist financing. Wang Wenhua's chapter identifies specific legal and policy issues that should be addressed in order to bolster China's efforts against cross-border money laundering, ranging from legislative questions, such whether money laundering should be criminalised on an 'all crimes' basis, to the challenges of international cooperation. Her practice-focused contribution is therefore a useful complement to Shi's comprehensive overview of the Chinese AML regulation. A more theoretical approach to the challenges of fighting transnational crime is represented in Petter Gottschalk's chapter on cybercrime, which looks at several case studies to discuss the characteristics of cybercriminals, ranging from fraudsters to biker gangs that engage in cybercrime.

The next section of the book could be more broadly described as the 'history' part of this volume. It brings together contributions that deal with cultural heritage crime and the protection of historical memory. Samuel Hardy provides an insight into the world of illicit metal detectorists who unlawfully appropriate antiquities in East Asian countries, including China. His meticulous and highly original empirical research, which is based on analysing open sources such as web forums and Facebook groups, sheds light on one form of transnational crime that may not be highly organised or centralised but, nevertheless, inflicts substantial damage on communities where it takes place. The issue of cultural and social significance of art crime is addressed in detail, albeit in a different context, by Naomi Oosterman in her chapter on the societal implications of two notable art thefts from Dutch museums, namely the Westfries Museum and Kunsthal. As she demonstrates, the consequences of these crimes reverberated beyond the Dutch art world and even had effect on the country's political discourse and foreign relations. In a variation on the theme developed by Oosterman, Emmanouil Billis critically examines the criminal law regulations concerning a somewhat different type of heritage, namely historical truth. By examining the trial in Greece of the German history professor Heinz Richter, he confronts the vexed issue of how far the reach of criminal law may extend when free speech and the freedom of academic research are at stake.

The following section of the book deals with financial crime and corruption. Relying on examples from Australian, UK and US laws, Simon Bronitt argues that the legitimacy and practical efficiency of anti-corruption rules should be of greater concern for legal scholarship than the minutiae of the legislation. The theme of legislative efficiency is also present in the next two chapters, which provide an overview of some of the major issues of financial crime legislation in China and will therefore be of particular interest to those readers who seek up-to-date information on the Chinese legislation and scholarly debates in the area. Liu Mingxiang's chapter deals with the law on credit card fraud in China. In addition to providing a thorough account of the existing legislation and practical challenges of its enforcement, the chapter elucidates some of the doctrinal debates as to whether a separate offence of credit card fraud is at all necessary, as well as highlights the occasional inconsistencies between criminal and banking laws. Cheng Lei's chapter offers a concise and accessible guide to the Chinese legislation on confiscation of the proceeds of financial crime. By analysing the challenges of confiscation, which is an indispensable criminal justice response to financial crime, the chapter complements and expands on Shi's and Liu's contributions.

The book concludes with three chapters on environmental crime, which is clearly a subject of growing concern around the world. The chapters in this section amply demonstrate the global nature of the threat, as well as the interconnectedness of modern states and need for international cooperation. Grazia Maria Vagliasindi offers a *tour d'horizon* of international responses to environmental crime, ranging from treaties such as the Convention on International Trade in Endangered Species of Wild Fauna and Flora to non-binding declarations to arrangements for international cooperation and information sharing. As Vagliasindi makes clear, there is no silver bullet to environmental crime and solutions must include a range of coordinated responses aimed at changing the underlying economic dynamics of supply and demand, as well as addressing the links of environmental crime with other types of crime and removing the challenges to international cooperation. Toine Spapens, Shanna Mehlbaum and Rudi Neve analyse the date from 13 major criminal investigations that involved the illicit export of waste materials from the Netherlands to China. The authors of the contribution combine academic and police experience. Among the major hindrances to the successful investigation of such cases is the lack of adequate information exchange between Dutch and Chinese authorities, and even the spontaneous information sharing in the EU is hardly always adequate – something that is ripe for change in view of the shared interest of states in preventing environmental crime. Finally, the chapter by Erika J. Techera and Jade Lindley is unique for this book in its focus on the Indo-Pacific ocean areas. Looking at illegal, unregulated and unreported (IUU) fishing through the lens of crime opportunity theory, it advocates multi-faceted regional responses grounded in the understanding of the economy of IUU. Once again, international cooperation is of essence, although at the same time the authors acknowledge its limits and underscore the necessity of understanding the motivations of states in addressing or not addressing IUU.

The study of transnational crime demands that we look beyond our national jurisdictions and consider causes and effects of crime, as well as criminal law and procedure, in other parts of the world. This book is intended to set the scene and awaken interest in European and Chinese issues. However, there are many more topics to consider for joint research than transnational crimes. Doctrinal legal comparisons of Chinese and European legal problems can be as enlightening as cross-border issues. The future books in this series will aim to delve even deeper into this world of similarities and differences and attempts to compare problems and solutions in two parts of the worlds that might have more in common in this field than previously thought.

2 The global governance of transnational crime

Implications for justice and the rule of law

Valsamis Mitsilegas

Introduction

The past three decades have witnessed the adoption at the global and regional level of a plethora of regulatory and legislative measures aimed at countering transnational crime. Rather than forming a homogenous body of norms, these measures have been adopted in a variety of forms and fora. The aim of this chapter is to provide a comprehensive typology of norm-making in transnational criminal law, by focusing on both the adoption of norms at the global level and on issues of implementation and compliance. Transnational criminal law is to be distinguished from international criminal law in this context in involving the production of norms which must be implemented by – and be enforced in – *domestic* criminal justice systems, being transformed in this process largely into domestic criminal law rules. When implemented in domestic systems, transnational criminal law norms thus have a significant impact on the relationship between the individual and the state and the protection of human rights at the domestic level. The essay will look in particular at how the making of transnational criminal law has shifted from traditional forms of international law-making – namely multilateral international treaties – to other forms of governance including regionalism, 'soft' or 'informal' law and 'global administrative law'. The next sections will thus examine the global governance of transnational crime under these headings. The interaction and inter-relationship between these forms of governance in the development of a multi-level paradigm of global governance of transnational crime will be highlighted and the implications of this paradigm on justice and the rule of law will be explored. Questions on justice will focus on issues of inter-state justice, but also the impact of transnational criminal law on domestic criminal justice systems. Questions on the rule of law will focus primarily on the process of global norm-making and, in particular, democracy, transparency and accountability, but will also explore questions of rule of law as judicial review, in addressing the changing paradigm of international law having a direct impact on individuals. A number of parallel and innovative processes of internationalisation and globalisation will be highlighted in this context and their impact on law-making in a complex global arena will be explored.

Legislating by multilateral conventions: the case of UN treaties on transnational crime

The classic example of global law-making, including in the field of transnational crime, is the multilateral convention and the key actor in this context has been the United Nations (UN). United Nations intervention in this context can be seen as traditional in that it attempts to promote global standards while rooted firmly within state sovereignty and equality.[1] The emergence of multilateral conventions in the field of transnational crime is inextricably linked with changes in the post-Cold War security landscape. The end of the Cold War has had broader implications for the reconfiguration of the global security agenda. The shift from the emphasis on military threats to the securitisation of broader phenomena has been well documented.[2] A key element of this securitisation shift has been the elevation of forms of criminality as security threats that require urgent and concerted response by governments.[3] In this securitisation process, perceived security threats have proliferated and assumed a chameleon nature over the years – from drug trafficking in the 1980s to organised crime in the 1990s and terrorism in the 2000s.[4] This evolving securitisation agenda has led to the production of what Nadelmann has termed 'global prohibition regimes', which involve the introduction of security standards by dominant societies and states – in particular the United States – and their internationalisation and internalisation by the rest of the world.[5] The globalisation of this securitisation agenda has been reflected in the intervention by the United Nations

1 See in this context also Walker, who notes that 'the UN system links law to a claimed monopoly of the means of legitimate violence in a manner that stands both as a powerful (if fitful) reminder of conventional understandings of the paradigm of state-centered legal authority and as a direct challenge to the dominance of that paradigm': Neil Walker, *Intimations of Global Law* (CUP 2015) 63.

2 See in particular Barry Buzan, *People, States and Fear. An Agenda for International Security Studies in the Post-Cold War Era* (Harvester Wheatsheaf 1991); Barry Buzan, 'New Patterns of Global Security in the Twenty-First Century' (1999) 67(3) *International Affairs* 431. In the context of securitisation and crime, see Didier Bigo, *Polices en Réseaux: L'Experiénce Européenne* (Presses de Sciences Po 1996).

3 On the securitisation process, see Barry Buzan, Ole Waever and Jaap de Wilde, *Security: A New Framework for Analysis* (Lynne Rienner 1998); and Ole Waever, 'Securitization and De-Securitization' in Ronnie D Lipschutz (ed.), *On Security* (Columbia University Press 1995) 46–86.

4 On this changing focus in the context of the development of money laundering countermeasures, see Valsamis Mitsilegas, 'Countering the Chameleon Threat of Dirty Money: "Hard" and "Soft" Law in the Emergence of a Global Regime against Money Laundering and Terrorist Finance' in Adam Edwards and Peter Gill (eds), *Transnational Organised Crime: Perspectives on Global Security* (Routledge 2003) 195–211.

5 Ethan Nadelmann, 'Global Prohibition Regimes: the Evolution of Norms in International Society' (1990) 44(4) *International Organization* 479, 525. On the dominance of the United States in this context see also Peter Andreas and Ethan Nadelmann, *Policing the Globe: Criminalization and Crime Control in International Relations* (OUP 2008); and on the role of powerful players such as the US more broadly see Gregory Shaffer, 'The Dimensions and Determinants of State Change' in Gregory Shaffer (ed.), *Transnational Legal Ordering and State Change* (CUP 2013) 36.

via the adoption of multilateral conventions in the field of transnational crime. A major step towards the globalisation of criminal law in this context was undertaken by the United Nations in the 1980s in the form of the conclusion of the 1988 Vienna Convention against Illicit Trafficking in Narcotic Drugs and Psychotropic Substances. To a great extent prompted by the so-called US 'war on drugs', the Convention introduced a number of detailed provisions on drug trafficking, as well as – for the first time – the criminalisation of money laundering at the global level.[6] The Vienna Convention was followed in ensuing decades by two further major UN Conventions in the field: the UN Convention on Transnational Organised Crime (UNTOC), and the UN Convention Against Corruption (UNCAC). UNTOC constitutes perhaps the most impressive contribution of a United Nations multilateral treaty towards the globalisation of criminal law. It was negotiated throughout the 1990s and signed symbolically in Palermo in 2000. Reflecting the growing securitisation of organised crime at the time, the Convention is an ambitious and comprehensive multilateral instrument aiming at combating and preventing organised crime. It contains provisions ranging from the criminalisation of participation in an organised crime group, money laundering and corruption, to provisions on judicial cooperation with regard to organised crime, police cooperation and the law of criminal procedure. The Convention is complemented by three Protocols, on human trafficking, human smuggling, and the illicit manufacturing of and trafficking in firearms.[7] UNTOC was followed by the adoption of the 2003 UN Convention against corruption (UNCAC). UNCAC aims to establish a comprehensive anticorruption framework, by focusing on both prevention and control.[8]

The adoption by the United Nations of multilateral conventions on transnational crime with a global reach poses significant challenges of implementation and compliance by state parties. More recent conventions have tried to address these challenges by the introduction of specific mechanisms of monitoring and review. Leading these mechanisms are the so-called 'Conferences of the Parties'.[9] The

6 For an analysis of the Vienna Convention, see William C Gilmore, *Dirty Money: The Evolution of International Measures to Counter Money Laundering and the Financing of Terrorism* (3rd edn, Council of Europe Press 2004) ch 3; see also David P Stewart, 'Internationalizing the War on Drugs: the UN Convention Against Illicit Traffic in Narcotic Drugs and Psychotropic Substances' (1990) 18 *Denver Journal of International Law and Policy* 387.

7 See David McClean, *Transnational Organized Crime: A Commentary on the UN Convention and its Protocols* (OUP 2007). For an overview of the background to and negotiating history of the Convention, see also Dimitri Vlassis, 'Drafting the United Nations Convention against Transnational Organized Crime' in Phil Williams and Dimitri Vlassis (eds), *Combating Transnational Crime: Concepts, Activities and Responses* (Frank Cass 2001) 356.

8 For an overview, see Philippa Webb, 'The United Nations Convention against Corruption: Global Achievement or Missed Opportunity?' (2005) 8 *Journal of International Economic Law* 191.

9 For a background and discussion of the legal nature of Conferences of the Parties see Malgosia Fitzmaurice, 'Law-Making and International Environmental Law: The Legal Character of Decisions of Conferences of the Parties' in Rain Liivoja and Jarna Petman (eds), *International Law-Making: Essays in Honour of Jan Klabbers* (Routledge 2014) 190–210.

establishment of Conferences of the Parties has been justified by the need to create strong regimes, as decision-making by a treaty body can be more efficient than the traditional consent-based treaty-making process.[10] In this context, Conferences of the Parties are viewed as autonomous institutional arrangements, introducing a model of inter-state collaboration that is more informal and more flexible, and often innovative in relation to norm creation and compliance.[11] Questions of compliance are multilateral in character and promote resolution in a cooperative rather than an adversarial manner.[12] Both the UNTOC and the UNCAC contain provisions on Conferences on the Parties. Article 32 UNTOC entrusts the Conference of the Parties to the Convention with the objectives of improving the capacity of States Parties to combat transnational organised crime and to promote and review the implementation of the Convention (Article 32(1)). According to Article 32(3), the Conference of the Parties will agree upon mechanisms for achieving these objectives inter alia by reviewing periodically the implementation of this Convention and making recommendations to improve this Convention and its implementation (Article 32(3)(d) and (e)). For these purposes, the Conference of the Parties must acquire the necessary knowledge of the measures taken by States Parties in implementing this Convention through information provided by them and through such supplemental review mechanisms as may be established by the Conference of the Parties (Article 32 (4)). A similar clause has been included in the UNCAC (see Article 63(1), 63(4) (e) and (f) and 63(5) respectively).

At the time of writing, it is under the UNCAC that review mechanisms have been mostly developed. Resolution 3/1 of the Conference of the State Parties adopted Terms of Reference of the Mechanism for the Review of Implementation of UNCAC. The guiding principles include commitments that the review mechanism must not produce any form of ranking (point 3(b)), must be non-adversarial and non-punitive (point 3(f)), must be an intergovernmental process (point 4), must not serve as an instrument for interfering in the domestic affairs of States Parties, but must respect the principles of equality and sovereignty of States Parties, and the review process must be conducted in a non-political and non-selective manner (point 5) and must take into account the levels of development of States Parties, as well as the diversity of judicial, legal, political, economic and social systems and differences in legal traditions (point 8). A system of peer review between states has been established (point 18). The review will be primarily a desk exercise based on the responses to states' self-assessment and

10 Daniel Costelloe and Malgosia Fitzmaurice, 'Lawmaking by Treaty: Conclusion of a Treaty and the Evolution of a Treaty Regime in Practice' in Catherine Brölmann and Yannik Radi (eds), *Research Handbook on the Theory and Practice of International Lawmaking* (Edward Elgar 2016) 118–128.

11 Robin R Churchill and Geir Ulfstein, 'Autonomous Institutional Arrangements in Multilateral Environmental Agreements: A Little-Noticed Phenomenon in International Law' (2000) 94 *American Journal of International Law* 623, 625.

12 Ibid. 645.

will be complemented by further means of direct dialogue, such as country visits, only if agreed by the state party under review (points 27 and 29). The country review reports will remain confidential, although state parties are encouraged – under their sovereign rights – to give some publicity (points 37 and 38). It can thus be seen that the monitoring mechanisms established by the UNCAC Conference of the Parties are firmly anchored within the principles of equality between states, state sovereignty and national diversity. The emphasis on these principles may be explained by the criticism levelled at existing attempts towards the introduction of global anti-corruption rankings, which have been seen as reflecting the interests of particular countries and parts of the world.[13] There are also limits to transparency with evaluation reports remaining in principle confidential. A similar model is envisaged in the development of concrete monitoring mechanisms for UNTOC, which are currently being developed.[14]

The above analysis has demonstrated the progress, but also the limits, in terms of norm-making and compliance by means of multilateral treaties with a global reach. In terms of norm-making, the international community has indeed legislated in major areas of transnational crime, including drug trafficking, money laundering, organised crime and corruption. However, there are aspects of these phenomena that have not been regulated by the UN Conventions analysed above. Moreover, the absence of similar multilateral treaties addressing other serious security threats, including terrorism and cyber-crime, is also striking. The limits to international norm-making in the field can be explained by the difficulties in reaching a global consensus on how to respond to such threats. This difficulty has led to what Krisch has termed 'the decay of consent' in international law.[15] Krisch notes that consent-based structure presents a structural bias against effective action on global public goods, especially given the large number of sovereign states today, increasingly, favouring more effective problem-solving mechanisms.[16] This trend towards moving away from an exclusive focus on global multilateral conventions can be clearly discerned in the field of security and transnational criminal law. Legal responses to the emerging global securitisation landscape take many different, overlapping and inter-related forms. The following sections will look at each of these in detail: from the turn to regional multilateralism (and focusing here on the activities of the Council of Europe), to the production of norms on transnational crime via 'informal', 'soft' or 'global administrative law' (with the examples of the Financial Action Task Force against Money Laundering and Terrorist Finance and the United Nations Security Council (FATF) emerging prominent in the

13 See Mlada Bukovansky, 'Corruption Rankings: Constructing and Contesting the Global Anti-Corruption Agenda' in Alexander Cooley and Jack Snyder (eds), *Ranking the World: Grading States as a Tool of Global Governance* (CUP 2015) 60–84.

14 On the terms of reference of the UNTOC review mechanism, see annex 1 to Conference of the Parties Resolution 5/5. On recent impetus towards the establishment of such a mechanism see Resolution 7/1 and the Progress Report submitted to the Conference of the Parties meeting in Vienna, 21–26 October 2016, CTOC/COP/2016/13, 29 July 2016.

15 Nico Krisch, 'The Decay of Consent: International Law in an Age of Global Public Goods' (2014) 108 *American Journal of International Law* 1.

16 Ibid. 4.

field). The emergence of these new regulatory avenues is significant not only in terms of norm-making, but also in terms of compliance and effective implementation – with the circumvention of the traditional multilateral UN route being explained or justified by the necessity not only to respond swiftly to perceived security threats, but also to achieve effective compliance in order to create a true global level-playing field in the fight against transnational crime.

From regionalisation to globalisation: the case of the council of Europe

The Council of Europe has been a major driver of regional standard setting in the field of serious and transnational crime, having emerged as a significant norm entrepreneur in the field.[17] The first wave of Council of Europe measures in the field adopted in the early years of the organisation consisted of a number of traditional Conventions on judicial cooperation in criminal matters including Conventions on extradition[18] and mutual legal assistance in criminal matters.[19] In the absence of express criminal law competence of what was then the European Community, these Conventions constituted the cornerstone of intergovernmental judicial cooperation between Western European countries, including European Union member states. The post-Cold War security landscape renewed legislative ambition in the field of transnational criminality by the Council of Europe, via the adoption since the 1990s of a series of comprehensive, avant-garde multilateral Conventions covering both substantive and procedural criminal law in areas such as money laundering[20] (followed by a convention on money laundering and terrorist finance),[21] corruption,[22] the suppression[23] and prevention[24] of terrorism and

17 On the Council of Europe as norm entrepreneur more generally, see Gwendolyn Sasse, 'The Council of Europe as a Norm Entrepreneur: The Political Strengths of a Weak International Institution' in Neil Walker and Jo Shaw (eds), *Europe's Constitutional Mosaic* (Hart 2011) 171–204.

18 European Convention on Extradition (adopted 13 December 1957, entered into force 18 April 1960) ETS 024.

19 European Convention on Mutual Legal Assistance in Criminal Matters (adopted 20 April 1959, entered into force 12 June 1962) ETS 030.

20 Convention on Laundering, Search, Seizure and Confiscation of the Proceeds of Crime (adopted 8 November 1990, entered into force 1 September 1993) ETS 141.

21 Council of Europe Convention on Laundering, Search, Seizure and Confiscation of the Proceeds from Crime and on the Financing of Terrorism (adopted 16 May 2005, entered into force 1 May 2008) ETS 198.

22 Criminal Law Convention on Corruption (adopted 27 January 1999, entered into force 1 July 2002) ETS 173. The Convention is complemented by a Civil Law Convention on Corruption (adopted 4 November 1999, entered into force 1 November 2003) ETS 174.

23 European Convention on the Suppression of Terrorism (adopted 27 January 1977, entered into force 4 August 1978) ETS 090.

24 Council of Europe Convention on the Prevention of Terrorism (adopted 16 May 2005, entered into force 1 June 2007) ETS 196.

cyber-crime.[25] The Council of Europe has thus produced a series of detailed and sophisticated legal standards to counter transnational criminality.[26] At the same time, it has acted as a catalyst for the strengthening of the legal framework in the field at both the EU and the global level. At the EU level, membership of the Council of Europe and compliance with Council of Europe standards has acted as a laboratory for membership of the European Union in the context of EU enlargement, with Council of Europe Conventions forming benchmarks with which compliance is required as a criterion of membership of the European Union. Such compliance is also a benchmark in the development of relations between the Union and its neighbours in the context of the European Neighbourhood Policy.[27] Council of Europe measures also serve as EU benchmarks in areas where the European Union is itself reluctant to legislate, such as anti-corruption law.[28]

At the global level, the Council of Europe has advanced and strengthened international norms against transnational crime via the adoption of comprehensive and pioneering Conventions.[29] Importantly, this has occurred in areas such as terrorism and cyber-crime, where Council of Europe conventions have been developing in the absence of a global consensus. Law-making by the Council of Europe acts as a laboratory for globalisation in this context. A number of Council of Europe Conventions in the field of transnational crime have been open for participation to non-European states. A prime example in this context is the Convention on cyber-crime, where the participation of the United States signals the evolution of a transatlantic enforcement regime where a global consensus in favour of this particular form of legislative intervention may be lacking.[30] This development poses a number of rule of law challenges. From the perspective of the Council of Europe legal order, participation in its regional conventions is allowed by states that are not its members and thus not bound by the entirety of its standards (including the European Convention on Human Rights). From the

25 Convention on Cybercrime (adopted 23 November 2001, entered into force 1 July 2004) ETS 185.

26 For an overview of the evolution of the activities of the Council of Europe in criminal matters, see Peter Csonka, 'Organised and Economic Crime (an overview of the Relevant Council of Europe Activities)', in Peter J Cullen and William C Gilmore, *Crime sans Frontières: International and European Legal Approaches* (Edinburgh University Press 1998) 93–99.

27 Valsamis Mitsilegas, 'The EU and the Implementation of International Norms in Criminal Matters' in Marise Cremona, Jörg Monar and Sara Poli (eds), *The External Dimension of the Area of Freedom, Security and Justice* (Peter Lang 2011, College of Europe Studies No. 13), 239–272.

28 Valsamis Mitsilegas, 'The Aims and Limits of EU Anti-Corruption Law' in Jeremy Horder and Peter Alldridge (eds), *Modern Bribery Law: Comparative Perspectives* (CUP 2013) 160.

29 See Gilmore, *Dirty Money* (n 6). See also as regards one of the first Conventions in this context Hans Nilsson, 'The Council of Europe Laundering Convention: A Recent Example of a Developing International Criminal Law' (1991) 2 *Criminal Law Forum* 419.

30 Jonathan Clough, 'The Council of Europe Convention on Cybercrime: Defining "Crime" in a Digital World' (2012) 23(4) *Criminal Law Forum* 363.

perspective of globalisation of criminal law, standards that have been developed and agreed in a specific regional context may de facto become global standards via the opening of participation to conventions by third states and in particular in areas of law that involve extraterritoriality (such is the case with elements of the cyber-crime convention). In a system of multi-level security governance, Council of Europe intervention may act as a legitimising factor for a number of initiatives that have not originated via traditional public international law means. A key example is recent legislation on the criminalisation and prevention of terrorism, notably via targeting the phenomenon of 'foreign fighters'. In this field, standards were first put forward by the United Nations Security Council in another example of the application of 'global administrative law'.[31] The key provisions in UN Security Council Resolution 2178 have been introduced in the Council of Europe legal order by the Additional Protocol to the Council of Europe Convention on the Prevention of Terrorism adopted by the Council of Europe.[32] The Council of Europe has thus legitimised sweeping and controversial changes in the criminal law of terrorism: in addition to widening the categories preparatory offences[33] the Protocol introduces a series of provisions expressly criminalising mobility and travel. These changes in turn are in the process of being legitimised further by the European Union, whose institutions are currently negotiating a revision of its counter-terrorism law to introduce the Council of Europe standards in the EU legal order.

The Council of Europe has not only been innovative in producing transnational criminal law norms. Its normative efforts have been coupled with strong efforts to secure compliance with these standards. In this context, a number of innovative compliance and implementation monitoring procedures have been put forward by the Council of Europe. These mechanisms go beyond the setup envisaged by the Conferences of the Parties in UN Conventions, whose provisions seem rather timid in comparison to the Council of Europe monitoring frameworks. Rather, the Council of Europe mechanisms are closer to invasive monitoring mechanisms introduced by bodies such as the FATF[34] and there is a high degree of interconnection between the Council of Europe and bodies and organisations such as the FATF and the European Union in terms of the development of multi-layered evaluation processes on the basis of a plethora of EU, regional and global standards. The first example of innovative compliance mechanisms relates to the mechanisms established within the framework of the Group of States Against Corruption (GRECO). Legal bases for GRECO can be found in the Council of Europe Civil and Criminal Law Conventions on

31 On the UN Security Council and global administrative law see section 5.

32 For a background to the Protocol see Nicola Piacente, 'The Contribution of the Council of Europe to the Fight against Foreign Terrorist Fighters' (2015) 1 *Eucrim* 12–15.

33 See the provisions on criminalising the participation in an association or group for the purpose of terrorism (Article 2) and receiving training for terrorism (Article 3).

34 See section 4 below.

Corruption.[35] According to the Conventions, GRECO will monitor their implementation. Ratification of or accession to the Conventions will entail automatic membership of GRECO for non-member states.[36] GRECO's objective is to improve the capacity of its members to fight corruption by monitoring their compliance with Council of Europe anti-corruption standards through a process of mutual evaluation and peer pressure. All members participate in, and submit themselves without restriction to, the mutual evaluation and compliance procedures, which include on-site visits and evaluations on the ground.[37]

A rigorous monitoring mechanism is thus introduced, which places emphasis on evaluation of law in action and on the achievement of compliance by members with Council of Europe anti-corruption standards. The potential of the regional evaluation mechanism set out by GRECO to promote anti-corruption standards more broadly is significant. It is noteworthy that membership of GRECO includes the United States, and that regional organisations such as the Organization of American States have observer status.[38] Moreover, the GRECO system is envisaged to be both mirrored and internalised at EU level as regards the evaluation of anti-corruption law: in its Communication on EU anti-corruption policy, the European Commission committed to setting up a new mechanism, the *EU Anti-Corruption Report*, to monitor and assess member states' efforts against corruption. Alongside this mechanism, the EU should participate in GRECO.[39] In addition to the efforts of GRECO, another innovative evaluation mechanism based upon peer review has been set up within the framework of the Council of Europe in order to ensure compliance with Council of Europe standards against transnational crime: the MONEYVAL system aims at ensuring compliance with Council of Europe anti-money laundering standards and beyond.[40] MONEYVAL was established to address in particular the fact that not all Council of Europe members are also members of the FATF, which, as will be seen below, is the main international body leading with regard to developing and ensuring compliance with detailed standards in the field of anti-money

35 'The Group of States against Corruption (GRECO) shall monitor the implementation of this Convention by the Parties': Criminal Law Convention on Corruption, Article 24; Civil Law Convention on Corruption, Article 14.

36 Articles 32 and 33 of the Criminal Law Convention; Articles 15 and 16 of the Civil Law Convention.

37 Council of Europe, *How Does Greco Work?* <www.coe.int/t/dghl/monitoring/greco/general/4.%20How%20does%20GRECO%20work_en.asp>.

38 Council of Europe, *GRECO, Members and Observers* < www.coe.int/t/dghl/monitoring/greco/general/members_en.asp>.

39 COM (2011) 308 final, 2.

40 Council of Europe, *Committee of Experts on the Evaluation of Anti-Mondey Laundering Measures and the Financing of Terrorism (MONEYVAL)* <www.coe.int/moneyval/>. For an overview, see Wolfgang Rau and John Ringguth, 'Evaluation in the Framework of the Council of Europe', in Anne Weyembergh and Serge de Biolley (eds), *Comment Évaluer le Droit Pénal Européen?* (Editions de l'Université de Bruxelles 2006) 33–44.

laundering.[41] MONEYVAL membership consists primarily of countries from Central and Eastern Europe, both EU and non-EU members. The establishment of a specific peer review mechanism for these states serves to ensure that the FATF peer review was complemented for non-members in Europe, but also serves to ensure compliance of these states with EU standards in the field – as MONEYVAL benchmarks are not limited to Council of Europe standards, but also include FATF, UN and EU anti-money laundering standards.[42] Both GRECO and MONEYVAL constitute attempts to legitimise further the production of norms not only by the Council of Europe, but also by other international fora, by focusing on their implementation based in a system of expert evaluation.

From 'soft' to 'informal' law: the case of the FATF

The establishment and operation of the Financial Action Task Force (FATF) represents perhaps the most prominent departure from the traditional paradigm of multilateral 'hard' law-making in the field of transnational criminal law. The FATF is an *ad hoc* body, established by the G7 in 1989 under the auspices of the OECD.[43] Its main normative output has been a series of Recommendations, evolving over time and covering a wide range of aspects of the fight against money laundering. The 40 FATF Recommendations produced in 1990 were revised in 1996, 2003 and 2012, with money laundering countermeasures being deemed necessary to counter a series of emerging and new threats, from drug trafficking to organised crime to terrorism.[44] The revisions of the FATF Recommendations have gone hand in hand with the renewal and gradual expansion of the FATF mandate to now include action against money laundering, the financing of terrorism and now proliferation of weapons of mass destruction.[45] The rapid evolution and expansion in the FATF mandate, standards and membership can be attributed to its informal nature[46] and network structure, which aims at flexibility and adaptability.[47] Although membership of the FATF is limited and its output takes the form of Recommendations,

41 Gilmore, *Dirty Money* (n 6) 206.

42 See the MONEYVAL terms of reference at Council Of Europe, *MONEYVAL Terms of Reference*, <www.coe.int/t/dghl/monitoring/moneyval/About/MONEYVALTERMS.pdf>.

43 For a detailed analysis of the role and work of the FATF, see Gilmore, *Dirty Money* (n 6) chs 4–6.

44 See Mitsilegas, 'Countering the Chameleon Threat of Dirty Money' (n 4).

45 *Financial Action Task Force Mandate (2012–2020)*, Washington DC, 20 April 2012.

46 On the concept of informal international law-making see Joost Pauwelyn, Ramses Wessel and Jan Wouters (eds), *Informal International Lawmaking* (OUP 2012); informal law-making is defined as dispensing with certain formalities traditionally linked to international law having to do with output, process, or the actors involved: Joost Pauwelyn, 'Informal International Lawmaking: Framing the Concept and Research Questions' 15. https://papers.ssrn.com/sol3/papers.cfm?abstract_id=1738464

47 On the network nature of the FATF see Anne-Marie Slaughter, *A New World Order* (Princeton University Press 2004). Slaughter highlights the advantages of what she calls

which could be characterised as 'soft law',[48] informal law,[49] or global administrative law,[50] in juxtaposition to standards adopted in the form of multilateral international treaties, their impact on global law reform in the field has been immense.[51] Such impact has been achieved in two ways: by the constant willingness of major international players, such as the EU (some of whose member states and the European Commission have played a part in shaping the FATF standards in the first place) to legitimise the FATF standards by implementing them with legislation in their internal legal orders;[52] and by accompanying the adoption of FATF Recommendations by a system of rigorous evaluation of their implementation and compliance by FATF members and non-members alike, which takes the form of mutual evaluation and peer review.[53] Over time, the FATF has developed detailed evaluation methodologies and guidelines.[54] These evaluation mechanisms have ensured that the FATF is a body with selective membership but global reach. The emphasis on the regional dimension has been key in ensuring the achievement of global compliance with FATF standards. There have been three ways in which the incorporation of a regional dimension has contributed to global compliance with FATF standards: the expansion of FATF membership to include non-Western countries from key, strategically important regions; the expansion of the FATF system and methodology via the establishment of a series of FATF regional-style

'government networks', marrying hard and soft power and using information, persuasion and socialisation: see 168 *et seq.*

48 In the context of the FATF, it can be argued that the regular revision of both mandate and standards has been easier compared with a more formal international organisation. See in this context Alan Boyle, 'Some Reflections on the Relationship of Treaties and Soft Law' (1999) 48 *International and Comparative Law Quarterly* 901, noting that soft law instruments are easier to amend or replace than treaties: 903.

49 See Pauwelyn, Wessel and Wouters (n 46).

50 On the concept of global administrative law see the chapter section 'The emergence of "global administrative law": the role of the UN Security Council' below.

51 For further discussion see Valsamis Mitsilegas, 'The European Union and the Globalisation of Criminal Law'(2009–2010) 12 *Cambridge Yearbook of European Legal Studies* 337.

52 All four EU money laundering Directives have been justified on the basis of the need to adjust the EU legal framework to the FATF requirements: on the interrelationship between EU and FATF law over time see Valsamis Mitsilegas, *Money Laundering Counter-Measures in the European Union: A New Paradigm of Security Governance versus Fundamental Legal Principles* (Kluwer Law International 2003); Valsamis Mitsilegas and Bill Gilmore, 'The EU legislative framework against money laundering and terrorist finance: A critical analysis in the light of evolving global standards' (2007) 56 *International and Comparative Law Quarterly* 119; and Valsamis Mitsilegas and Niovi Vavoula, 'The Evolving EU Anti-Money Laundering Regime. Challenges for Fundamental Rights and the Rule of Law' (2016) 23 *Maastricht Journal of European and Comparative Law* 261.

53 Michael Levi and William Gilmore, 'Terrorist Finance, Money Laundering and the Rise and Rise of Mutual Evaluation: A New Paradigm for Crime Control?' (2002) 4 *European Journal of Law Reform* 337.

54 FATF, *Methodology for Assessing Technical Compliance with the FATF Recommendations and the Effectiveness of AML/CFT Systems* (2016).

bodies; and the inclusion of regional elements in assessing compliance with FATF standards, most notably when extending such assessment beyond FATF members.

The growing importance of the regional dimension is reflected in the evolution of the membership of the FATF – which, being initially essentially a G7 initiative consisted primarily of G7 and related Western countries as well as the European Commission.[55] Since its establishment, FATF membership has expanded significantly to include regional powers such as Russia, China, India, Mexico, Argentina and Brazil.[56] This move reflects the strategic importance of these countries in an era of financial globalisation and the changing balance of power in the global financial and political system. It has been seen as increasing the efficiency and legitimacy of the FATF[57] – with the expansion of FATF membership in these terms ensuring the representation of broader national and regional interests beyond a narrow Western perspective. This is particularly relevant as regards the development and adoption of FATF standards. The importance of the regional dimension in the work of the FATF is also evident in the organisation's criteria for membership. A fundamental criterion for FATF membership is the strategic importance of the jurisdiction, one of the indicators in this context being its regional prominence in efforts against money laundering and terrorist finance. Membership should also lead to the enhancement of the geographical balance of the FATF. Additional technical membership criteria include (in addition to adhering to the FATF standards and evaluation process) full and active membership of a relevant FATF-style regional body.[58] This 'club' drives not only the development of the FATF Recommendations, but also their implementation by FATF members and beyond. A major weapon in this context is a 'naming and shaming' process, consisting of identifying and engaging with jurisdictions that have strategic deficiencies and carried out by the FATF's International Co-operation Review Group (ICRG), which reviews and monitors a large number of potentially high-risk and non-cooperative jurisdictions around the world. Initial referral to the ICRG is based on information on threats, vulnerabilities or particular risks emanating from a specific jurisdiction that comes to the ICRG's attention. Such information includes, but is not exclusively based on, the results of mutual evaluation reports (MERs); or the lack of a clear commitment to implementing the FATF standards through non-participation in any of the

55 In addition to the participants in the G7 summit establishing the FATF (Canada, France, Germany, Italy, Japan, United Kingdom, United States and the Commission…) eight other states (Australia, Austria, Belgium, Luxembourg, Netherlands, Spain, Sweden and Switzerland) were invited to take part: Gilmore, *Dirty Money* (n 6) 89.

56 See Gilmore, *Dirty Money* (n 6). For a more specific regional dimension, see Maíra R Machado, 'Similar in their Differences: Transnational Legal Processes Addressing Money Laundering in Brazil and Argentina' in Gregory Shaffer (ed), *Transnational Legal Ordering and State Change* (CUP 2013).

57 Rainer Hülsse and Dieter Kerwer, 'Global Standards in Action: Insights from Anti-Money Laundering Regulation' (2007) 14 *Organization* 625.

58 <www.fatf-gafi.org/pages/aboutus/membersandobservers/fatfmembershippolicy.html>.

FATF-style regional bodies. Jurisdictions that are identified as having serious AML/CFT threats and vulnerabilities or posing significant risks are referred to the ICRG for a preliminary or prima facie review conducted by one of the four regional review groups, covering, respectively: the Africa/Middle East, the Americas, the Asia/Pacific, and the Europe/Eurasia regions. Based upon reports from these groups, the FATF decides whether it should conduct a more in-depth, targeted review of the relevant jurisdiction's strategic AML/CFT deficiencies. The FATF specifically requests high-level political commitment to implement these action plans.

On the basis of the results of the ICRG review, jurisdictions may be publicly identified in the FATF Public Statement. The Public Statement identifies two groups of countries, namely jurisdictions for which the FATF calls on its members and non-members to apply countermeasures and jurisdictions for which the FATF calls only on its members to consider the risks arising from the deficiencies associated with the countries. This second category includes jurisdictions that have not made sufficient progress in addressing the deficiencies or have not committed to an action plan developed with the FATF to address the deficiencies.[59] Since 2008, the FATF has issued public statements, three times a year, expressing concerns and calling for particular actions from FATF members and other jurisdictions. The classification of states in this context has evolved over time. The most recent FATF statement at the time of writing called on its members and other jurisdictions to apply countermeasures in the case of the Democratic People's Republic of Korea[60]; called for the application of enhanced due diligence measures in the case of Iran;[61]identified eight jurisdictions with strategic deficiencies[62]; and one jurisdiction (Guyana) that has been 'de-listed', i.e. no longer subject to the FATF on-going compliance process.[63] The recent documents confirm a process of on-going monitoring and assessment on a global scale.

The above analysis demonstrates that the FATF Recommendations are 'soft' law with hard teeth, with the FATF creating a global normative orthodoxy in the field of money laundering and terrorist finance. However, the evolution of the FATF continues to pose fundamental rule of law challenges. A primary challenge lies at the level of production of anti-money laundering norms. As mentioned above, the FATF is a single-agenda body with renewable mandate, informal structures and selective membership, something which gives flexibility in adopting and revising its standards. A number of authors have stressed the advantages

59 FATF Annual Report 11–12.

60 FATF Public Statement, 21 October 2016 < www.fatf-gafi.org/publications/high-riskand non-cooperativejurisdictions/documents/public-statement-october-2016.html>.

61 Ibid.

62 FATF, 'Improving Global AML/CFT Compliance: On-Going Process 21 October 2016' < www.fatf-gafi.org/publications/high-riskandnon-cooperativejurisdictions/documents/fatf-comploance-october-2-16.html>.

63 Ibid.

of informality, with Pollack and Shaffer noting that formal legal instruments such as treaties are particularly problematic

> where it presupposes a fixed condition when situations of uncertainty demand constant experimentation and adjustment, where it requires uniformity when a tolerance of national diversity is needed, and where it is difficult to change when frequent change may be essential'.[64]

The flexibility of 'soft' or 'informal' law is a particular asset coupled with the ensuing strong compliance mechanisms. As Boister notes,

> while treaty provisions are coupled with only very weak powers for enforcement of implementation, soft law is faster and cheaper to make than treaty law and is thus more adaptive and can be combined with fairly coercive name and shame tools to ensure implementation.[65]

However, the production of norms by the FATF raises significant challenges of democratic participation, transparency and accountability. Particular challenges arise in this context by the fact that norms are produced by a club with selective membership and then imposed by a sophisticated and invasive system of multi-level implementation monitoring across the globe; and by the fact that norms are produced behind closed doors, mainly by experts representing national executives. The uncritical emphasis and reliance on expertise serves to depoliticise the issues and shield them from political debate.[66] The FATF has responded to these criticisms by introducing public consultations regarding the revision of its Recommendations.[67] However, the FATF norm-making process leaves much to be desired in terms of participatory and transparent debate. A particular challenge in this context is that FATF is a single-agenda body, which has to justify its existence in order for its mandate to be renewed. This does not allow a more rounded debate on the necessity and content of further anti-money laundering

64 Mark A Pollack and Gregory C Shaffer, 'The Interaction of Formal and Informal International Lawmaking' in Gregory Shaffer (ed.), *Transnational Legal Ordering and State Change* (CUP 2013) 246.

65 Neil Boister, 'Further Reflections on the Concept of Transnational Criminal Law' (2015) 6(1) *Transnational Legal Theory* 9, 23.

66 On various aspects of such 'depoliticisation', see: Alexander Somek, *Administration without Sovereignty* (University of Iowa Legal Studies Research Paper 09–04, January 2009); Jan Klabbers, 'Institutional Ambivalence by Design: Soft Organizations in International Law' (2001) 70 *Nordic Journal of International Law* 403; and David Kennedy, 'Challenging Expert Rule: The Politics of Global Governance' (2005) 27 *Sydney Law Review* 5 (talking *inter alia* about 'the expert consensus'). For a more positive view, emphasising the benefits of professional socialisation, see Slaughter (n 47).

67 For a recent example, see Public Consultation on the Revision of Recommendation 8 (Non-profit organisations) < www.fatf-gafi.org/publications/fatfrecommendations/documents/public-consultation-npo-r8.html>.

standards, or the balancing of enforcement or efficiency considerations with broader fundamental rights or rule of law imperatives.

The emergence of 'global administrative law': the role of the UN Security Council

Calls for global emergency counter-terrorism action post-9/11 have not resulted in the adoption of measures in the form of the traditional multilateral 'hard law' Conventions at the level of the United Nations. Rather, global standards have been adopted and promoted principally under the format of what legal scholars have labelled as 'global administrative law'.[68] It has been noted that 'underlying the emergence of global administrative law is the vast increase in the reach and forms of transgovernmental regulation and administration designed to address the consequences of globalized interdependence in such fields as security' and that

> much in the detail and implementation of such regulation is determined by transnational administrative bodies – including international organizations and informal groups of officials – that perform administrative functions but are not directly subject to control by national governments or domestic legal systems or, in the case of treaty-based regimes, the states parties to the treaty.[69]

It is contested whether all or some of the norms included under the rubric of 'global administrative law' can really be classified as 'law'.[70] However, the term is a useful analytical tool in focusing on the *process* of the adoption of norms and in this context highlighting key differences between the development of global norms in this context and the traditional adoption of multilateral legally binding treaties. The production of normative standards at the level of 'global administrative law' or 'government networks' differs from the adoption of multilateral, expressly legally binding standards at the multilateral level in four main respects: standards are put forward by a limited number of states without the need for a global consensus; standards are adopted with a minimum of transparency; standards are adopted speedily (a factor that may explain the appeal of this form of normative production in times of perceived emergency); and standards are not explicitly legally binding rules of general application, but in reality have far-reaching consequences for law reform around the world.

68 Benedict Kingsbury, Nico Krisch and Richard B Stewart, 'The Emergence of Global Administrative Law' (2004–05) 68 *Law and Contemporary Problems* 15.

69 Ibid 16.

70 See in this context Benedict Kingsbury, 'The Concept of "Law" in Global Administrative Law' (2009) 20 *European Journal of International Law* 23; and Alexander Somek 'The Concept of "Law" in Global Administrative Law: A Reply to Benedict Kingsbury' (2009) 20 *European Journal of International Law* 985.

The adoption of preventive counter-terrorism sanctions by the UN Security Council constitutes a prime example of Global Administrative Law in this context. The production of normative standards in criminal matters by the UN Security Council has been linked to global counter-terrorism efforts as part of a two-fold strategy. The first element of this strategy has been the adoption, beginning pre-9/11, of a set of Resolutions targeting specifically the Taliban, Osama bin Laden, Al-Qaida and those associated with them. The first step in this direction has been Resolution 1267 (1999), which imposed a series of restrictive measures against the Taliban, including an arms embargo, banning travel and the freezing of funds. Resolution 1333 (2000) extended the freezing regime expressly to individuals in the Al-Qaida organisation and requested the Sanctions Committee to maintain an updated list of the individuals and entities designated as being associated with bin Laden, including those in Al-Qaida.[71] The next substantive amendment to the sanctions regime came about after 9/11, with Resolution 1390 (2002). The latter adjusted the content of Resolution 1267 to take into account political developments since its adoption but continued and consolidated the freezing regime established in paragraph 4(b) thereof. The emphasis on the adoption of legislative measures is even more prominent in the second element of the Security Council counter-terrorism strategy. Resolution 1373 (2001), adopted less than three weeks after the 9/11 attacks, called upon all States in particular to prevent and suppress the financing of terrorist acts; criminalise terrorism finance; and extend the freezing regime to cover in general persons who commit or attempt to commit terrorist acts or participate in or facilitate the commission of such acts, entities owned or controlled directly or indirectly by such persons and persons and entities acting on their behalf or direction.[72]

In this manner, the international community witnessed the production of global normative standards in the field of counter-terrorism outside the framework of the multilateral treaty. This shift did not go unnoticed by international lawyers, who stressed the Security Council's 'legislative' role.[73] In this context, it has been pointed out that Resolution 1373 is of general and abstract character and does not name a single country, society or group of people[74]; that with Resolution 1373, together with the related efforts of its 1267 Sanctions Committee, the Council is no longer responding with discrete action directed at a particular state because of a concrete threat to peace arising from a specific incident[75]; and that Resolution 1373 imposed general obligations on all states for an indefinite period, while Resolution 1267 set up a sanctions committee with

71 Para 8(c).

72 Para 1(a)-(c).

73 See in particular Stefan Talmon 'The Security Council as World Legislature' (2005) 99 *American Journal of International Law* 175; José Enrique Alvarez 'Hegemonic International Law Revisited' (2003) 97 *American Journal of International Law* 873.

74 Talmon (n 73) 176–177.

75 Alvarez (n 73) 874.

court-like powers to identify and freeze the assets of individuals, groups and corporations.[76] This production of normative standards by the Security Council has been criticised as undemocratic on the grounds of the limited transparency of Security Council negotiations,[77] of the adoption of the Resolutions (in particular 1373) speedily as emergency measures,[78] and last, but not least, on the ground of the selective membership of the Security Council. It has been forcefully pointed out that 'a patently unrepresentative and undemocratic body such as the Council is arguably unsuitable for international lawmaking' and that 'Council practice may be criticised as contrary to the basic structure of international law as a consent-based legal order'.[79] It has also been argued that the Resolutions 'circumvent the "vehicle *par excellence* of community interest", namely the multilateral treaty' and that as such they serve to promote the interests of a limited number of state actors.[80] As Cohen has noted,

> the assumption of legislative power and its actual legislation thus have a double status: general laws are being made by an (unelected, unrepresentative) executive body and constitutional change in the allocation of powers is being perpetrated by that same body insofar as it ascribes to itself the competence and capacity to legislate for the world, thereby introducing a radically new way of global law-making.[81]

It must be noted in this context that the Resolutions do not only impose an extensive normative restrictive counter-terrorism framework as such, but also aim to ensure and accelerate the implementation of the enforcement standards adopted in a pre-existing multilateral treaty, the 1999 Convention for the Suppression of the Financing of Terrorism.[82] In a departure from the consensus required for the adoption of legally binding provisions in a multilateral international treaty, in the case of the UN Security Council far-reaching norms are produced by a body operating with a limited agenda, membership, transparency or scrutiny. What makes this departure even more striking is that, in the counter-terrorism Resolutions, the individual (targeted by a series of sanctions) enters directly the realm of a system designed to address primarily inter-state relations.[83] What renders the reach of these Resolutions even more far-reaching is that, in

76 Ian Johnstone 'Legislation and Adjudication in the UN Security Council: Bringing Down the Deliberative Deficit' (2008) 102 *American Journal of International Law* 275, 283.

77 See in particular Talmon (n 73) 190.

78 See Talmon (n 73) 187, and the detailed analysis of Johnstone (n 76) 284.

79 Talmon (n 73) 179.

80 Alvarez (n 73) 874–875.

81 Jean L Cohen, *Globalization and Sovereignty: Rethinking Legality, Legitimacy, and Constitutionalism* (CUP 2012) 278.

82 See in this context the criticism of Alvarez (n 73) 875.

83 See in this context in particular Paul C Szasz 'The Security Council Starts Legislating' (2002) 96 *American Journal of International Law* 901; Johnstone (n 76) 295.

addition to the fact that they target individuals directly, they leave (in particular Resolution 1267) states and international organisations, such as the European Union, with very limited discretion as to how to implement them. As Krisch has noted, insofar as member state implementation is necessary to give measures effect, states' action is reduced to a subordinate, non-discretionary role in the overall administrative machinery directed by the Council and its committees, resulting in the significant reduction of the distance between national and international law in this domain and leading to an increasing enmeshment between those layers.[84]

Some of the rule of law challenges posed by the production of norms by the Security Council have been addressed by the judiciary, and in particular by the European Court of Justice in its *Kadi* litigation. In the first round of the *Kadi* rulings, referred to in this chapter as *Kadi I*, the Court of Justice stressed the requirement for the EU to comply with fundamental rights in the implementation of the Security Council Resolutions and found that uncritical automatic implementation ran contrary to the right to judicial protection as enshrined in the EU legal order – and, at the same time, affirming the autonomy of the EU constitutional order.[85] As in the case of the FATF, the Security Council responded to this criticism by introducing changes to its internal listing processes. Resolution 1822 (2008) introduced the requirement for listing proposals to identify those parts of the statement of case that may be publicly released, including for use by the Sanctions Committee for development of the summary described below or for the purpose of notifying or informing the listed individual or entity, and those parts which may be released upon request to interested States.[86] The Resolution also provides that the Sanctions Committee, when it adds a name to its Consolidated List, is to make accessible on its website 'a narrative summary of reasons for listing' and that it is to make accessible on the same site 'narrative summaries of reasons for listing' names on that list before the adoption of Resolution 1822 (2008).[87] A further Security Council Resolution, 1904 (2009), established an 'Office of the Ombudsperson', whose task is to assist the Sanctions Committee in the consideration of delisting requests. The person appointed to be the Ombudsperson must be an individual of high moral character, impartiality and integrity with high qualifications and experience in relevant fields, including law, human rights, counter-terrorism, and sanctions.[88] A subsequent Resolution, 1989 (2011), extended the mandate and support of the

84 Nico Krisch, *Beyond Constitutionalism: The Pluralist Structure of Postnational Law* (OUP 2010) 156–157.

85 Joined Cases C-402/05 P and C-415/05 P, *Yassin Abdullah Kadi and Al Barakaat International Foundation v Council and Commission* [2008] ECR I-6351. From the plethora of commentaries, see Valsamis Mitsilegas, 'The European Union and the Globalisation of Criminal Law' (2009–2010) 12 *Cambridge Yearbook of European Legal Studies* 337.

86 Para 12.

87 Para 13.

88 Para 20.

Ombudsperson and included detailed provisions on listing and de-listing procedures.[89] The Security Council continues thus to have the ultimate decision-making power on delisting and is not obliged to follow a de-listing recommendation by the Ombudsperson.[90]

This new scheme of listing was examined by the Court of Justice in the *Kadi II* litigation.[91] While attempting to accommodate to some extent security considerations, the Court of Justice has adopted in *Kadi II* a rigorous, substantive test of judicial review of listing decisions by the European judiciary. The Court reiterated that such a judicial review is indispensable to ensure a fair balance between the maintenance of international peace and security and the protection of the fundamental rights and freedoms of the person concerned, those being shared values of the UN and the European Union.[92] While the emphasis on shared values may have been included to diffuse potential tensions with regard to the conflict between EU law and UN Security Council measures, the Court did not hesitate to emphasise the need to protect human rights in the face of a UN framework providing with limited safeguards. The Court reiterated the substantial negative impact of sanctions to the affected individuals[93] and went on to say that the improvements at UN level with regard to listing do not provide the guarantee of effective judicial protection to the affected individual.[94] The Court of Justice thus confirmed again, as in *Kadi I*, the autonomy of the EU legal order based on the respect for the rule of law and fundamental rights. While the Court's ruling in *Kadi I* has had a noticeable impact in improving listing procedures at UN level, the Court of Justice in *Kadi II* sent a clear message that such improvements can by no means equate to effective judicial protection. The Court of Justice continued to remind the international community that it is the individual who should be the focus of authorities in the invasive process of the imposition of restrictive sanctions. At the same time, the Court of Justice in *Kadi II* sent a clear message with regard to the relationship between the executive and the judiciary: the executive cannot use secrecy and confidentiality to evade judicial scrutiny, especially when the protection of fundamental rights is at stake.[95] However, it must be noted that the Court focused on procedural justice and refrained from ruling on the impact of terrorist listings on substantive human rights of the affected individuals, such as the right to property, and did not question (perhaps unsurprisingly) the very existence of the sanctions system

89 Para 12–35.

90 Para 23.

91 Resulting in Joined Cases C-584/10 P, C-593/10 P and C-595/10 P, *European Commission v Kadi*.

92 Para 131.

93 Para 132.

94 Para 133.

95 Valsamis Mitsilegas, 'The European Union and the Global Governance of Crime' in Valsamis Mitsilegas, Peter Alldridge and Leonidas Cheliotis (eds), *Globalisation, Criminal Law and Criminal Justice: Theoretical, Comparative and Transnational Perspectives* (Hart 2015) 189.

and the elevation of the UN Security Council into a legislator. This practice is continuing, with the recent adoption of a UN Resolution on 'foreign fighters' being a key example. As with the post-9/11 Resolutions, the 'foreign fighters' Resolutions have gone through a process of legitimisation via the adoption of legislation – in Europe, this has occurred as seen above with the Council of Europe and currently with the European Union.

Conclusion

This chapter has provided a typology of norm-making in the field of transnational criminal law and has painted a complex, multi-layered landscape of global security governance. Traditional forms of international law-making – in the form of United Nations treaties – have emerged in the past three decades to address major perceived security threats including drug trafficking, money laundering, organised crime and corruption. The more recent treaties – the 2000 Palermo Convention and UNCAC in 2003 – have placed emphasis not only on standard-setting, but also on compliance, by establishing a series of monitoring mechanisms albeit on the basis of the principles of equality and sovereignty of states parties. This model of global law-making has been deemed to be limited by key global players (and in particular the United States and the European Union). The lack of global consensus has meant that the international community has not managed to reach consensus on all major areas of security concern (terrorism and cyber-crime are examples in this context). At the same time, regulatory and legal responses reflected the need to react to perceived security threats as a matter of urgency (in particular post-9/11) and as a matter of priority and sustained focus (in particular in the development of a global anti-money laundering regime). They also reflected a greater emphasis towards effective implementation and compliance across the globe, in an effort to create a global regulatory and legal level-playing field. These factors explain the emergence of forms of governance parallel to the traditional model of international conventions. These forms of governance have emerged at three levels: at the regional level; at the level of 'soft' or 'informal' law; and at the level of 'global administrative law'. Rather than being mutually exclusive, these levels of governance of transnational crime are inter-related and mutually reinforcing. In all areas of transnational crime examined in this essay, regulation in one level of governance has resulted in regulation in another level of governance. The emergence of a brand new global framework to counter money laundering and terrorist finance exemplifies this trend: norms have emerged in the UN system (in both the Vienna and Palermo Conventions), at the regional level (in the Council of Europe, the EU and the regional bodies of the FATF), and at the level of the UN Security Council. Global anti-money laundering governance has also witnessed the emergence in the form of the FATF of a new international institution with a single agenda, entrusted specifically to counter money laundering and terrorist finance.

The emergence of this paradigm of global multi-level governance in the field of transnational crime poses significant challenges for justice and the rule of law. As a starting point, it must be remembered that this is a paradigm centred on enforcement, with the norms adopted having a significant impact on individual rights. In a system of transnational criminal law, the norms adopted at global level have a domestic reach, in creating criminal law obligations at the national level and at times – as in the case of sanctions imposed by the Security Council – having a direct impact on individuals. Both the way in which global norms are produced and their impact challenge perceptions and the substance of justice at the international and domestic level. At the international level, a key issue is justice among states, which is an aspect of the principle of equality among states. On a number of occasions – and in particular in cases of less traditional forms of norm-making including by the FATF and the UN Security Council – we have seen that norms are pushed through by a select club of states, which then attempt to impose standards globally. This form of governance gives little space to a plurality of voices across the globe. The shift towards regionalism can be explained as an attempt to address this injustice and take into account diversity, but the very foundations and processes of global norm-making have not changed significantly over time. At the domestic level, the issue of justice is linked to the protection of fundamental rights and, in particular, the right to judicial protection. The justice deficit in this context has been clearly demonstrated in the case of terrorist sanctions imposed by the UN Security Council, where invasive action has been adopted against specific individuals behind closed doors and with very little transparency or justification. Challenges to justice in this context are inextricably linked to challenges for the rule of law. In its *Kadi* litigation the Court of Justice has highlighted these challenges for the protection of fundamental rights by insisting on the need for full judicial scrutiny of executive action. But the rule of law challenges are not limited to judicial review. The system of governance established in particular by informal and global administrative law raises major questions of democracy, transparency, accountability and participation in the process of global norm-making in transnational criminal law. Notwithstanding attempts to improve procedures at the FATF and UN Security Council, a plethora of global enforcement standards are being depoliticised and produced behind closed doors by experts from a select group of states – and are then presented as an orthodoxy for the whole world to adopt. Fundamental rule of law requirements and the impact of these measures and transnational criminal law on individual rights make this form of governance increasingly untenable.

Part I

Money laundering, terrorist financing and cybercrime

3 Introduction to anti-money laundering regulation in China

Institutions, legal framework and practices

Shi Yanan

Anti-money laundering laws and regulations in China

Laws

Criminal code

In China, the act of money laundering was first stipulated as a crime in the Decision on the Prohibition of Narcotic Drugs, enacted by the Standing Committee of the National People's Congress (NPC) in 1990. Article 4 of this decision provided: 'Whoever cover up or conceal the illicit nature and source of the property gained by selling drugs, shall be sentenced to fixed-term imprisonment of not more than seven years, criminal detention or public surveillance, and may also be fined.'[1]

Article 120a states that:

> Whoever provides funds to any terrorist organisation or individual who engages in terrorism shall be sentenced to fixed-term imprisonment of not more than five years, criminal detention, public surveillance or deprivation of political rights, and shall also be fined; if the circumstances are serious, he shall be sentenced to fixed-term imprisonment of not less than five years, and he shall also be fined or his property shall be confiscated. Where a unit commits the crime mentioned in the preceding paragraph, it shall be fined, and the persons who are directly in charge and the other persons who are directly responsible for the offence shall be punished in accordance with the provisions of the preceding paragraph.

Article 191 of the current Criminal Code of China, which was revised respectively by Amendment 3 enacted in 2001 and Amendment 6 enacted in 2006, states that:

1 This paper uses the English translations of Chinese legislation available at <www.npc.gov.cn/englishnpc/Law/Frameset-page6.html>.

> Whoever, while knowing that the funds are proceeds illegally obtained from drug-related crimes, crimes committed by organisations of criminal gangs, terrorist crimes, crimes of smuggling, graft and bribery, crimes of disrupting the order of financial management, crimes of financial fraud, commits any of the following acts in order to cover up or conceal the source or nature of the funds shall, in addition to being confiscated of the said proceeds and gains, be sentenced to fixed-term imprisonment of not more than five years or criminal detention and shall also, or shall only be fined not less than five percent but not more than 20 percent of the amount of money laundered; if the circumstances are serious, he shall be sentenced to fixed-term imprisonment of not less than five but not more than 10 years and shall also be fined not less than five percent but not more than 20 percent of the amount of money laundered: (1) providing fund accounts; (2) helping exchange property into cash, any financial bills, or negotiable securities; (3) helping transfer capital through transferring accounts or any other form of settlement; (4) helping remit funds to any other country; or (5) covering up or concealing by any other means the nature or source of the illegally obtained proceeds and the gains derived therefrom. Where a unit commits any of the crimes mentioned in the preceding paragraph, it shall be fined, and the persons who are directly in charge and the other persons who are directly responsible for the crime shall be sentenced to fixed-term imprisonment of not more than five years or criminal detention; if the circumstances are serious, he shall be sentenced to fixed-term imprisonment of not less than five but not more than 10 years.

Article 312 of the Criminal Code, revised by Amendment 6, states that:

> Whoever knowingly hides, transfers, purchases, helps to sell or use other ways to cover up or conceal the goods gained through crimes and their proceeds, shall be sentenced to fixed-term imprisonment of not more than three years, criminal detention or public surveillance, and shall also, or shall only, be fined; if the circumstances are serious, he shall be sentenced to fixed-term imprisonment of not less than three years but not more than seven years, and shall also be fined.

Article 349 of the Criminal Code states that:

> Whoever harbors, transfers or covers up narcotic drugs or the pecuniary and other gains from drug crimes shall be sentenced to fixed-term imprisonment of no more than three years, criminal detention or public surveillance; if the circumstances are serious, he shall be sentenced to fixed-term imprisonment of not less than three years but not more than 10 years.

The crimes provided for by Articles 120a, 191, 312 and 349 are all related to so-called money laundering. However, in China only the crime provided for by Article 191 is called the crime of money laundering. The crime provided for by

Article 120a is called the crime of providing funds for terrorist activity, while the crime provided for by Article 312 is called the crime of covering up or concealing the goods gained through crimes and criminal proceeds. Finally, the crime provided for by Article 349 is called the crime of harbouring, transferring or covering up narcotic drugs or proceeds gained through drug crimes, according to the judicial interpretation issued by the Supreme People's Court (SPC) and Supreme People's Procuratorate (SPP). These four crimes overlap. For example, the penalty provided for by Article 191 is more severe than that under Article 312, so when both are applicable, the former will be applied in priority.

The criminalisation of money laundering in the Criminal Code shows the effect of international conventions, such as the United Nations Convention against Illicit Traffic in Narcotic Drugs and Psychotropic Substances,[2] the conventions on combating terrorism, the United Nations Convention against Transnational Organized Crime, and the United Nations Convention against Corruption, etc.

Anti-money laundering law

The Anti-Money Laundering Law, adopted at the 24th meeting of the Standing Committee of the 10th National People's Congress of the People's Republic of China (PRC) on 31 October 2006, came into force on 1 January 2007. There are seven chapters in this law, which include: general provisions, supervision over anti-money laundering, the obligation of financial institutions to fight against money laundering, anti-money laundering investigation, international cooperation in anti-money laundering, legal responsibility and supplementary provisions.

This law contains a legal definition of money laundering. According to Article 2 of this law, anti-money laundering refers to the adoption of relevant measures according to the provisions of this law to prevent any money laundering that is designed to cover up or conceal, by various means, the sources and nature of the criminal gains, and proceeds derived from drug-related crimes, crimes committed by organisations of criminal gangs, terrorist crimes, crimes of smuggling, graft and bribery, crimes of disrupting the order of financial management, crimes of financial fraud, etc.

The law establishes the duties of the financial institutions and special non-financial institutions. Article 3 states that financial institutions established within the territory of PRC and special non-financial institutions are required to comply with anti-money laundering obligations. They shall, in accordance with law, adopt preventive and monitoring measures by establishing sound systems for establishing their clients' identities, preserving the data for clients' identities and records of transactions, and set up a reporting system for transactions involving large sums of money and suspicious transactions. Here, financial institutions

2 Angran Gu, 'Illustration to the Draft to the Decision on the Prohibition Against Narcotic Drugs' (25 October 1990) <www.npc.gov.cn/wxzl/gongbao/2000-12/27/content_5002497.htm>.

include policy-oriented banks, commercial banks, credit cooperatives, postal saving and remittance institutions, trust investment companies, securities companies, futures brokerage companies and insurance companies that are established according to law to engage in financial business. The definition of financial institutions also covers institutions that are determined by the State Council's administrative department in charge of anti-money laundering to engage in financial business. Special non-financial institutions shall also comply with anti-money laundering obligations. The scope of such obligations is determined by the State Council's administrative department in charge of anti-money laundering in conjunction with other relevant departments.

Other legal instruments

Article 5 of the Decision on Relevant Issues of Further Strengthening Anti-Terrorist Work, enacted by the Standing Committee of NPC on 31 October 2011, states that when the department for public security of the State Council releases the list of terrorist organisations and individuals, it can freeze the funds or other properties related to such organisations and persons. Financial institutions and special non-financial institutions shall freeze the funds and other properties of terrorist organisations and individuals immediately, and report to the department for public security of the National State Security Council and the department in charge of anti-money laundering of the State Council.

On the basis of this decision and relevant authorisation, the PBC, the Ministry for Public Security and the Ministry for National Security, referring to the United Nations Security Council Resolutions 1267 and 1373 the recommendations of the Financial Action Task Force (FATF), drafted the Administrative Measures on Freezing the Assets relating to Terrorist Activities.[3] This regulation was published on 10 January 2014.

Departmental rules

Before the promulgation of the Anti-Money Laundering Law, departmental rules[4] made by the People's Bank of China included the Provisions on Anti-Money Laundering through Financial Institutions (1 March 2003), the Measures on the Administration of Reporting Large and Suspicious Payment Transactions of Renminbi (1 March 2003) and the Measures on the Administration of Financial Institutions Reporting Large and Doubtful Foreign Exchange Funds Trade (1 March 2003).

After the promulgation of the Anti-Money Laundering Law, the People's Bank of China alone or along with Ministry of Public Security or other ministries has

3 PBC, *China Anti-Money Laundering Report* (People's Bank of China 2013).
4 Departmental rules mean the regulations made by the Departments under the State Council.

made many departmental rules, which form a practical framework of anti-money laundering in China.

Provisions on anti-money laundering through financial institutions (came into force on 1 January 2007)

According to the Anti-Money Laundering Law and this departmental regulation, the PBC shall be the anti-money laundering administrative department of the State Council. It shall supervise and administer the anti-money laundering work of the financial institutions. The China Banking Regulatory Commission (CBRC), China Securities Regulatory Commission (CSRC) and China Insurance Regulatory Commission (CIRC) shall, according to their respective functions, exercise their duties of anti-money laundering supervision and administration. During the course of anti-money laundering supervision and administration, the PBC shall cooperate with the relevant departments, institutions and judicial organs of the State Council. According to the authorisation of the State Council, the PBC shall carry out international cooperation in respect of anti-money laundering on behalf of the Chinese Government.

The PBC's functions on anti-money laundering supervision and administration are: (1) to formulate, jointly with the CBRC, CSRC and CIRC, anti-money laundering by-laws for financial institutions; (2) to be responsible for monitoring the laundering of funds in RMB and in foreign currencies; (3) to supervise and inspect the financial institutions' compliance with anti-money laundering obligations; (4) to investigate the suspicious transactions within its scope of functions; (5) to report to investigative authorities any transaction involving money laundering; (6) to exchange the relevant anti-money laundering information and materials with overseas anti-money laundering institutions in pursuance of the pertinent laws and administrative regulations; (7) to perform other functions as prescribed by the State Council.

The PBC has established the China Anti-Money Laundering Monitoring and Analysing Centre (CALMAC), which exercises the following functions: (1) to accept and analyse the large transactions reports in RMB or in foreign currencies and suspicious transaction reports; (2) to establish a national anti-money laundering database so as to properly preserve the information about large-sum transactions and suspicious transactions as reported by financial institutions; (3) to report the analysis results to the PBC according to the relevant provisions; (4) to require the financial institutions to timely report large-sum transactions in RMB or in foreign currencies as well as suspicious transactions; (5) to exchange information and materials with the relevant overseas institutions upon approval of the People's Bank of China; (6) to perform other functions as prescribed by the PBC.

According to this regulation, financial institutions, including all of their branches, must establish a sound internal anti-money laundering control system in accordance with the law, set up a special anti-money laundering department or designate an internal department to take charge of the anti-money laundering work, formulate internal operating procedures and control measures for anti-money laundering and offer anti-money laundering training to its staff members so as to enhance their anti-money laundering capability.

Financial institutions must set up and implement a client identity identification system with the following functions: (1) to identify the identity of any client with whom it establishes a business relationship or a one-off financial business. This requires the financial institution to see the client's genuine and valid identity certificate or any other identity document, verify and register it, and timely update the client's identity information if it is changed; (2) to inquire about the purpose and nature of the transaction and effectively identify the beneficiary of the transaction; (3) to re-identify the identity of the client if it finds any abnormality or if it has any doubt about the genuineness, validity and completeness of the client's identity materials obtained earlier; (4) to ensure that any overseas financial institution, with an agency relationship or similar relationship, effectively identifies the identity of the clients to be able to obtain the clients' identity information from the overseas financial institution. Where a financial institution, during the course of performing its anti-money laundering obligations, finds any suspected crime, it must submit a written timely report to the local branch of the PBC and to the local public security organ, and assist the judicial organ and administrative law enforcement organ in investigation of the money laundering activities.

The PBC and its branch institutions may, when necessary, take the following measures to conduct anti-money laundering inspections on the spot: (1) to carry out inspections by entering into a financial institution; (2) to query the staff members of a financial institution about the relevant information and demand them to make an explanation about the inspection items; (3) to consult and copy a financial institution's documents and materials relating to the inspection items, and seal up and preserve the documents and materials that are likely to be moved away, destroyed, concealed or altered; (4) to check the computer system used by a financial institution to manage the business data.

When a financial institution violates these Provisions, the PBC or its branch institution, such as a central sub-branch at the prefecture level or above, shall punish it in accordance with the Anti-Money Laundering Law and may, according to different circumstances, propose that the CBRC, CSRC or CIRC take the following measures: (1) order the financial institution to stop business for rectification, or to revoke its business license; (2) disqualify the directly liable directors, senior managers and other directly liable persons from assuming their respective position, and to prohibit them from working in the financial sector; (3) order the financial institution to impose a disciplinary sanction on the directly liable directors, senior managers and other directly liable persons.

Measures on the administration of reporting large and suspicious payment transactions (came into force on 1 March 2007)

According to this regulation, PBC and its branch institutions shall supervise and inspect the financial institutions' reports of large-sum transactions and suspicious transactions. The CALMAC is responsible for accepting reports of large-sum transactions and suspicious transactions in RMB and in foreign currencies. If the CALMAC finds that the basic contents of a financial institution's report of large-sum transaction or suspicious transaction are not complete or there is any error in the report, it may issue to the reporting financial institution a notice of supplement or correction. The financial institution shall make a supplement or correction within five working days after it receives the notice of supplement or correction.

A financial institution shall set up special anti-money laundering posts and explicitly appoint full-time staff members to be responsible for reporting large-sum transactions and suspicious transactions. It will work out internal management rules and operating procedures for the reporting of large-sum transactions and suspicious transactions according to these measures and submit them to the PBC for archival purposes. It will also supervise and administer its subsidiaries' implementation of the rules on the reporting of large-sum transactions and suspicious transactions. It must report the following large-sum transactions to the CALMAC in these circumstances: (1) a single transaction or the total of RMB transaction(s) or foreign currency transaction(s) on a single day in the form of deposit of cash, withdrawal of cash, settlement or sale of foreign exchange in cash, exchange of notes, cash remittance, payment of cash instrument reaches 200,000 yuan or more, or reaches the equivalent value of US $10,000 or more; (2) a single transfer or the total of transfers on the current day between the bank accounts of legal persons, other organisations and individuals and individual commercial households reaches 2 million yuan more, or reaches the equivalent value of US$200,000 or more; (3) a single transfer or total of transfers on the current day between the bank accounts of natural persons, or between the bank account of natural person and the bank account of a legal person, any other organisation or individual industrial and commercial household, reaches 500,000 yuan or more, or reaches the equivalent value of US$100,000 or more; (4) a single transnational transaction or the total of transnational transactions on the current day, to which one party is a natural person, reaches the equivalent value of US$10,000 or more.

Detailed rules for anti-money laundering investigations (for trial omplementation) (came into force on 21 May 2007)

According to this regulation, if the PBC or its branch institution at the provincial level finds any of the following suspicious transactions and if it is necessary to verify them, it may conduct an anti-money laundering investigation of the following transactions: (1) a suspicious transaction reported by a financial institution under the relevant provisions; (2) a suspicious transaction found in the process of anti-money laundering supervision and administration; (3) a suspicious transaction reported by a central sub-branch of the PBC in a prefecture or city at the prefecture level or sub-branch of the PBC in a county or city at the county level; (4) a suspicious transaction circulated through a notice by any other administrative organ or by the judicial organ; (5) a suspicious transaction exposed by any entity or individual; (6) a suspicious transaction known through a foreign-related channel; (7) any other suspicious transaction, which it is reasonable to investigate and verify.

Administrative measures for financial institutions' reporting of transactions suspected of financing for terrorist purposes (came into force on 21 June 2007)

'Financing for terrorist purposes' in this regulation refers to the following types of behaviour: (1) raising, possessing or using funds or other forms of property by terrorist organisations or terrorists; (2) assisting terrorist organisations, terrorists, terrorism or terrorist criminal activities with funds or other forms of property; (3) possessing, using or raising funds or other forms of property for the purpose for terrorist purposes or terrorist criminal activities; (4) possessing, using or raising funds or other forms of property for terrorist organisations or terrorists. The PBC and its branches shall supervise and examine the transactions suspected of financing for terrorist purposes as reported by financial institutions.

Administrative measures for the on-site inspections for anti-money laundering (for trial implementation) (came into force on 4 June 2007)

The anti-money laundering law enforcement departments of the PBC and of its branch institutions are responsible for the on-site inspections for anti-money laundering. The on-site inspections for anti-money laundering include the preparations for on-site inspections, execution of on-site inspections, treatments in on-site inspections, etc.

The People's Bank of China, China Banking Regulatory Commission, China Securities Regulatory Commission, and China Insurance Regulatory Commission: measures on the administration of client identity verification materials and transaction recording of financial institutions

A financial institution shall, according to the legal provisions on anti-money laundering and anti-terrorist financing, establish and improve internal working rules in respect of client identity identification, client materials and transaction recording. Designated special persons should take charge of the compliance management of anti-money laundering and anti-terrorist financing and reasonably design the work flow and operation norms, in order to make internal audits at regular intervals for the purpose of evaluating whether the internal operation rules are sound and effective, as well as timely amend and improve relevance by laws.

Measures on anti-money laundering and anti-terrorist financing through payment institutions (came into force on 5 March 2012)

'Payment institution' refers to the non-financial institution which has got the certificate for payment business in accordance with the Administration Measures on Non-Financial Institution Payment Service.

According to this regulation, the headquarters of payment institutions shall set up comprehensive and uniform internal anti-money laundering and anti-terrorist financing rules, which shall include: (1) measures for establishing the client's identity; (2) materials accepted as proof of client's identity and measures of storage of payment record; (3) the standard of suspicious payment and the procedure of analysing reports; (4) the measures of internal auditing and training on anti-money laundering and anti-terrorist financing; (5) internal process for assisting anti-money laundering and anti-terrorist financing investigations; (6) secret anti-money laundering and anti-terrorist financing measures; (7) other measures of preventing money laundering and terrorist financing. The payment institution shall set up specific organs or appoint some internal organ to be in charge of anti-money laundering and terrorist financing.

Administrative measures for the freezing of assets relating to terrorist activities (came into force on 10 January 2014)

This regulation requires all the financial institutions and special non-financial institutions in the territory of the PRC, to strictly take freezing measures according to the list of terrorist organisations and individual issued by the Ministry for Public Security. They shall have in place internal processes for freezing the assets relating to terrorist activities, and supervise their branches or affiliated institutions. Furthermore, they shall appoint specific organs or personnel to focus on the performance of relevant obligations while protecting the client's identity information and trading information. This regulation also provides for the coordination between financial institutions and the public security organs.

Judicial interpretation

The Supreme People's Court: interpretation of several issues concerning the specific application of law in the trials of money laundering and other criminal cases (came into force on 11 November 2009)

This interpretation has clarified the meaning of some key elements of Articles 191 and 312. In case of the judgment of 'knowingly', the judges are required to take into account subjective and objective factors. Examples of those are the defendant's cognitive ability, the circumstances of his contact to the goods gained through crimes and relevant proceeds, the fact of exchanging and transferring of such property and his confession, etc.

The anti-money laundering agencies in China and their functions

Responsibilities of agencies related to anti-money laundering

The People's Bank of China; the Supreme People's Court, the Supreme People's Procuratorate; the General Office of the State Council; the Ministry of Foreign Affairs; the Ministry of Public Security; the Ministry of State Security; the Ministry of Supervision, the Ministry of Justice; the Ministry of Finance; the

Ministry of Construction; the Ministry of Commerce; the General Administration of Customs; the State Administration of Taxation; the State Administration of Industry and Commerce; the State Administration of Radio, Film and Television; the Legal Affairs Office of the State Council; the China Banking Regulatory Commission; the China Securities Regulatory Commission; the China Insurance Regulatory Commission; the Post Office; the Foreign Exchange Bureau; the General Staff Department of the Chinese People's Liberation Army and other 23 departments; are the members of inter-departmental joint meetings on anti-money laundering while the PBC is the leading institution of the joint meetings with the permission of the State Council. The joint meetings are the mechanism to coordinate the relevant agencies to control and fight against money laundering.

According to the laws and other legal instruments:

- The responsibility of PBC is to: undertake specific tasks in the organisation and coordination of national anti-money laundering work; undertake international cooperation and exchange work; guide and arrange anti-money laundering work in the financial industry, study and formulate anti-money laundering policies and measures in financial industry and the supervisory reporting regime; collect, track and analyse the data on RMB, foreign currency and other suspicious transactions provided by other departments; transfer those suspected of a crime to judicial departments; cooperate with judicial agencies in the investigation of money laundering; formulate proposals for anti-money laundering policy; coordinate and manage foreign cooperation in the anti-money laundering field. The PBC also coordinates anti-money laundering activities in relation to non-financial industries that have been identified by the relevant departments to pose high money-laundering risks.
- The responsibility of the SPC is to: supervise and guide the trial of money laundering crimes and issue timely judicial interpretation about the relevant legal problems encountered in trials.
- The responsibility of the SPP is to: supervise and guide the arrest, prosecution and supervision; investigate crimes committed by public officials, issue timely judicial interpretation about the relevant legal problems encountered in the work of procuratorates.
- The responsibility of the Ministry for Foreign Affairs is to: study the relevant policies about international cooperation against money laundering; study and give assistance to international or regional anti-money laundering organisations that China participates in; study and provide assistance in anti-money laundering cooperation between governments and perform its duties in accordance with relevant international conventions.
- The responsibility of the Ministry for Public Security is to: organise, coordinate and direct local public security organs in relation to preventive anti-money laundering work and detect and investigate suspicious financial transactions.

- The responsibility of the Ministry of State Security is to: take part in intelligence gathering on money laundering crimes, study relevant programs of information sharing and cooperation; carry out investigations into suspicious activities involving foreign affairs or foreign nationals through international cooperation and other channels.
- The responsibility of the Ministry of Supervision is to: investigate and deal with illegality involving governmental administrative departments, national civil servant and other persons appointed by the governmental administrative departments; strengthen the design of the anti-money laundering framework; facilitate information sharing and cooperation mechanisms in the fight against corruption and corruption-related money laundering.
- The responsibility of the Ministry of Justice is to: supervise anti-money laundering compliance in the legal and notary services; coordinate judicial assistance in money laundering cases according to relevant treaties and conventions, especially for recovering the stolen funds overseas.
- The responsibility of the Ministry of Finance is to: make the budgetary provisions for anti-money laundering work; take further steps to strengthen the management of financial funds and accounts; study and strengthen the supervision of state-owned financial assets and state-owned property; establish the system of recovering money involved in money laundering back to the national treasury; study and establish accounting firms, evaluating institutions and other intermediary organisations; carry out anti-money laundering work with the assistance of certified public accountants, appraisers and other practitioners; make use of international bilateral and multilateral cooperation as well as relevant international forums to carry out anti-money laundering work.
- The responsibility of the Ministry of Construction is to: carry out anti-money laundering work in the real estate industry and study the policies and measures for carrying out anti-money laundering work in real estate industry.
- The responsibility of the Ministry of Commerce is to: participate in the strengthening of the management of the fields and regions where money laundering is relatively frequent; supervise anti-money laundering compliance in foreign-funded enterprises and make relevant policy recommendations; participate in strengthening the supervision of import and export trades and the prevention of trade-based money laundering
- The responsibility of the General Administration of Customs is to: study and establish a supervisory and investigative system of fighting against cross-border money laundering; strengthen the supervision of inbound and outbound currency flows, bankbook, securities and articles made of gold and silver in the process of import and export trades; prevent trade-based money laundering; cooperate with relevant departments closely and facilitate information sharing in relation to import and export trades.
- The responsibility of the State Administration of Taxation is to: participate in the study of the policies and measures against tax evasion and establish appropriate mechanisms for information sharing and law enforcement cooperation in conjunction with relevant departments.

- The responsibility of the State Administration of Industry and Commerce is to: regulate market access; strengthen anti-money laundering supervision; establish the anti-money information communication and reporting system with the People's Bank of China, the Ministry of Public Security, the Ministry of State Security, the State Administration of Taxation, the General Administration of Customs and other relevant departments and cooperate with relevant departments to carry out anti-money laundering supervision in non-financial industries.
- The responsibility of the State Administration of Radio, Film and Television is to: participate in anti-money laundering education and raise people's awareness of anti-money laundering.
- The responsibility of the General Office of the State Council is to: participate in drawing up anti-money laundering laws and regulations and participate in legislative investigation of special laws and regulations for anti-money laundering.
- The responsibility of the China Banking Regulatory Commission is to: give assistance to PBC to study the anti-money laundering policies and measures in banking industry and the supervisory reporting system of suspicious transactions, assist the PBC in developing supervisory guidance for anti-money laundering in the banking industry and assist the PBC in the supervision of the banking industry.
- The responsibility of the China Securities Regulatory Commission is to: cooperate with PBC to study the anti-money laundering policies in securities and futures industry as well as to supervise the system for reporting suspicious transactions, formulate the anti-money laundering regulations and systems as well as supervisory guidance in securities and futures industry, be in charge of supervising how the securities and futures industry carry out anti-money laundering regulations, study the important problems of anti-money laundering in international and domestic securities and futures industry and put forward policy recommendations.
- The responsibility of the China Insurance Regulatory Commission is to: be in charge of the anti-money laundering work in insurance industry while the PBC will organise and coordinate the work; participate in the supervision of suspicious transaction reporting by the insurance industry; formulate the supervisory guidance for the insurance industry; carry out on-site and off-site supervision of anti-money laundering compliance in the insurance industry; study the important problems of anti-money laundering in international and domestic insurance industries and put forward policy recommendations.
- The responsibility of the Post Office is to: assist PBC and CBRC in studying the anti-money laundering policies and measures of postal savings businesses and in supervising the reporting of suspicious transactions; supervise anti-money laundering compliance of the postal remittance systems.
- The responsibility of the Foreign Exchange Bureau is to: under the unified leadership of PBC, take charge of supervising and managing the transaction reporting task of wholesale and foreign exchange funds; formulate and improve the transaction reporting system of wholesale and foreign exchange funds;

Table 3.1 The anti-money laundering bureau

General Office	International Cooperation Office	Policy Supervision Office	Security Management Office	Anti-Money Laundering Investigation Office

monitor abnormal cross-border capital flows; collect, filter and analyse the transaction information of wholesale and foreign exchange funds; punish non-compliance; transfer suspicious cases to relevant law enforcement agencies; cooperate with relevant law enforcement agencies; fight against 'underground banks' and other illegal foreign exchange activities; manage and guide financial organisations in anti-money laundering compliance relevant to foreign exchange business; participate in the studying of uniform reporting standards of suspicious financial transactions for domestic currency and foreign currency.

- The responsibility of the General Staff Department of the Chinese People's Liberation Army is to: collect and provide the intelligence information on money-laundering crimes; assist in the location of criminals who have fled abroad; participate in international cooperation on anti-money laundering; strengthen the fight against money laundering activities in the border areas.

The organisational structure of the anti-money laundering bureau of PBC

The functions of the anti-money laundering bureau of the PBC are to undertake the task of organising and coordinating national anti-money laundering policies; study and protocol anti-money laundering rules and policies in financial institutions; undertake the task of international cooperation on anti-money laundering; collect, track and analyse RMB, foreign currency and other suspicious transactions reported by other departments. Furthermore, it is required to transfer those suspected of a crime to judicial departments; assist judicial departments in the investigation of suspected money laundering; undertake the task of security and protection in the system of the PBC; formulate prevention measures and, finally, organise the protection and armed escort for the movement of gold, silver, cash and securities in the system of the PBC.

Current conditions of money laundering in China and achievements of PBC and other agencies in anti-money laundering

Current conditions of money laundering in China

There are ten usual typologies of money laundering in China[5]:

5 See Zhao Zhan, Jun Liu and Jie Liu, *Explanation to Anti-Money Laundering and Practical Management* (China People's Public Security Press 2008); Lixin Yan and Zhen Zhang, *The*

1 The use of financial institutions to transfer illicit proceeds. For example, Wu, a staff member of the China Bank, stole 4 billion yuan of foreign exchange, of which US$87,000 was sent to Singapore via other countries. In the end, the High Court of Singapore returned this money to the China Bank.
2 The transportation of drug trafficking proceeds into China. For example, Dong (a US citizen) and Zheng (a Chinese citizen living in the US) attempted to launder the money from drug crimes. In February 1993, they were arrested by the police in Fujian, and US$1.4 million was confiscated.
3 The use of export trade. For example, Zhang (a Hong Kong citizen) smuggled 20,000 grams of gold to mainland China. In order to transfer the dirty money back to Hong Kong, he signed an agreement with Hong Kong's Qiuyi company and promised to pay the debt of Qiuyi in mainland China while Qiuyi would pay the relevant money to him in Hong Kong.
4 Money laundering under the pretext of investing in China. Gangs abroad, such as the Yakuza in Japan, favour the technique of laundering dirty money by investing in China the proceeds of smuggling and trafficking drugs.
5 The use of a shell company to launder dirty money. Criminals set up hotels, night clubs and other kinds of companies, which help mix their dirty money with legitimate income.
6 The use of a fake name to deposit money or purchase financial bills. Corrupt officials often resort to anonymity when they dispose of the proceeds of bribery.
7 Illegal transfer of capital. This means that the criminal signs the banker's acceptance bill without having any business rationale for the transaction, whereupon the money is transferred many times until its origin cannot be determined.
8 The laundering of dirty money through an underground bank. Based on the types of currency and services, underground banks can be divided into three kinds: (1) running local currency; (2) running foreign exchange; (3) running comprehensively. For example, in 1993, Li Kuide from Taiwan of China, set up the Sanya Jiahong Real Estate Company in Hainan. From 1998, he used this company as an underground bank to manage the exchange business of the Taiwanese currency, Hong Kong dollars, US dollars and Renminbi. Until 2004, his underground bank had traded foreign exchange of about 520 million yuan, while some underground banks set up bank accounts in China and abroad, and had their own independent settlement systems. On one hand, they supply the companies or individuals from abroad with RMB in China and accept foreign

Basic Course of Anti-Money Laundering (Fudan University Press 2008); Jie Chen, Bei Bei Zhang and Jie Deng Yang, *Chinese Strategies of Anti-Money Laundering in a Global Context* (China Book Press 2013).

currencies abroad, while on the other hand, they provide foreign currencies to companies or individuals from China and get RMB in China.[6] Judging from the current situation, underground banks play a significant role in illicit cross-border transfer of money and are involved in large-scale capital flight. For example, the money involved in the Weihai, Shandong Province '11·14' cross-border illicit trading in foreign exchange case uncovered in 2002 amounted to as much as US$50 million. The underground bank of Guangdong Xu had illicitly traded foreign exchange for 500 million Hong Kong dollars for its more than a dozen clients before being banned. Underground banks are not only concentrated in the southeast coastal areas, but also exist in the border trade areas. Criminals always set up several underground banks in different cities, which show a clear trend in a broad area.[7]

9 The use of private lending to launder money, meaning that the criminal lends the dirty money to small companies or individuals, and the latter may return the money to the appointed bank account of some companies related to the criminal.
10 The laundering of dirty money through an insurance company. The criminal buys any kind of insurance with the dirty money, and then revises the contract clause with insurance company to get back the insurance fee by legal means from the insurance company.

Nowadays, money laundering activities are managed through networks by electronic business, online auction, online banks and online gambling.

6 The main process of such transaction is as follows: a client who needs foreign currency should provide an underground bank with Renminbi or deposit the money into a designated bank account. Then the underground bank will calculate the exact amount of foreign currency according to the exchange rate of the black market on that day, and request its partner abroad to put the money into the bank account that the client appoints. The settlement model of the underground bank in China and its partner abroad is called 'offset balance'. When foreign cash is not abundant, the underground bank will buy foreign cash from others (always called 'exchange experts') and send to its partner abroad. Before 1998, 'exchange experts' got the foreign currency by using fake import contract and fake customs declaration. After 1998, the government changed the relevant institutions, so they could not use fake documents to get foreign currency. Now big underground banks usually own their companies and have a network of clients. They always balance the income and expenditure by repeated bucketing business with foreign companies, which are often called 'Dashu' in the underground banks business circles. It is mostly the illegal business enterprises that engage in the illicit foreign exchange transactions through underground banks. It is not safe to keep the illicit proceeds in the country, and they make every effort to transfer them to abroad by the use of foreign exchange and Renminbi, in order to transfer assets and evade the payment of duties. See Xiaohong Zhao and Chunlei Xie, 'Present Investigation of Underground Banks and Research on Countermeasures of Prevention and Combat' (2003) 1 Jinan Finance 15.

7 Yuan Wen, 'Underground Banks, No Escape in the Sunshine' *Guangming Daily* (Beijing, 29 November 2004) <www.gmw.cn/01gmrb/2004-11/29/content_140006.htm>.

Achievements of PBC and other agencies in anti-money laundering

In 2011, the CAMLAC received 336 million reports on large payments and 5.411 million reports on suspicious payments. The PBC discovered and received reports alerting it to 8,585 cases of money laundering, carried out 7,803 amoney laundering investigations on the basis of 1,593 important reports and transferred 595 cases to the investigative organisations. Local investigative organisations had 146 cases on file for investigation based on reports filed by the branches of the PBC. Meanwhile, the PBC cooperated with investigative organisations to investigate 982 cases of suspected money laundering. The CAMLAC transferred 56 suspicious transaction reports to the Supreme People's Procuratorate, the Ministry of Public Security and the Ministry of Supervision in the Central Commission for Discipline Inspection. Furthermore, it accepted and heard 311 cases investigated by the Supreme People's Procuratorate, the Ministry of Public Security and the Ministry of Supervision in the Central Commission for Discipline Inspection, General Administration of Customs and other departments.

In total, 11 defendants were charged with money laundering (Article 191 of CL), and 34,931 defendants were charged with covering up or concealing the source of goods through crimes and relevant proceeds (Article 312 of CL), while 118 defendants were charged with harbouring, transferring or covering up narcotic drugs or proceeds gained through drug crimes (Article 349 of CL).

During this year, the Ministry for Public Security, in cooperation with PBC and National Foreign Exchange Bureau, successfully investigated over 40 criminal cases of managing underground banks in China.[8]

In 2012, the CAMLAC received 328 million reports on large payments and 2.9 million reports on suspicious payments. The PBC discovered and received reports alerting it to 4,800 cases of money laundering, carried out 2,235 anti-money laundering investigations based on 530 important reports and transferred 490 cases to the investigative organisations. Local investigative organisations had 100 cases on file for investigation based on reports filed by the branches of the PBC. Meanwhile, the financial system cooperated with investigative organisations to investigate 1,034 suspected money laundering cases and predicate crimes. The CAMLAC transferred 87 suspicious transaction reports to the Ministry of Public Security and other departments, sent out 35 notifications, accepted and heard 507 cases and gave feedback to the departments whose investigations it assisted.

In total, 16 defendants were charged with money laundering (Article 191 of CL), and 33,659 defendants were charged with covering up or concealing the source of goods through crimes and relevant proceeds (Article 312 of CL), while 146 defendants were charged with harbouring, transferring, covering up narcotic drugs or proceeds gained through drug crimes (Article 349 of CL).[9]

8 PBC, *China Anti-Money Laundering Report* (2011).
9 PBC, *China Anti-Money Laundering Report* (2012).

In 2013, the CAMLAC received 381 million reports on large payments and 2.5 million reports on suspicious payments. The PBC discovered and received reports alerting it to 4,854 cases of money laundering and carried out 3,832 anti-money laundering investigations based on 473 important reports while it transferred 474 cases to the investigative organisations. Local investigative organisations had 168 cases on file for investigation based on reports filed by the branches of the PBC. Meanwhile, the financial system cooperated with investigative organisations to investigate 618 suspected money laundering cases and predicate crimes. The CAMLAC transferred 165 suspicious transaction reports to the Ministry of Public Security and other departments, sent out 39 notifications, accepted and heard 989 cases and gave feedback to the institutions whose investigations it assisted. These numbers exceed the total of the numbers from the preceding two years.

A total of 15 defendants were charged with money laundering (Article 191 of CL), and 28,233 defendants were charged with covering up or concealing the source of goods through crimes and relevant proceeds (Article 312 of CL). Finally, 112 defendants were charged with harbouring, transferring or covering up narcotic drugs or proceeds gained through drug crimes (Article 349 of CL), and 13 defendants were charged with providing funds to terrorist organisations or individuals (Article 120a of CL).[10]

10 PBC, *China Anti-Money Laundering Report* (2013).

4 Acts of charity and acts of terrorism

Regulation and prosecution

Clive Walker

Background

The attention given to the financing of terrorism has intensified since the attacks on 11 September 2001 for two reasons. First, international terrorism outruns local neighbourhoods and so garners its resources through dispersed channels beyond individual nations. The second reason is that the impact of *jihadi* terrorism has energized international condemnation and the universal demand for reaction. This shifting international attitude was signalled, *inter alia*, by the International Convention for the Suppression of the Financing of Terrorism,[1] though it is notable that just four ratifications, including by the United Kingdom, were lodged before 9/11. Also starting in 1999, the United Nations Security Council passed resolutions against support for individuals and groups associated with the Taliban and al-Qa'ida, commencing with Resolution 1267. These policies were reinforced by the Security Council Resolution 1373 of 28 September 2001 and were reflected in later resolutions against al-Qa'ida and Islamic State.[2] Endorsement and enforcement has also been undertaken by the European Union.[3]

One important aspect of the intensification of *jihadi* terrorism, and the focus on countering terrorism finances since 9/11, is that charities have fallen under closer scrutiny as potential channels of terrorism finance. Underlying characteristics within charities that give rise to vulnerability include enhanced public trust through the embodying of ideals of civic volunteerism, diversity of financial activities, cash intensiveness, a lighter regulatory regime than for financial institutions, complex multiple donor patterns, and the involvement of politically committed individuals.[4]

1 International Convention for the Suppression of the Financing of Terrorism (adopted 9 December 1999, entered into force 10 April 2002) (2000) 39 ILM 270.

2 UNSC Res 1989 (17 June 2011) UN Doc S/RES/1989; UNSC Res 2253 (17 December 2015) UN Doc S/RES/2253.

3 Council Regulation (EC) 2580/2001 of 27 December 2001; Council Regulation (EC) 881/2002 of 27 May 2002.

4 Tamar Barkay, 'Regulation and Voluntarism' (2009) 3(4) Regulation & Governance 360.

The potential link between charities and terrorism finance was indicated as an innate risk by the Financial Action Task Force (FATF) in October 2001, when it issued its Special Recommendation VIII on Terrorism Financing (as revised in 2012). The FATF has identified three categories of charity abuse.[5] The first concerns the use of bogus charities as fronts for terrorists. One rare but clear example in the United Kingdom concerned the prosecution in *R v Irfan Naseer and others*, involving a group from Birmingham who planned suicide attacks.[6] There was evidence that they posed as collectors for the Muslim Aid charity and carried out street and door-to-door collections in Birmingham and Leicester; they collected £12,100 but the court was told they also lost £9,149.39 in foreign currency trades. The second, more widespread, link is the fraudulent (or at least furtive) diversion of properly raised funds, which are subverted to terrorist purposes. This second category will sometimes arise from humanitarian work abroad in regions of conflict (such as Afghanistan, Pakistan, Palestine, Somalia and, hitherto, Sri Lanka) where financial probity may be compromised by the unavoidability of working alongside protagonists within the conflict. The third example involves broader exploitation of a charitable umbrella, such as through the recruitment and payment of extremists or for the propagation of a militant ideology.

These depictions of the salience of charities in contemporary terrorism financing underplay the personal commitment that drives terrorism and the personal integrity of charity workers. Reliance upon charities as sources of finance may also compromise the independence of terrorist groups.[7] The allegations of complicity in terrorism also overplay the analogy to criminal racketeering. Thus, the worldwide outlay of al-Qa'ida has been estimated at up to US$30m per annum,[8] but individual operations often involve modest costs, much of which is derived and defrayed by individual protagonists reliant on lawful sources rather than group or state sponsorship. Exceptionally, the ambitious attacks on 11 September 2001 did consume up to US$500,000 in travel and accommodation expenses.[9] However, the 11 March 2003 Madrid bombers incurred costs of just €8,315,[10] while

5 Financial Action Task Force, 'Terrorist Financing' (28 February 2008) 10–11 <www.fatf-gafi.org/media/fatf/documents/reports/FATF%20Terrorist%20Financing%20Typologies%20Report.pdf>.

6 *R v Irfan Naseer and others* (Woolwich Crown Court, 21 February 2013). See also Crown Prosecution Service, 'The Counter-Terrorism Division of the Crown Prosecution Service (CPS) – Cases Concluded in 2013' <www.cps.gov.uk/publications/prosecution/ctd_2013.html#a01>.

7 Michael Freeman, 'The Sources of Terrorist Financing: Theory and Typology' (2011) 34 *Studies in Conflict & Terrorism* 461, 471.

8 European Union Committee, *Money Laundering and the Financing of Terrorism* (HL 2008–09 132–I) para 9.

9 National Commission on Terrorist Attacks upon the United States, Final Report (US Government Publishing Office 2004) 172.

10 Thomas Baumert, 'The Impact of Terrorist Attacks on the Stock Markets' in Mikel Buesa and Thomas Baumert (eds), *The Economic Repercussions of Terrorism* (OUP 2010) 181.

the 7 July 2005 London bombers left another light financial footprint of around £8,000.[11] As for Islamic State, its huge wealth derives from various sources such as oil trading and the exploitation of the population under its control; it has no need to subvert charities.[12]

Consequently, the qualitative prominence of the anti-terrorism financing activities and legislation is not evidently correlated with quantitative impact. Nevertheless, the policy of attacking terrorism finance persists. More cynical explanations are that it is less contentious to curtail property rights than expressive rights, and that the focus represents a state ploy to assert control over non-governmental actors especially those linked to diaspora communities.[13] Conversely, tight financial regulation embodies the sound preventive purpose of stemming even larger flow of resources to terrorism.[14]

So far as the United Kingdom law is concerned, legislation against the funding of Irish and international terrorism has burgeoned over the past three decades, with attention to *jihadi* terrorism merely reinforcing well-established tactics.[15] The current code is executed by the Terrorism Act 2000, Pt III, comprising several offences, extensive powers of seizure and forfeiture, and civil forfeiture through cash seizures. These measures were supplemented by Anti-Terrorism, Crime and Security Act 2001. Part I replaced and extended beyond internal or external borders the cash seizure powers in the Terrorism Act 2000. There were also new measures to extend the scope of investigative and freezing powers, including account monitoring and customer information orders. Freezing powers are further regulated by the Counter-Terrorism Act 2008, Part V. Next, litigation about international sanctions produced the al-Qa'ida and Taliban (Asset Freezing) Regulations 2010 (SI 2010/1197) and the Terrorist Asset-Freezing etc. Act 2010. This legislation is applied in ways now specified in the 'CONTEST' strategy.[16]

The mechanisms for the governance of charities in regard to terrorism financing are manifold, but, beyond a brief exposition, the key questions to be tackled in this paper will involve the following. First, what has been the incidence of the interaction between UK-based charities and terrorism? Second, what has been the impact of regulation and legal interventions in terms of dampening that

11 Home Office, *Report of the Official Account of the Bombings in London on the 7th July 2005* (HC 2005–06 1087) paras 63–64.

12 Financial Action Task Force, 'Financing of the Terrorist Organisation Islamic State in Iraq and the Levant (ISIL)' (February 2015) <www.fatf-gafi.org/media/fatf/documents/reports/Financing-of-the-terrorist-organisation-ISIL.pdf>.

13 Mark Sidel, 'The Third Sector, Human Security, and Anti-Terrorism: The United States and Beyond' (2006) 17(3) *Voluntas* 199, 203.

14 Michael Levi, 'Combating the Financing of Terrorism' (2010) 50(4) *British Journal of Criminology* 650, 663.

15 Clive Walker, *Terrorism and the Law* (OUP 2011) chap 9.

16 Home Office, *Countering International Terrorism* (Cm 6888, 2006); Home Office, *CONTEST: The United Kingdom's Strategy for Countering Terrorism* (Cm 9048, 2015).

interaction with terrorism? Third, what have been the other, often unexpected, consequences of regulation and legal interventions?

Regulatory and legal mechanisms applied to suspected charitable financing of terrorism

Whether within strict law or administrative regulation, including self-regulation, the following essential elements of state governance emerge: the specification of rules and standards; the monitoring of compliance; and the establishment of enforcement devices. These elements will be corralled at two levels: 'internal governance' (inward looking) and 'external governance' (externally imposed and enforced).

Internal governance

Internal privately sited governance, operating beyond the state apparatus, is a growing phenomenon. Internal governance is applied to charities' demands that each organization should monitor its own business and procedures to rule out terrorism financing. Of course, 'external' rules also set and enforce the standards, so it is not wholly 'internal', but the charity must police itself, in the same way that money-laundering counteraction depends primarily on high standards of vigilance by financial institutions themselves.

The external rules that enforce the parameters for watchfulness against terrorism financing include the following. First, there is a general duty not to withhold information about terrorism, breach of which is a criminal offence. The offence is committed under section 38B(2) of the Terrorism Act 2000.[17] An offence occurs where a person, without reasonable excuse, does not disclose information which:

> . . . he knows or believes might be of material assistance
> (a) in preventing the commission by another person of an act of terrorism, or
> (b) in securing the apprehension, prosecution or conviction of another person, in the United Kingdom, for an offence involving the commission, preparation or instigation of an act of terrorism.

This extraordinary measure applies to the trustees of charities. There is no record of any trustee being prosecuted, but the offence is applied by the police across a broad spectrum as a reminder and even a threat.

A more onerous duty along the same lines is imposed by section 19(1) of the Terrorism Act 2000. When a person believes or suspects that another person has committed an offence under either of sections 15 to 18 on the basis of information accruing in the course of a trade, profession, business or employment, an

17 Clive Walker, 'Conscripting the Public in Terrorism Policing' (2010) 6 *Criminal Law Review* 441.

offence is committed if the information is not disclosed to a police officer or member of the National Crime Agency (NCA) or the Charity Commission as soon as reasonably practicable. The width of the duty is striking. It is sufficient to have a subjective belief or suspicion that can only be safely suppressed if the intermediary has a 'reasonable excuse' under sub-section (3). This defence is not subject to the interpretive rule in section 118, which ensures that only an evidential burden is imposed. It is arguable that this switch is fair only in the context of professionals who are trained and keep records; the extension to voluntary enterprises is more dubious. Under section 19(7), the duty has a global reach to equivalent transactions overseas.

In the original drafting of the Terrorism Act 2000, the government emphasised the confinement of the onerous duty under section 19 to professionals handling finance, though it recognised that family and business relations may overlap within small enterprises. However, the reach of section 19 was stretched by the Counter-Terrorism Act 2008, section 77, arising from allegations about the terrorist abuse of charities.[18] Section 77 inserts, as section 22A of the Terrorism Act 2000, a revised definition of 'employment', which encompasses both paid and unpaid employment and can even include voluntary work. In this way, unpaid volunteers who are the trustees of a charity must act with the same insight as professional forensic accountants. The Home Office misleadingly described the amendment as 'a very minor change to close a possible gap in the current provisions'.[19] The result might be to deter community-spirited individuals, since the burden placed on charities to lodge Suspicious Activity Reports (SARs) may be stricter in law than is recognized in practice. In 2006, just 48 SARs were issued from the charitable sector, a dearth of suspicion that officialdom found 'hard to explain',[20] especially as defensive reporting is commonplace in most other sectors. The trend has markedly changed, perhaps related to the growth of Islamic State: in 2014–15, 1,899 SARs were terrorist-related, albeit out of a total of 381,882.[21]

An even stricter duty to disclose is imposed on the 'regulated sector' by Schedule 2, Part III, of the Anti-Terrorism, Crime and Security Act 2001. This duty is imposed instead of, and not additional to, section 19 on most businesses

18 HM Treasury and Home Office, 'The Financial Challenge to Crime and Terrorism' (February 2007) <http://webarchive.nationalarchives.gov.uk/+/http:/www.hm-treasury.gov.uk/media/C/B/financialchallenge_crime_280207.pdf>; Home Office and HM Treasury, 'Review of Safeguards to Protect the Charitable Sector (England and Wales) from Terrorist Abuse' (2007).

19 Home Office, 'Possible Measures for Inclusion into a Future Counter-Terrorism Bill' (25 July 2007), para 22.

20 Home Office and HM Treasury ('The Financial Challenge to Crime and Terrorism' n 18), paras 3.3; 3.6.

21 National Crime Agency, 'Suspicious Activity Reports (SARs) Annual Report 2015' (2016) 31; Annex D <www.nationalcrimeagency.gov.uk/publications/677-sars-annual-report-2015/file>.

handling substantial financial activity. Under section 21A (inserted into the Terrorism Act 2000), a person in that sector commits an offence by knowing or suspecting or having reasonable grounds for knowing or suspecting, that another person has attempted or committed an offence under either of sections 15 to 18 (including offences committed or attempted outside the UK), unless that information is disclosed as soon as practicable to a constable, officer of the NCA, or the employer's nominated officer. The duty is subject to a reasonable excuse not to disclose and to exceptions for privileged legal advice. The objective standard of liability, which can arise without subjective awareness of any suspicion, is justified by the '[g]reater awareness and higher standards of reporting in the financial sector'.[22] Charities do not generally fall within the 'regulated sector', but the indispensable financial institutions that handle their transactions do so. For instance, the Royal Bank of Scotland was fined £5.6m (including a 30 per cent discount for early settlement) by the Financial Services Authority in 2010 for failing to ensure funds were not transferred to people or organizations on sanctions lists, leading to an 'unacceptable risk' of facilitating terrorist financing.

More serious criticisms and stiffer regulatory penalties arising from terrorism financing links have been suffered by financial institutions in the United States.[23] Some of these problems relate to the keeping of accounts for charities that are alleged to be channelling money to terrorist groups (such as HAMAS). An additional and virulent form of governance in that jurisdiction is civil law action under the Anti-Terrorism Act 1996 (18 USC s 2333), whereby a bank with a US branch and assets can be made liable for complicity in terrorism funding by its charity client and thereby made responsible for a proximate cause that led to the deaths of US citizens in terrorist attacks in Israel. The Jordan-based Arab Bank, which had maintained an account for the Saudi Committee for the Support of the Intifada al Quds, was the first to lose such a civil action in 2014.[24] British banks have also encountered this form of challenge, and litigation is pending against NatWest for its maintenance of an account for a charity, in this case Interpal, the details of which will be given below.[25]

External governance

External governance over charities is principally exerted by regulatory measures as applied by the Charity Commission, operating under Part II of the Charities Act 2011 as amended by the Charities (Protection and Social Investment) Act 2016.

22 Home Office, 'Regulatory Impact Assessment: Terrorist Property' (2001), para 8.
23 US Senate Permanent Sub-Committee on Investigations, *US Vulnerability to Money Laundering, Drugs and Terrorist Financing* (US Senate 2012).
24 *Linde v Arab Bank, PLC* (2015) 97 F Supp 3d 287 (EDNY).
25 *Weiss v National Westminster Bank* (2014), 768 F3d 202 (USCA 2nd Cir).

In the context of alleged links to terrorism, there may be two triggers for investigation. One is that the charity may be overstepping the boundaries of its charitable status by supporting political purposes or activities sympathetic to those of terrorist groups. The demarcation line between 'political' and 'charitable' is often difficult to draw. For its part, the Charity Commission warns against the adoption of any political purpose and against any political activities as a core business, though political campaigns in support of charitable purposes may be acceptable.[26] This first potential problem has not been the prime issue in the context of links to terrorism, either in terms of political activism or the content of the cause being espoused. Instead, the alleged infraction is of a second kind – that money is misused to fund activities that are, in part, political or social but also are in part violent.

The enforcement powers of the Charity Commission are indicated in sections 76 to 87 of the Charities Act 2011. The powers arise at any time after an inquiry has been instituted under section 46 either for general or particular purposes. Information-gathering and inquiry powers then arise under sections 46 to 49. The Commission may suspend or remove any trustee, officer, agent or employee of the charity, divest or restrain property, restrict transactions, appoint managers and receivers, or establish a scheme for the administration of the charity. Most drastic of all, by section 34(1)(a), the commission 'must remove from the register … any institution which it no longer considers is a charity'.

These powers sound sweeping and are claimed to be 'far in advance of the requirements imposed on charities in most of the rest of the world'.[27] But they have been sparingly invoked[28] and are, in practice, circumscribed by two limitations.

The first is that while charities with a turnover above a specified amount (£5,000) must register under section 30 of the Charities Act 2011, not-for-profit bodies may choose against adopting the format of a charity. Charitable status brings concrete tax advantages as well as garnering social approbation and social capital. But the status of charity also triggers oversight and potential interference. Some religious groups are suspicious of this meddling and prefer not to register as charities.[29] That pathway may be taken by minorities who are less conversant with British norms and structures, with mosques providing a case in point. It is reckoned that 1,834 mosques are operative in the United

26 Charity Commission, 'Speaking Out – Campaigning and Political Activity by Charities' (London, CC9, 2008).

27 Home Office and HM Treasury (n 18), para 3.

28 Charity Commission, 'Charities Back on Track 2011–12: Themes and lessons from the Charity Commission's investigations and regulatory casework' (2012) 32 <www.gov.uk/government/uploads/system/uploads/attachment_data/file/494666/Charities_Back_on_Track_2011_12.pdf>.

29 Brian Lucas and Anne Robinson, 'Religion as a Head of Charity' in Myles McGregor-Lowndes and Kerry O'Halloran (eds), *Modernising Charity Law* (Edward Elgar Publishing 2010).

Kingdom.[30] The Charity Commission exercises jurisdiction over a minority and records in its *Annual Report 2009/10* that,

> Through outreach work undertaken by the Faith and Social Cohesion Unit set up in 2007, the Commission has also successfully identified and increased the number of mosques registered with us to 593, a 79% increase from the previous figure of 331.[31]

The second limitation is that policing and enforcement have not been priorities in the constitution and culture of the Charity Commission. Thus, the statutory objectives in section 14 of the Charities Act 2011 include legal compliance by charity trustees with their legal obligations in exercising control and management of the administration of their charities but just one objective amongst several as follows:

1 The public confidence objective: The public confidence objective is to increase public trust and confidence in charities.
2 The public benefit objective: The public benefit objective is to promote awareness and understanding of the operation of the public benefit requirement.
3 The compliance objective: The compliance objective is to promote compliance by charity trustees with their legal obligations in exercising control and management of the administration of their charities.
4 The charitable resources objective: The charitable resources objective is to promote the effective use of charitable resources.
5 The accountability objective: The accountability objective is to enhance the accountability of charities to donors, beneficiaries and the general public.

In this way, the Commission has been depicted as a 'green-light' regulator rather than a 'red-light' regulator.[32] Its mission and approach is based around the facilitation of charities to adapt to their legal environment,[33] as is reflected in words such as 'enabling' and 'promoting'. Even in connection with its work in the legal sphere, its mission statement does not communicate a punitive role but is depicted as 'enabling' legal compliance rather than 'enforcing' or 'imposing' it. Because of this approach, more formal policing agencies have found it hard to take over investigations started by the Charity Commission since it pursues a distinct culture and does not aim to collect 'evidence'.[34] Others have referred to

30 'UK Mosque Statistics / Masjid Statistics' (23 September 2015) <www.muslimsinbritain.org/resources/masjid_report.pdf>.
31 Charity Commission, 'Annual Report 2009/10' (HC 2009–10 260) 7.
32 Carol Harlow and Richard Rawlings, *Law and Administration* (3rd edn, CUP 2009) chap 1.
33 Elizabeth A Bloodgood and Joannie Tremblay-Boire, 'International NGOs and National Regulation in an Age of Terrorism' (2011) 22(1) *Voluntas* 142.
34 Home Office and HM Treasury (n 18), para 3.20.

the predilection of the Charity Commission and indeed the government for 'soft power'.[35]

The general stance of the Commission is further underlined by the statutory 'general functions' of the Commission in section 15(1)(3), which, without mention of any punitive or prohibitory sanction, refers to 'Identifying and investigating apparent misconduct or mismanagement in the administration of charities and taking remedial or protective action in connection with misconduct or mismanagement in the administration of charities.'

The 'green-light' approach of the Charity Commission can be further evidenced by its six general duties as set forth in section 16 of the Charities Act 2011. General Duty 2 states that, 'So far as is reasonably practicable, the Charity Commission must, in performing its functions, act in a way which is compatible with the encouragement of (a) all forms of charitable giving, and (b) voluntary participation in charity work'. Furthermore, in performing all its functions, the commission is required by General Duty 4 to 'have regard to the principles of best regulatory practice (including the principles under which regulatory activities should be proportionate, accountable, consistent, transparent and targeted only at cases in which action is needed)'.

As mentioned earlier, some correction to the perceived indulgence has been provided by the Charities (Protection and Social Investment) Act 2016 by stiffening and extending the powers of the Charity Commission. Henceforth, the Commission will be enabled to issue public warnings (section 1). The Act next extends the grounds for automatic disqualification from becoming a trustee to include convictions for serious terrorism offences (section 9) and introduces a process enabling the Commission to disqualify someone it considers to be unfit for trusteeship (section 10), including on the grounds of convictions abroad, for misconduct or mismanagement, or for activities damaging to public trust and confidence in a charity. The charity itself can be wound up under section 7 or its property applied to another charity under section 8.

The claim that the Charity Commission has been hitherto hobbled, in part as a matter of framing by law and in part as a self-induced restraining organisational culture, may be next tested by an examination of the application of its powers in practice.

Application of external governance

Designated charities

A distinction may be drawn between those charities that have become designated under the international sanctions regime pursuant to United Nations Security Council Resolutions 1267 and 1373 (and EU equivalents) and other targeted charities. The UN sanctions mechanisms amount to a novel form of international

35 Peter W Edge, 'Hard Law and Soft Power' (2010) 12 *Rutgers Journal of Law & Religion* 358.

financial outlawry against specified persons and organisations that is not dependent on criminal conviction. They are enforced in the United Kingdom by a combination of the Al-Qaida (Asset-Freezing) Regulations 2011 (SI 2011/2742) and the Terrorist Asset-Freezing etc. Act 2010.[36]

By and large, cases involving designation are straightforward but are not very significant for charities. Most charities listed in the targeted financial sanctions lists have not been openly active in any United Kingdom jurisdiction. One exception is the Sanabel Relief Agency. This charity, whose purpose was to provide relief to Muslims in destitute parts of the world, had registered in 2000 and maintained branches in Birmingham, London, Manchester and Middlesbrough. It was effectively closed in 2006 following international sanctions listing by the United Nations because of links to the Libyan Islamic Fighting Group.[37] Next, the Islamic Foundation, founded in 1973 and based in Leicester, was subject to action when the Charity Commission detected in 2003 that two trustees appeared to be named in the international sanctions listings. The Commission immediately suspended the named trustees but discovered that the two trustees did not reside in the United Kingdom and had not been active in the administration of the charity since 1999 and 2000. Nevertheless, they subsequently resigned. At the same time, the Charity Commission sounded a note of futile defiance in the face of international listings: 'As an independent statutory regulator, the Commission will make its own decisions on the law and facts of the case.'[38]

Non-designated registered charities

Assuming a charity is not internationally designated, then regulatory action is much less straightforward. The version of 'green-light' regulation adopted here is not that the Charity Commission wholly ignores allegations of terrorism. Rather, the question is what happens during, and as a result of, those investigations. By way of evidence of past practice until recent times, four cases should be highlighted.

One concerned the Ikhlas Foundation, which was registered in 1997 and whose main work was reflected in its adopted working title of the 'Muslim Prisoner Support Group' and especially related to prisoners impugned for involvement in terrorism. The group has been of serial concern to the Charity Commission because of the activities of various trustees.[39] In 2007, Mohammed al-Ghabra, a trustee, was removed after he was accused of facilitating terrorism

36 See Independent Reviewer of the Terrorism Legislation, *Reports on the Operation of the Terrorist Asset Freezing Etc Act 2010* (Home Office, 2011–14).

37 Case T-134/11 *Al Faqih v Commission* [2015] OJ C 429/14.

38 Charity Commission, 'Inquiry: The Islamic Foundation' (4 February 2004).

39 Charity Commission, 'Inquiry Report: Al Ikhlas Foundation' (15 October 2008); 'Inquiry Report: Al Ikhlas Foundation' (16 March 2010).

training in Pakistan and was designated by the UN and by the HM Treasury in December 2006.[40] The Charity Commission was apparently unaware of this designation until informed in July 2007. The other trustees resisted any disciplinary action, taking the view that they would be 'considered as hypocrites' if they shunned a colleague because of this official condemnation while at the same time seeking to aid prisoners.[41] The Charity Commission removed him as a trustee in October 2007 and prevented his further participation. However, it imposed no sanction on the remaining trustees even though it viewed them as inadequately recognizing or managing the risks involved with their work. Instead, the inquiry was closed on the commitment by remaining trustees to strengthen their governance within three months.

That undertaking by the trustees did not seem to bear much fruit. A second inquiry began in 2008, when another trustee, Abbas Taj, was suspended by the Commission (and later resigned) following his arrest in 2008 and conviction in 2009 for conspiring in an arson attack. The attack was made on the home of Martin Rynja, owner of Gibson Square Books, which published *The Jewel of Medina*, a novel by US author Shelley Jones that controversially tackles the subject of the Prophet Muhammad's third wife, Aisha, who is said to have been married at the age of nine. Whatever the theological arguments surrounding those ancient events, the subsequent wrongdoing was stark. Taj had helped two other men to go to the publisher's house, where they poured diesel through the letterbox and lit a fire. Two other trustees were also disciplined on unconnected, less serious grounds (for bankruptcy and failing to attend meetings with the Commission). The Commission recorded that the trustees had failed to deliver on their previous commitments.[42] Despite this recurrently woeful record, the Commission concluded its second inquiry by issuing a direction under section 19A by which the trustees were set a further few months after December 2009 to regularize their meetings and membership and to conduct a risk assessment and take action to mitigate risks. Given that the charity had a very modest income of around £5,000 per annum, the risk of terrorism financing should not be exaggerated. Nevertheless, the patience of the Charity Commission accorded to this serially delinquent charity was astonishing, though the Ikhlas Foundation has since been removed from the Register of Charities.

More prominently reported, policing action in regard to a trustee next relates to the removal of Abu Hamza, from the North London Central Mosque (Finsbury Park) in 2004.[43] This mosque became notorious in the late 1990s as a site for 'extremists', many of them foreign émigrés, who were accused of infiltrating the mosque, intimidating moderate locals, and preaching hatred and violence. For a while, the Charity Commission sought to work with all shades of trustees,

40 *HM Treasury v al-Ghabra* [2010] UKSC 2.
41 Charity Commission (n 39) para 16.
42 Charity Commission (n 39) paras 38; 39.
43 Abdul H Baker, 'A View from the Inside' (2008) 73 *Criminal Justice Matters* 24.

including Abu Hamza. The decisive turning point came when the mosque premises were raided by police on 20 January 2003, whereupon the commission suspended and later removed Abu Hamza as trustee of the charity and also closed a bank account that he had secretly operated. Abu Hamza was later convicted of solicitation to murder.[44] Following completion of his sentence, he was extradited to the USA and convicted in 2015 in respect of terrorism offences, including raising money for fighters in Afghanistan from 1999 to 2001.[45] While this later treatment represents a 'red-light' approach, it took several years for decisive action to be implemented by the Commission and such action was impelled by police intervention and boosted by media hostility.

The third case, Iqra, involved arguably the most notorious trustees of all.[46] Iqra, a bookshop and learning centre in the Beeston, Leeds, registered as a charity in 2003. However, its activities came to an abrupt halt in 2005, when it was confirmed that two of the 7 July bombers, Mohammed Siddique Khan and Shehzad Tanweer, had acted as trustees. The police raided its premises, as a result of which the remaining trustees claimed that the charity had become inoperative. Another trustee, Khalid Kaliq, was convicted in 2008 of terrorist-related offences not directly related to Iqra. Yet, not until 2009 did the Charity Commission decide to launch a formal inquiry, and even that step seems to have been prompted by media concerns. In the event, the Commission found no evidence that Iqra's finances or premises had been used for the preparation of the 7 July attacks, and it can hardly be blamed for not detecting more astutely than the police or security agencies that some of its trustees were developing into active terrorists.[47] However, the Commission found that extremist materials had been possessed and also admitted that no action had been taken over the fact that no reports or accounts had ever been filed by the trustees. Awakening from this stupor, the Commission took steps to seize the remaining trust money (£12,500).

Trustee links to Rashid Rauf, who was implicated in the transatlantic airline liquid bomb plot in 2006, was the reason for another inquiry into the Crescent Relief charity, which was involved in relief work in Kashmir and Indonesia.[48] The inquiry began in 2006 but was held up until 2011 not only because of the various prosecutions but also because of the failure to keep records and the difficulties of obtaining evidence from abroad. The outcome of the inquiry was inconclusive, but it was sustained that financial controls had been inadequate and that there had been an ongoing lack of candour and effective management by the trustees. Despite all these serious shortcomings, the Commission concluded that

44 *R v Abu Hamza* [2006] EWCA Crim 2918.

45 *Hamza v Secretary of State for the Home Department* [2012] EWHC 2736 (Admin).

46 Charity Commission, 'Inquiry Report: Iqra' (22 February 2011).

47 Lady Justice Hallett, 'Coroner's Inquests into the London Bombings of 7 July 2005: Report under Rule 43 of The Coroner's Rules 1984' (6 May 2011) para 21.

48 Charity Commission, 'Inquiry Report: Crescent Relief' (29 September 2011).

the future good intentions of the trustees should be recognized by ordering them to take action within a set time-frame and to submit regular reports. Compliance was confirmed in a *Supplementary Report* later in 2011.

Moving from a focus on wayward trustees to more general allegations, several other charities have been the subject of investigations because of suspicions of links to terrorism. The most persistent allegations have concerned Interpal, the Palestinian Relief and Development Fund, which was established in Britain in 1994 to provide relief to Palestinians in the Occupied Territories, Lebanon and Jordan. Allegations of connections with HAMAS have been made, but not sustained, on several distinct occasions.[49] HAMAS is not proscribed in the United Kingdom (though the related HAMAS-Izz al-Din al-Qassem Brigades are banned). The charity faced an acute threat to its existence when it was listed as linked to HAMAS by the US Treasury on 22 August 2003, whereupon its activities were investigated by the Charity Commission. The BBC Panorama programme, *Faith, Hate and Charity*, issued fresh allegations in 2006 and thereby prompted another Charity Commission investigation in 2007. Its report in 2009 was critical of the due diligence and monitoring procedures then in place, but Interpal was again cleared of promoting terrorist ideology or activities. The Charity Commission appreciated the 'challenging' environment in which Palestinian charities must work but recognized that 'Humanitarian assistance cannot be denied to people because they support, actively or otherwise, or are sympathetic towards the work or aims of a political body, such as Hamas.[50]

Another strand of the attack on Interpal, mentioned earlier, has taken the form of a civil law action brought against its bankers, including *Weiss v NatWest*.[51] Interpal's bank accounts with the NatWest were closed in 2007. The Islamic Bank of Britain also ended its links with Interpal in 2008 because of pressure from Lloyds TSB, which acted as its clearing bank. This process of 'de-risking' or 'de-banking' not only of listed persons or entities but also of Muslim organizations that operate in conflict zones or have political objectives (including some mosques) is difficult to challenge[52] and has become increasingly common as shall be discussed later.

Linkage with HAMAS, via the al-Ihsan Charitable Society, was the charge levelled against Muslim Aid, founded in 1985 and with operations in 70 countries. Money was set aside for al-Ihsan in 2005, but there was no transfer because al-Ihsan became designated within the UK only on 27 June 2005. The Commission's reaction was to provide regulatory advice and guidance to the trustees.[53]

49 Ben Smith, 'Interpal' (SNIA/6678, House of Commons Library 2013).

50 Charity Commission, 'Inquiry Report: Palestinian Relief and Development Fund (Interpal)' (27 February 2009) paras 176; 183.

51 See https://www.osenlaw.com/case/natwest-case.

52 *Dahabshiil Transfer Service v Barclays Bank* [2013] EWHC 3379 (Ch).

53 Charity Commission, 'Regulatory Case Report: Muslim Aid' (17 December 2010).

Another set of allegations regarding HAMAS arose in connection with the group Viva Palestina, a project that responded to the Israeli incursion into Gaza in December 2008 and seeks to provide aid convoys.[54] The two founding trustees were George Galloway, at the time a Member of Parliament, and Sabah al-Mukhtar, president of the Arab Lawyers Association in the UK. The Charity Commission opened an inquiry in 2009 because of alarm about its non-registration as a charity as well as uncertainty around the control and ultimate application of funds. Its bank (the Islamic Bank of Britain) had frozen its funds because of these concerns and then terminated its relationship, as a result of which monies received after the freeze had to be returned to donors. Charitable registration was imposed in 2009 on the instructions of the Commission, subsequent to which the founding trustees resigned since the categorization was contrary to their wishes. The attempt by the trustees to add two additional and explicitly political (and thereby non-charitable) purposes to the constitution of the body was viewed as *ultra vires* by the Commission as well as not divesting the funding held of its charitable status. In summary, there was an unusually quick and robust response in this case, even though the main problems related to the proper handling of funds rather than the financing of terrorism. Perhaps the publicity attached from the outset of the controversy, magnified by the involvement of George Galloway, made the Commission unusually sensitive to being depicted as inactive or supine. Nevertheless, the dispute has dragged on, after a statutory inquiry in 2013, assets have been frozen and an Interim Manager imposed in 2014.

Several other investigations have concerned Tamil charities accused of involvement with the Liberation Tigers of Tamil Eelam ('LTTE' – the Tamil Tigers), a proscribed organization under the Terrorism Act 2000. The Charity Commission began in 2000 investigating the Tamils Rehabilitation Organisation ('TRO'), which was founded in 1985 in Tamil Nadu, India, to provide relief to Tamil refugees, and then moved in 1987 to Jaffna. The investigation found that the charity exerted little control once its relief money had been transmitted to Sri Lanka, where local representatives had liaised with LTTE representatives.[55] The Commission organized for an interim manager to be appointed to take over the administration of the charity and then agreed for a new charity, the Tamil Support Foundation, to take over its assets in 2005. The Tamils Rehabilitation Organisation was then struck off the register, though on the basis that it was defunct rather than because of abusive practices.

Tamil charities continued to be treated with some indulgence. The charity, Sivayogam, was registered in 1995 as an organization that worked with Tamils both in London and in northern Sri Lanka. Concerns surfaced in 2005 when it became apparent that the leading trustee, Nagendram Seevaratnam, had professed LTTE sympathies going back some decades, including an admission of

54 Charity Commission, 'Inquiry Report: Viva Palestina' (4 March 2010).

55 Charity Commission, 'Inquiry Report: Tamils Rehabilitation Organisation' (2 February 2006).

membership before 1991. The inquiry instigated by the Charity Commission found problems with the selection and monitoring of local partners in Sri Lanka, that the financial accounting involved interest-free loans and cash transactions that increased risks, and that the said trustee remained a dominant figure who admitted supporting the LTTE in 2006 and 2007.[56] In another example of its 'green-light' style, the Charity Commission imposed the sanction of removal as a trustee but otherwise sought to work with the impugned charity to improve its standards. Even the attempted removal was reversed by the First-Tier Tribunal (Charity), which viewed the trustee's statements as merely 'unwise and unguarded' in circumstances where he had not been 'warned that his own statements might be used against him or advised of his right to obtain legal advice'.[57] The tribunal did still accept that he had maintained contact with the LTTE, though that fact did not make it necessary or desirable to remove him, and it also found that the investigation had not properly translated all relevant evidence regarding due diligence. Furthermore, the tribunal endorsed a 'green-light' regulatory approach, stating that:

> If there had remained any legitimate regulatory concerns following a proper examination of the evidence originally provided to it, the Tribunal concludes that it would have been appropriate for the Respondent to work with the charity to improve its processes before considering exercising its regulatory powers. As it was, the Respondent exercised its regulatory powers without considering the evidence with which it had been provided.[58]

Seevaratnam later chose to resign from the charity.[59]

Assessment of governance responses

The incidence of terrorism financing by charities is not large. However, the wrongdoing has persisted over many years, and the Charity Commission may be generally assessed to have a poor track record in response. Powerful critics coalesced in five official reports between 2011 and 2014.

First, the Home Office commented in its 2011 paper on *Prevent Strategy* that 'The Charity Commission must be seen to be capable of taking robust and vigorous action against charities that are involved in terrorist activity or have links to terrorist organisations'.[60] The accompanying independent survey by Lord Carlile was more candidly critical of the Commission:

56 Charity Commission, 'Inquiry Report: Sivayogam' (31 August 2010).

57 *Nagendram Seevaratnam v Charity Commission for England and Wales and Her Majesty's Attorney General* (CA/2008/0001, 13 October 2009) para 6.52.

58 Ibid., para 6.75.

59 Charity Commission (n 55) para 180.

60 Home Office, *Prevent Strategy* (Cm 8092, 2011) para 10.203.

> The Charity Commission has a very important role as guardian of the governance of charities. They must be seen to take robust and vigorous action against charities involved in terrorism and extremism. Trustees must be left in no doubt of their responsibilities. Further discussion and work between central government and charities is needed to secure the reputation of the Commission as a valuable participant in this area of work.[61]

The second relevant report was by Lord Hodgson in 2012, *Trusted and independent: giving charity back to charities – review of the Charities Act 2006*. Lord Hodgson not only called for automatic trustee disqualification following any conviction of a terrorism offence (which would not make much difference) but also and more tellingly that the Charity Commission should take 'a more robust approach to potentially failing organisations' and 'proactive as well as reactive steps' in cases of abuse. [62]

Third, the National Audit Office in its report, *The regulatory effectiveness of the Charity Commission*, made the following bleak findings:

> The Commission continues to make little use of its statutory enforcement powers. ... The Commission can be slow to act when investigating regulatory concerns. ... The Commission does not take tough enough action in some of the most serious regulatory cases. .... The Commission relies heavily on trustees' assurances, but should do more to check whether trustees have actually complied. ... The Commission is reactive rather than proactive, making insufficient use of the information it holds to identify risk.[63]

Fourth, the House of Commons Public Accounts Committee thoroughly lambasted the Charity Commission, concluding that it had 'no coherent strategy for delivering clearly defined priorities within its broad remit', had 'not regulated the charity sector effectively', had 'little confidence in the Commission's ability to put right its problems and failings'.[64]

Fifth, the House of Commons Home Affairs Committee, in *An inquiry into Counter-terrorism*, expressed similar concerns and recommended 'that the Charity Commission be granted extra resources and stronger legal powers to counter the abuse of charities by terrorists. We also recommend that the Charity Commission be able to undertake unannounced inspections in order to audit their accounts'.[65]

These criticisms of the Charity Commission must now be read subject to three provisos. One is that legislation has now been put in place to strengthen the

61 Lord Carlile, 'Report to the Home Secretary of Independent Oversight of Prevent Review and Strategy' (May 2011) para 60.

62 Lord Hodgson, 'Trusted and Independent: Giving Charity Back to Charities – Review of the Charities Act 2006' (July 2012) paras 4.29; 5.28.

63 National Audit Office, 'The Regulatory Effectiveness of the Charity Commission' (HC 2013–14 813) paras 15–19.

64 Public Accounts Committee, *The Charity Commission* (HC 2013–14 792) paras 2; 3; 6.

65 Home Affairs Committee, *An Inquiry into Counter-Terrorism* (HC 2013–14 231).

powers of the Commission, as had been promised by the Cabinet Office in 2013.[66] The Charities (Protection and Social Investment) Act 2016 has been considered above. Second, further administrative efforts have been instituted to tighten the regulations covering terrorism financing. Third, there are competing public interests that may legitimately affect the degree and manner of intervention by the regulators. These two further points will now be considered.

As for administrative efforts, the Home Office and HM Treasury reviewed the regime in their 2007 report, *Review of Safeguards to Protect the Charitable Sector (England and Wales) from Terrorist Abuse*, which assessed the channelling of funds by charities to terrorists to be 'extremely rare'.[67] Nevertheless, the Charity Commission was urged to reinforce awareness of risk factors. The Charity Commission responded in 2008 by publishing its *Counter-Terrorism Strategy*. It reiterated that the instances of infiltration or abuse remain 'extremely rare' but, when detected, are subject to 'zero tolerance'.[68]

In pursuance of its strategy, various further administrative actions have been undertaken to improve trustee awareness, including oversight through a Proactive Monitoring Unit, cooperation between enforcement agencies, and greater intervention. Published advice has been elaborated through the issuance of an *Operational Guidance (OG96)* (2007) and a *Compliance Toolkit* (2011), including advice about the work of the Counter Terrorism Team which forms part of the Intensive Casework Unit in Compliance and Support.[69] The documentation was impressively expanded in 2013, when the Commission issued several much fuller versions of the *Compliance Toolkits*. A subvention of £1m in 2007 also allowed the Commission to establish a Faith and Social Cohesion Unit with the objective of engaging with faith communities (primarily Muslim) to register and to assist faith-based charities in their management standards. These extra initiatives were not initially sufficient to nudge cultural practices away from the 'greenlight' approach. But a change of personnel, including the appointment in 2012 of a new Chairman, William Shawcross, and in 2013 of Peter Clarke (an ex-police officer who had been a national commander in counter-terrorism) as a Board member, did markedly change practices and outlooks. Thus, the volume of investigatory work increased significantly, and terrorism became an explicit priority.[70]

Moving next to the competing public goods that might properly preclude or at least restrain the sanctioning of charities for terrorism financing, countervailing

66 Cabinet Office, 'Tackling Extremism in the UK' (December 2013).

67 Home Office and HM Treasury (n 18), para 2.10.

68 Charity Commission, Counter-Terrorism Strategy (July 2008, revised September 2015) <www.gov.uk/government/uploads/system/uploads/attachment_data/file/465994/counter-terrorism_strategy.pdf>.

69 Charity Commission, 'Compliance Toolkit: Protecting Charities from Harm' (September 2013) <www.gov.uk/government/collections/protecting-charities-from-harm-compliance-toolkit>.

70 Charity Commission, 'Annual Report and Accounts 2013 to 2014' (HC 2014–15)1;

considerations are that British society should not appear to be stone-hearted in the face of the most difficult humanitarian crises in conflict zones, such as in Palestine, Somalia and Sri Lanka. Such a stance might even aggravate the situation by encouraging less regulated and less cooperative activities, even resulting in a strategic defeat: 'In that event, the government ironically would have exacerbated, not reduced, one ultimate goal of fundamentalist and radical terrorists: the disruption of globalism.'[71] An illustration of such upheaval arises from the United Nations listing of al-Barakaat group in Somalia from 2001 to 2009,[72] a process that some claim to have deepened the crisis in that country and to have encouraged hostility to Western values. The hazards for humanitarian relief have been highlighted in several reports.[73] The UK government has sought to establish 'safe corridors for such relief, especially in Somalia'.[74] However, other oversight agencies, including the police, may not be as tolerant in their application of the law. There have been 40 prosecutions for offences under section 15 to 19 of the Terrorism Act 2000 between 2001 and 2013 in Britain.[75] Many offenders have received substantial sentences, including several who would regard themselves as charitable workers.

Conclusions and future governance

The United Kingdom approach to charities assailed by the taint of terrorism funding has been one of understanding if not, at times, downright indulgence, contrary to the impression given by other commentators.[76] As well as the 'green-light' approach to charitable trusts themselves, their bankers are seemingly rarely at risk beyond the legal shark pools of the US civil courts. However, the official stance becomes markedly less benevolent when individual volunteers within the tainted charities are identified as sympathizers of extremist groups or as well-meaning couriers. Thus, it is usually worthy individuals who must pay the price

71 Nina J Crimm, 'High Alert: The Government's War on the Financing of Terrorism and its Implications for Donors, Domestic Charitable Organizations, and Global Philanthropy' (2004) 45(4) *William & Mary Law Review* 1341.

72 Case T-85/09 *Kadi v Commission* [2010] ECR II–5177.

73 Kate Mackintosh and Patrick Duplat, 'Study of the Impact of Donor Counter-Terrorism Measures on Principled Humanitarian Action' (UNOCHA, July 2013) <https://docs.unocha.org/sites/dms/documents/ct_study_full_report.pdf>; Tom Keatinge, Uncharitable Behaviour (Demos, December 2014) <www.demos.co.uk/files/DEMOSuncharitablebehaviourREPORT.pdf>; Clay Lowery and Vijaya Ramachandran, 'Unintended Consequences of Anti Money Laundering Policies for Poor Countries' (Center for Global Development, 2015) <www.cgdev.org/sites/default/files/CGD-WG-Report-Unintended-Consequences-AML-Policies-2015.pdf>.

74 Tracy Durner and Liat Shetret, 'Understanding Bank De-Risking and its Effects in Financial Inclusion' (Global Center on Comparative Security, November 2015) <www.globalcenter.org/wp-content/uploads/2015/11/rr-bank-de-risking-181115-en.pdf>.

75 Clive Walker, *The Anti-Terrorism Legislation* (3rd edn, OUP 2014) Table 3.1.

76 Levi (n 14) 650.

for relief work at the margins of legality and not those voluntary or financial institutions which have failed to manage risk or have even turned a blind eye. This serial indulgence of abuses has done no favour to charities seeking to engage public support for oppressed people. Therefore, the changed stance after 2012 is welcome.

Notwithstanding the need to eradicate terrorism sympathies from charitable structures, it would be counter-productive to swing entirely towards criminal prosecution and asset forfeiture, a stance which would unduly ignore competing public goods and would create conflict with the voluntary sector and its many public sympathizers. The Commission should rightly retain a supportive and enabling approach to charities. This role has been well served by its decision to undertake more intensive work with those involved in convoys to Syria.[77] One other possible tactic might include the creation of a 'safe passage' to countries affected by conflict, whereby only larger, more capable, and more experienced charities are encouraged to be active, leaving smaller, often newly established groups to act as their suppliers otherwise they will risk substantial oversight costs. Various further techniques have been suggested, such as the 'whitelisting' of approved charities and greater incentives for disclosure. The prioritisation of financial intelligence-gathering should also be considered.[78] A financial investigation approach may produce fairer treatment between organizations and individuals involved in charitable work and may be easier to square with such desirable objectives as building the 'big (civil) society' and harmonious community relations. This financial investigation approach is not best placed in the hands of the Charity Commission but should primarily be conducted by a formal police body. The roles left for the Charity Commission should be as standard-setter by continuing to promulgate operational guidance, as standard-monitor (with alerts back to the police financial investigators if alarms are sounded), and as standard-applier once the police financial investigators find no criminal wrongdoing but grounds for concern about practices and risk. In this way, the heaviest price for terrorism financing should be paid by professional profit-takers and recipient perpetrators of terrorism.

Postscript

Since the writing of this manuscript (in mid-2016), developments have included: a revision by the FATF of guidance on SR VIII (http://www.fatf-gafi.org/publications/fatfgeneral/documents/outcomes-plenary-october-2016.html); and the passage of the (UK) Sanctions and Anti Money Laundering Act 2018, which allows more flexible licensing of humanitarian activities.

77 Charity Commission (n 69) 26.

78 Mark Pieth, 'Terrorism Financing Mechanisms and Policy Dilemmas' in Jeanne K Giraldo and Harold A Trinkunas (eds), *Terrorism Financing and State Responses* (Stanford University Press 2007).

5 On the improvement of criminal legislation and criminal policy to deter cross-border money laundering in China[1]

Wang Wenhua

The current situation of cross-border money laundering in China

According to an announcement made by the Procuratorate of Guangdong Province, the former manager of Nanhai Real Estate Limited Company, Li Jixiang (hereafter referred to as 'Li'), who fled to Australia for eight years, was under investigation by the Australia Federal Police for money laundering.[2] On 14 September 2011, the jury of the Supreme Court of Queensland, Australia, found Li guilty of nine charges of money laundering and using illegal proceeds. The day after, the Court sentenced Li to 14 years' imprisonment for money laundering with no less than ten years to be served and according to Article 4 in Division 400 of the Australia Criminal Code Act 1995, 12 years' imprisonment for dealing in proceeds of crime with no less than nine years to be served. The judge ordered all the sentences to be served concurrently from 13 September 2011 and for a total of 26 years' imprisonment; parole shall not be granted until at least nine years have been served. Of the 40 million yuan that were transferred by Li to Australia, nearly 30 million yuan were recovered. So far, the case that was followed by the Procuratorate of Guangdong Province for eight years has come to an end, which is referred to as 'the First Case of Judicial Assistance between Australia and China'.

There were other cross-border money laundering cases successfully investigated by the Chinese police, for example: (1) money laundering by Yu Zhendong, Xu Chaofan and Xu Guojun, three former managers of Kaiping Office of the Bank of China's Guangdong Provincial Branch in south China's Guangdong Province; (2) smuggling, bribing and money laundering by Lai Changxing, a leader of the Xiamen Yuanhua Smuggling Group; (3) money laundering through underground banking by Singaporean Shanghainese Luo Huaitao.[3]

1 This chapter is the result of a project on 'Supporting the Intelligent Mind in the New Era' launched by the Ministry of Education of China.

2 Lin Xiahong, Liu Yiming, 'The Outlaw Official was Sentenced to 26 Years in Prison in Australia' *Guangzhou Daily* (Guangzhou, 23 September 2011) <http://news.xinhuanet.com/politics/2011-09/23/c_122076444.htm>.

3 Kang Shuhua, 'On the Present Situation, Cause and Countermeasures of Money Laundering' (2006) 26 (4) *Academic Forum of Nandu* 81.

As the economic globalisation and China's reform and opening up develops, more cross-border money laundering crimes involve China. According to a report issued by the Financial Action Task Force on Money Laundering, an important trend of international money laundering crime is the spread from developed countries to developing countries. In the context of financial globalisation, countries lacking comprehensive financial regulations are bound to become hard-hit areas of laundering crime. A survey made by the School of Finance of the Central University of Economics and Finance of China shows that the underground economy of China in 2005 was almost 6 trillion yuan, of which money laundering took up 930 billion yuan. In fact, no one knows exactly how much money has been laundered every year. The channels to legitimise illegal proceeds vary. Besides commonly known ways such as travelling abroad, shopping, gambling (gambling on the internet included), smuggling and false trading, money launderers have made it a bigger business by obtaining mortgages on illegal proceeds, getting legitimate loans from banks, quitting soon after purchasing an insurance of high premiums, and through stock markets and underground banks. By underground banks only, at least 200 billion yuan of illegal money can be laundered and transferred abroad every year, which amounts to 2% of the GDP of China.[4] Some overseas branches of state-owned companies in China even become professional facilities for money laundering.

Cross-border money laundering makes it possible for illegal proceeds to be transferred at high frequency among states, which not only becomes the breeding ground for bribery, corruption, smuggling, financial fraud and terrorism, serving all kinds of criminal groups at convenience, but also becomes a disturbance to the forecasting of real money demand of a country. It jeopardises regular judicial activities, undermines financial management and free market competition, brings about instability to international capital operation and the investment market and, as a result, damage the economy at a regional or even international scale.

Based on an overview of the legislative and judicial accomplishments of China, this article will discuss several issues: (1) the jurisdiction over cross-border money laundering; (2) whether the range of the predicate offences of money laundering should be broadened to cover all crimes; (3) whether all the charges of money laundering should be stipulated in criminal law; (4) whether we should make any supplement to the means of act of money laundering crime; (5) whether the *mens rea* of money laundering should be limited to *knowingly*; (6) whether self-laundering can constitute a money laundering offence; and (7) how to strengthen the cooperation between mainland China and Hong Kong, Macao and other jurisdictions in criminal judicature and law enforcement against cross-border money laundering crime.

4 'Money Laundering Exceeds 200 Billion Yuan Every Year in China' (*Souhu Finance*, 10 October 2015) <http://mt.sohu.com/20151010/n422909361.shtml>.

Legislative and judicial responses to money laundering in China

China has been actively engaged in the international cooperation against money laundering and has signed, approved and implemented a series of international legal documents on anti-money laundering, including The International Drug Control Conventions, United Nations Convention against Transnational Organized Crime, International Convention for the Suppression of the Financing of Terrorism and United Nations Convention against Corruption. China takes measures against money laundering mainly through criminal legislation, preventive legislation and legal practice.

Criminal legislation

The Criminal Law of China (1979) did not grant money laundering the status as an independent crime. It was after China ratified and acceded to The International Drug Control Conventions on 4 September 1990, in order to honour its obligations under the Convention and to combat drug related crimes, that the Standing Committee of National People's Congress passed the Decision of Prohibition Against Narcotic Drugs, which stipulated the crime of concealment or withholding the illegal nature or source of gains from drug dealing. Later, the Criminal Law of China (1997) stipulated for the first time money laundering offences. After China participated in the drafting of and thereafter signed the International Convention for the Suppression of the Financing of Terrorism and the United Nations Convention against Transnational Organized Crime, the Amendment III of the Criminal Law of the People's Republic of China amended Article 191, in which terrorist offences were added as a predicate offence for money laundering, 'serious circumstance' was implemented as a requirement for an offence to constitute money laundering and the severity of the penalty was increased. In 2006, the Amendment VI to the Criminal Law of the People's Republic of China added to the predicate offences corruption, bribery, disrupting the financial management order and financial fraud. By the time the Amendment VII to the Criminal Law of the People's Republic of China was issued, which criminalised concealing ill-gotten money and the gains therefrom, the criminal legislation against money laundering crimes has gradually developed into a comprehensive system.

Although the crime of money laundering is stipulated in Article 191 of the Criminal Law of China, there are actually four clauses altogether governing activities related to money laundering, including Article 191 (money laundering), Article 312 (concealing illegal proceeds and gains therefrom), Article 349 (sheltering, transferring or concealing drugs or gains from drug dealing) and Article 120(1) (funding terrorism). Funding terrorism is not a typical money laundering offence, however, the international community at large regards terrorist financing as an inversion of money laundering and the Interpretation of the Supreme People's Court on Several Issues concerning the Specific Application of Law in the Trial of Money Laundering and Other Criminal Cases, which was promulgated in China on 11 November 2009, specified and interpreted terrorist financing crime in the context of money laundering crime. Therefore, money laundering crimes should be understood in a broad way in which the aforesaid four charges should all be included.

The preventive legislation

The Anti-Money Laundering Law of the People's Republic of China was promulgated in 2006. As a comprehensive statute, it is composed of 37 articles of seven chapters covering general provisions, anti-money laundering supervision, anti-money obligations of financial institutions, anti-money laundering investigation, international anti-money laundering cooperation, legal liabilities and miscellaneous provisions. Other statutes dealing with anti-money laundering include Provisions on Anti-money Laundering through Financial Institutions, Administrative Measures for the Financial Institutions' Report of Large-sum Transactions and Doubtful Transactions, the Detailed Rules for Anti-money Laundering Investigations (for Trial Implementation), Administrative Measures for Financial Institutions' Reporting of Transactions Suspected of Financing for Terrorist Purposes, the Administrative Measures for the On-site Inspections for Anti-money Laundering (for Trial Implementation) and Measures on the Administration of Client Identity Identification and Materials and Transaction Recording of Financial Institutions. It should be recognised that China has made a first step towards the establishment of anti-money laundering legislation system.

Legal practice relating to anti-money laundering

As mentioned at the beginning of this chapter, China has prosecuted several cross-border money laundering cases, which indicates the severe situation where laundering crimes frequently take place but also displays China's accomplishments in combating money laundering. By now, enforcement bodies have been established in all the major departments against money laundering crime, including the Anti-Money Laundering Bureau of the People's Bank of China, the Economic Crime Investigation Department of the Ministry of Public Security, the Supervision and Inspection Department of the State Administration of Foreign Exchange and China Anti-Money Laundering Monitoring and Analysis Center. All the branches of the Bank of China have established specialised anti-money laundering agencies with professional staff since 2004. With both full-time and part-time employees at count, there are over 4,000 people working for the People's Bank of China in the area of anti-money laundering. Moreover, China has made great progress in the international cooperation on anti-money laundering by fulfilling its role in international and regional anti-money laundering campaigns. In February 2005, China became an observer of the Financial Action Task Force (FATF) and on 28 June 2007 a member thereof, which is a big step forward in the international cooperation to combat money laundering crime. In October 2005, the Eurasian Group on Combating Money and

Financing of Terrorism (EAG), a regional group against money laundering and terrorism financing with largest area covered and most people involved, was established in Moscow and China was one of the founding members.

The judicial dilemma of fighting cross-border money laundering in China

Although the anti-money laundering legislation system of China has been established, the progress of law enforcement is lagging behind. Since money laundering offences were stipulated in the Criminal Law of China in 1997, it was not until the Guangzhou Wangzhao money laundering case[5] in April 2004 that the court ruled on the charge of money laundering. By the end of 2007, only five cases were affirmed of money laundering in which ten people were sentenced to imprisonment of ten years where the property laundered was 130 million yuan. Therefore, the Mutual Evaluation of China released by FATF in 2007 suggested that Article 191 of the Criminal Law of China was not effectively implemented, since in only few cases were suspects charged with money laundering offence.

It is an undisputable fact that money laundering is marginalised in the judicial practice in China. 'Although money laundering is an independent offence in the legislation, it can only be tracked down as an attachment and thereafter be tried on the premise of the establishment of the former in judicial practice.'[6] This is an even more pressing issue when applied to international money laundering. The cause of this problem is that on the one hand, by taking advantage of transnational channels, cross-border laundering conceals and legitimises the illicit proceeds through the conversion of the forms of illicit property in an increasingly internationalised way, rendering illicit proceeds deeply hidden and well disguised and creating more obstacles for the investigation. On the other hand, there is still plenty of room for China to improve its legislation, judicature and law enforcement on money laundering crimes.

For example, the charges of money laundering offences are stipulated in separate chapters in the criminal law. Some money laundering activities cannot be pursued under the money laundering provisions of Article 191, but are charged under sheltering and concealing illegal proceeds and gains therefrom, Article 312, or illegal dealing, Article 225, which makes it impossible to calculate

5 Defendant Wang Zhao assisted others by purchasing 60 per cent of shares of the Guangzhou Baiye Forest Company with money gained from drug dealing and helped with the transfer of the money. Later, he renamed the company as Lixin Company and transferred the illegal proceeds as legal income of the wood business. In March 2004, he was found guilty of money laundering by the People's Court of Zhuhai Region in Guangdong Province and sentenced to imprisonment for a year and six months with a fine of 275,000 yuan and confiscation of illegal proceeds including a ML 320 Benz. For reference see, Kang Shuhua, 'On the Present Situation, Cause and Countermeasures of Money Laundering' (2006) 26 (4) *Academic Forum of Nandu* 81.

6 Lin Anmin, 'The Problems and Solutions of Legislation on Money Laundering' (2010) 2 *Journal of Fujian Police College* 64.

the exact number of money laundering cases. What is more, in international money laundering cases, more problems arise. Problems in the legislative field include jurisdiction over cross-border money laundering cases, the *actus reus* elements of money laundering, whether to broaden the scope of predicate offence of money laundering to all crimes, whether to prescribe money laundering offences in one clause, whether the *mens rea* element of laundering crime should be limited to *willful*, whether self-laundering can constitute a money laundering offense, and whether money laundering and its predicate offences should be combined for punishment. In the area of criminal policy, we face the problem of whether to expand anti-money laundering offences in law enforcement, and how to enhance China's cooperation with other countries and territories as well as with Hong Kong, Macao and Taiwan in transnational judicial and law enforcement activities. These issues, directly or indirectly, influence the advancement of international cooperation to combat cross-border money laundering and the outcome thereof, which should be discussed in depth.

Improving the criminal law against cross-border money laundering in China

How to determine the jurisdiction over cross-border money laundering cases

Not only can money laundering and its predicate offences happen in different countries, but the steps of placement, layering and integration in money laundering offences tend to take place in different countries. Therefore, the primary issue to be solved to ensure effective prosecution and punishment for money laundering is the reasonable determination of the jurisdiction.

Article 6 of the United Nations Convention Against Transnational Organized Crime and article 23(2)(c) of the United Nations Convention Against Corruption stipulate that

> predicate offences shall include offences committed both within and outside the jurisdiction of the State Party in question. However, offences committed outside the jurisdiction of a State Party shall constitute predicate offences only when the relevant conduct is a criminal offence under the domestic law of the State where it is committed and would be a criminal offence under the domestic law of the State Party implementing or applying this article had it been committed there.

This is the principle of double criminality under which the predicate offence can be committed within or outside the territory of a state, but in the latter case, such conduct should constitute a criminal offence both in the state of conduct and the state presiding over the trial, in order to be established as the predicate offence of money laundering crime.

However, Europe takes a step further than UN Conventions in deciding the jurisdiction over money laundering offences. Article 6(2)(a) of the Council of

Europe's Convention on Laundering, Search, Seizure and Confiscation of the Proceeds from Crime provides that 'it shall not matter whether the predicate offence was subject to the criminal jurisdiction of the Party'. Article 1(C) of the EU Council Directive on Prevention of the Use of Financial System for the Purpose of Money Laundering (1991) provides that 'money laundering shall be regarded as such even where the activities which generated the property to be laundered were perpetrated in the territory of another Member State or in that of a third country'. According to these provisions, where the money to be laundered is the proceeds of crimes committed within the territory of a third country, even if the predicate activities do not constitute crimes in the third country, the charge of money laundering can still be established. The same has been provided in the Organization of American States' Model Regulations Concerning Offence Connected to Illicit Drug Trafficking and Related Offences. 'The adoption of jurisdiction beyond country border has been accepted by more countries.'[7] This is of great significance for China in combating cross-border crimes. For example, even if gambling does not constitute a crime in Mainland China, where it is conducted, as long as it constitutes the predicate offence in a money laundering case in Hong Kong, it should be charged as money laundering and subjected to the jurisdiction of Hong Kong.[8]

Both Article 15 of United Nations Convention against Transnational Organized Crime and Article 42 of United Nations Convention against Corruption have established the principle of universal jurisdiction. Each State Party shall exercise its jurisdiction over cross-border money laundering crime. In accordance with the principle of prosecution or extradition, any State Party shall have the obligation to combat money laundering. When an offender is arrested by a certain state, if not extradited to another state party, he should be charged in accordance with domestic law. What is more, it is also an important aspect of international cooperation to recover and return the proceeds of money laundering to countries that suffered the loss.

More specific rules include Article 15 of United Nations Convention against Transnational Organized Crime and Article 47 of United Nations Convention against Corruption, which provide rules for consultative jurisdiction.

> State Parties shall consider the possibility of transferring to one another proceedings for the prosecution of an offence established in accordance with this Convention in cases where such transfer is considered to be in the interests of the proper administration of justice, in particular in cases where several jurisdictions are involved, with a view to concentrating the prosecution.

7 Huang Boqing, 'International Cooperation on the Anti Money-Laundering Mechanism' (2007) 1 *Justice of China* 102.

8 Chen Hui, 'The Anti-Money Laundering Research on the Issue of China's Interregional Criminal Judicial Assistance among the Mainland, Hong Kong and Macao' (2006) 8 (5) *Journal of SWUPL* 32.

This is the legal basis in an international convention for international cooperation in the prosecution of money laundering. Therefore, where a State Party refuses to surrender its jurisdiction, it is sensible and practical for other states to give assistance to the prosecution process before considering the possibility of extradition and transfer.[9] The 'First Case of Judicial Cooperation between China and Australia – Money Laundering by Li' is a typical example of consultative jurisdiction.

At present, a prominent feature of cross-border money laundering is laundering through the internet. How to choose the jurisdiction of money laundering on the internet? The Convention on Cybercrime (2001) issued by the Council of Europe provides rules on jurisdiction in Chapter 2, Section 3. Apart from the adoption of the traditional principle of nationality and principle of territoriality, with regard to the conflict of jurisdiction, it provides that 'When more than one Party claims jurisdiction over an alleged offence established in accordance with this Convention, the Parties involved shall, where appropriate, consult with a view to determining the most appropriate jurisdiction for prosecution.' Therefore, for money laundering activities on the internet, the primary jurisdiction should be exercised according to where the activity occurs or results, with the offender's nationality as an additional option of jurisdiction. It should be noted, however, that there might be more than one place involved in a specific case, where the primary jurisdiction should be determined according to the principle of judicial convenience. The Convention should be taken for reference in China.

Whether the range of predicate offences of money laundering should be broadened to cover all crimes

It is not only a matter of legislative technique to broaden the scope of predicate offences for money laundering, but it depends on whether there are similar offences and whether enough is in store for prosecution. Different provisions on money laundering have been provided in countries and territories, which can be divided into three types:

1. Provisions that only stipulate money laundering activities relating to illegal proceeds of drug crimes
2. Provisions that stipulate several predicate crimes that give rise to money laundering
3. Provisions that stipulate all crimes as giving rise to money laundering activities or certain serious money laundering offences.

The United Nations Convention against Transnational Organized Crime has expanded the predicate offence of money laundering to all serious crime,

9 Chen Lei, 'On the Prospect of the Research and Practice in the International Cooperation of Prosecutions' *Procuratorial Daily* (Beijing, 14 October 2011) Section 3.

especially crimes involving organised criminal groups, corruption, obstruction of justice and offences punishable by a maximum deprivation of liberty of at least four years or more. The United Nations Convention against Corruption draws out the maximum range and the minimum range of the predicate offences of money laundering. 'The widest range of predicate offences' include all crimes stipulated in the domestic law that may generate illegal proceeds, because the Convention only requires 'knowing that such property is the proceeds of crime' without limiting the specific kind of crime as the source of generation. The narrowest range includes all crimes stipulated in the Convention which should be incorporated into the domestic law of all State Parties, including bribery of national public officials in Article 15, bribery of foreign public officials and officials of public international organisations in Article 16, embezzlement, misappropriation or other diversion of property by a public official in Article 17, trading in influence in Article 18, abuse of functions in Article 19, illicit enrichment in Article 20, bribery in the private sector in Article 21, embezzlement of property in the private sector in Article 22, concealment in Article 24 and obstruction of justice in Article 25.

After having become a party to the above two Conventions, China has to take its international responsibility and coordinate domestic law with the Conventions. The Amendment VI to the Criminal Law of the People's Republic of China amended the predicate offences of money laundering crime by covering seven offences including drug-related crime, organisational crime of any gangland, terrorist crime, crime of smuggling, crime of corruption or bribery, crime of disrupting the financial management order and crime of financial fraud. As mentioned before, although only Article 191 uses the term 'money laundering', there are four articles providing for the criminalisation of money laundering activities. An issue that has been discussed for years is whether to broaden the range of predicate offence of money laundering to all crimes. The supporting view is based on Article 23(2)(2) of the United Nations Convention against Corruption which provides that 'Each State Party shall include as predicate offences at a minimum a comprehensive range of criminal offences established in accordance with this Convention', claiming that there is a distance between the Convention and what has been provided in Chapter 8 of the Criminal Law of China, for the latter cannot cover all corruption crimes in the Convention, such as abuse of functions, which renders the PRC Criminal Law unable to reach the bottom line of the Convention.

The author believes that if there is only one clause stipulating money laundering offences in the Criminal Law, it is necessary to expand the scope of predicate offences, if not, then it should not be necessary. For the present Criminal Law of China, there are four clauses stipulating money laundering offences, each of which has its own scope of predicate offences, and thus the four clauses should be coordinated for implementation rather than be in conflict or in deficiency. Such coordination has been realised by the promulgation of the Interpretation of the Supreme People's Court on Several Issues concerning the Specific Application of Law in the Trial of Money Laundering and Other Criminal Cases on 11 November 2009, which provides in Article 4 that 'The term "upstream crimes" as mentioned in this Article refers to the various criminal acts which generate the crime-related income or proceeds therefrom as prescribed in Articles 191, 312 and 349 of the Criminal Law.'

In this way, can China get rid of its name of having failed to meet the standards of the range of predicate offences in the United Nations Convention against Corruption? The answer seems to be in the negative. Based on earlier discussions, although the Interpretation has expanded the scope of predicate offences to crimes in Article 191, Article 312 and Article 349 that generate illegal proceeds, it is only an interpretation in nature. However, in a narrow sense, money laundering crime means Article 191, which still leads to difficulties in determining the predicate offences in judicial practice. In other words, because of the inconsistencies between form and content, Article 4 of Interpretation did not give a satisfactory answer to the debate on the range of predicate offences.

Then what is the answer? China could take reference from the two Conventions and Article 3 of the Money Laundering Prevention Act of Taiwan, which applies money laundering to primary offences that are punished by imprisonment of more than five years. The 'primary offence' means the predicate offence, which could be supplemented with a list of specific charges. A base line of the legal penalty of the predicate offence could also be drawn as four or five years at least.

Whether all the charges of money laundering should be stipulated in the Criminal Law

Should all the charges of money laundering be put into a particular section of a chapter, or even into a single article in the Criminal Law of China? Should the money laundering crime be stipulated separately or integrally?

The United Nations Convention against Transnational Organized Crime stipulates money laundering activities in a single chapter, whereas the United Nations Convention against Corruption sets different rules for money laundering and concealment, namely to establish independent rule for concealment as Article 24 after the laundering of proceeds of crime in Article 23, where the former provides that

> when committed intentionally after the commission of any of the offences established in accordance with this Convention without having participated in such offences, the concealment or continued retention of property when the person involved knows that such property is the result of any of the offences established in accordance with this Convention

with the premise of 'without prejudice to the provisions of Article 24'. There are some countries, such as Russia, that adopt a single charge of money laundering,[10]

10 Wang Xin, 'Analysis of the Enlightenment of Russian Legislation for Anti-Laundering' (2010) 1 *Law Science Magazine* 107.

whereas China has developed separate rules for prevention and deterrence. The four clauses providing for four charges belong to different kinds of crimes: Funding Terrorism belongs to Crimes of Endangering Public Security, Money Laundering belongs to the Crimes of Undermining the Order of Financial Management under the Chapter of Crimes of Undermining the Order of Socialist Market Economy, the Disguise and Concealment of Illegal Proceeds and Gains Thereof belongs to Crimes of Disrupting Justice under the Chapter of Crimes of Disrupting the Order of Social Administration, and the Shelter, Transfer and Concealment of Drugs and Drug-related Proceeds belongs to Crimes of Smuggling, Trafficking, Transporting, and Manufacturing Drugs under the Chapter of Crimes of Disrupting the Order of Social Administration. It is obvious that money laundering crimes are stipulated separately, which is optimal for the overall protection of legal interest. However, to promote the implementation of money laundering law, it is advisable to put together all the provisions. The author believes that for the convenience of legal practice and realisation of the guiding rule of law, it is better to put all provisions on money laundering into a single article. Specifically, the present Article 312 and Article 349 should be placed after paragraph 1 of Article 191, combining the three into one article and each paragraph stipulating a certain act of money laundering, all together referred to as special rules for money laundering offences. On the other hand, the charge of sheltering, transferring or selling illegal proceeds in Chapter 6 of Crimes of Disrupting the Order of Social Administration should remain the traditional charges of illegal proceeds because they are different in nature from money laundering. And Article 349 should be deleted because it has been covered by other provisions governing money laundering and activities related to illegal proceeds.

Whether the actus reus elements of money laundering offence should be amended

Article 191 in the present Criminal Law of China lists five ways of committing money laundering. Money laundering is a conduct of assistance in nature, and often involves conversion and transfer through financial institutions and underground banks. Money laundering is getting increasingly frequent and calls have been made for new approaches to fight laundering. Some launderers make use of the latest financial products as important tools through financial markets while others wash their money by means of pawning, leasing, purchasing, investment, lotteries and gambling. Therefore, the Interpretation of the Supreme People's Court on Several Issues concerning the Specific Application of Law in the Trial of Money Laundering and Other Criminal Cases in 2009 provides that 'assisting in the transfer or conversion of the crime-related income or proceeds therefrom by means of pawn, leasing, purchase and sale, investment' shall constitute money laundering. Under extensive interpretation, these types of money laundering can be included in paragraph 1(5) of Article 191 'covering up or concealing the source or nature of crime-related income or proceeds therefrom by any other means'. However, because paragraphs 1(1) to 1(4) of Article 191 mainly govern money laundering through the banking system, whether the transfer, disguise and concealment through the non-banking system can be included in paragraph 1(5) of Article 191 remains in dispute. To answer this question, the interpretation issued by the People's Supreme Court of China holds that the fundamental difference among the three kinds of money laundering activities lies in their predicate offences instead of their specific approach.

The author believes that the answer to this question is connected to the latter. Without an integrated provision for money laundering crime, it leaves inconsistency in practice and difficulty in interpretation. Whether to expand the conduct element of money laundering to 'through financial transactions and other transactions' depends on whether money laundering crime can be integrated into one charge or in one article. Currently, no adjustment can be made to the four charges of money laundering. It is therefore better to stipulate the ways of pawning, leasing, purchase and sale, investment listed in the interpretation of Article 191 of the Criminal Law to clarify the intent of the legislation.

Whether the mens rea *element of money laundering should be limited to knowingly*

The Criminal Law of China limits the *mens rea* element of money laundering to 'wilful' and the offender must clearly know that the money laundered is the proceed of drug-related crime, organised crime, terrorism, smuggling, corruption or bribery, disrupting the financial management order or financial fraud. The United Nations Convention against Corruption also specifies money laundering as an intent crime in Article 23, Chapter 3, laundering of proceeds of crime. For a long time, there have been different understandings of 'knowingly' and the establishment of proof is difficult, which is one of the main reasons why only a few suspects have been charged with money laundering in China since the offence was established in law.

The criminal law of Taiwan provides that a money laundering offence can be established without a requirement of knowledge, but the offender must have the intent to commit the crime. Article 2 of the Money Laundering Prevention Act does not specify knowledge as an element and Article 9(3) provides that the legal representative of a legal entity or any natural person who has fulfilled the due diligence and with best effort to prevent money laundering shall be exempted from responsibility, which means that money laundering can only be established if committed wilfully.[11] Therefore, offenders with indirect intention can also commit a money laundering offence. The legal basis lies in Recommendation 6 of the FATF's Forty Recommendations, which provide that 'the offense of money laundering should apply at least to knowing money laundering activity,

11 Dong Shitan, 'Comparison of Legal Theories on the Crime of Laundering in Taiwan and Macao' (2006) 3 *Journal of Fujian Public Safety College* 75.

including the concept that knowledge may be inferred from objective factual circumstances'.[12]

The author believes that the key is in how to understand and interpret 'knowingly'. Article 1 of The Interpretation of the Supreme People's Court on Several Issues concerning the Specific Application of Law in the Trial of Money Laundering and Other Criminal Cases (2009) provides a clear definition of 'knowingly':

> The word "knows" as prescribed in Article 191 and Article 312 of the Criminal Law shall be determined in consideration of such subjective and objective factors as the cognitive ability of the defendant, the information on the contact with other's crime-related income or proceeds therefrom, the type and amount of the crime-related income or proceeds therefrom, the ways of conversion or transfer of the crime-related income or proceeds therefrom and the confession of the defendant. Under any of the following circumstances, it may be determined that the defendant knows that the alleged property is crime-related income or proceeds therefrom, except that there is evidence that he really does not know: (1) while knowing that another person is engaged in criminal activities, assisting the person in the conversion or transfer of the property; (2) assisting in the conversion or transfer of the property by illegal means without any justifiable reason; (3) acquiring the property at a price obviously lower than the market price without any justifiable reason; (4) assisting in the conversion or transfer of the property by charging a "handling fee" which is obviously higher than the market price without any justifiable reason; (5) assisting another person in scattering a large amount of cash in several bank accounts or transferring the same frequently among different bank accounts without any justifiable reason; (6) assisting a close relative or any other person close to him in the conversion or transfer of the property which is obviously inconsistent with his occupation or property status; or (7) any other circumstance under which the actor may be determined as knowing.

The promulgation of this interpretation clarified the standard of 'knowing' in judicial practice and ceased disagreement among theories.

However, is the *mens rea* of money laundering only limited to 'knowingly', or can negligence constitute money laundering? The Chinese legislation only stipulates the intentional commission of the laundering offence in the Criminal Law of China, *but the Convention on Laundering, Search, Seizure and Confiscation of the Proceeds from Crime formulated* by the Council of Europe in 1990 offers explicit suggestions to all State Parties that where an offender who ought to have assumed that the property was criminal proceeds committed intentionally the

12 Quoted from Tang Ruoyu, 'A Brief Comparison of Money Laundering Crime in Mainland China and Taiwan' (1999) 3 *The Jurist* 105.

conversion, transfer, concealment, disguise, acquisition, possession or use, such activities should be criminalised. For example, paragraph 5 of Article 261 of the German Criminal Code provides that any offender, who, acting negligently, is unaware of the source of property stipulated in paragraph 1, should be sentenced to imprisonment for no more than two years or be fined. The Federal Supreme Court of Germany finds the key word 'negligence' as a *mens rea* element of extreme carelessness or disregard of the source of the proceeds. The Court further holds that what should be punished is the offender's failure to fulfil the legal obligation of deliberation in the transaction.[13] Prosecutor Jiang Zhi from Macao, China, also believes that 'money laundering activities committed out of negligence by particular financial and non-financial entities such as banks, security agencies, insurance companies, the futures traders, currency exchange agencies, gambling operators and pawnshops should be criminalized.'[14]

The reason why only a few money laundering crimes are charged under money laundering offences in China is that the standard of proof, 'knowingly', is difficult to establish in most cases. So far, it is not common for institutions that are obliged to report money laundering transactions and yet failed because of gross negligence to be punished by law. It should be acknowledged that it is the working direction of the Criminal Law of China to implement money laundering offences committed negligently. There are countries and territories, China included, that have established a system by which banks, brokers and other entities are required to report suspicious transactions and are liable if they ever failed to identify such transactions out of gross negligence. International conventions require the criminalisation of wilful money laundering as a minimum, which is by no means an obstacle for States to criminalise money laundering offences committed negligently.

Whether self-laundering can constitute a money laundering offence

According to the traditional theory of Double Jeopardy, although the disposal of illegal proceeds after the commission of a crime may constitute an independent offence, the act of disposal should be included into the previous offence and instead of combining the punishment of all offences, the offender should only be charged with and thereafter punished by the most serious one. Therefore, it is not necessary to criminalise the conduct of disposal after the commission of a crime. The disposal of property and illegal proceeds generated from the commission of any of the seven predicate offences is similar to handling stolen goods, which according to the theory of impunity prevents responsibility for the later

13 Wang Xin, 'Analysis of the Criminal Legislation on Anti-Money Laundering in Germany and Its Enlightenment' (2012) 1 *Journal of Henan Administrative Institute of Politics and Law* 132.

14 Jiang Zhi, 'On Several Issues about Money Laundering Crimes' (9 April 2012) <www.mp.gov.mo/gb/int/articles-2003-04a.html>.

acts. In general, an offender should only be charged with the predicate offence, unless the legal penalty for the money laundering offence is higher. However, this is impossible in China because the legal punishment of any predicate offence is higher than that for money laundering, which can also explain why there have been only a few cases of money laundering though the present criminal law has been making constant improvements to the provisions of money laundering offences.

In fact, it has become an international trend to criminalise self-laundering. Since the laundering crime has become independent from its predicate offence, the two have become different types of crimes, followed by the trend of international anti-money laundering legislation to regard the subject of responsibility in predicate offences as an eligible subject to money laundering, namely to criminalise self-laundering. The Palermo Convention and The Forty Recommendations (2003) issued by FATF also include similar provisions. Most countries have criminalised self-laundering as a money laundering offence. Only a few countries of the civil law system do not apply such rules according to the theory of impunity for later acts.[15] The Money Laundering Prevention Act of Taiwan stipulates that the offence of money laundering shall be applied to people who committed the predicate offence.[16] The criminal code in Hong Kong used to rule that money laundering crime can only apply to those who did not commit predicate offences, which can be evidenced by the charge of 'assisting others to maintain drug crime proceed'. Now Hong Kong has removed the word 'assisting', so that the subject of money laundering offences is broadened to cover the predicate offender. As for the criminal law in Macao, the *actus reus* elements of money laundering in organised crime cases, although only applying to natural persons, include both the offender of the predicate offence and the money laundering offence.[17]

It should be kept in mind that the punishment for money laundering, either self-laundering or assisting laundering, should not be higher than that of the predicate offence. For example, the criminal law in Macao[18] provides that the legal penalty for money laundering not be higher than that of the predicate offences that generate the property being laundered.

Whether money laundering and the predicate offence should be combined for punishment

Some scholars point out that the complex process of money laundering has greatly changed the nature, form, source, direction, possession and ownership of

15 Lin Anmin, 'The Problems and Solutions of Legislation on Money Laundering' (2010) 2 *Journal of Fujian Police College* 64.

16 Tang Ruoyu, 'A Brief Comparison of Money Laundering Crime in Mainland China and Taiwan' (1999) 3 *The Jurist* 105.

17 Tong Weihua, 'The Research on Regional Money Laundering Crime' (10 June 2006) <www.criminallawbnu.cn>.

18 Dong Shitan, 'Comparison of Legal Theories on the Crime of Laundering in Taiwan and Macao' (2006) 3 *Journal of Fujian Public Safety College* 75.

the ill-gotten property, which provides legal coverage to ensure the transfer of illicit proceeds. Money laundering, as a process of legalising the illegal proceeds, is an independent offence from its predicate offence, jeopardising two different legal interests and instead of applying the principle of impunity, it should be combined for punishment with its predicate offence. What is more, from the standpoint of jurisdiction, the cross-border nature of money laundering indicates that money laundering and its predicate offences tend to happen outside the territory of one state, which means that if people who committed predicate offences are excluded from the subject of money laundering, it will be unfavourable to the exercise of criminal jurisdiction.[19]

Even so, new problems can still arise. If people who committed predicate offences and participated in money laundering should be punished for both crimes, should those who committed theft, robbery or fraud and then disguise and conceal the ill-gotten gains and proceeds therefrom be subjected to combined punishment of Article 312 and the predicate offence? It is true that the traditional charge of ill-gotten gains, stipulated as 'the concealment or selling of property gained through crime' in the Criminal Law of China 1979, was different from money laundering, however, it has evolved to become similar to money laundering when the Criminal Law of China 1997 amended the *actus reus* of this offence and named it the offence to conceal, transfer, purchase or sell the gains of crime. Later, the Amendment VI to the Criminal Law of the People's Republic of China refined this article to the concealment or disguising of property gained through crime or the proceeds therefrom, so that the *actus reus* includes not only concealing, transferring, purchasing and selling, but also any other ways to disguise and hide the source of ill-gotten gains. Besides property gained from crime, it also covers the proceeds of the property gained from predicate offences, creating very little difference between Article 312 and Article 191 except for the different ranges of predicate offences. The intention of such implementation was to coordinate Article 312 with the money laundering offence. Therefore, if the punishment under Article 191 can be combined with that of its predicate offence, while Article 312 and its predicate offence should exert punishment separately, it will surely lead to inconsistency in its enforcement.

Another view holds that if the offender only conceals, transfers or sells gains from a predicate offence, such conduct mainly hampers the investigation without harming other legal interests, so that the principle of impunity for the later offence can be applied to establish the predicate offence only. On the other hand, for people who committed crimes such as stealing, fraud, seizing by force, robbery, drug-related crime, smuggling, corruption or bribery, as long as the gains of crime and proceeds therefrom are used for cash smuggling, deposition in financial institutions, underground bank laundering, insurance purchase,

19 He Ping, 'Self-launderer Can Constitute Money Laundering Crime' *Procuratorial Daily* (Beijing, 6 January 2010) Section 3.

investment in real estate and other ways of disguise through cash intense industries, auctioning or gambling, combined punishment should be imposed.[20]

Such a view has its merits but will bring about inconsistency in the administration of justice. One act of disguise or concealment of criminal gains or the proceeds therefrom would lead to two different results, either separate punishment when the offender only conceals, transfers or sells the proceeds, or combined punishment when the offender disposes of the proceeds to disguise and conceal the source and nature thereof, which is clearly not a proper rule to be followed. The key to solving this problem is to stipulate all money laundering offences in one article and retain the traditional offence of ill-gotten gains that is different in nature from money laundering in Chapter 6. Also, one paragraph should be added to Article 191 providing that anyone who committed a predicate offence and participated in money laundering activities thereafter, where the money laundering offence can be established, should be charged and punished for both the money laundering offence and the predicate offence.

Improving the criminal policy against cross-border money laundering policy in China

Law enforcement: whether to expand the subject of anti-money laundering obligations

As the saying goes, banks either stand for or against money laundering. Banks are playing the leading role in combating money laundering activities. However, both the Anti-Money Laundering Law of the People's Republic of China and Administrative Measures for Financial Institutions' Reporting of Transactions Suspected of Financing for Terrorist Purposes limit the subject of obligation to prevent money laundering and terrorist financing to financial institutions, which is too narrow. In present practice, the People's Bank of China is in charge of the supervision and control of money laundering transactions and the collection of information, whereas the investigation agency, the police bureau, is released from its duty of active investigation and the reports of money laundering activities submitted by financial institutions are used only as clues to track down predicate offences. This has weakened the fight against money laundering activities.

For financial institutions under the obligation to combat laundering, it is in fact very hard to take effective measures against money laundering. The People's Bank of China and its subordinate bodies such as China Anti-Money Laundering Monitoring and Analysis Center are in great shortage of specialised staff who are equipped with enough knowledge and experience to be able to fulfil their duty.[21] It is sometimes even the case that banks, driven by economic interests, refuse to

20 Ibid.

21 Lin Anmin, 'The Problem and Solution of Legislation on Money Laundering' (2010) 2 *Journal of Fujian Police College* 64.

cooperate with the investigation and retain a record of suspicious transactions in the name of the protection of their client's privacy.

Adopted on 4 December 2001, the Directive of the European Parliament and of the Council Amending Council Directive on Prevention of the Use of the Financial System for the Purpose of Money Laundering provides that the Directive applies to financial institutions, and legal or natural persons acting in the profession of auditors, external accountants, tax advisors, real estate agents, notaries and other independent legal professionals, dealers in high-value goods and casinos.[22] Faced with the challenge to combat money laundering, China should expand anti-money laundering obligations to non-financial institutions and other professions.

Transnational criminal cases and law enforcement: how to enhance cooperation with other countries and territories as well as with Hong Kong, Macao and Taiwan against money laundering

In order to strengthen the judicial and executive cooperation among countries, legal instruments including the United Nations Convention against Corruption and the United Nations Convention against Transnational Organized Crime provide rules about extradition, legal assistance in investigations and prosecutions, sharing information and resources and administrative cooperation, but the key lies in law enforcement by all State Parties. The money laundering cases solved by the joint investigation between China and Australia as introduced at the beginning of this article is a good example.

Transnational money laundering means the elements of money laundering activities take place in different countries, whereas trans-boundary money laundering (or interregional money laundering) means although money laundering activity takes place in China, it crosses different jurisdictions from the Mainland to Hong Kong and/or Macao. For both transnational and trans-boundary money laundering, at least one of the three elements, the money laundering conduct, the money laundering offender and the object to be laundered, should cross borders. The money laundering activities conducted in China are marked by a combination of transnational and trans-boundary features. After Hong Kong and Macao returned to China, Mainland China has witnessed its economic development at high speed with increasing demand for capital flow and trading volume on a yearly basis. As an international financial and shipping centre, Hong Kong enjoys great freedom in financing and relatively flexible regulation, and Macao is known for well-developed tourism and gambling. Hong Kong and Macao belong to different jurisdictions than Mainland China with different regulations and punishment for money laundering activities. Therefore, money launderers regard Hong Kong and Macao as an important gateway to take advantage of the conflicts and loopholes in regulations of the three jurisdictions

22 Wang Xin, 'Analysis about Its Enlightenment of Russian Legislation for Anti-Laundering' (2010) 1 *Law Science Magazine* 107.

and to get ill-gotten gains laundered abroad. 'Mainland China, Hong Kong and Macao are the hardest-hit area of money laundering crime ... the trans-boundary money laundering among the three regions is always in combination with transnational money laundering.'[23] A considerable amount of money is being laundered between Mainland China and the two special administrative regions.

> From March to December in 2003, the foreign exchange volume of large-sum transnational transactions in individual accounts from mainland China to other regions and countries amounted to 0.654 billion. Hong Kong and US America, ranking the first two among the top ten inflow countries and territories, takes account of 47.64% of the capital flow, with Macao ranking the ninth. During the same period, 2.251 billion dollars of large-sum foreign exchange in individual accounts flew in to the mainland China from Hong Kong, USA and other 10 countries and territories.[24]

The Criminal Code of Hong Kong provides for two types of money laundering offences: relating to proceeds of drug-related crime, and proceeds of other crimes, namely serious crimes. The scope of predicate offences extensively covers all illegal proceeds. As for the definition of money laundering, the Criminal Code of Hong Kong only provides general rules like 'the disposal of proceeds from drug-related crime or other crimes under prosecution'. In Macao, the Financial System Act 1993, the Organized Crime Act 1997 and the Amendment of the Article 10 of the Organized Crime Act make up the three primary rules regulating money laundering activities. Similarly, the criminal law of Macao defines money laundering as the conduct of conversion, transfer or concealment of illegal property, which hardly leaves any loopholes in the definition.

The fight against cross-border money laundering calls for a consensus in ideas and exchange of experience in legislation, judicial approaches and law enforcement between Mainland China and other jurisdictions. Also, a comprehensive system of legislative coordination, judicial assistance, cooperation in supervision and exchange of staff and culture should be established with a permanent mechanism of anti-money laundering cooperation to strengthen the bonds between the legal systems. The cooperation is challenged by the differences in legal systems from Mainland China, Hong Kong and Macao, but at the same time is encouraged by the convergence of the three regions as a nation, so that the conflict in legislation can be eliminated and the fight against money laundering will be more effective. A few suggestions are offered in this article:

23 Tong Weihua, 'The Research on Regional Money Laundering Crime' (10 June 2006) <www.criminallawbnu.cn>.

24 State Administration of Foreign Exchange, *The Report of Anti Money Laundering in the Field of Foreign Exchange* (2004) 55. Quoted from Zhang Changlong, 'The Construction of the Anti-Money Laundering Cooperation Mechanisms among the Inland and Hong Kong and Macao' (2008) 23 (4) *Legal Forum* 134.

First, the inconsistency among statutes needs to be eliminated, convergence of anti-money laundering regulations applicable in China, Hong Kong and Macao encouraged and favourable conditions for judicial and law enforcement cooperation created. We can follow the example of the Convention on Laundering, Search, Seizure and Confiscation of the Proceeds from Crime, the Council Directive on Prevention of the Use of Financial System for the Purpose of Money Laundering and the Organization of American States' Model Regulations Concerning Offence Connected to Illicit Drug Trafficking and Related Offences to refine our legal system and formulate a Regional Anti-Money Laundering Agreement.

Second, the jurisdiction over cross-border money laundering crime should be well determined. The primary rules to be followed should be the principle of actual control and the 'first seized' principle, namely, where the competent authority establishes the case first, there the jurisdiction should be exercised.

Third, the risk of money laundering should be taken into consideration when formulating specific economic policy and measures. The Deputy Chairman of the Panel on Security of the Legislative Council of the Hong Kong Special Administrative Region of the People's Republic of China expressed his concern that 'under the current system, Hong Kong cannot at all identify whether the source of cash flow from the Mainland is legal or not'.[25] Should it remain unchanged, the situation will go against our effort to combat cross-border money laundering.

Taiwan passed the Money Laundering Prevention Act in October 1996 as the first law on the prevention of money laundering in Asia, which came into force in April 1997[26] and was implemented twice in part. The Investigation Bureau of the Ministry of Justice of Taiwan set up its Anti-Money Laundering Division in April 1997, specialising in the prevention of money laundering activities. Anti-money laundering cooperation should be strengthened not only among mainland China, Hong Kong and Macao, but also between China and Taiwan, therefore, China needs to make a further step in judicial activities and enforcement of anti-money laundering legislation. For example, the first and most important step to take is to raise awareness among financial institutions and police bureaus to take their responsibility in active investigations and provide support with advanced technology.

Conclusion

The importance of international cooperation in the combating of money laundering has been fully acknowledged by countries around the world so that judicial

25 Xia Wenhui, 'Investment Immigrants from Mainland China Will Give Rise to the Black Hole of Money Laundering in Hong Kong' *International Herald Leader* (Beijing, 12 September 2003) 4.

26 Dong Shitan, 'Comparison of Legal Theories on the Crime of Laundering in Taiwan and Macao' (2006) 3 *Journal of Fujian Public Safety College* 75.

and executive departments and financial supervisory institutions are focused on the promotion of international cooperation. The deterrence effect of cross-border money laundering legislation not only helps in reducing international financial crime but also cuts off the channels for other cross-border crimes. However, the fight against money laundering is faced with great challenges, especially cross-border money laundering. 'In fact, even in countries where a comprehensive system of anti-money laundering law has been established, the conviction rates of suspicious transaction remains low, only a few in a thousand cases.'[27]

Back to the case in the beginning of this article, had Australia not concluded an extradition treaty with China, the Procuratorate of Guangdong Province would have received a request for judicial assistance and would then have reported the case to the Supreme People's Procuratorate of China with a proposal for direct cooperation between China and Australia. In this way, the police of Australia brought a prosecution against Li and the Supreme Court of Queensland found Li guilty of money laundering and launched the asset recovery process. The case was tackled by the joint investigation of competent authorities in Guangdong and Australia, with assistance provided by the Hong Kong police and the Chinese police arranged for 13 witnesses to testify by remote video link. In the meantime, the police of Australia launched a civil procedure to confiscate the illegal gains. It is a successful precedent of international cooperation to combat cross-border money laundering crime. To conclude, a well-established domestic law and international convention system is the first step to combat money laundering, but it takes an indispensable and enduring effort to make progress in legislation, judicial and law enforcement practice and only by practical and effective cooperation among countries, can we make further steps to prevent and disrupt cross-border money laundering.

In spite of those limited areas of non-compliance with current international requirements, China has still made dramatic progress during the next years. However, we should bear in mind that solutions against money laundering mean much more than merely building up a legislative framework or anti-money laundering regulatory system. Criminal policy is as important and effective as the criminal law itself in fighting money laundering. For instance, how to create a favourable domestic environment that can make current AML measures as effective as possible is another key element. With lots of scholars condemning the omission of supervision of banks in China, are they well aware of the fact that the most popular way of laundering in China is by using underground banks, which are out of the reach of bank supervision? When scholars are not satisfied with the passivity in tracing dirty money in China, have they noticed the popular use of cash and fake ID cards in China? In fact, China has its own local barriers in anti-money laundering and has been making great efforts in preventing ID card counterfeiting and reducing the use of cash. The more you know about China the more you will find out about how much China has contributed to the world in fighting transnational money laundering.

27 Kang Shuhua, 'On the Present Situation, Cause and Countermeasures of Money Laundering' (2006) 26 (4) *Academic Forum of Nandu* 81.

6 Transnational cybercrime and cybercrime by transnational organisations

Petter Gottschalk

Introduction

Traditional crime generally concerns personal or property offences that law enforcement has continued to combat for centuries. Cybercrime is characterised by being technologically advanced, it can occur almost instantaneously and it is extremely difficult to observe and detect. Cybercrime is sometimes easy to track, as digital detectives can follow electronic traces. While the crime scene in terms of computers involved may be easy to track, the criminals as actors are more difficult to find and prosecute. The problem of offender identification occurs because of the relative anonymity afforded by the Internet as well as the transcendence of geographical and physical limitations in cyberspace. Also, decentralised peer-to-peer networks may prevent material from being tracked to a specific location, and sophisticated encryption lets criminals keep online chats private from those policing the web.

Transnational cybercrime encompasses illegal activities carried out across national borders[1] using information technology. Criminals are able to take advantage of a virtually limitless pool of potential victims. This is the case, for example, in online grooming where paedophile offenders find child victims across borders.[2] Similarly, transnational music piracy is committed through a multitude of modi operandi.[3] Also, financial crime in terms of, for example, electronic money laundering is frequently transnational between banking sectors with different legislations and secrecy practices.[4]

1 Petter Gottschalk and Vesna Markovic, 'Transnational Criminal Organizations (TCOs): The Case of Combating Criminal Biker Gangs' (2016) 11(1) *International Journal of Criminal Justice Sciences* 30.

2 Julia Davidson and Petter Gottschalk, 'The Context of Online Abuse: Policy and Legislation' in Stephen Webster, Julia Davidson and Antonia Bifulco (eds), *Online Offending Behavior and Child Victimization* (Palgrave Macmillan 2015) 1–10.

3 George E Higgins, Scott E Wolfe and Catherine D Marcum, 'Music Piracy and Neutralization: A Preliminary Trajectory Analysis from Short-Term Longitudinal Data' (2008) 2(2) *International Journal of Cyber Criminology* 324.

4 Cathrine Filstad and Petter Gottschalk, 'Characteristics of White-Collar Criminals: A Norwegian Study' (2012) 15(2) *Journal of Money Laundering Control* 175.

This chapter addresses the issues of transnational cybercrime and cybercrime by transnational criminal organisations. Two cases of transnational cybercrime are presented: online grooming and CEO fraud. One case of transnational criminal organisations is presented: Hells Angels Motorcycle club.

This chapter applies both an offender-based and an offence-based perspective on crime: offence-based with respect to online grooming and CEO fraud, and offender-based with respect to Hells Angels. The chapter focuses on offenders who abuse the Internet to commit crime. While online grooming as well as CEO fraud are typical examples of transnational cybercrime, Hells Angels is a typical transnational organisation where we so far know little about their cybercrime. We know that they are involved in drugs, and we can assume that it involves a form of online shopping and transnational money transfers in electronic channels not regulated by governments.

The case of online grooming

The sexual abuse of young people via the Internet is an international problem, a crime without geographical boundaries. Adults use the Internet to befriend and establish an emotional connection with a child, in order to entice them into meeting. As more young people use the Internet to socially network with friends, the potential for contact with sexual offenders will increase. There is, however, limited information available about the behaviours of Internet sexual offenders to inform effective risk management strategies for policy makers, law enforcement agencies, parents, and young people. In response to this, the European Commission Safer Internet Plus Program commissioned a consortium of leading experts from the UK and across Europe to develop an understanding of the different ways in which sexual offenders approach, communicate and 'groom' young people online. Davidson and Gottschalk[5] report findings from the European project based on interviews of both experts and offenders in the UK, Belgium, Italy and Norway.

There is growing evidence that adults use the Internet to an increasing extent to access children and young people for the purposes of sexual abuse. Internet sex offender behaviour includes the construction of sites to be used for the exchange of information, experiences, and indecent images of children; the organisation of criminal activities that seek to use children for prostitution purposes and that produce indecent images of children at a professional level and the organisation of sexual tourism. The definition of an online groomer is someone who has initiated online contact with a child with the intention of establishing a sexual relationship involving cyber-sex or sex with physical contact. Child grooming is a process that commences with sex offenders choosing a target area that is likely to attract

5 Davidson and Gottschalk (n 2).

children.[6] In the physical world, this could be venues visited by children such as schools, shopping malls or playgrounds. A process of grooming commences when offenders take a particular interest in the child and make them feel special with the intention of forming a bond as a precursor of abuse. The Internet has greatly facilitated this process in the virtual world in terms of geographic location, speed of contact and range of number of contacts.

Groomers will often offer incentives such as money, gifts, concert tickets, modelling contracts, day trips, phones and games as part of the grooming process or to encourage young people to produce and send personal images. Internet sexual offenders are currently defined as falling into two principal categories, which are not mutually exclusive: Those who use the Internet to target and groom children for the purposes of sexual abuse; and those who produce and/or download indecent illegal images of children from the Internet and distribute them.

Recent advances in computer technology have been aiding sex offenders, stalkers, child pornographers, child traffickers, and others with the intent of exploiting children. While such offences occurred prior to the Internet, the advent of the new technology two decades ago has allowed for easier and faster distribution of pornographic materials and communication across national and international boundaries. The dynamics of this opportunism are the subject of ongoing discussion. It seems to be through the exploration of sexual themes and seeking out adult pornography on the Internet that offenders' previous deviant sexual interests are reawakened.

The Internet provides the opportunity to join a virtual community where people with similar interests can communicate and find useful information. 'Myspace' and other similar social networking sites encompass thriving 'communities' where young people engage in countless hours of photo sharing. In addition to Myspace, other social networking and blogging sites such as Friendster.com, Facebook.com and MyYearbook.com, allow users to post pictures, videos and blogs and send emails and instant messaging. Myspace and Facebook differ in security aspects in that Myspace is open to anyone, and has loose age restrictions, while Facebook users are encouraged and often required to register using their real name. The anonymity, availability of extremely sensitive personal information and ease of contacting people, make social networking sites a useful tool for online child sex offenders in general, but specifically for online groomers. Usage by young people develops, whereby if young people want to get to know each other better, then they may move into more private arenas such as MSN. This intensifies the communication and, if the relationship is developed further, then the private space of web cameras is utilised.

While many of these sites have age restrictions, it is possible for offenders to misrepresent their age. Also, in order to hide their IP addresses and locations,

6 Llian Alys, Kristina Massey and Stephen Tong, 'Investigative Decision Making: Missing People and Sexual Offences, Crossroads to an Uncertain Future' (2013) 10(2) *Journal of Investigative Psychology and Offender Profiling* 140.

offenders can piggyback on insecure Wi-Fi connections or use proxy servers. Decentralised peer-to-peer networks prevent material from being tracked to a specific server, and encryption lets them keep online chats private from those policing the Internet.

Therefore, technologies around social networking sites allow relatively easy access to children by online groomers, with children having frequent and open access to such sites at younger ages. Once in contact with a child, the online groomers can use various incentives to encourage the child's participation, towards the goal of sexual contact.

The case of CEO fraud

CEOs typically enjoy substantial individual freedom in their professions with little or no control. The CEO is the only person at that hierarchical level in the organisation. Below the CEO, there are a number of executives at the same hierarchical level. Above the CEO, there are a number of board members at the same hierarchical level. But the CEO is alone at his or her level. The CEO is supposed to be controlled by the board, but the board only meets once in a while to discuss business cases. Executives below the CEO are typically appointed by the CEO and tend to be loyal to the CEO. Therefore, power, influence and freedom are characteristics of CEOs.

CEO power and influence can be illustrated by what is labelled CEO fraud in law enforcement. CEO fraud is not fraud by CEOs. Rather, CEO fraud is fraud committed by someone claiming to be the CEO. If someone claims to be the CEO, most people in the organisation will do what they are told. As long as they believe that the message stems from the real CEO, they are completely obedient and do as they are told by the fake CEO. The U.S. Federal Bureau of Investigation (FBI) warned in 2016 about a dramatic increase in CEO fraud, e-mail scams in which the attacker spoofs a message from the boss and tricks someone at the organisation into wiring funds to the fraudsters. The FBI estimates these scams cost organisations in the United States more than one billion dollars per year. Organisations that are victimised by CEO fraud can be characterised by a combination of CEO power and obedience culture.

Some of the surprises for new CEOs arise from time and knowledge limitations – there is so much to do in complex new areas, with imperfect information and never enough time. Others stem from unexpected and unfamiliar new roles and altered professional relationships. Still others occur because of the frequent paradox that the more power you have, the harder it is to use it. While several of the challenges may appear familiar, Porter et al. discovered that nothing in a leader's background, even running a large business within his or her company fully prepare them to be CEO.[7] Given the required struggle for CEOs to succeed under such circumstances, their

7 Michael E Porter, Jay W Lorsch, and Nitin Nohria, 'Seven surprises for new CEOs' (2004) *Harvard Business Review* 62.

subordinates have to cope with initiatives and decisions that may seem random without any clear pattern. After a while with a new CEO, little will surprise those who have to execute CEO decisions. This opens up companies to CEO fraud, where external criminals can take advantage of an institutional climate where every decision by a CEO is expected to be executed, whether or not the decision makes sense.

CEOs have long been recognised as the principal architects of corporate strategy and major catalysts of organisational change, and the extent to which CEOs can effect change in corporate strategy is thought to be determined largely by the power they possess, and how they decide to apply it.[8] Thus, CEO fraud is enabled by change initiatives, where CEO behaviour itself changes in ways so that there is no suspicion when deviant requests for money transfers occur.

While strategy development as well as organisational change may be at the centre of CEO work, many CEOs spend much more time on other – and more minor – matters and issues. Conflicts between individuals in the organisation take time to resolve and sudden media attention can steal even more time – and sometimes sleep – from important strategic thinking. Trivial matters tend to occupy much of CEO time. Given an understanding for a stressful situation among employees, CEO fraud is enabled based on the lack of formal rules guiding CEO decision-making and implementation.

Many CEOs discover that they are alone, particularly in difficult times. They have nobody on their side at the same organisational level with whom they can openly discuss how to get out of a crisis situation. Rather, others in an organisation may speculate whether or not the CEO will survive in the position and act accordingly to rescue their own future in the organisation. Therefore, employees who receive strange requests from an alleged CEO will be reluctant to contact the real CEO to check whether or not they should execute a money transfer as requested.

Problem-solving is at the core of CEO work. Mindsets are conceived as distinct cognitive operations that facilitate problem-solving. The concept dates back to the end of the nineteenth century and the experimental psychologist Oswald Külpe, who showed that most human thinking happens without images (imageless thoughts) and that most of it also occurs outside of our awareness. The resulting term, 'Bewusstseinslage', literally a 'state of mind', was later translated into the concept of mindsets, 'Einstellung'. Subordinates tend to spend time speculating on the mindset of the CEO and thus feel distant from communicating with the CEO.

Külpe showed that subjects would single out the features related to their tasks, while unimportant or irrelevant features were rejected from their attention. For example, faced with the task of observing the number of letters presented to them, subjects may be totally unable to recall the colour and may even deny that

8 Petter Gottschalk, *CEOs and White-Collar Crime: A Convenience Perspective* (Palgrave Macmillan 2017).

colour has been experienced at all. This is the original meaning of the term 'mindset': the brain is 'set' to perceive the world according to predefined criteria. In the course of his research, it was observed that, while given tasks were conscious initially, after a few repetitions the tasks would gradually disappear from consciousness. Upon increased practice, conscious awareness concerning the task waned, although the task could be completed even if there was no awareness of it.[9] Subjects had no phenomenological awareness of inner speech at the time of study, i.e. there was no longer conscious reflection about the tasks. The original purpose is duly forgotten and appearance of the stimulus automatically activated the prescribed conduct. In our perspective of speculation with lack of communication, subordinates can be fearful of the possible response by the CEO if they contact the person concerning a requested money transfer. Again, this phenomenon is an enabler of CEO fraud.

The word 'set' in 'mindset' describes how the actor is perceptually prepared or 'set' to detect and respond to a given situation,[10] a cognitive recognition pattern that is automatically evoked when scanning the environment. The core aspect is that mindsets are a) caused by repetitive tasks; b) automatic behaviours set in play with little or no awareness; and c) replace personality-based dispositions with mindset content. Mindsets can be extremely effective in terms of seizing business opportunities, but are in themselves neither lawful nor unlawful since the ethical implications may not be a part of the mindset. Instead, they may be seen as automated recognition of opportunity with instrumental value as profit maximising in a competitive setting.

Bigley and Wiersema[11] argue that CEOs' cognitive orientation should influence how they wield their power to affect corporate strategy. On the other hand, predictions about a CEO's use of power require an understanding of the CEO's cognitive orientation toward his or her firm's strategy, because power is simply the ability to bring about a preferred or intended effect. Hypothesised association between a CEO's cognitive orientation and corporate strategy presupposes that the CEO has sufficient power to bring about the preferred or intended effects.

At the core of a CEO's mindset we sometimes find himself or herself. Being alone at the top with rivalling executives as main contacts, the CEO has to enter the role of team player without really believing that it will work. There is no top management team and the CEO is alone. Over time, a CEO may focus more and more on managing the role rather than managing the company.

Not all CEOs work for change. Some are more committed to status quo – particularly to their organisation's current strategy and leadership profile – than

9 Oshrit Cohen-Kdoshay and Nachshon Meiran, 'The Representation of Instructions in Working Memory leads to Autonomous Response Activation: Evidence from the first trials in the Flanker Paradigm' (2007) 60 *Quarterly Journal of Experimental Psychology* 1140.

10 Ibid.

11 Gregory A Bigley and Margarethe F Wiersema, 'New CEOs and Corporate Strategic Refocusing: How Experience as Heir Apparent influences the Use of Power' (2002) 47(4) *Administrative Science Quarterly* 707.

others. Hambrick et al.[12] found that many organisations do not adapt effectively to changes in their environments because of CEO commitment to status quo. Organisational inertia can thus be caused by the CEO, making the organisation unable to change at the same rate as its environment. McClelland et al.[13] found that CEO commitment to status quo is influenced by variables at the individual, firm, and industry levels. Increasing CEO age and tenure are associated with greater status quo commitment. CEOs in firms with financial slack view change more favourably. In contrast, CEOs at firms with liquidity problems may be more committed to the status quo out of necessity.

CEOs' mindsets and strategic beliefs are likely to be instantiated to a significant degree in their firms' current strategies. When a top executive seeking advice confirms and/or restores his or her confidence in the correctness of strategic beliefs, the CEO will be less inclined to alter firm strategy. The mindsets of CEOs are expected to cause them to be the principal architects of corporate strategy and major catalysts of organisational change.[14] Belonging to their mindsets is how to use power and secrecy, building alliances with some people and keeping others in the dark about their dispositions, as shown by Bigley and Wiersma.[15] McDonald and Westphal[16] theorised that relatively poor firm performance can prompt CEOs to seek more advice from executives of other firms who are their friends or similar to them and less advice from acquaintances or dissimilar others and suggest how and why this pattern of advice seeking could reduce firms' propensity to change corporate strategy in response to poor performance.

Similarly, CEOs can have a tendency to listen more to executives in their top management teams who confirm rather than disconfirm their beliefs. Differential association theory postulates that CEO learning occurs in association with those who find their behaviour and thinking favourable and in isolation from those who find it unfavourable. Differential association is the process whereby one is exposed to normative definitions favourable or unfavourable to illegal or law-abiding behaviour. Whether CEOs engage in white-collar crime is largely based on their socialisation within certain peer groups.[17]

12 Donald C Hambrick, Vilmos F Misangyi, and Chuljin A Park, 'The Quad Model for Identifying a Corporate Director's Potential for Effective Monitoring: Toward a New Theory of Board Sufficiency' (2015) 40(3) *Academy of Management Review* 323.

13 Patrick L McClelland, Xin Liang, and Vincent L Barker, 'CEO Commitment to Status Quo: Replication and Extension using Content Analysis' (2010) 36(5) *Journal of Management* 1251.

14 Bigley and Wiersma (n 11).

15 Ibid.

16 Michael L McDonald and James D Westphal 'Getting by with the Advice of Their Friends: CEOs' Advice Networks and Firms' Strategic Responses to Poor Performance' (2003) 48(1) *Administrative Science Quarterly* 1.

17 Kristy Holtfreter, 'General Theory, Gender-Specific Theory, and White-Collar Crime' (2015) 22(4) *Journal of Financial Crime* 422.

McDonald and Westphal[18] tested their hypothesis that relatively poor firm performance can prompt CEOs to seek self-confirming advice. The results from a large sample confirm their hypothesis and show that executives' social network ties can influence firms' responses to economic adversity, in particular by inhibiting strategic change in response to relatively poor organisational performance. Additional findings indicate that CEOs' advice-seeking in response to low performance may ultimately have negative consequences for subsequent performance, suggesting how CEOs' social network ties could play an indirect role in organisational decline and downward spirals in form performance.

The case of Hells Angels

One per cent (1%) of biker clubs demonstrates non-conformist behaviour, including anti-social and criminal behaviour.[19] Outlaw biker groups are organised in units that are registered as legal entities. Nevertheless, most of them are criminal matrix organisations where the motorcycle clubs themselves are legal, while activities of club members are often illegal. This combination of legal and illegal can be labelled matrix organisations, where the horizontal axis is legal (the club), while the vertical axis is illegal (the projects).

Lavigne described criminal bikers in this way:

> The darkness of crime lies not in its villainy or horror, but in the souls of those who choose to live their lives in the abyss. A man who toils from youth to old age to violate the line that divides civilization from wilderness, who proclaims he is not of society, but an outsider sworn to break its laws and rules, yet who readily seeks refuge in its lenient legal system, embraces its judicial paternalism and gains substance from its moral weakness; whose very existence as an outlaw is defined by society's being, is but a shadow of the real world, bereft of freedom and doomed to tag along in society's wake.[20]

Outlaw biker groups as criminal organisations can be compared to legal organisations such as manufacturing companies and auditing firms. In a criminal organisation, management is exercised by clear and explicit rules laid out for its members.[21] In a legal organisation, management is exercised by clear and explicit goals for business performance. Table 6.1 illustrates some of the differences between criminal and legal organisations. In terms of recruitment, a criminal

18 McDonald and Westphal (n 16).

19 Tom Barker, 'One Percent Biker Clubs: A Description' (2005) 9(1) *Trends in Organized Crime* 101; Tom Barker, 'American Based Biker Gangs: International Organized Crime' (2011) 36(3) *American Journal of Criminal Justice* 207.

20 Yves Lavigne, *Hells Angels: Into the Abyss* (Harper Collins Publishers 1996).

21 Carlo Morselli, 'Hells Angels in Springtime' (2009) 23 *Trends in Organized Crime* 145.

Table 6.1 Comparison of criminal and legal organisations

Characteristic	*Criminal biker organisation*	*Legal business organisation*
Management	Rules how to conduct illegal business	Goals for business performance
Organisation	Network, matrix, and support groups	Hierarchy and subsidiaries
Recruitment	Successful crime and similar lifestyle	Labour market based on education and experience
Leadership	Control of member activities and lifestyle	Control of work outcome and performance
Relationships	Tight brotherhood based on common values	Loose ties based on cooperation at work
Finance	Cash and accounts in unstable secrecy states	Budgets and accounts in stable states
Marketing	Bribes, threats and adventures	Advertisements, corruption, and power games

organisation engages in selective recruitment of new members,[22] while a legal organisation turns to the labour market to identify candidates.

Hells Angels Motorcycle Club (HAMC) was founded in 1948 in San Bernardino in California. Today, the outlaw group has close to 3,000 members in close to 250 chapters around the world in nearly 60 countries. Like many network organisations, a large number of individuals are associated with the club in various capacities – often wearing the sign 81 as letter numbers for HA. HAMC maintains a strong core leadership. Each chapter has a charter and a clearly defined division of labour between the international organisation and itself.[23] With a history spanning more than half a century, the HAMC has developed into a vast organisation, with chapters spanning across five continents.[24]

Morselli studied criminal market activities of the HAMC in Canada.[25] He found that the HAMC organisation is a hierarchical structure with clear and explicit rules laid out for its members. Their criminal market activities are characterised by flexibility rather than the rigid confines of a formal organisation.

Some gangs have legally registered their names and insignia in order to protect their reputation. For instance, the HAMC has registered its trademarks. HAMC has successfully sued Disney Pictures to change a movie script and legally forced

22 Robert J Thomas, 'Crucibles of Leadership Development' (2008) 49(3) *Sloan Management Review* 15.

23 Ibid.

24 Morselli (n 21).

25 Ibid.

an author who used the HAMC winged death head on the cover of his book not to publish their icon. HAMC only had to legally threaten Marvel Comics in order to prevent them from using the name Hell's Angel for one of their comic characters.[26]

When HAMC are suing companies worldwide for trademark infringements in order to protect their reputation and economic interest, it tells us how society lets a deviant and outlaw group assimilate into a larger system. Trademark protection is an example of the cultural politics of the outlaws, i.e. the ways in which social and economic exclusion and inclusion are negotiated in socio-cultural practice. Trademark protection also tells about ways in which the proliferating internal boundaries of society, often grounded in relations of inequality, are crossed and challenged by those deemed expelled, with the mechanisms used by agents of the dominant system to control them.

Thomas argues that HAMC has 'mastered the art of turning crucible experiences into leadership gold'.[27] He characterises HAMC as a large, durable, complex, multiunit, multinational entity that has grown rapidly. The organisation has closed its own borders and engages in selective recruitment of new members, and it rarely admits converts into the top leadership ranks. The most visible crucible is the motorcycle run – an event remarkable in its functional similarity to that of a tour of duty.

Thomas suggests that HAMC is best known for two things: its violent past – including murders, drug wars and gang fights – and its longevity.[28] As an organisation, it seems like a paradox that a group that purports not to follow society's rules, or any other rules, maintains a strict code of conduct.

Maturity describes the transition from an initial to a more advanced state, possibly through a number of intermediate states.[29] The evolutionary improvement can be defined in terms of discrete maturity levels. The fundamental underlying assumption of maturity models is that a higher level of maturity will result in better performance. Maturity models reflect the degree to which an organisation has success.

A stage model is a theoretical approach to a phenomenon where stages are (1) sequential in nature, (2) occur as a hierarchical progression that is not easily reversed, and (3) involve a broad range of organisational activities and structures. Benchmark variables, such as membership, affiliates and behaviour, are used to indicate characteristics in each stage of growth. A one-dimensional continuum is established for each benchmark variable.

26 Carol Fleischhaker, 'Piercing the Power of the Patch: How Trademark Law Could Diminish the Power of Gang Insignia' (2011) 14(1) *The Journal of World Intellectual Property* 21.

27 Thomas (n 22) 15.

28 Thomas (n 22).

29 Imed Boughzala and Gert-Jan de Vreede, 'Evaluating Team Collaboration Quality: The Development and Field Application of a Collaboration Maturity Model' (2015) 32(3) *Journal of Management Information Systems* 1129.

The concept of maturity models and stages of growth has been applied to a variety of organisational phenomena to determine maturity levels. Maturity models identify sequential, hierarchical and cumulative levels for development over time. The first topic is to decide on the number of stages. Stage models have a limited number of stages, which are conceptualised and defined in significantly different forms from one to another. The second topic is to identify the dominant problems for each stage, indicating that for each of them there is a pattern of primary concerns. The third topic is to identify workable benchmark variables. Benchmark variables indicate the theoretical characteristics in each stage of growth. The fourth and final topic is concerned with paths of evolution. Stage models indicate that growth proceeds from the initial to the final stage, via intermediary ones.

All stages of growth models share a common underlying logic. Organisations undergo transformations in their design characteristics over time, which enable them to face new tasks or problems that growth elicits. Problems, tasks or environments may differ from model to model, but they all suggest that stages emerge in a well-defined sequence, so that the solution of one set of problems or challenges leads to the emergence of a new set of problems or challenges that the organisation must address. Each stage comes with its own difficulties that the organisation has to resolve and each resolution leads yet to another problem in need of a resolution. This key principle of the growth model may be illustrated by referring to the problems common to legal organisations, where they will survive or collapse depending on their ability to develop and mature over time. Solving the developmental task of one stage, leads to the next problem demanding solution.

A stage model considers degrees of criminal cooperation based on the fundamental principle of social organising. It indicates maturity levels for criminal cooperation based on patterns of criminal organising and elements of social organisations.

Criminal organisations may develop through four stages over time, as illustrated in Figure 6.1. In the beginning, the gang is randomly selecting targets for crime and carries out their activities without plan or coordination. At the highest level of a value-based organisation, gang members share core values that determine how and why they do what they do, based on competence and a strategy.

Criminal organisations at four levels, as illustrated in Figure 6.1, can be characterised by management, structure, relations, actors, leadership and corruption, as listed in Table 6.2. Management develops from rules via knowledge and goals to a culture where rules are implicitly guiding behavior. Members develop from amateurs and generalists to specialists and experts in fields such as trade, finance, intelligence, and marketing.

Criteria to determine maturity for HAMC include exploitation of law, businesses that cut across legal and illegal markets, trademark protection, reputation, prosperity, followers, and law enforcement avoidance.

We define a maturity model for HAMC in terms of four stages. The first stage is characterised by establishing territories both geographically and in terms of illegal markets. Threats and power are applied to succeed in establishing the club in competition with rivalry gangs. The final stage is characterised by entering into legal arrangements by running legal businesses and keeping

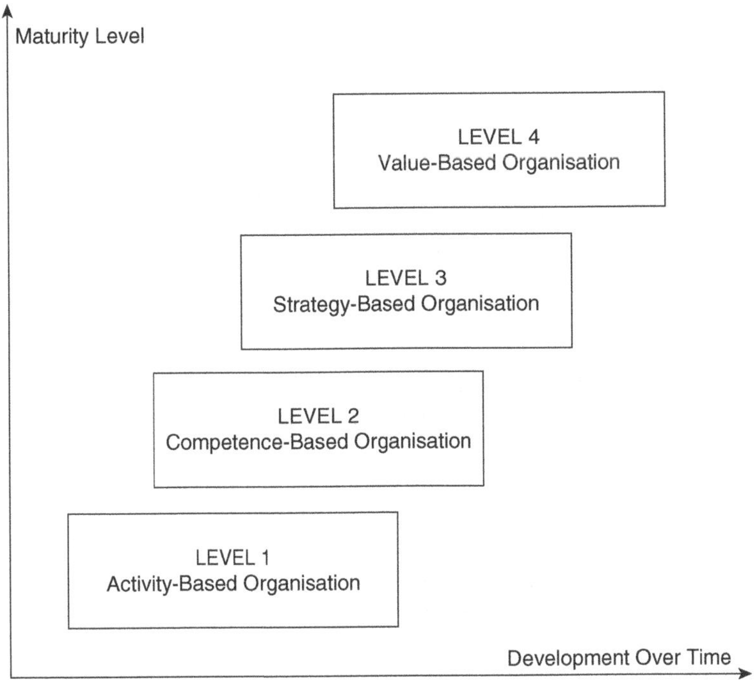

Figure 6.1 Maturity levels for criminal organisations

Table 6.2 Characteristics of the development model for criminal organisations

	Level 1 activity-based organisation	*Level 2 competence-based organisation*	*Level 3 strategy-based organisation*	*Level 4 value-based organisation*
Management	Rules	Knowledge	Goals	Culture
Structure	Gang	Network	Hierarchy	Matrix
Relationships	Friendship	Resources	Commitments	Community
Actors	Amateurs	Generalists	Specialists	Experts
Leadership	Dramatic	Organisational	Ambitious	Charismatic
Corruption	Random	Selective	Goal-oriented	Continuous

professional relations with banks, attorneys and government representatives, while at the same time keeping secrecy around their club activities. The maturity model is illustrated in Figure 6.2.

Characteristics of each maturity level in Figure 6.2 can be identified in terms of structure, activities and reputation as illustrated in Table 6.3. The first stage of

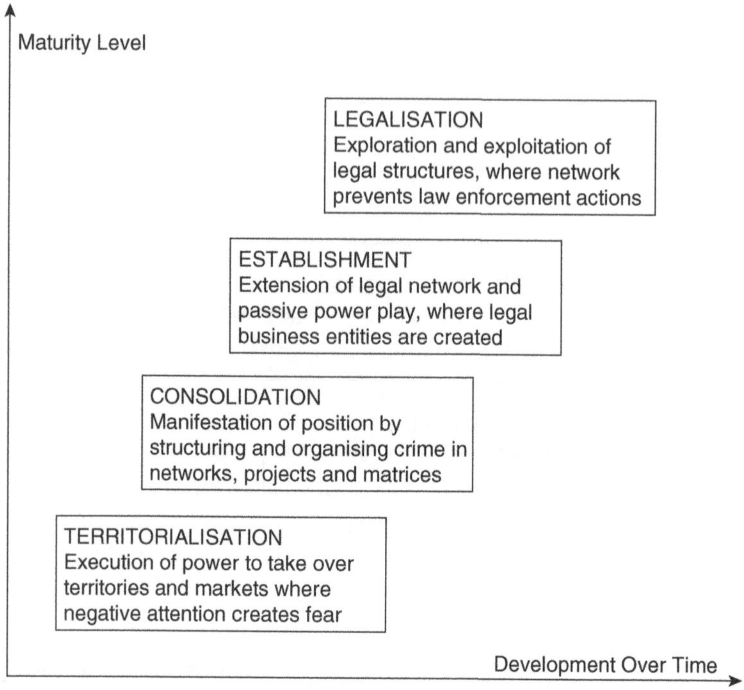

Figure 6.2 Maturity model for Hells Angels MC

territorialisation is characterised by a loose structure where members initiate crime with some coordination among them, by violent and risky activities, and by a reputation of dangerous criminals. The final stage of legalisation is characterised by a legal base organisation in the club that sets up project organisations separate from the club that carry out criminal activities. This is a matrix organisation, where the vertical chapters are legal, while the horizontal projects are illegal. Criminal activities are hidden in legal activities, and the club is seeking a positive and respectful reputation based on social activities.

As an example, Hells Angels MC Norway is seeking positive attention by means of social activities. Their spokesman is a hero in Norway because of a number of publicity stunts where he participates in adventures and helps disabled children. When he comments on members being convicted of crime, he says that they were unlucky and stupid, and that their actions have nothing to do with the club. Wood and Alleyne[30] found that gangs achieve positive attention by

30 Jane L Wood and Emma Alleyne, 'Street Gang Theory and Research: Where are we now and where do we go from here?' (2010) 15(2) *Aggression and Violent Behavior* 100.

Table 6.3 Characteristics of maturity levels for Hells Angels MC

	Structure	*Activities*	*Reputation*
Territorialisation	Individual violent member initiatives with some coordination among them	Violent behaviour, risk taking and random crime	Dangerous criminals seeking negative publicity
Consolidation	Coordinated individual profit-oriented activities	Trade in drugs, manipulation, threats and fraud among rivals and suppliers	Negative attention and respect in the underworld
Establishment	Management by outsourcing of criminal activities	Threats of violence, management and arbitration among criminals	Attention avoidance and power base construction in criminal markets
Legalisation	Base organisation sets up and monitors criminal projects	Mixture of legal and illegal activities and businesses, money laundering	Seeking positive attention by means of social activities

providing financial aid (albeit from drug trade profits) to disadvantaged communities, by providing law and order services, by providing security escorts for recreational programs and by assisting impoverished households by supplying groceries, free transportation, and manpower.

Conclusion

Transnational cybercriminals include online groomers, CEO fraudsters, and Hells Angels members as presented in this article. The extent to which HAMC use the Internet is dependent on the local chapter's maturity level. At the lower stages of territorialisation and consolidation, the Internet is mainly used for threats and other violent purposes. At higher stages, the Internet serves as a communication channel to enable drug trade and money laundering.

CEO fraud is characterised by the organisational opportunity that arises both from CEO behaviour and from subordinates' reactions to CEO behaviour. The CEO is responsible for change, and the personal behaviour of a CEO can be unpredictable, thereby opening up opportunities for other actors claiming to be the CEO. The lack of knowledge combined with speculations about CEO behaviour among subordinates can cause CEO fraud to come as no surprise to them.

Transnational cybercrime in the area of online grooming has created a market for paedophiles where they can buy and sell images, videos and access to children. For many paedophiles, a personal computer in a safe environment at home makes them feel comfortable in grooming children globally.

Part II

Art crime and historical memory

7 ‘Paint it black’

‘Simple’ and increasingly ‘professional’ looting of antiquities with metal-detectors in East Asia

Samuel Hardy

Introduction

‘Metal-detectors’ are a range of instruments of electromagnetic induction that are used to find metals on and behind surfaces, underground and/or underwater. While metal-detectors have a wider range of uses, the practice of ‘metal-detecting’ is the search for metal objects for collection. Metal-detecting is sometimes conducted to find lost property such as jewellery and other recently deposited objects, which are commonly categorised as modern losses. However, as is suggested by a common alternative identifier, ‘treasure-hunting’, and by specialised ‘coin-shooting’, ‘relic-hunting’ and ‘treasure-hunting’ detectors, common targets are ancient artefacts, historic objects or otherwise cultural goods.

Metal-detecting can be a hobby, a business and a crime, which is conducted by visitors (who are, primarily, tourists) as well as residents and citizens. The scale of loss of cultural objects *to metal-detecting* in East Asia is not yet known. However, a lot of cultural property is lost to metal-detecting in Western Europe,[1] Eastern Europe[2] and beyond; a lot of cultural property is lost to looting in some territories of East Asia; and, the ‘humble’[3] metal-detector is amongst the ‘simple[st]’[4] and most efficient tools for looting in East Asia, whether that looting is performed by a part-time criminal entrepreneur or an organised crime group. So, practice among detectorists is instructive for understanding of practice among looters and traffickers.

1 Samuel Hardy, ‘Quantitative Analysis of Open-Source Data on Metal Detecting for Cultural Property: Estimation of the Scale and Intensity of Metal Detecting and the Quantity of Metal-Detected Cultural Goods’ (2017) *Cogent Social Sciences* 3 <http://dx.doi.org/10.1080/23311886.2017.1298397>.

2 Samuel Hardy, ‘“Black Archaeology” in Eastern Europe: Metal Detecting, Illicit Trafficking of Cultural Objects and “Legal Nihilism” in Belarus, Poland, Russia and Ukraine’ (2018) *Public Archaeology* <https://doi.org/10.1080/14655187.2017.1410050>.

3 Yan Wang, ‘Traffic Boom’ (*News China*, September 2011) <http://old.newschinamag.com/magazine/traffic-boom1>.

4 Ke Shao, ‘After Tip-Off, Police Roll up Nationwide Tomb Raiding Gangs’ (*Sixth Tone*, 3 October 2017) <www.sixthtone.com/news/1000946/after-tip-off%2C-police-roll-up-nationwide-tomb-raiding-gangs>.

Method

Due to a lack of legislation and/or precision in legislation, typically, at least some form of metal-detecting activity is not illegal according to the letter of the law and/or not prosecutable in practice. For example, eyewitness testimony or video recording as well as the product of the act may be required for conviction. Due to a dearth of offline monitoring and/or online monitoring, potential offenders may rarely be identified offline and may never be identified online. Hence, illicit detectorists may hide in plain sight, visible amongst (at least ostensibly) licit detectorists. These actors often form online communities, where they study metal-detecting and interpretation of cultural objects, as well as buy, sell and exchange metal-detecting equipment and cultural objects.

In order to gather such evidence, Google Scholar was searched for 'antiquities' and 'looting' plus 'territory name' in English. Facebook Groups, Facebook Pages, Google Scholar and Google Web were searched for 'metal detecting' or 'treasure hunting' plus 'territory name' in English. Facebook Groups, Facebook Pages and (albeit cursorily) Google Web were searched for 'metal' and 'detecting' plus 'territory name', then 'treasure' and 'hunting' plus 'territory name', in English, Chinese, Hmong, Japanese, Korean and Mongolian. Google Web searches minimised results about security by including 'forum'.

China, Tibet, Hong Kong and Macau

Cultural property law on the mainland, incorporating Tibet

In China and Tibet,[5] antiquities underground or on the ground belong to the state; excavation and export are licensed activities.[6] When export is not prohibited, it is licensed, for *ethnic minority* cultural relics from 1966 or before; *historically, artistically or scientifically valuable* cultural relics from 1949 or before; or *any* cultural relics from 1911 or before.[7]

Thus, unlicensed detecting for modern losses would appear to be legal. Yet modern losses would exclude all cultural objects from 1911 or before, some cultural objects from as recently as 1949 and some other cultural objects from as recently as 1966. Furthermore, looters commonly identify their activity as 'robbery of tombs [dàomù]'[8] or 'tomb-robbery [mù jié]'.[9] This leaves little

5 Officially, Tibet Autonomous Region or Xizang Autonomous Region.

6 Law on the Protection of Cultural Relics 1982; Z Liu, *The Case for Repatriating China's Cultural Objects* (Springer 2016) 43–46.

7 Export Criteria for Cultural Relics 2007.

8 This form of the term was identified in Frank Fang and Larry Ong, 'China Fights Losing Battle against Tomb Robbers' (*Epoch Times*, 16 March 2016) <www.theepochtimes.com/n3/1993683-china-fights-losing-battle-against-tomb-raiders/>.

9 This form of the term was machine-translated from English, then confirmed as used by the community.

doubt about its targets, its (il)legality and their understanding of its (il) legality. With a grinning wink, a detectorist in China told detectorists abroad that it was not permitted to use a detector to extract cultural objects, yet it was permitted to collect cultural objects that had (ostensibly) been acquired from the market.[10]

While capital punishment for cultural property crime has technically been ended, antiquities traffickers continue to be 'sentenced to death with a two-year reprieve'.[11] Evidently, at least in relation to other offences, this peculiar sentence does sometimes result in the application of the death penalty.[12]

Even when someone has published their own material that demonstrates their own illicit activity, there remains a risk that (re)publication would put them at (greater) risk of capital punishment. Rather than creating a permanent record of this activity that is out of the control of the actor, potentially incriminating statements are anonymised. They are augmented with already formally published material, such as reports in newspapers, in order to outline the online management and scale of potentially illicit activity.

Cultural property law in Hong Kong

In Hong Kong,[13] it is illegal 'to excavate and search for antiquities' at a monument (or proposed monument) with a detector without a licence. It is also illegal to 'remove' any 'relic', any object that was made or modified by a human before 1800, from a monument (or proposed monument), or to 'remove' any believed relic from its findspot without a licence or emergency.[14] Yet, it is implicitly permitted to conduct unlicensed detecting at unprotected sites, thereby to recover objects that have only been made or modified by a human since 1800.

Cultural property law in Macau

In Macau,[15] all 'archaeological finds[...] are owned by SARM [achados arqueológicos[...] são propriedade da RAEM]' and should be curated in a museum or other cultural heritage institution. Both 'destruction of archaeological objects or

10 Source withheld.

11 E.g. Xinhua, 'Tomb-Raiding Gang Leader Faces Death' (*Shanghai Daily*, 15 April 2016) <www.shanghaidaily.com/national/Tombraiding-gang-leader-faces-death/shdaily.shtml>.

12 Cf Xiang Ji, 'Corruption and the Death Penalty in China' (*Capital in the North*, 14 July 2013) <http://thecapitalinthenorth.blogspot.co.uk/2013/07/corruption-and-death-penalty-in-china.html>.

13 Officially, Hong Kong Special Administrative Region.

14 Antiquities and Monuments Ordinance to provide for the preservation of objects of historical, archaeological and palaeontological interest and for matters ancillary thereto or connected therewith 1997.

15 Officially, Macau Special Administrative Region.

remains [destruição de objectos ou vestígios arqueológicos]' and unlicensed export are prohibited.[16]

The scale of potentially illicit activity

Looting is 'simple' and increasingly 'professional'.[17] Yet, considering the legal situation, online communities cannot be expected to provide meaningful evidence of the scale of potentially illicit activity. The broader political situation may discourage online management. For instance, internet connections and even mobile connections in Tibet and Xinjiang are periodically shut down, sometimes for months.[18] Still, a wide range of online forums for treasure hunters number in single digits, tens, hundreds and thousands. Some online forums for ancient coin dealing number in the tens of thousands. As well as detecting by local residents in the centrally administered regions, there is at least some evidence of beachcombing detecting by permanent foreign residents, flexpatriates and tourists in the special autonomous regions (SARs) of Macau and Hong Kong.

However, in recent years, a foreign resident in Hong Kong seemingly could not find any local online community and sought advice in an international forum.[19] Still now, there appear to be very few, very small online communities for detectorists in the SARs, such as one with around seven members[20] and another with around four members.[21]

Due to the social situation, many detectorists in the SARs may engage online in national Chinese-language communities or international English-language communities. Nonetheless, significant detecting populations elsewhere sustain local as well as national and international online communities, so the dearth of online communities in the SARs does suggest a dearth of detectorists there.

It is very difficult to make an empirical estimate of the scale of looting in any territory, let alone in a geographical, socioeconomic and political entity such as China. It is exceptionally difficult to infer a national estimate from regional data, since the relative proportions of 'professional' and 'amateur' looters, as well as the total rates of looters, vary within as well as between provinces.

16 Lei de Salvaguarda do Património Cultural 2013.

17 Fang and Ong (n 8).

18 Oiwan Lam, 'In Tibet and Uyghur Regions, Internet Blackouts Are the Norm' (*Global Voices*, 17 December 2013) <https://advox.globalvoices.org/2013/12/17/in-chinas-ethnic-minority-regions-internet-blackouts-are-the-norm/>.

19 sonnie, 'Hello from Hong Kong' (*TreasureClassifieds*, 24 April 2014) <https://web.archive.org/web/20170222035448/http://forum.treasureclassifieds.com/Thread-hello-from-hong-kong?pid=5804#pid5804>.

20 Metal Detecting Club Hong Kong, 'Metal Detecting Club Hong Kong' (*Facebook*, 24 November 2017) <www.facebook.com/groups/682090825187239/>; it is also known as the Hong Kong Metal Detecting Club.

21 Metal Detecting Hong Kong, 'Metal Detecting Hong Kong' (*Facebook*, 24 November 2017) <www.facebook.com/groups/mdhongkong/>.

Nonetheless, it has been estimated that there are perhaps 100,000 'professional' looters, according to two insiders in Shaanxi province,[22] or 'full-time' looters, according to the Chinese Academy of Social Sciences[23] and a member of the Archaeologist Association of Jiangsu, Ni Fangliu.[24] These seem to be alternative phrasings of the estimate that, by 2010, there were 'already over 100,000[...] grave robbers', including full-time 'professional[s]' *and* part-time 'amateur[s]' who supplemented incomes from agriculture and other labour (according to an insider, cited by state newspaper Chu Tian Jin Bao).[25]

That estimate was made with regard to just six provinces.[26] Thus, there were apparently 100,000 looters amongst then approximately 330,380,000 inhabitants of Gansu, Hebei, Henan, Hunan, Shaanxi and Shanxi.[27] For a range of reasons, regions outside this sample may have fewer 'amateur' or entrepreneurial criminals. For example, Xinjiang[28] is exceptionally securitised, so exceptionally rare sites are plundered by atypically few, well-connected, professional criminals.[29] Yet other provinces, such as Anhui and Jiangsu, are known looting 'hotspots' on a par with Hebei, Henan, Shaanxi and Shanxi.[30]

Despite the massive flows of cultural objects across China's borders, that number of looters might still seem to be overestimated. However, there is also an internal market of tens of millions of private collectors,[31] due to which there has been an observable shift in consumer markets.[32] At least some of those collectors deliberately collect 'recently looted objects to avoid the risk of buying fakes'.[33]

22 Yan Zhang, 'Tomb Raiders Remain a Menace' (*China Daily*, 7 September 2011) <www.chinadaily.com.cn/cndy/2011-09/07/content_13635838.htm>.

23 Wang (n 3).

24 Celine Ge, 'China's Ancient Treasures under Siege from Army of Tomb Raiders' (*South China Morning Post*, 4 December 2015) <www.scmp.com/lifestyle/article/1885832/chinas-ancient-treasures-under-siege-army-tomb-raiders>.

25 Fang and Ong (n 8).

26 Ibid.

27 Gansu had around 25,600,000 residents; Hebei, 71,940,000; Henan, 94,050,000; Hunan, 65,700,000; Shaanxi, 37,350,000; and Shanxi, 35,740,000. Cf National Bureau of Statistics of China, 'China Statistical Yearbook 2015' (*National Bureau of Statistics of China*, 2016) <https://web.archive.org/web/20161110070410/http://www.stats.gov.cn/tjsj/ndsj/2015/html/EN0205.jpg>.

28 Officially, Xinjiang Uygur Autonomous Region.

29 Gino Caspari, 'The Impact of Looting on Archaeology in the Eurasian Steppe – a Case Study' (Workshop on Radiocarbon Dating and Protection of Cultural Heritage, Zurich, 16–17 November 2017).

30 Wang (n 3).

31 Reportedly, there are 70,000,000, though that would suggest a rate of about 1 collector per 19 inhabitants. See Wang (n 3).

32 William Chak and Ricardo Pinto, 'O Caçador de Tesouros [The Treasure Hunter]' (*Ponto Final*, 6 August 2017) <https://pontofinalmacau.wordpress.com/2017/08/06/o-cacador-de-tesouros/>.

33 Amy Qin, 'Tomb Robbing Makes Comeback in China' (*New York Times*, 15 July 2017) <www.nytimes.com/2017/07/15/world/asia/china-tomb-robbing-qin-dynasty.html>.

Furthermore, according to public police data, between the mid-2000s and the mid-2010s, full-time looting operations have come to span '[from] Xinjiang in the northwest [to] Guangdong in the southeast'.[34] Plus, in recent years, 'thousands' more migrant urban labourers and farmers have been inspired to start tomb-raiding by popular culture, in the form of novels, television series and films.[35] This is compounding existing threats to ethnic minorities in regions that are subject to intensive development and consequent influxes of migrant workers, such as Tibet.[36]

Thus, it is possible to assume that there is perhaps one looter in 3,304 inhabitants. On that basis, it is possible to infer the activity of perhaps 405,869 looters across China (in a population of then 1,340,910,000[37]). This estimate is an estimate of the number of looters, instead of an estimate of the number of detectorists. However, as noted, metal-detecting is a simple and efficient means of looting.[38] So, practice among detectorists is still instructive for understanding of practice among looters and traffickers.

Metal-detecting and online management

The internet caused a 'big bang' for looting and trafficking.[39] Self-education, 'professional' training, equipment, co-offenders – from looters to advisers to financiers – and antiquities are 'easily accessible' through online forums of specialist communities, as well as chat rooms, e-commerce platforms and online marketplaces.[40] For example, looter Zhuanshengdianlunhui advertised a profit-sharing tomb-looting enterprise in the Ancient Tomb Bar of Baidu Tieba: 'Apprentices and Partners Wanted! Those who are brave and diligent give me your contact details'.[41] He found 65 applicants, 'many of whom provided their QQ numbers' for online contact.[42]

Discussions on Baidu, amoBBS and other online platforms address such subjects as the technical capacity of detectors; the purchase of detectors; the home-made, hand-built manufacture of 'do-it-yourself metal-detectors [DIY jīnshǔ tàncè qì]', including the sale of complete kits for assembly; the usage of detectors to find treasure; and the nature of the treasure. One seemingly

34 Ge (n 24).
35 Ge (n 24); Qin (n 33).
36 RFA, 'The Plunder of Tibet's Treasures' (*RFA*, 1 August 2005) <www.rfa.org/english/news/arts/tibet_artifacts-20050801.html>.
37 For population estimates, see National Bureau of Statistics of China (n 27).
38 Wang (n 3); Shao (n 4).
39 Ge (n 24).
40 Chao Wang, 'The Amateur Tomb Raiders Pilfering China's Artifacts' (*Sixth Tone*, 9 September 2016) <www.sixthtone.com/news/1301/chinese-tomb-raiders>; see also Ge (n 24); Fang and Ong (n 8).
41 Ge (n 24).
42 Ibid.

full-time, entrepreneurial detectorist seeks international advice on detecting devices; appeals for manufacturers and/or distributors, in order to become their promoter and/or dealer; and negotiates his trades on Facebook.[43]

Detectorists use other online communities, too, such as ones for technology experts and arts and crafts enthusiasts. Naturally, this enables them to get the benefit of the wisdom of specialists in other subjects. Treasure-hunters' use of generic communities, and the size of specialist treasure-hunting communities, may also partly be explained by active enforcement of laws and policies on handling of antiquities, as suspect actors scatter from disrupted networks and novice participants do not immediately find specialist communities.

Activity is also discussed in foreign detecting forums. Affirming the expected, a detectorist-and-collector in South Korea revealed that he knew that 'coins [were] being found on a weekly basis', because he was buying 'Chinese coins from a coin dealer in NY State who gets them from a contact' in China.[44] This demonstrates not only the existence of regional markets among 'source countries', but also the potential complexity of supply chains, as antiquities flow out of one source country in East Asia, through a market country in North America, then into another source country in East Asia.

In one case, according to an accomplice abroad, an illicit antiquities dealer in China was 'aware' that, 'by law', 'anything found in the soil should be handed over to the local government', but he 'kn[ew] where to look and when to do it'.[45] He wanted to hunt for 'old artifacts',[46] buried hoards of coins, jewellery, statues and boxes of those who had been forcibly displaced by the Cultural Revolution.[47] To avoid the risk of buying a counterfeit detector via Taobao in China, the dealer arranged for a non-detectorist to buy and import a detector from the USA.[48] To do so, the non-detectorist sought and received technical advice from the members of an online forum in the USA. According to a foreign resident detectorist in China, dealers would get into 'big trouble' if they sold religious relics in public, but they do sell such relics, they just 'do it in private' instead.[49]

At least some foreign residents conduct dangerous, but legal, detecting for modern militaria in Hong Kong. Some explicitly reject 'insensitive' detecting of

43 Source withheld.

44 hikeinmts, 'Metal Detecting in China' (*TreasureNet*, 18 May 2009) <www.treasurenet.com/forums/asia/79629-metal-detecting-china.html#post1391046>.

45 ansumei, 'Newbie Question' (*TreasureNet*, 23 October 2017c) <www.treasurenet.com/forums/tool-shed/556765-newbie-question.html#post5580747>.

46 ansumei, 'Newbie Question' (*TreasureNet*, 22 October 2017b) <www.treasurenet.com/forums/tool-shed/556765-newbie-question.html#post5579566>.

47 ansumei, 'Metal Detecting in China' (*TreasureNet*, 23 October 2017d) <www.treasurenet.com/forums/asia/79629-metal-detecting-china-3.html#post5580819>.

48 ansumei, 'Metal Detecting in China (*TreasureNet*, 22 October 2017a) <www.treasurenet.com/forums/asia/79629-metal-detecting-china-2.html#post5579549>.

49 Source withheld.

such material 'for [their] own gratification',[50] rather than for the advancement of historical understanding. Still, there does not appear to be a significant amount of detecting by foreign residents or international tourists.

One permanent foreign resident, who appeared to have been in China for more than a decade, stated that he had 'never' even 'heard' of any others.[51] Another said that there were 'not many'.[52]

That permanent foreign resident, from the United Kingdom in western China, does it 'regularly'. He has 'never' been stopped, been questioned or feared any risk of negative consequences for his actions. However, that may be because there are laws for 'everything', yet almost no enforcement of any of those laws, in his opinion. It may also be because he detects in sparsely populated, mountainous and rural areas, which manifestly makes it more difficult for those laws to be enforced.[53]

He extracts relics, such as Qing Dynasty coins; twentieth-century conflict archaeology, such as civil war militaria; and other cultural objects, such as Communist symbols.[54] The twentieth-century militaria and symbols are probably not protected, at least as *cultural* objects. However, the Qing Dynasty reigned from 30 October 1644 to 12 February 1912. It seems unlikely that all of his many Qing Dynasty coins were minted in the final 43 days of its 97,614-day reign.

Metal-detecting tourism

Indicating the potential value of cultural goods that are extracted through 'tourist' detecting, reportedly, a 'Professional Treasure Hunter' spent 'around $1200 for a round trip from Egypt to Hong Kong'[55] and 'made a profit overall',[56] after two weeks in Hong Kong and four weeks in Thailand, when all of the finds were from beachcombing and underwater detecting and most of the finds were modern losses.

Like Macau and Hong Kong, the centrally administered regions of China probably experience at least *some* detecting tourism, as it features in online forums for detectorists in other countries. One detectorist from Russia,

50 E.g. Craig, 'Finds and Discoveries in HK' (*Gwulo: Old Hong Kong*, 6 April 2009) <https://gwulo.com/comment/8333#comment-8333>.

51 Source withheld.

52 Source withheld.

53 Source withheld.

54 Source withheld.

55 Orosurf, 'Longest Trip Ever to a Detecting Site, Going to Hong Kong' (*TreasueQuest*, 22 November 2011) <www.treasurequestxlt.com/community/index.php?threads/longest-trip-ever-to-a-detecting-site-going-to-hong-kong.50674/>.

56 Orosurf, 'Back Again, It's Been a Long Trip' (*TreasureQuest*, 28 March 2012) <www.treasurequestxlt.com/community/index.php?threads/back-again-its-been-a-long-trip.52657/#post-681048>.

who wanted to hunt twentieth-century conflict archaeology in China, had been discouraged when he learned that detecting there was 'prohibited'.[57] However, he smiled once he realised that the situation in China was 'just like in Russia', 'forbidden, but [the] state doesn't persue [*sic* – pursue] it hardly'.[58] In other words, it was not possible legally, but it was 'possible practical[ly]'.[59]

While the strategy is more widespread, there is an exceptionally active online detectorist in the USA, who relentlessly queries the existence or meaning of prohibitive or restrictive laws, seemingly in order to spread the perception that permissive regulation is the international standard. As well as at least two detectorists who were permanent foreign residents in China, elsewhere in the same thread of conversation, he queried the detectorist in Russia who had decided not to detect in China.

> Even if you *could* remember the forum where you read that, and even if you *did* have a link, here's what would probably happen: The 'source' there would merely be someone saying 'it's illegal'. Death penalty, etc[...]. And if you were to find the person who typed *that*, and had asked him: 'What is your source?', he too would probably answer: '*I read it on a forum somewhere*'.[60]

He discourages detectorists from 'asking purist archies [archaeologists] and lawyers',[61] as applicable laws are not 'applied' in practice, '[u]nless someone [takes] out a treasure chest and start[s] making a big news stink about it'.[62] In a similar fashion, one of the permanent foreign residents in China advised others not to attract attention, unless they had the government's permission. Otherwise, they would spoil the activity for 'everyone'.[63] This would not make sense unless 'everyone' was doing it without the government's permission.

Taiwan

Cultural property law

As the Taiwanese government was the Chinese government in 1930, it imple mented the Law of Preservation of Antiquities. This established state ownership

57 SilverReciever, 'Metal Detecting in China' (*TreasureNet*, 12 April 2017a) <www.treasurenet.com/forums/asia/79629-metal-detecting-china.html#post5366787>.

58 SilverReciever, 'Metal Detecting in China' (*TreasureNet*, 13 April 2017b) <www.treasurenet.com/forums/asia/79629-metal-detecting-china-2.html#post5367765>.

59 SilverReciever 2017b (n 58).

60 Tom_in_CA, 'Metal Detecting in China' (*TreasureNet*, 13 April 2017a) <www.treasurenet.com/forums/asia/79629-metal-detecting-china-2.html#post5367905>.

61 Tom_in_CA 2017a (n 60).

62 Tom_in_CA, 'Metal Detecting in China' (*TreasureNet*, 27 May 2017b) <www.treasurenet.com/forums/asia/79629-metal-detecting-china-2.html#post5416025>.

63 Source withheld.

of antiquities underground or on the ground, state licensing of excavation and state licensing of export.[64]

However, due to a 2005 amendment to the 1982 Cultural Property Preservation Law, 'chance finds' underground or underwater are 'not unequivocally national property' anymore.[65] If they are willing to take the risk of a legal challenge, alleged 'chance finders' and collectors may assert ownership.

The level of risk is unclear. A USA-based detectorist queried the existence of a law against detecting (in China, due to a misremembering of his acquaintance's activity in Taiwan), then commented, '[n]ot that it would stop' his acquaintance anyway, 'but it [would] give him a chuckle'.[66] Still, detecting for antiquities may be legal and detectorists must be assumed to be licit detectorists.

Metal-detecting, online management and the scale of potentially illicit activity

By some accounts, there are 'many' aspiring detectorists in Taiwan, yet there does not appear to be a significant market for detectors, as there is only one 'ridiculously expensive' distributor.[67] Still, detectorists may simply equip themselves through online distributors instead.[68]

Nonetheless, there appears to be very little trace of online management. Seemingly, some detectorists themselves do not know and cannot find online communities, so they appeal for detecting partners in generic forums.[69]

Although it is comparatively very small, one Facebook group grew from 24 to 54 members within the space of a year.[70] It is unlikely that the offline detecting population has more than doubled within the same period. This tentatively

64 Kwang-Tzuu Chen, 'The Protection of Archaeological Sites in Taiwan' (2011) *Conservation and Management of Archaeological Sites* 58, 61–62.

65 Ibid 71.

66 Tom_in_CA, 'Metal detecting in China' (*TreasureNet*, 15 December 2016a) <https://web.archive.org/web/20170227222050/http://www.treasurenet.com/forums/asia/79629-metal-detecting-china.html#post5217809>; see also Tom_in_CA, 'Metal Detecting in China' (*TreasureNet*, 16 December 2016b) <https://web.archive.org/web/20170227222352/http://www.treasurenet.com/forums/asia/79629-metal-detecting-china.html#post5218606>.

67 brobronek, 'Metal Detecting and Gold Prospecting' (*Taipei Forum*, 8 July 2013c) <https://web.archive.org/web/20170222031702/http://www.expat.com/forum/viewtopic.php?id=252535#1348862>.

68 Cf discussion under brobronek, 'Metal Detecting and Gold Prospecting' (*Taipei Forum*, 18 April 2013b) <https://web.archive.org/web/20170222030055/http://www.expat.com/forum/viewtopic.php?id=252535#1189312>.

69 E.g. discussion under brobronek, 'Gold Panning or Metal Detecting????' (*Forumosa*, 15 April 2013a) <http://forumosa.com/taiwan/viewtopic.php?p=1512227#p1512227>; brobronek 2013b (n 53); see also DeepdiggerKen27, 'Metal Detecting in Taiwan' (*Forumosa*, 30 November 2016) <http://tw.forumosa.com/t/metal-detecting-in-taiwan/156803>.

70 Metal Detecting Taiwan, 'Metal Detecting Taiwan' (*Facebook*, 27 January 2017–24 November 2017) <www.facebook.com/groups/987051558018599/>.

suggests that existing yet offline detectorists may be shifting towards online management of their offline activity, thereby becoming visible.

Outside designated, legally-protected sites, 'especially' on private land, the legal uncertainty has produced 'serious problems with treasure-hunting'.[71] This again suggests that there is a significantly greater number of local detectorists, who are either undervisible, because they participate in internationalised Chinese-language online communities, or invisible, because they operate offline.

The total number of active detectorists may still be very small. One online forum was founded by a local resident who was married to a permanent foreign resident from the USA,[72] so it should have become a hub of activity for Chinese-language and English-language detectorists. Yet it was 'archived' – closed – due to 'lack of activity'.[73]

Some foreign residents both prospect for raw gold and detect for ancient coins and other relics. As well as to find partners, they use online forums to identify finds.[74] Detecting tourists, who collaborate with local residents as well as foreign residents, are also active. A USA-based Chinese detectorist has engaged in detecting tourism in Taiwan '[without] any problem in the world' and has 'corresponded with hunters from there', too.[75]

Even at the smallest scale, this may involve foreign exploitation of local knowledge and extraction of assets. Upon digging up some votive offerings at the site of a former 'temple or shrine', one seemingly Germany-based intermittent foreign resident begrudgingly shared some of the Qing Dynasty coins with the local who had identified the site and some other local observers, because he did not want to tell them that he was 'raiding' their 'fancy little old temple site' and they were 'not part of the fun'.[76] Then, he 'pretended' to leave, waited to be alone in the dark and resumed detecting with a 'head-mounted light [headlamp]'.[77] Then, he went back 'around midnight' the next night and dug up yet more coins.[78]

71 Chen (n 64) 71.

72 wekali, 'New Member in Taiwan' (*Friendly Metal Detecting Forum*, 25 May 2009) <https://metaldetectingforum.com/showpost.php?p=315365&postcount=1>.

73 wekali, '[Untitled]' (*wekali*, 29 November 2017) <http://web.archive.org/web/20171124053613/http://wekali.conforums.com/index.cgi>.

74 E.g. discussion under Benjamin52, 'Found Chinese Temple Cache with Silver Coin in Taiwan Today' (*TreasureNet*, 16 April 2014a) <http://web.archive.org/web/20170516022701/http://www.treasurenet.com/forums/metal-detecting/410794-found-chinese-temple-cache-silver-coin-taiwan-today-pics.html#post3958024>.

75 Tom_in_CA 2016a (n 66); see also Tom_in_CA 2016b (n 66).

76 Benjamin52 2014a (n 74).

77 Benjamin52 2014a (n 74).

78 Benjamin52, 'Found Chinese Temple Cache with Silver Coin in Taiwan Today' (*TreasureNet*, 16 April 2014b) <http://web.archive.org/web/20170516022701/> <http://www.treasurenet.com/forums/metal-detecting/410794-found-chinese-temple-cache-silver-coin-taiwan-today-pics.html#post3961038>.

Japan

Cultural property law

When any owner or other occupant of land uncovers 'remains' or other 'unearthed articles', they must notify the Commissioner for Cultural Affairs 'without altering the status quo of such remains', except for minimal emergency interventions. Ownerless goods or 'lost property' must be reported to the police. When 'buried object[s]' are 'object[s] of cultural property', those objects are taken by the police and delivered to a board of education. Ownerless cultural goods belong either to the exchequer or to the prefecture – in other words, either way, the state. Moreover, it is specifically illegal to damage, discard or conceal 'important cultural property', or otherwise to alter a historic site, destroy it, damage it or cause it to deteriorate.[79]

Metal-detecting and online management

One permanent foreign resident from the USA recognises that it is generally 'not okay to just find things' in Japan, so detecting 'can be a hassle', because it is 'misunderstood'. Presumably, there is an innocuous reason that, whenever they detect anywhere other than beaches and parks, it is 'at night and [they] have a look out in place'; they have extracted 'some real valuables that way'.[80]

A USA-based detectorist instead suggested that as long as he was 'discreet' and 'stay[ed] away from obvious historic landmark[s]', the temporary migrant worker would be able to detect 'unbothered'.[81] Likewise, a then Japan-based detectorist implied that 'no one' would 'bother' anyone who was detecting illegally, 'as long as' the detectorist was 'not creating trouble'.[82] One USA-based detectorist cautioned that '*"anything"* found by any *"method"* including *"Eye Balling"* must be turned into [*sic* – turned in to] the *"Police"*'.[83] Another Japan-based detectorist reassured that, according to a more experienced personal acquaintance, there was 'enough ambiguity about stuff dug out of the dirt' for detectorists 'to work fairly unhindered'.[84] Elsewhere, a Sweden-based detectorist suggested with a

79 Law for the Protection of Cultural Property 2007.

80 HolyCheese300, 'U Want a Great Paying Job??' (*GaijinPot Forums*, 13 March 2010) <https://forum.gaijinpot.com/forum/working-in-japan/career-discussion/74159-u-want-a-great-paying-job?p=1113990#post1113990>.

81 Tom_in_CA, 'Metal Detecting in Japan' (*TreasureNet*, 3 August 2008) <www.treasurenet.com/forums/general-discussion/93188-metal-detecting-japan.html#post973530>.

82 Radu, 'Metal Detecting in Japan' (*TreasureNet*, 3 September 2009) <www.treasurenet.com/forums/general-discussion/93188-metal-detecting-japan.html#post1523438>.

83 La Beep, 'Metal Detecting in Japan' (*TreasureNet*, 4 August 2008) <www.treasurenet.com/forums/general-discussion/93188-metal-detecting-japan.html#post974085>.

84 Discrimination Dave, 'Metal Detecting in Japan' (*TreasureNet*, 20 September 2008) <www.treasurenet.com/forums/general-discussion/93188-metal-detecting-japan.html#post1036432>.

wink that, if the police 'stop[ped someone] on the beach with [their] goodies', they would 'still [be] on the beach', so they could argue that they could not report and deliver their finds until they went to the police station 'later'.[85]

Yet another permanent foreign resident learned that 'anything' that was found, then not delivered to the police, was 'considered [to be] stolen property!'[86] Consequently, he sought 'a connection with the local police'.[87] He found 'a friend with a connection in the department', with whom he secured 'an informal meeting'.[88] Through his friend, he 'found out' that, if he went 'to sell any precious metals, the buying shops' would not 'check with the police', so 'some "padding" [might] be possible'.[89] He would 'probably prefer to only pad with the things that probably weren't lost [within] the last 3 months'[90] because, '[i]f most people respect the law, it would look pretty bad' if one who did not was 'a crazy foreigner'.[91] Yet, his explicit plan was not to report and deliver those finds for which he had plausible deniability, then to sell those finds to buyers who would not establish the illicit nature of the finds, who would then unknowingly destroy the evidence that linked the illicit finds to the illicit finder. In other words, his explicit plan was not to respect the law. He noted that he would also be the 'benefactor' if it became a 'pain' for the police to process 'new finds every weekend'.[92]

A USA-based (non-visiting) detectorist complained that the relevant laws and guidelines were 'riddled with words [such as] "cultural" and "historic" and "antiquities" and so forth' when, 'if someone is hunting the tourist beaches (where it's predominantly jewelry hunting, not "antiquities")', it was 'no problem'.[93] However, a USA-based dealer in 'relics' (of militaria) had

85 Dano Sverige, 'Japan Lost Items Law' (*TreasureNet*, 8 May 2011) <www.treasurenet.com/forums/general-discussion/236829-japan-lost-items-law.html#post2339731>.

86 JapanBeachMan, 'Japan Lost Items Law' (*TreasureNet*, 8 May 2011a) <www.treasurenet.com/forums/general-discussion/236829-japan-lost-items-law.html#post2339547>.

87 JapanBeachMan (n 86).

88 JapanBeachMan, 'Japan Lost Items Law' (*TreasureNet*, 8 May 2011b) <www.treasurenet.com/forums/general-discussion/236829-japan-lost-items-law.html#post2339583>.

89 JapanBeachMan, 'Japan Lost Items Law' (*TreasureNet*, 10 May 2011c) <www.treasurenet.com/forums/general-discussion/236829-japan-lost-items-law.html#post2342159>.

90 It is not clear whether this is a misunderstanding of the law or wishful thinking about the process. Necessarily, the police release lost property that has not been claimed within three months of the delivery of the property to the police. Obviously, the police do not release lost property that has not been claimed within three months of the report of its loss. First, property might not be found and delivered to the police within three months of the report of its loss. Second, the police would only know that property had not been claimed within three months of its loss, if they could identify the object and the date of its loss, in which case they would have identified the rightful owner.

91 JapanBeachMan 2011c (n 89).

92 JapanBeachMan 2011c (n 89).

93 Tom_in_CA, 'Metal Detecting in Japan' (*TreasureNet*, 3 August 2012) <www.treasurenet.com/forums/general-discussion/93188-metal-detecting-japan-2.html#post2880466>.

'racked up some treasure' while 'MDing Okinawa's beaches',[94] as he appeared to demonstrate with a photograph of 32 mineral-encrusted swords and two mineral-encrusted pistols.

Public discussion of the law demonstrates not only standard language games and legal obfuscation, but also moral regulation by the public and destruction of evidence by detectorists. One foreign resident had sought out conversation amongst detectorists, appealed for ethical conduct and highlighted key clauses in legislation and other official documentation that were publicly available in English.[95]

Another apparently foreign resident, who had been targeting historic Samurai sites,[96] explained that he had 'gone looking for[...] relics'.[97] He 'thought' that he had 'treaded [*sic* – trodden] very carefully', although 'maybe' he had 'not and ha[d] been noticed'.[98] Hence, he had 'had some of [his] posts deleted', '[j]ust in case', and planned 'to ask' a moderator or an administrator 'to remove' other implicitly incriminating evidence.[99]

The scale of potentially illicit activity

According to authorised national distributors for two international manufacturers, detecting is 'still virtually unknown in Japan', so it is currently a 'great opportunity'.[100] Although there are local hobbyists, including ones who use non-local usernames, detectorists agree that 'very few people[...] metal detect

94 wilkere, 'Metal Detecting in Japan- Did Pretty Good Today' (*TreasureNet*, 2 February 2010) <www.treasurenet.com/forums/today-s-finds/160198-metal-detecting-japan-did-pretty-good-today.html#post1715583>.

95 E.g. Nekentros, 'Metal Detecting in Japan' (*TreasureNet*, 3 August 2012) <www.treasurenet.com/forums/general-discussion/93188-metal-detecting-japan-2.html#post2880071>.

96 E.g. Kiwisan, 'Samurai Militaria and Coins Japan' (*Friendly Metal Detecting Forums*, 24 December 2011b) <https://metaldetectingforum.com/showpost.php?p=1054824&postcount=1>.

97 E.g. Kiwisan, 'Some of Us Have Been Noticed. In a Good Way? Hmm.' (*Friendly Metal Detecting Forums*, 21 November 2012b) <http://web.archive.org/web/20170121024520/https://metaldetectingforum.com/group.php?do=discuss&gmid=8811>.

98 Kiwisan, 'Some of Us Have Been Noticed. In a Good Way? Hmm.' (*Friendly Metal Detecting Forums*, 20 November 2012a) <http://web.archive.org/web/20170121024520/ https://metaldetectingforum.com/group.php?do=discuss&gmid=8811>; see also stewart73, 'Some of Us Have Been Noticed. In a Good Way? Hmm.' (*Friendly Metal Detecting Forums*, 21 November 2012) <https://metaldetectingforum.com/group.php?do=discuss&gmid=8811>.

99 Kiwisan 2012b (n 97).

100 Metal Detecting Japan/MCC Trading, 'I Just Want to Let Everyone Know that Jun and I Are Authorized Minelab and Garrett Distributors' (*Facebook*, 8 October 2016) <www.facebook.com/metaldetectingjapan/posts/353752804961901>.

in Japan'.[101] It is such a 'vere [*sic* – very] very rare hobby' that one detectorist had 'never seen another MD'er'.[102] He had gone beachcombing and intended to go underwater detecting 'at night', for which he sought advice on waterproof devices.[103]

Many online detectorists appear to be foreign residents. One foreign resident, who also 'hadnt [*sic* – hadn't] seen anyone else' do it there, suggested that there might be so few other detectorists simply because international brands charged 66 per cent more for their products in Japan than elsewhere.[104] However, another detectorist recommended 'buy[ing a detector] from a forum member with a good rep[utation]'.[105] Such a private trade would circumvent the public market and incidentally reduce public sales figures.

Alongside a couple of even smaller online communities, one English-language Facebook business page has around 77 fans.[106] Yet, one social group in an international forum has around 86 members.[107] As such, these numbers seem to be unrepresentatively low. Thus, they cannot be used as minimum numbers to estimate the size of the detecting community.

Metal-detecting and online management

As elsewhere, detectorists find detecting partners, and organise partnered and group detecting of archaeological sites, through international forums. Less knowledgeable hobbyists get identifications from more knowledgeable hobbyists, as more knowledgeable detectorists may get identifications from cultural heritage professionals. For instance, 'lol [laughing out loud]', one explained that, if he is 'completely stuck' for an answer, he consults 'a co-worker[...] in the archeology department, who knows' that he has a detector.[108]

Techniques that are developed by detectorists in one territory are shared with detectorists elsewhere, so their collective intelligence circumvents regulation.

101 Coins4Cheese (n 65).

102 MarkTwa8n, 'Emerald Beach Okinawa Japan' (*Thunting*, 20 April 2010) <www.thunting.com/smf/beach_shallow_water/emerald_beach_okinawa_japan-t13678.0.html;msg86556#msg86556>.

103 Ibid.

104 Ern in Japan, 'Why I Have Not Seen Any Japanese Metal Detecting' (*UK and European Metal Detecting Forum*, 28 June 2011) <www.metaldetectingforum.co.uk/viewtopic.php?f=10&t=13121#p111571>.

105 OBN, 'Detector for Japan' (*TreasureNet*, 14 May 2014) <www.treasurenet.com/forums/beach-shallow-water/415388-detector-japan.html#post4004193>.

106 Metal Detecting Japan/MCC Trading, 'Metal Detecting Japan/MCC Trading' (*Facebook*, 24 November 2017) <www.facebook.com/metaldetectingjapan/>.

107 Detecting Japan, 'Detecting Japan' (*Friendly Metal Detecting Forum*, 24 November 2017) <https://metaldetectingforum.com/group.php?groupid=91>.

108 Kiwisan, 'A Few Mysterious Bits from the Hills of Japan' (*Friendly Metal Detecting Forums*, 21 December 2011a) <https://metaldetectingforum.com/showpost.php?p=1051822&postcount=14>.

Once, an aspiring detecting tourist asked an online forum in the USA about the legality of detecting in Thailand. A USAF/NATO crew chief, who had served in Japan (as well as Germany and the UK),[109] responded. He shared techniques for undocumented export–import that had 'worked in other places'.[110] The USAF/NATO personnel recommended: 'Paint everything black and mail it out[...]. I personally have a C-5′ military cargo transport aircraft 'that brings me and my treasure home'.[111]

When he and his detecting partner(s) 'recovered the bones, dog tag [identity tag], watch, and few coins' of a Japanese soldier in Okinawa,[112] they appear not to have delivered the dog tag to the Japan Self-Defense Forces (JSDF), for the identification and return of the missing person to their family. Rather, he 'traded that dog tag for a very nice Japanese bayonet (that [he] still ha[s])' in the USA.[113] He did not say what they did with the soldier's other possessions or bodily remains.

Metal-detecting tourism

There is evidence of detecting tourism in both directions between Japan and the rest of the world. One USA-based detectorist advertised its possibilities by noting that he 'still [had] a Japanese WWII dog tag', which he had removed from the USAF's Yokota Air Force Base.[114]

Like finding partners for everyday detecting, detecting tourists find international hosts online. An experienced detectorist abroad offered to assist an inexperienced detectorist in Japan by engaging in couchsurfing, profit-sharing detecting tourism. He would bring 'two detectors', 'hunt everyday [*sic* – every day] and split the proceeds'.[115] Meanwhile, a foreign wife–local husband detecting couple in Japan proposed a detecting 'exchange'[116] with detectorists in Austria, where unlicensed detecting is 'prohibited',[117] or elsewhere in Europe.

109 Cf Steve (Fairfield), 'Detectorist Veterans. Front and Center ...' (*Old California Metal Detecting Forum*, 3 May 2004c) <http://cadetecting.proboards.com/post/60655/thread>.

110 Steve (Fairfield), 'Detecting in Thailand. Is it Legal?' (*Old California Metal Detecting Forum*, 5 April 2004b) <http://cadetecting.proboards.com/post/60279/thread>.

111 Steve (Fairfield) 2004b (n 110).

112 Steve (Fairfield), 'To Sell or Not to Sell' (*Old California Metal Detecting Forum*, 30 March 2004a) <http://cadetecting.proboards.com/post/40821/thread>.

113 Steve (Fairfield) 2004a (n 112).

114 kc10bull, 'Detector for Japan' (*TreasureNet*, 14 May 2014) <www.treasurenet.com/forums/beach-shallow-water/415388-detector-japan.html#post4004313>.

115 hookahman, 'Detector for Japan' (*TreasureNet*, 16 May 2014) <www.treasurenet.com/forums/beach-shallow-water/415388-detector-japan.html#post4007770>.

116 sofia, 'Going to Austria, from Japan, Exchange Mding?' (*TreasureNet*, 10 June 2013) <www.treasurenet.com/forums/europe-other/358942-going-austria-japan-exchange-mding.html#post3416028>.

117 Raimund Karl, 'On the Highway to Hell: Thoughts on the Unintended Consequences for Portable Antiquities of SS11(1) Austrian Denkmalschutzgesetz' (2011) 2 *The Historic Environment* 111, 114.

The Korean Peninsula (North Korea and South Korea)

Potential capital punishment of cultural property crime in the Democratic People's Republic of Korea (DPRK)

In North Korea, exceptionally harmful theft, trafficking and illicit trade of personal wealth, national wealth and state assets, which encompass all cultural assets, are punishable by death.[118] Offences specifically include trafficking of metal goods, which encompass all metal cultural goods.

Cultural property law in the Republic of Korea (RoK)

In South Korea, the Cultural Heritage Committee of the Cultural Heritage Administration controls excavation of buried cultural heritage. When any 'buried cultural heritage' is discovered, it should be reported to the Cultural Heritage Administration 'without making any changes in the existing state'. It is illegal to 'excavat[e] buried cultural heritage', or any site that is 'deemed to conceal the buried cultural heritage', without permission from the Cultural Heritage Administration. It is also illegal to facilitate unlicensed excavation, to conceal movable cultural heritage, to engage in unlicensed export and to facilitate unlicensed export. Furthermore, it is illegal to attempt to commit, or to conspire to commit, any of those acts.[119]

The scale of potentially illicit activity

Due to totalitarian control, abject poverty and almost entirely absent internet, there appears to be little potential for either detecting or online management in North Korea. According to local detectorists, even South Korea has only 'just started' detecting,[120] although it is quickly becoming 'very fashionable'.[121]

Yet, an English-language social network only has around three members, of whom two are detectorists abroad, including the administrator.[122] While the membership statistics are not displayed, based on the number of conversation threads and the number of posts in those threads, a Korean-language online

118 YNA, 'N. Korea Revised Cultural Asset Protection Law to Include Intangible Heritage' (*YNA*, 15 November 2012) <http://english.yonhapnews.co.kr/northkorea/2012/11/15/2/0401000000AEN20121115005400315F.HTML>; Death Penalty Worldwide, 'Death Penalty Database: North Korea' (*Death Penalty Database*, 3 June 2014) <www.deathpenaltyworldwide.org/country-search-post.cfm?country=north%20korea>.

119 Cultural Heritage Protection Act 2007.

120 Yong Jun Lee, 'A New Challenge' (*Minelab*, 17 April 2013) <www.minelab.com/usa/go-minelabbing/success-stories/a-new-challenge>.

121 Yong Jun Lee, 'Scary Greed' (*Minelab*, 17 September 2014) <www.minelab.com/usa/go-minelabbing/success-stories/scary-greed>.

122 Metal Detecting KOREA, 'Metal Detecting KOREA' (*Facebook*, 24 November 2017) <www.facebook.com/groups/mdkorea/>.

forum may have as few as two members.[123] However, more Korea-based detectorists are visible in online forums elsewhere. These numbers are unrepresentatively low and cannot be used as minimum numbers to estimate the size of the detecting community.

Metal-detecting and online management

As elsewhere within the region, many Korea-based detectorists seem to be foreign residents; some Korea-based detectorists are also active in other countries in the region. This may partly be due to extreme overpricing of international brands,[124] which limits the potential for local participation. They exchange information on 'productive sites' and identification of finds. One advertised that 'most' of his 'korean [*sic* – Korean] holed coins have been found using a detector', so he had 'many varieties not listed in any reference book'.[125] If there were 'many' *types* that had *never* been documented, they would be exceptionally significant and their unscientific extraction and disappearance into the private market would be exceptionally harmful. However, it should be remembered that, elsewhere, fake objects have been advertised as 'metal-detector finds', in order to lend false legitimacy.[126]

One USA-based detectorist appeared to be a cautious, licit detectorist, as he had warned detectorists elsewhere that 'relic hunting' for militaria was 'sometimes illegal'.[127] He had found 'religious items', '[m]ost' of which he had left, some of which he had taken.[128] He presented two that had been 'in the middle of nowhere'.[129] He had also found coins, arrowheads, axe heads and other unidentified objects.[130]

123 Detector, 'Poleom [Forum]' (*Detector*, 24 November 2017) <www.detector.co.kr/forumLog/forum.php>.

124 echo, 'Why I Have Not Seen Any Japanese Metal Detecting' (*UK and European Metal Detecting Forum*, 28 June 2011) <https://web.archive.org/web/20170226090615/http://www.metaldetectingforum.co.uk/viewtopic.php?f=10&t=13121>.

125 william smith, 'Most of My Korean Holed Coins Have Been Found Using a Metal Detector, So I Have Many Varieties Not Listed in Any Reference Book' (*World Coins and Paper Money Traders and Collectors*, 26 April 2006) <http://web.archive.org/web/20180127025619/http://www.coinswappers.com/html/asia.html>.

126 E.g. in the United Kingdom, cf David Brown, 'Metal Detector User David Hutchings Jailed for Selling Fake Coins' (*Times*, 11 May 2009) <www.thetimes.co.uk/article/metal-detector-user-david-hutchings-jailed-for-selling-fake-coins-7rjx8vsb5gh>.

127 Matt Pfeil, 'I've Never Been down There, but I Could Imagine There Would Be Plenty' (*Facebook*, 4 December 2016d) <www.facebook.com/groups/MetalDetectingThailandAndGlobalDiggers/permalink/1757522147833973/?comment_id=1758257927760395>.

128 Matt Pfeil, 'I've Only Found a Couple Religious Items While Detecting in Korea' (*Facebook*, 15 August 2016a) <www.facebook.com/groups/MetalDetectingThailandAndGlobalDiggers/permalink/1712538982332290/>.

129 Pfeil 2016a (n 128).

130 Matt Pfeil, 'A Charm I Found out on an Old Mountain Trail in Korea about 7' in the Dirt' (*Facebook*, 26 November 2016b) <www.facebook.com/groups/MetalDetectingThailandAnd

Mongolia

Cultural property law

Unlicensed 'use of special tools and metal detectors' is prohibited specifically 'in the area of immovable historical and cultural memorials'. Furthermore, unlicensed 'paleontological and archaeological prospecting, excavation and research' are prohibited generally. In addition, unlicensed export of cultural objects is prohibited.[131] Like the other territories under discussion, while these laws have been instituted in principle, they have not been implemented effectively in practice, due to a dearth of monitoring and enforcement.[132] Even with increased technical capacity for law enforcement, effective control would be difficult.

According to the General Police Department, smuggling methods are becoming 'more advanced[…] more difficult to catch'.[133] However, they do not need to be very advanced to be very effective. As an illicit dealer spontaneously advised a perceived customer, 'just wear it as a necklace when you go through customs, and no one will stop you'.[134]

Online management and the scale of potentially illicit activity

There does not appear to be significant evidence of online management of detecting in Mongolia. One local detectorist sought advice on the targeting of sites on a generic English-language thread on Reddit.[135] There are various potential reasons.

The historically nomadic society may have produced and consumed relatively few metal objects, which it deposited sparsely across an expansive territory. So it may simply be less productive to engage in detecting there.

While internet access in Mongolia is similar to China in overall proportions of populations, Mongolia has a much smaller population in the country with a much rarer language internationally, so the Mongolian-language detecting population may simply be too small to sustain a significant online community.

GlobalDiggers/permalink/1754516968134491/>; Matt Pfeil, 'What I Have Before You Is Your Average Sized Soju Shot Glass that Somehow Made Its Way from a Bar in Korea to My Home in California' (*Facebook*, 3 December 2016c) <www.facebook.com/groups/MetalDetectingThailandAndGlobalDiggers/permalink/1757662167819971/>.

131 Law on the Protection of Cultural Heritage 2014.

132 James Williams, 'Protecting Archaeological Sites for Mongolian Nomads' (*Cultural Survival*, March 2004) <www.culturalsurvival.org/publications/cultural-survival-quarterly/protecting-archaeological-sites-mongolian-nomads>.

133 Mendbayar Zoljargal, 'Mongolian and Chinese Gang of Antique Smugglers Caught in the Act' (*UB Post*, 27 February 2014) <http://ubpost.mongolnews.mn/?p=8125>.

134 Oliver Steeds, 'The Hidden Grave of History's Greatest Warrior' (*Newsweek*, 3 December 2012) <www.newsweek.com/hidden-grave-historys-greatest-warrior-63527>.

135 ScorchedRabbit, 'Metal Detecting near UB' (*Reddit*, 4 May 2016) <www.reddit.com/r/mongolia/comments/4hsuxz/metal_detecting_near_ub/>.

More fundamentally, there is an intense cultural prohibition on grave-robbing. There is a 'detest[ation]' of 'any attempt to touch graves, or even wander around graveyards', such that 'burial spots are forbidden areas' that people are expected not to enter.[136] Even licensed professionals, who have performed surveys, have refrained from scientific excavations.

However, according to an artisanal miner, while detecting was 'not popular' before, it is now 'increas[ing]' in popularity.[137] There is evidence of 'treasure hunting', both before and 'particularly' since marketisation in 1990, when Buddhist objects with religious value gained financial value as well.[138]

Metal-detecting

An archaeological survey documented that 'robbers[...] with metal detectors'[139] had been caught in the act at the monastery of Züün Khural and that there was evidence of 'loot[ing]',[140] 'loot[ing]'[141] by 'treasure hunters'[142] with detectors, at the monasteries of Tariatyn Deed Khuree, Khoshuu Khural and Guchin Jas.

Identified in another report,[143] there is an online dealer of metal-detected cultural objects with around 3,715 fans.[144] Based on a poll elsewhere, which indicated that 6.58 per cent of online detectorists were not active detectorists,[145]

136 Mongolia Today, 'In Search of Chinggis Khaan Misterious Tomb' (*Mongolia Today*, 26 February 2000) <http://web.archive.org/web/20150108215507/http://www.mongoliatoday.com/?p=321>.

137 BAATAR, 'Hello from Mongolia' (*Thunting*, 13 September 2009) <www.thunting.com/smf/new_user_introduction/hello_from_mongolia-t7944.0.html;msg49670#msg49670>.

138 Renske Franken, Guido Verboom and Sue Byrne, 'Tov Pilot Survey Report 2005' (*Mongolia's Buddhist Monasteries Project*, 2005) <www.mongoliantemples.org/index.php/en/2014-07-01-06-34-46/2014-07-01-06-58-17/the-pilot-survey-report>.

139 Mongolia's Buddhist Monasteries Project, 'Züün Khural' (*Mongolia's Buddhist Monasteries Project*, 2007a) <www.mongoliantemples.org/index.php/mn/%D0%B3%D0%B0%D0%B7%D1%80%D1%8B%D0%BD-%D0%B7%D1%83%D1%80%D0%B0%D0%B3/1021?view=oldtemplemn>.

140 Mongolia's Buddhist Monasteries Project, 'Tariatyn Deed Khuree' (*Mongolia's Buddhist Monasteries Project*, 2007b) <www.mongoliantemples.org/index.php/mn/2014-07-01-06-18-41/old-temples/1094?view=oldtempleen>.

141 Mongolia's Buddhist Monasteries Project, 'Khoshuu Khural' (*Mongolia's Buddhist Monasteries Project*, 2007c) <www.mongoliantemples.org/index.php/en/component/domm/1960?view=oldtempleen>.

142 Mongolia's Buddhist Monasteries Project, 'Guchin Jas' (*Mongolia's Buddhist Monasteries Project*, 2007d) <www.mongoliantemples.org/index.php/mn/2014-07-01-06-18-41/old-temples/1436?view=oldtempleen>.

143 William Taylor, 'Beyond Genghis Khan: How Looting Threatens to Erase Mongolia's History' (*Guardian*, 26 October 2017) <www.theguardian.com/science/blog/2017/oct/26/beyond-ghengis-khan-how-looting-threatens-to-erase-mongolias-history>.

144 Ertnii Edlel Avna, 'Ertnii Edlel Avna [Take Ancient Objects]' (*Facebook*, 27 November 2017) <www.facebook.com/Эртний-эдлэл-авна-1260730577274843/>.

145 Marc, 'How Often Do You Metal Detect?' (*TreasureNet*, 16 February 2004) <www.treasurenet.com/forums/voting-booth/720-how-often-do-you-metal-detect.html>.

it is possible to infer that there are at least 3,471 active detectorists among a population of around 3,027,398 (as of 2016). Thus, it is possible to infer that there is at least one illicit detectorist amongst 872 people.

As advertised by a detector manufacturer, there is also detecting tourism. Some detectorists work in pairs and target 'artifacts' such as 'rare coin[s] or jewelry', including 'medieval Chinese coins' and seventeenth to nineteenth-century objects, across Mongolia (e.g. lecturer Vladimir Pavlovskiy, who 'display[s]' some finds in the museum of G. I. Nevelskoi Maritime State University, Vladivostok, Russia).[146]

Crisis antiquities trafficking

Between the 1990s and the 2000s, privatisation and industrialisation increased poverty. Thus, poverty-stricken herders turned to subsistence digging for a supplementary income, 'sell[ing] precious objects, such as antiquities, to tourists'.[147] Since then, natural disasters have been ravaging herders' livestock, in cycles that are being intensified by climate change and worsened by human action to compensate for the consequent poverty and insecurity.[148]

Hence, according to archaeologist Prof. Ulambayar Erdenebat, illicit digging of precious metal grave goods has increased even more, as a matter of 'survival'; exploiting the situation, intermediaries contract 'locals to dig up burial sites'.[149]

Discussion

Dangerous business

In East Asia as elsewhere, cultural property crime can be a dangerous business. Looters are gassed by their energy generators[150] and buried alive in collapsed holes.[151] Metal-detecting of (especially twentieth-century) conflict archaeology is

146 Vladimir Pavlovskiy, 'Detecting Stone' (*Minelab*, 9 January 2014) <www.minelab.com/usa/go-minelabbing/success-stories/detecting-stone->.

147 Williams (n 132).

148 Joanna Chiu, 'Climate Change in Mongolia Destroying Pastures on Which Nomadic Herders Rely' (*Guardian*, 10 March 2016) <www.theguardian.com/global-development/2016/mar/10/climate-change-mongolia-destroying-pastures-nomadic-herders-dzud>; Patrick Kingsley, 'Nomads No More: Why Mongolian Herders Are Moving to the City' (*Guardian*, 5 January 2017) <www.theguardian.com/world/2017/jan/05/mongolian-herders-moving-to-city-climate-change>.

149 Steeds (n 134).

150 ECNS, 'Chinese Grave Robbers Poison Themselves Inside Ancient Tomb' (*ECNS*, 10 March 2017) <www.ecns.cn/2017/03-10/248836.shtml>.

151 Donna Fu, 'Grave robbers' search for treasure buries them alive' (*Sixth Tone*, 28 November 2016) <www.sixthtone.com/news/grave-robbers%E2%80%99-search-treasure-buries-them-alive#>.

dangerous to the community as well as to the metal-detectorists, as munitions sometimes explode *after* extraction.[152] Unexploded ordnance (UXO) is cause to be 'careful' across the region.[153] Yet its unsafe extraction persists, even in licit detecting.

For instance, in South Korea, a permanent foreign resident military historian and his colleague had metal-detected a nineteenth-century battlefield site, where they found militaria and 'other relics'.[154] The academic detectorists 'gave' a 'live Schenkl [artillery] shell' to the Korea Army Museum 'for deactivation'.[155] In other words, they appear to have removed the object and transported the unstable explosive to a public institution, rather than marked the location and alerted professional explosive ordnance disposal (EOD) technicians.

Diversity in crime, diversity in consumption

There is diversity in the perpetrators and mechanisms of cultural property crime in East Asia. Looting/trafficking is a means of subsistence for poor and insecure members of local communities; a source of profit for criminal entrepreneurs, networks and groups, including illicit excavation tourism operators;[156] and a means of asset extraction for tourists and expatriates, where the assets are sometimes converted into financial assets through sale, sometimes kept as cultural assets through collection.

Risky goods encompass all kinds of cultural objects, even human remains, for example, from Tibet.[157] Looted, stolen and/or illegally exported goods are commonly trafficked in 'boutique' operations, for assembly of personal collections,

152 André Schoellen, 'Problem Metalldetektoren: Militärische Kampfmittel als Rettungsanker für Unser Archäologisches Erbe? [The Problem of Metal Detectors: Military Ordnance as a Lifeline for Our Heritage?]' (2015) 38 *Archäologische Informationen* 331, 336.

153 Stefan Burford, 'I Haven't but Would Imagine that There Would Still Be Lots of Ordinance Left There, Careful' (*Facebook*, 3 December 2016) <www.facebook.com/groups/MetalDetectingThailandAndGlobalDiggers/permalink/1757522147833973/?comment_id=1757545761164945>; Pfeil 2016d (n 127).

154 Thomas Duvernay, 'These Are Various Items a Colleague of Mine and I Found on Ganghwa Island, Korea, Where the First Military Action between the US and Korea Took Place (1871)' (*Facebook*, 22 October 2015) <www.facebook.com/groups/424903424382673/permalink/431348223738193/>.

155 Duvernay (n 154).

156 Shuzhong He, 'Illicit Excavation in Contemporary China' in Neil Brodie, Jenny Doole and Colin Renfrew (eds) *Trade in Illicit Antiquities: The Destruction of the World's Archaeological Heritage* (McDonald Institute for Archaeological Research 2001) 23.

157 Duncan Chappell and Damien Huffer, 'Protecting Cultural Heritage: A Review of Some Contemporary Developments in Australia and Near Environs' in Duncan Chappell and Saskia Hufnagel (eds), *Contemporary Perspectives on the Detection, Investigation and Prosecution of Art Crime: Australasian, European and North American Perspectives* (Ashgate 2015) 252.

disorganised sale into grey markets or pre-arranged delivery to market-end dealers and collectors. They are also trafficked in industrial supply chains by organised crime groups, for example, in China[158] and Mongolia.[159]

Such criminals sometimes conduct looting-to-order for collectors or dealers[160] and 'often' traffic cultural goods online.[161] Activity is often facilitated and sometimes even performed by corrupt law enforcement agents, government officials and/or archaeologists.[162]

As well as global markets, there are thriving regional and national markets, which drive the looting. For example, according to an illicit dealer in Ulan Bator, collectors in China are the primary consumers of antiquities from Mongolia as well as China.[163] Meanwhile, in Taiwan, Japan and South Korea, tourists and expatriates appear to constitute significant numbers of extractors as well as consumers.

Throughout the process, from extraction to consumption, the internet facilitates the functioning of the illicit trade. This encompasses selection, purchase and use of equipment; identification of targets; extraction, processing and transfer of assets; and identification of trainers, advisers, financiers, partners and sellers/ buyers.

Paint it black: the practical impossibility of source-end control

As demonstrated by testimony from detectorists across the region, they can use homemade, hand-built metal-detectors, so ownership of detectors is extremely difficult to trace. They can go detecting in obscure locations or at night, so that use of detectors (or, more generally, extraction of cultural objects) is extremely difficult to identify. They can engage in private online trading, so that handling of metal-detected (or otherwise extracted) cultural goods is extremely difficult to trace.

If detectorists illicitly export more unwieldy portable/movable cultural heritage, and 'portableised'[164] immovable cultural heritage (which has been extracted

158 According to the Ministry of Public Security of China, cited by Zhang (n 22); see also China Daily, 'Protection of Relics Needs More Resources' (ECNS, 18 November 2010) <www.china.org.cn/china/2010-11/18/content_21369720.htm>; He (n 156) 19–21.

159 Zoljargal (n 133).

160 Samuel Hardy, 'Is Looting-to-Order "Just a Myth"? Open-Source Analysis of Theft-to-Order of Cultural Property' 2015 *Cogent Social Sciences* 1 <http://dx.doi.org/10.1080/23311886.2015.1087110>) 14; see also Caspari (n 29); Lie Ma, 'Return of the Stolen Sarcophagus' (*China Daily*, 25 June 2010) <www.chinadaily.com.cn/china/2010-06/25/content_10018044.htm>; Zoljargal (n 133).

161 According to the Ministry of Public Security of China, cited by Zhang (n 22).

162 RFA (n 36); Zhang (n 22); Fang and Ong (n 8).

163 Steeds (n 134).

164 Paul Barford, 'Katie Paul: The U.S. Market in Cambodian Cultural Property' (*Portable Antiquity and Cultural Heritage Issues*, 24 October 2017) <http://paul-barford.blogspot.com/2017/10/katie-paul-us-market-in-cambodian.html>.

from something that was not supposed to circulate as a matter of course), they may need to use more complex smuggling methods. However, if detectorists illicitly export 'very' portable antiquities, such as jewellery or coins, they may simply wear it or mail it. Hence, source-end regulation is necessary, but insufficient; market-end regulation is essential, to minimise the potential for profit that drives the extraction.

8 From canvas to ashes

Understanding the implications of the Westfries Museum and Kunsthal thefts for the Dutch art world

Naomi Oosterman

Introduction

Art crimes can have severe consequences for international and local art worlds, affecting their cultural infrastructure, institutions, and sometimes even causing political distress. In the last 12 years, two major art thefts occurred in the Netherlands: one theft in 2005 in Hoorn at the Westfries Museum and one theft in 2012 in Rotterdam at the Kunsthal. Both thefts instigated (inter) national controversy on different levels. They furthermore had profound implications for Dutch cultural policy and local politics. This chapter is part of a larger research project concerning the criminal dynamics of art theft in the European Union. This chapter is mostly a conceptual case study of these two thefts; however, it is empirically embedded in a larger quantitative research project, which analyses all art thefts as registered by the Interpol Works of Art Database (henceforth WoA) since 1950 in 15 European Union countries. From this established database, I extracted the Netherlands as a singular case to frame the two thefts discussed in this paper. This case study discusses the thefts, the conceptual framework in which these thefts can be embedded, and the implications the thefts had on the Dutch art world. This paper aims to provide a sociological framework for the study of art crime.

The thefts

In the dead of night, from Sunday 9 to Monday 10 January 2005, 24 paintings and 70 pieces of silver were stolen from the Westfries Museum in Hoorn, the Netherlands. Amongst the paintings were works by Jan van Goyen, Jacob Waben, and Matthias Withoos, all painters from the Dutch Golden Age. The criminals were able to enter the museum through a small cellar door. They left a devastating scene. Glass doors were shattered, wooden panels were destroyed and valuable porcelain was smashed into hundreds of pieces. The museum was equipped with a high-tech security surveillance system. However, during the theft, the system failed to deliver any signal to the authorities. According to the police, the criminals had manipulated the security system on the eve of the theft. In contrast to their rough treatment of the museum grounds, they took their time to carefully remove the canvases from their frames. Apart from two pieces, all artworks, including the silverware, were owned by the museum itself. However, they were not insured due to the insurance premium being too high. The estimated value of the artworks was roughly around €250,000 to €1.3 million.

However poorly the Westfries Museum was treated, the Kunsthal in Rotterdam, the Netherlands, was barely touched. Apart from an emergency door that was opened, and seven empty spots on the wall, there was no sign of a forced break in. However, damage to the collection was severe. In the night of 15 to 16 October 2012, seven paintings by Lucian Freud, Pablo Picasso, Jacob Meijer de Haan, Henri Matisse, Paul Gauguin and Claude Monet were stolen. In quantity, the theft seemed a whole lot less. Although far fewer objects were taken than the 94 items stolen from Hoorn, the insured value of the Rotterdam artworks was approximately €18.1 million. According to reports made by the museum and the police, the criminals were mostly interested in the size of the paintings. Only smaller, 'hand-held' paintings were stolen that night. The Kunsthal did not own any of the paintings that were stolen. All paintings belonged to the Triton Family Foundation, one of the most influential collectors in the art world. It took the criminals only 2 minutes and 48 seconds to break in, steal the paintings, and leave the museum grounds. No fewer than four alarm systems went off the moment they managed to open the security door of the museum, however, it took five minutes for the police (11 for the private security company working for the Kunsthal) to arrive at the scene of the crime. By this time, the criminals and the artworks were gone. It did not help that the museum staff sent the police away almost immediately. Although the security door was unlocked, there were no other signs of a break-in. When the museum staff found out that the seven pieces had been stolen, it took almost two hours for the police to be informed and take action.[1]

The Westfries Museum and Kunsthal thefts are without doubt two of the biggest thefts in the Dutch art world since the beginning of the twenty-first century, both in terms of cultural and economic value.[2] Both were solved in very different ways. They had a significant influence on Dutch cultural policy concerning the protection and securitisation of artworks in Dutch museums. Before we can discuss what implications these thefts have for Dutch policy and how they were solved, we first need to understand the conceptual implications that art theft can have on a society.

1 Lex Boon, 'De kunst van het stelen: Het tragische lot van de geroofde Kunsthalwerken' (*NRC*, 17 October 2013) <www.nrc.nl/kunsthal/> accessed 10 February 2017; Westfries Museum, 'Westfriese roofkunst in Oekraïne, maar onbereikbaar' <http://wfm.nl/gestolen-kunst/> accessed 5 January 2017.

2 The biggest recorded art crime in Dutch history was that of the Van Gogh Museum theft in 1991 in Amsterdam, in which 20 paintings by Van Gogh were stolen, with an estimated value of €500 million.

The cultural diamond

In order to fully grasp the significant impact that these art thefts can have on society, we must first understand the relationship that art has with society. Art can be seen as a 'mirror' of society,[3] the provider of role models and deviants,[4] a way of symbolic control over subordinate classes,[5] or a leisurely activity.[6] Nevertheless, even though it is tempting to view the relationship between art and society as a direct link, it is often only one part of society that gets reflected by art. One specific group that is subordinated; or gets to subordinate. We do not merely and without criticism accept role models just because they are on television or, in this case, because their art is placed within a museum. Art has a seemingly ambiguous position within society. The numerous scholars listed here are the tip of the iceberg concerning sociological theory. The sheer concept of 'what is art' is ambiguous and there is no clear consensus as to what constitutes art or the art world.[7] Before we consider the position of art and the art world, we must first discuss how culture relates to society as a whole.

In order to understand art and culture sociologically, Griswold developed the idea of the cultural diamond.[8] The diamond is shaped like a kite, with each of the four corners representing different actors within the cultural field.

The actors reflected in the cultural diamond are (1) art, (2), producers of art, (3) consumers of art, and (4) the wider society. According to Griswold, in order to understand the position of art within society, one must take into account all four corners of the kite, as well as the six links. The cultural diamond almost functions as a metaphor, a heuristic device that sets out the idea that relationships between these four points exist. An explanation of this diamond is that an artist, or a group of artists creates art, but that alone is not enough for art to find its place within society. Instead, it reaches a particular public, a group of individuals that is embedded within a social system. How the consumers on the other side use art, what meanings they attribute to it and how it eventually reaches the general society is mediated by these individuals. It is furthermore affected by their attitudes and values, their social networks, and their (social) location. Society affects artists, the producers, the consumers, and through these: art. The cultural diamond cannot be seen as a conclusive theory. It does not aim to explain what the relationship between these points is; only that some of these relationships exist.

3 Pierre Bourdieu, *Distinction: A social critique of the judgement of taste* (Routledge 1984).
4 Victoria Alexander, *Museum and money: The impact of funding on exhibitions, scholarship, and management* (Indiana University Press 1996).
5 Antonio Gramsci, *Selections from the prison notebooks of Antonio Gramsci* (Lawrence & Wishart 1971).
6 Robert Herbert, *Impressionism: Art, leisure, and Parisian society* (Yale University Press 1988).
7 Howard Becker, *Art Worlds* (University of California Press 1982); Pierre Bourdieu and Randal Johnson, *The field of cultural production: Essays on art and literature* (Columbia University Press 1993); Cynthia Freeland, *But is it art? An introduction to art theory* (OUP 2001).
8 Wendy Griswold, *Cultures and Societies in a changing world* (Sage 1994).

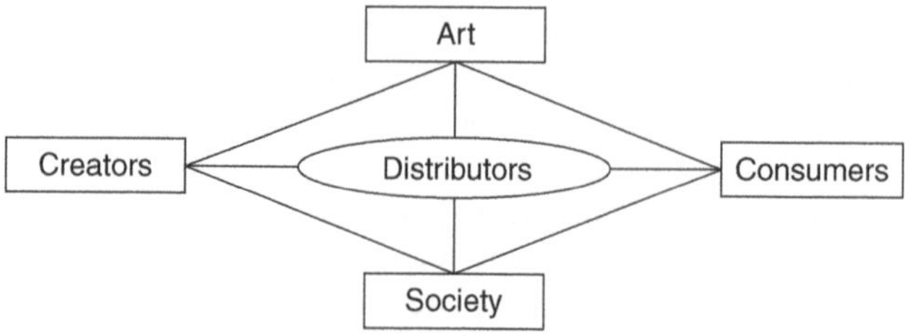

Figure 8.1 Modified cultural diamond as by Victoria Alexander (1996)

One thing that the cultural diamond is missing, which is important for this paper, is the definition of the distributor. In order for art to reach consumers (or in this case criminals) or for producers to reach consumers, one must rely on certain networks, organisations or persons. The modified cultural diamond as proposed by Alexander acknowledges the existence of these networks, and names them the distributors.[9]

Alexander's modified cultural diamond

For this case study, I reviewed the thefts from two particular museums. In this modified cultural diamond, we can see that many forms of art become divorced from the artist after they have entered the distribution system. Museums and galleries often circulate their artworks. The Kunsthal in Rotterdam is technically not even a museum, it has no own permanent collection or a depot, it is purely an exhibition space, completely reliant on borrowing artworks. The Westfries Museum, however, owned their artworks, apart from two of the artworks. In either case, museums are distributor and therefore powerful gatekeepers (Figure 8.1).

The modified cultural diamond shows that the link between art objects and society is not a simple, direct link. In Alexander's diamond, the direct link between the art object and society is dismantled and much more ambiguous. It suggests that objects are shaped and mediated by both the producers and the consumers of culture. The distributors function as a filtering system, determining which cultural product will reach consumers and the society as a whole. It is worth bearing in mind that society consists of different audiences and not a homogenous group.

Museums therefore act as gatekeepers, exhibiting what is considered valuable art, both in terms of economic and cultural value, and can therefore not only attract the interested art lover, but also the criminal who is interested in money.

9 Victoria Alexander, *Sociology of the arts: Exploring fine and popular forms* (Wiley-Blackwell 2003).

Art worlds

In order to sociologically understand the concept of art theft as discussed in this chapter, we must take into account two important aspects. First of all, we need to understand that the creation of an artistic work is not an endeavour undertaken by a single person. The artistic endeavour of the creation, distribution, and consumption of art is done by many people. Any dissemination of such artworks in society could not have been completed without distributors. These distributors, which include museums, galleries, and art dealers, are fundamental to both the creation and the display of art. This signals the second important aspect under consideration when discussing art theft: there is not always *one* owner of an artwork, and the owner might not always be the *creator* of this piece. Therefore, we need to understand the power relations within our studied artistic field. The determination of the hegemonic elite in the artistic field is important to understanding the economic, political, and cultural hierarchy that exists. When discussing these art thefts and the related deviance, we furthermore need to understand and identify the subordinated classes within the field. The power relations within this field might influence the way that we deal with art theft. It is important that we both determine the definition of ownership in respect to cultural objects and that we identify legislation. Ownership in the sociological sense can be considered different than that in the legal sense.

In order to understand this gatekeeping procedure, we need to understand that art worlds have a very specific *modus operandi*. Many theorists have discussed the notion of these so-called *art worlds*, most prominently Howard Becker, who introduced the term in 1982. Becker argues that the arts are embedded in art worlds. He considers an art world to be 'the network of people whose cooperative activity, organised via their joint knowledge of conventional means of doing things, produces the kind of artworks that the art world is noted for'.[10] Some of these art worlds are small, like an experimental theatre group and others are large, such as the pop music industry. In his theorisation of the art world, Becker argues that works of art are not created by a sole artist, but are instead shaped by the whole system of the art world. Every aspect of that system therefore provides a set of resources and constraints for the production of art.

Art is thus deemed to be a collective activity. In order to understand art sociologically, Becker considers art to be a process rather than the finished product. He considers the production of art to be a collective endeavour. In regard to consumers, or the audience, Becker argues that if there is no audience, there is no art. A work has to be both made and appreciated.

Art needs an audience; art is a collective activity. This generates the assumption that there is a specific division of labour within the art world. Becker divides all people dealing with an artwork (be it a play, painting, or rock music) into two main categories. One he considers to be the *core personnel*. This core personnel

10 Becker (n 7) 1.

are at the centre of the making of the artwork. These people are considered to possess special skill and creativity of an artist. Others help, for instance, with design, marketing, public relations and finance. Becker considers these to be the support personnel. These are labelled as people that work as a matter of craft. They are given a lower status than the core personnel.

The division between core and support personnel is not a conclusive one, nor is it a clear line. Some art worlds have a large number of fine distinctions. An example of this is the film industry where the director, screenwriter, and actors can be seen as the core personnel, but the supporting actors, cameramen, and stuntmen might be labelled as support personnel, albeit important ones. A caterer or a driver could be seen as furthest away from the artistic core. All of the personnel combined are in some aspect responsible for the final product. The tasks are therefore bundled, as Becker calls it, and this is what is interesting when we are looking at art crime.

Looking at Becker's art world theory, we can conclude that determining the ownership of artworks can cause difficulties. In Becker's model we see that multiple people are involved in some way with the final artistic product. In the case of art theft, this concerns the notion of ownership of cultural objects, closely linked to national heritage. Even though some of the works belonged to the Westfries Museum, and others belonged to the Triton Collection, art objects are often seen as an (inter-) national heritage, and thus philosophically 'owned' by those who cherish (art) history.

Bourdieu[11] proposes a similar model to Becker's, calling it a model of artistic fields. The two terms (art world and artistic fields) can often be used synonymously. Artistic fields, however, also encompass the notion of both power relations and the social construction of ideas within the specific field. Generally, in Bourdieu's sociology of the arts, the key concept is the consideration that modernisation is a 'long-term process of differentiation that has transformed societies into specialised fields of action'.[12] These fields not only include art, but also economics, politics, sports, and so on. Each field is ordered via specific rules. In Bourdieu's terms, modern societies refer to interconnected spaces that together form a field of power. Within this field of power, elites compete with each other for economic, political and cultural hegemony over subordinated classes.[13]

The definition of ownership of cultural objects has proven to be both difficult and fascinating.[14] All artworks need production and distribution. Museums are mere distributors of art, meaning that they not are able to perform the

11 Pierre Bourdieu and Randal Johnson, *The field of cultural production: Essays on art and literature* (Columbia University Press 1993).

12 Gordon Fyfe, *Art, power and modernity* (Continuum Books 2000) 24.

13 Ibid.

14 Kelly Ann Falconer, 'When honor will not suffice: The need for a legally binding international agreement regarding ownership of Nazi-looted art' (2000) 21 *University of Pennsylvania Journal of International Economic Law* 383; Susan Scafidi, 'Intellectual property and cultural products' (2001) 81 *Boston University Law Review* 793; Jennifer Kramer, *Switchbacks: Art, ownership, and Nuxalk national identity* (UBC Press 2011).

production on their own (hence the core and support personnel), so many have to rely on a form of patronage, or public sales. In case of patronage, the patron can lend artworks to museums, but in terms of the policing arrow as discussed below, is also able to control the art.[15] This was especially the case with the Kunsthal, whose artworks were on loan from the Cordia Family, owners of the Triton Foundation Collection. Some patrons even dictate the content of artworks today,[16] as was more common practice during the Renaissance (Medici) and the Soviet Union (Soviet Realism).[17] Modern day patrons are not just the wealthy philanthropist, but can also be artistic and cultural institutions, such as museums, galleries, and theatres. The government can also be a patron as is the case in the Netherlands with the Rijksmuseum, which is mostly funded by the government and in essence by Dutch tax payers.

The theory above shows that as there is not one specific creator of art, there might also not be a sole owner of artworks. Some argue that specifically classical cultural objects, such as objects presented in museums, are owned by 'the public', as some argue that cultural heritage belongs to everyone since it links people together through shared history,[18] or more simply, because national museums are funded by tax money.[19] It is therefore easy to understand that the thefts that we discuss in this paper have severe consequences on many different levels. One of the answers to the question of implications and consequences can be found within the policing of art crime in the Netherlands.

The art crime policing arrow

Already in 2004, at the beginning of the Dutch EU presidency, it was established that European Union member states should have an art crime database, be it physical or digital. After the Westfries Museum theft, this EU policy measure quickly became reality in the Netherlands, with the implementation of a Dutch national database, resembling the Interpol database. In the following years, many European countries and Interpol member states created art crime databases, making it easier to share intelligence about missing artworks across borders. In that sense, these databases function as intelligence-led policing mechanisms: they

15 Alexander, *Museum and money* (n 4); Alexander (n 9).

16 Ibid.

17 Ibid.

18 Richard Handler 'An anthropological definition of the museum and its purpose' (1993) 17 *Museum Anthropology* 33; James Cuno, *Who owns anitiquity?: Museums and the battle over out ancient heritage* (Princeton University Press 2010); Ian Hodder 'Cultural heritage rights: From ownership and descent to justice and well-being' (2010) 83 *Anthropology Quarterly* 861.

19 Jesse Helms, 'Is it art or tax-paid obscenity: The NEA controversy' (1994) 2 *Journal of Law and Policy* 99; Jeol Feinberg, 'Not with my tax money: The problem of justifying government subsidies for the arts' (1994) 8 *Public Affairs Quarterly* 101; Anne-Marie Rhodes, 'Big picture, fine print: The intersection of art and tax' (2003) 26 *Columbia Journal of Law and Arts* 179.

are actively used by police forces in Europe for information-sharing and detection purposes. However, a truly operational policing capacity is almost non-existent. Therefore, many of the police forces, the Dutch included, rely on these databases in the case of a theft.

When a work of art gets stolen, the local authorities in the city/country where the theft took place form the most crucial element in the following chain of events. When the local authorities initially get the report of a stolen or missing artwork, they need to act quickly, and internationally, in order to decrease the possibility of the artwork(s) disappearing for ever. The local authorities need to contact other law-enforcement agencies internationally. This is especially important for thefts that take place within the European Union. With semi-open borders, artworks can travel as easily across countries with small chances of getting caught. Furthermore, potential purchasers need to be informed. These could be private collectors, dealers or museums and other organisations within the art community. Lastly, but not less importantly, organisations that maintain databases need to be informed. A stolen work of art, whether it is a painting, antiquity, sculpture or vase, can be seen as moveable property. It is therefore important that the report of a theft is made with haste.

The way that both national police forces and Interpol (should) operate is conceptualised in the arrow in Figure 8.2.

The art crime arrow of policing is both a descriptive and conceptual overview of the policing of art crime within the European Union; and specifically in the

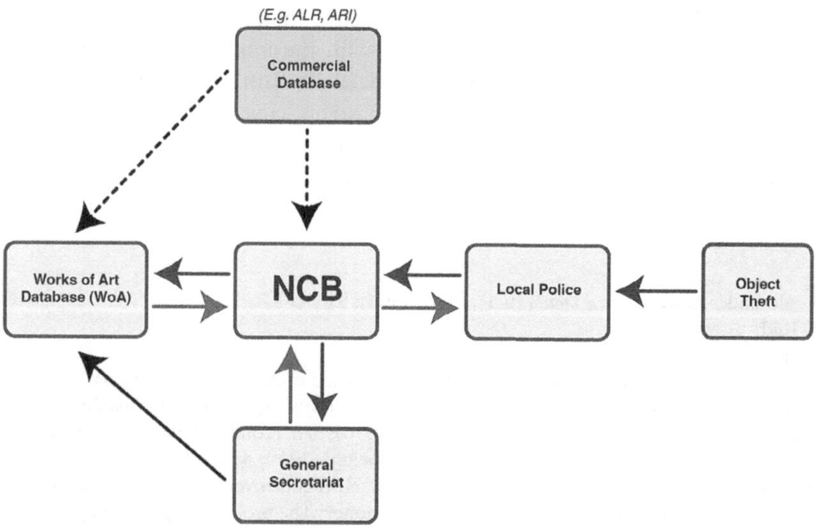

Figure 8.2 Art crime policing arrow

Netherlands during the Kunsthal and Westfries Museum thefts. Descriptively it shows the movement of information and policing. It almost always starts with the theft of a cultural object. This might be from a museum, an auction house, or a private household. However, theft via a direct crime or through the police is not always the starting point. The starting point sometimes lies with a provenance check from an auction house that holds a 'doubtful' object. The disputed object has been compared to the Interpol (or other commercial) databases and was flagged. In a sense the individual actors described in the arrow are all members (or guardians) of a network forming strong links of law-abiding citizens and institutions.[20]

However, in the case of a theft, the local police forces will initially contact the local National Coordinating Bureau (NCB). The NCB is the official representation of Interpol in its member states. Very, often the NCB consists of high-ranked detectives in the national police forces. The NCB is the first to decide if the information given by the local police (who get their information from the victim) should be transferred to the WoA. Here we already witness something that can be considered as a 'leaky pipeline effect'. Even though the leaky pipeline effect is mostly studied with issues concerning gender and minorities,[21] we see a similar effect with the exclusion of cultural objects from the WoA. Often, objects that have not been catalogued correctly will not be entered into the database. Only when an object has been catalogued through OBJECT-ID, will it be considered for inclusion.[22] These inclusion criteria are not solely based on bureaucratic measures, they seem to reflect a cognitive structure that determines these judgement processes: there is a social power relationship.[23] Often, 'famous' artworks, or artworks from highly canonised artists (e.g. high cultural value) make it to the Interpol database directly. Another example are artworks that not only have a high cultural value, but also a high economic value. They avoid the leaky pipeline and are often directly added to the database. The

20 Patricia L Brantingham, 'Environment, routine and situation: Toward a pattern theory of crime' (1993) 5 *Advances in Criminological Theory* 259.

21 Jasmin Joecks, Kerstin Pull and Uschi Backes-Gellner, 'Childbearing and (female) research productivity: A personnel economics perspective on the leaky pipeline' (2014) 84 *Journal of Business Economics* 517; Donald A. Barr, Maria Elena Gonzalez, Stanley F. Wanat, 'The leaky pipeline: Factors associated with early decline in interest in premedical studies among under-represented minority undergraduate students' (2008) 83 *Academic Medicine* 503; Jacob Clark Blickenstaff, 'Women and science careers: Leaky pipeline or gender filter?' (2005) 17 *Gender and Education* 369.

22 OBJECT-ID is an international framework for describing cultural objects (ICOM). It is a checklist concerning (amongst other things) materials and techniques, object type, technical measurements, inscriptions, and time periods. The Works of Art Database will allow only those artworks that have been correctly catalogued through this system. Object ID is an official trademark of the J. Paul Getty Trust and is thus under licensed agreement.

23 Pierre Bourdieu, '*The forms of capital*'. *Handbook of theory and research for the sociology of capital* (Greenwood Press 1986).

institutionally 'high' artworks are legitimised, and thus separated from their 'lower' counterparts.[24]

These high artworks dominate the ones from artists that are less canonised, less famous and less economically valuable. The highly canonised artworks can be seen as '(...) stakes and instruments of struggle, rescuing them thereby from the meaninglessness and uselessness to which they would be just as necessarily doomed in another field or another state of the same field'.[25] Specifically, this indicates that the artworks in the Interpol database are linked by relationships that are shaped by the structure of the field. In that sense, determining the efficacy of these databases, and perhaps more important, their cultural value, we can argue that the power relations within this field contribute to the scope and structure (which art is incorporated) of art crime databases. Another important element is the principle of artistic fields as discussed in the previous paragraph. The Cordia family is a powerful collectors couple from the Netherlands and a very powerful player in the Dutch (and international) art world. In light of Bourdieu, we could discuss that the Cordia family is part of one of the most dominant classes, sufficient in cultural, economic, and social capital, and thus their 'predicament' supported by the other dominant classes in the art world.[26] The Cordia Family is not only one of the dominant players in the Dutch art world, they are also the owners of the 'Triton Collection', the collection of which several works were stolen during the Kunsthal theft.

In terms of power and prestige, looking back at the arrow, the NCBs function as a gatekeeper and thus indirectly decide on the inclusion and exclusion criteria of the WoA. By following this system, the NCB seemingly holds the dominating power to what extent certain objects will come to the attention of the database. More importantly, through the NCB the *legitimisation* of certain artworks gets institutionalised. Like in Alexander's (1996) modified diamond, the embedding of a distributor node (NCBs) breaks the direct link between art object and society (in this case, WoA). The WoA here can be seen as the society of information, as a whole. It incorporates wider norms and values, laws, and social structures.

Just like the art world, gatekeepers (either as an organisational outcome, or individual decision), do not necessarily shape what art is created (*vis insita*), however, they do have the power to determine which objects, from all that are created, are viewed by the public and are thus considered important (*lex insita*).[27]

24 Diana Crane, *The transformation of the avant-garde: The New York art world, 1940–1985* (University of Chicago Press 1987); Paul DiMaggio, 'Classification in art' (1987) 52 *American Sociological Review* 440.

25 Pierre Bourdieu, *The rules of art: Genesis and structure of the literary field.* (Polity Press 1996).

26 Pierre Bourdieu, *In other words: Essays towards a reflexive sociology.* (Stanford University Press 1990); Pierre Bourdieu, *Distinction. A social critique of the judgement of taste* (Routledge 1984).

27 Alexander (n 9); Howard Becker, *Art Worlds* (University of California Press 1982); Pierre Bourdieu, *Distinction. A social critique of the judgement of taste* (Routledge 1984); Paul M. Hirsch, 'Processing fads and fashions: An organization-set analysis of cultural industry systems' (1972) 77 *American Journal of Sociology* 639.

This filtering, as we can see from the arrow, in this case is done by local police authorities. The objects of theft are immediately filtered in term of importance and value as mentioned previously. The big discrepancy between Becker and Bourdieu's theory on the one hand, and the operationalisation of art crime policing on the other, is that the gatekeeping in the policing arrow is rarely done by 'natives'.[28] It is often carried out by police officers that do not have any art-historical background, therefore creating an extra difficulty in determining the (cultural) value of the work for the database. In a sense, police officers function as boundary personnel.[29]

Ending up in the 'tip' of the arrow is the preferred outcome, i.e. full inclusion and legitimisation of these artworks. There are two 'external' organisations that are visible within the arrow. One are the commercial databases such as the Art Loss Register (ALR) and Art Recovery International (ARI) and the other is Interpol's General Secretariat. The WoA will only communicate with its General Secretariat if there is a suspicion that other forms of crime, other than art crime, were involved. Commercial databases operate almost completely outside of this arrow, as they only request information on certain objects or will contact Interpol when they have possibly located a stolen work of art. Vice versa, Interpol will not request any information from commercial organisations. The local police, who are often charged with the active investigation of the theft, only report to the NCB, but does have an indirect influence on the type of artworks that get included and thus legitimised within the WoA.

As mentioned before, the level of priority for the local police (and further down the line the NCBs) depends on factors of canonisation of the artist/object and the value of the objects. They initially function as distributors in this model. This, together with the police often lacking an art historical background, fuels the hypothesis that only legitimised and economically valuable artworks receive a quick and uneventful route towards the database.

What happened to the artworks in the Kunsthal and Westfries museum?

As mentioned at the beginning of this chapter, both cases luckily were resolved, however, not necessarily without any loss or damage. The paintings from the Kunsthal theft were kept for a short period of time in an apartment in Rotterdam, before being smuggled to Romania by the Romanian criminals involved.[30] Only three months later, after the Kunsthal theft was reported as the 'theft of the century', were the criminals and the paintings located in the small village of Carcaliu in Romania. It was one of the largest art crime operations of the past

28 Howard Becker, *Art worlds* (University of California Press 1982); Pierre Bourdieu, *Distinction. A social critique of the judgement of taste* (Routledge 1984).

29 Alexander (n 4); Hirsch (n 27).

30 Boon (n 1)..

decade for the Dutch national police: 25 detectives were put on the case and multiple undercover stings were conducted in cooperation between the Dutch and Romanian Police and Interpol. The whereabouts of the stolen paintings were established by phone tapping. Unfortunately, the police arrested the three very young culprits without them being in possession of the paintings. In an act of motherly love, one of the criminals' mothers burned at least some of the paintings in the bathroom of her house in that same village of Carcaliu.[31] Those paintings were destroyed beyond repair and all criminals involved were charged with various crimes that involved sentences ranging from a €10,000 fine to four years' imprisonment. As of the time of writing of this paper, the case has not yet been resolved due to an appeal to the Romanian High Court made in 2014.

As quickly as the paintings, or the remains thereof, were found in the Rotterdam case, so long did it take for the Westfries Museum pieces to be returned.[32] For a very long time after the theft, until early 2014, there was no trace of the missing artworks. In 2014, on a Ukrainian website, one of the paintings suddenly emerged. What happened in the two years until the return of five of the stolen paintings was an politically laden negotiation between the Dutch government, Ukrainian government and a splinter group of the extreme right-wing Organisation of Ukrainian Nationalists (OUN). The OUN was in possession of 24 paintings from the Hoorn museum and insisted that their value was €50 million. It took the intervention of a well-known Dutch art crime researcher, Arthur Brand, to negotiate a lower price. This happened in negotiations with the nationalist movement and the national government in Kiev. In July 2017, the MH17 passenger flight from Amsterdam to Kuala Lumpur was taken down, possibly accidentally, by a militant group in eastern Ukraine.[33] This caused a hardening of the debate between the Netherlands and Ukraine, as now not only the paintings needed to be repatriated, but also black boxes, intelligence, and information about the perpetrators needed to surface. Both the cases of the Westfries Museum theft and the MH17 plane crash led to political tensions between the Netherlands, Ukraine and Russia. However, two years later, in October 2016 the 24 paintings made their way back to Hoorn and had a festive reunion with their museum, 11 years after they originally left. Exactly how this came to be, and how much money was necessary, is unknown. The paintings, however, were in fairly good condition and are currently being restored to their former glory.

31 A forensic team of the Romanian National History Museum found traces of at least four oil paintings. However, other works were made on cardboard, and would leave no traces when burned. The court rules that it therefore can not be 100 per cent sure that the criminals had burned the paintings. Therefore, they have only been charged with theft.

32 Redactie, 'Westfries Museum heeft gestolen doeken elf jaar na roof terug' *De Volkskrant* (Amsterdam, 16 September 2016) <www.volkskrant.nl/binnenland/westfries-museum-heeft-gestolen-doeken-elf-jaar-na-roof-terug~a4378212/> accessed on 14 February 2017.

33 Ibid.

The two thefts illustrate the often ambiguous relationship that art has with society and the politics therein. The case of the Westfries Museum theft is the most prominent, showing how due to stolen artworks and complicated international cooperation between police forces, countries can develop complicated relationships with one another. Another implication that is indirectly related to the theft from the Westfries Museum is that of the 'Ukraine Referendum' in the Netherlands in the summer of 2016. The Dutch voted against the EU association agreement with Ukraine, and the research conducted afterwards showed this was mostly due to the MH17 crash. Illustrative of this are the comments by the Director of the Security Service of Ukraine, who argued that (in light of the Ukraine Referendum) that: 'the news of the recovery of the stolen art could have resulted in a positive influence on the Ukraine Referendum'.[34]

However, the case of the Kunsthal theft shows that the international policing of art crime, and the cooperation therein can be very fruitful. What should be taken into account was that there were no fewer than 25 detectives on the case, which is highly unusual for an art crime case. Despite the fact that the artworks were destroyed before recovery, due to the extensive collaboration between the Dutch and Romanian police, and Interpol, the case was resolved quickly, albeit with unimaginably damaging results to international heritage, and the reputation of the Dutch art museum.

The Kunsthal theft was was not only a blow to art history and heritage, but especially to the reputation of the Netherlands as a nation (and the Kunsthal as an institution) that can safeguard their art. During my fieldwork in the Netherlands, I interviewed several museum curators, who all agreed that the damage to their reputation was one that was most feared. In the case of the Kunsthal, it seemed that every measure was made to make sure that art investors, collectors and international institutions would not fear a collaboration with institutions in the Netherlands.

Conclusion

This chapter aimed to enhance our understanding of the implications of art theft on the art world, the Netherlands in particular, and discussed some of the consequences this has for the Dutch art world. Furthermore, this chapter gave a sociological perspective on the policing of art crime, providing the model of the 'art crime policing arrow'. The impact of art theft, as illustrated by the two cases of the Kunsthal and the Westfries Museum, was felt not only within the art world, but even in politics. The necessity of a well-functioning police unit became clear with the destruction of the artworks stolen from the Kunsthal in Rotterdam.

34 Redactie, 'Vondst roofkunst had Oekraïne-Referendum kunnen beïnvloeden' (*NOS*, 14 April 2016) <https://nos.nl/artikel/2099212-vondst-roofkunst-had-oekraine-referendum-kunnen-beinvloeden.html> accessed on 13 April 2018.

Nevertheless, despite these high-profile thefts and the need for an operational art crime police force, the Dutch Art and Antiques Unit consists of no more than four people dedicated to working on art crime in the Netherlands on a daily basis. Seeing that the Kunsthal theft needed no fewer than 25 detectives to be resolved, this can be considered an alarming statistic in the Dutch efforts to counter crimes against art.

From resolving the Westfries Museum theft, it is clear that there is furthermore a need for a functioning, operational, international cooperation between states. Often, stolen works of art move across national borders,[35] complicating law enforcement. As seen in Hoorn, it can take several years before cases are resolved due to complicated international cooperation between states. Furthermore, the implications for Ukraine, as the nation where the artworks were recovered, were political. A possible direct consequence of these thefts was the negative outcome of the Ukraine Referendum in the Netherlands in 2016.

35 INTERPOL, *Assessing crimes against cultural property. A survey of INTERPOL member countries 2013–2016* (2017) ch 2.

9 Expression crimes and the creation and protection of historical memory by means of criminal law

Emmanouil Billis

Introduction

Basic theories and principles of criminal law such as the legal interest theory, the principles of harm and legality, and the criminal law theory of the act all apply, more or less strictly, in most (not only Western) legal orders. The criminalisation of internal thoughts, moral beliefs, and personal opinions, however, is a grey policy area. Even in countries with longstanding constitutional traditions in safeguarding civil rights and liberties, penal laws may result in restrictions on fundamental freedoms, such as the freedoms of personal expression, science, and research.

Apart from the classic speech offences, contemporary provisions of international and European criminal law have created crimes concerning the public and racist condonation or denial of crimes of genocide, war crimes, crimes against humanity, and of the Holocaust. These are all included in the offence category of the so-called 'expression crimes'. Their cross-border dimension becomes particularly evident when committed via the internet, e.g., in scientific or personal blogs, or through the international publication of books and articles. Based on a recent high-profile trial in Greece against a German history professor, this paper examines, *inter alia*, the feasibility of protecting or creating historical memory by way of decisions of criminal courts and legal acts of parliaments. It also addresses the question of whether it would be preferable, in terms of transnational and transitional justice, to resolve controversies about crucial historical events by means of science and outside the criminal courts.

The protection of historical memory by means of criminal law

Historical memory can be violated not only at domestic level but also by means of transnational conduct. At the same time, it can be preserved and protected under supranational criminal law provisions and within the framework of international institutions. The normative and philosophical core of historical memory, namely historical truth, is undoubtedly a legal interest that is a part of the culture of many nations, a significant factor for transitional justice, and a standard lesson for contemporary and future generations in terms of not repeating past criminal mistakes. This is manifested, first and foremost, in the formal responses and the recognition of historical facts regarding mass killings and war crimes, both at national and at international level, through decisions of political bodies and fora, for example the Council of Europe (CoE) and the United Nations – e.g., in the case of the Holocaust,[1] the Genocide in Rwanda,[2] or the Armenian Genocide[3] – or through decisions of international criminal courts. In fact, in the opinion of at least some scholars, one of the purposes of international criminal trials, also in terms of transitional justice, is to establish a historical record.[4]

This is also why we are currently witnessing the adoption, by the international community, of international legal provisions promoting, in the national states, the penalisation of conduct that involves denying historical facts about mass atrocities or negating the recognition of their truth. In Europe, in particular, the supranational legal acts of the European Union (EU) and the third pillar instruments have had an important impact on re-shaping and harmonising the relevant national criminal laws. One basic example is the Framework Decision 2008/913/JHA of 28 November 2008 on combating certain forms and expressions of racism and xenophobia by means of criminal law.[5] Article 1 of this Framework Decision (FD) specifies that the EU member states shall, among

1 See, e.g. UNGA Res 61/255 (26 January 2007) UN Doc A/RES/61/255 condemning any denial of the Holocaust as a historical event.

2 UNSC Res 2150 (16 April 2014) UN Doc S/RES/2150.

3 CoE Declaration 320 (14 May 2001).

4 On the purposes of international criminal trials, see Emmanouil Billis, *Die Rolle des Richters im adversatorischen und im inquisitorischen Beweisverfahren* (Duncker & Humblot 2015) 423–425; Robert Cryer, Håkan Friman, Darryl Robinson, and Elizabeth Wilmshurst, *An Introduction to International Criminal Law and Procedure* (3rd edn, CUP 2014) 28–45; Jean Galbraith, 'The Pace of International Criminal Justice' (2009) 31(1) *Mich. J. Int'l L.* 3179, 84–97; Mirjan R Damaška, 'What is the Point of International Criminal Justice?' (2008) 83 *Chi.-Kent L. Rev* 329, 331–340; Albin Eser, 'Procedural Structure and Features of International Criminal Justice: Lessons from the ICTY' in Bert Swart, Alexander Zahar, and Göran Sluiter (eds), *The Legacy of the International Criminal Tribunal for the Former Yugoslavia* (OUP 2011) 109–117; Nandor Knust, *Strafrecht und Gacaca* (Duncker & Humblot 2013) 40–97; Jens Ohlin, 'Goals of International Criminal Justice and International Criminal Procedure' in Goran Sluiter, Håkan Friman, Suzannah Linton, Sergey Vasiliev, and Salvatore Zappalà (eds), *International Criminal Procedure* (OUP 2013) 55–68. See also: Report of the Secretary-General, 'The Rule of Law and Transitional Justice in Conflict and Post-conflict Societies' (23 August 2004) UN Doc S/2004/616 § 38; Preamble of the Rome Statute; Assembly of States Parties, 'Strategic Plan of the International Criminal Court (υπό III)', ICC-ASP/5/6, Fifth session (4 August 2006).

5 For additional information, see the European Parliament Resolution 2013/2543(RSP) of 14 March 2013 on strengthening the fight against racism, xenophobia and hate crime European Parliament Resolution 2012/2554(RSP) of 15 March 2012 on discriminatory internet sites and government reactions. According to the Report from the Commission to the European Parliament and the Council on the implementation of Council Framework Decision 2008/913/JHA (COM/2014/027 of 27 January 2014), 'a number of Member States have not transposed fully and/or correctly all the provisions of the Framework Decision, namely in relation to the offences of denying, condoning and grossly trivialising certain crimes. [...] Thirteen Member States (BE, CZ, DK, DE, EE, EL, IE, HU, NL, AT, FI, SE and UK) have no criminal-law provisions governing this conduct. DE and NL state that national case law applicable to Holocaust denial and/or trivialisation would also apply to the conduct covered by this article.'

other things, render punishable the conduct of publicly condoning, denying, or grossly trivialising crimes of genocide, crimes against humanity, and war crimes,[6] if they are directed against a group of persons or a member of such a group defined by reference to race, colour, religion, descent, or national or ethnic origin. This conduct is further qualified by requiring 'a manner likely to incite violence or hatred against such a group or a member of such a group', or, as an alternative, conduct that is 'either carried out in a manner likely to disturb public order or is threatening, abusive, or insulting'.[7] The FD of 2008 also includes provisions on instigation, aiding and abetting, the appropriate criminal penalties, the liability of legal persons, the freedom of expression, association, and the press, the requirements of prosecution, as well as issues of jurisdiction.

In terms of the jurisdictional issues, the problems that arise are especially complex in cases involving modern forms of transnational crime. This is especially true regarding violations of historical memory via the internet and the tremendous opportunities and tools this electronic medium provides to potential perpetrators. Aside from traditional books and magazines, which can be published and distributed nationally and internationally in all the traditional ways or online, today, there is an abundance of scientific or journalist blogs as well as different online social platforms, giving people a chance to express their opinions much more quickly and to reach a much broader audience. Simply by sitting in front of a computer in his or her own country, a person can write and publish online material on past events that may offend persons in another country or their historical memory, and others may easily view and download this material to their home computers. At the same time, it is far from easy to trace or effectively prosecute perpetrators due to technical difficulties related to the physical location of the servers, terminals, and electronic tools used in the commission of the act, conflicting jurisdictional claims, or difficulties at the level of judicial assistance.[8]

This is why the development of international and supranational legislation with respect to internet crimes has become more active in recent decades, including in terms of aspects of transnational crime. A prime example is the CoE Budapest Convention on Cybercrime,[9] along with the Additional Protocol to the Convention on Cybercrime, concerning the criminalisation of acts of a racist and

6 As these crimes are defined in the Statute of the International Criminal Court (ICC) or crimes defined in article 6 of the Charter of the International Military Tribunal appended to the London Agreement of 8 August 1945.

7 See also Article 6 of the Additional Protocol to the Convention on Cybercrime, concerning the criminalisation of acts of a racist and xenophobic nature committed through computer systems (adopted 28 January 2013, entered into force 1 March 2006) ETS 189.

8 See also, in a similar context, Emmanouil Billis and Panagiotis Gkaniatsos, 'Minors as Victims in the Age of Information and Communication Technologies' (2011) 2 *Eucrim – the European Criminal Law Associations' Forum* 82, 83–84 with further references.

9 Convention on Cybercrime (adopted 23 November 2001, entered into force 1 July 2004) ETS 185.

xenophobic nature committed through computer systems.[10] These legal instruments include provisions on the material definition of computer-related offences,[11] issues of procedural and international cooperation, as well as jurisdictional questions that are primarily answered based on the principle of territoriality.[12] Important in the context of hate crimes and the denial of historical facts is also Article 9 of the FD[13] on racism and xenophobia, which includes specific provisions for cases where the crimes under consideration were committed through an information system.[14] These (definitely imperfect) provisions aim to strengthen the fight against racists and deniers of historical atrocities by reducing their chances to avoid criminal prosecution for lack of jurisdiction.

Scientific freedom versus legally protected historical memory

So far, this chapter has focused only on the effective preservation of historical memory regarding significant criminal events at national, transnational, and international levels by means of the law. On the other side of the spectrum, however, are the freedoms, particularly the freedom of internal thoughts and the freedoms of speech, expression, and science. The present chapter will focus next on the potential conflict between these constitutional values and opposing legal-policy objectives, using the example of a recent criminal trial in Greece against a German professor of history who stood accused of denying and trivialising crimes committed by the Nazi invaders on the Greek island of Crete during the Second World War.

Relevant basic principles and rules of Greek criminal law

The Greek Constitution regulates the system of government of Greece, which is that of a Parliamentary Republic, on the basis of the separation of powers. The Constitution[15] of 1975 also provides for the following elements, which are of great significance for any legal system in order to operate in an effective, protective, and fair manner: the democratic and representative character of the

10 Additional Protocol to the Convention on Cybercrime (n 7).

11 *Inter alia*, the Convention refers to computer fraud and child pornography, while Article 6 of the Protocol specifically refers to the denial, gross minimisation, approval or justification of genocide or crimes against humanity through a computer system.

12 Article 22 of the Budapest Convention.

13 See also Article 12 of the Directive 2013/40/EU.

14 See also the European Parliament Resolution 2013/2543(RSP) of 14 March 2013 on strengthening the fight against racism, xenophobia and hate crime and the European Parliament Resolution 2012/2554(RSP) of 15 March 2012 on discriminatory internet sites and government reactions, as well as the Report from the Commission to the European Parliament and the Council on the implementation of Council Framework Decision 2008/913/JHA (COM/2014/027 of 27 January 2014).

15 The English translation of the Greek Constitution is available at <www.hellenicparliament.gr/en/Vouli-ton-Ellinon/To-Politevma/Syntagma/> accessed January 2017.

system of government; the state's primary obligation to respect and protect human dignity by guaranteeing equality, personal freedom, and the protection of fundamental rights and freedoms, including the freedoms of personal expression, the press, arts and sciences, research, and teaching; as well as the principle of the rule of law.[16]

In the context of a liberal and democratically shaped criminal law, the rule-of-law principle is implemented primarily by means of the principle of legality of crimes and punishments, all aspects of which are fully enshrined in Article 7 of the Constitution in conjunction with Articles 1–2 of the Greek Penal Code[17] (PC). Moreover, the Penal Code establishes in an abstract and general way the constitutive elements of the crime and defines the criminal offence as the wrongful act imputable to the perpetrator and punishable by law (Article 14 PC). Hence, penal punishment always presupposes an act ('omissions' are also included) that is wrongful and imputable to the perpetrator. The criminalisation of conditions related only to the internal world of a person that do not also constitute external conduct is not permitted. The act, which is specific human conduct (commission or omission), is a '*sine qua non* element' of the criminal offence.[18] Punishment can only be imposed due to acts, not due to mere personal thoughts and beliefs.[19] Internal thoughts and beliefs not associated with a direct and (from a social perspective) important change in the outside world are not considered acts under the Greek criminal law. Generally, the Greek state cannot control, forbid, or shape ideologies, personal convictions, or moral values by penalising conduct with no external and direct impact. Overall, criminal law represents the *ultima ratio* instrument of social regulation and control by the state. The criminalisation of a specific conduct that does not violate fundamental socio-ethical values, so-called legal interests, is not acceptable. The legislature may only regulates external conduct and, at the same time, must respect

16 For more details, see Emmanouil Billis., 'Introduction to the basic characteristics and fundamental principles of the criminal law and Penal Code of Greece' in Emmanouil Billis (ed.), *The Greek Penal Code: English Translation by Vasiliki Chalkiadaki and Emmanouil Billis* (Max Planck Institute for Foreign and International Criminal Law 2017) 1–4 and Emmanouil Billis, 'National Characteristics, Fundamental Principles, and History of Criminal Law in Greece' in Ulrich Sieber, Susanne Forster, and Konstanze Jarvers (eds), *National Criminal Law in a Comparative Legal Context, Vol. 1.2, Introduction to National Systems: Australia, Côte d'Ivoire, Greece, South Korea* (Duncker & Humblot 2013) 192–195, 222–228.

17 Law 1492/1950 (in conjunction with Presidential Decree 283/1985). For the English translation of the Greek Penal Code, see Emmanouil Billis (ed), *The Greek Penal Code: English Translation by Vasiliki Chalkiadaki and Emmanouil Billis* (Max Planck Institute for Foreign and International Criminal Law 2017). In the present chapter all translations of the Greek PC are the author's own.

18 I Giannidis, 'Arthro 14' [Άρθρο 14] (Article 14), in Spinellis (ed.), *Systematiki Ermineia tou Poinikou Kodika Arthra 1–133* [Συστηματική Ερμηνεία του Ποινικού Κώδικα Άρθρα 1–133] (Penal Code Commentary articles 1–133) (Athens 2005) p. 143 (in Greek).

19 C Mylonopoulos, *Poiniko Dikaio – Geniko Meros I* [Ποινικό Δίκαιο – Γενικό Μέρος Ι] (Criminal law – general part I) (Athens 2007) 95 (in Greek).

(constitutionally recognised) liberties. It is also argued that specific conduct is penalised primarily for the purpose of preventing harm (violation or endangerment) to others (principle of harm).[20]

The legal interest theory, the principle of harm, the principle of legality, the theory that substantive criminal law shall, as a rule, focus on the act rather than the personality of its perpetrator, all these theories and principles as implemented in Greece originate in the criminal law traditions of Germany and France. Until recently, Greece has been strict in applying these principles, especially the prohibition on criminalising internal thoughts, morals beliefs, and opinions. In all likelihood, this is a response to the arbitrariness and absoluteness present during the era of the military dictatorship (1967 to 1974), which included the suspension of basic human rights guarantees and of the European Convention on Human Rights (ECHR).[21] However, the broad liberal reform of the criminal justice system introduced by the Constitution of 1975, following the end of the military dictatorship period, seems to be facing new challenges these days. In recent years, penal provisions of international and supranational origin have been adopted that may result in broadly limiting fundamental freedoms such as the freedom of personal expression and the freedoms of science and research.

Naturally, freedoms, even constitutional ones, may have limits. However, these limits, especially if imposed by criminal law, must respect the proportionality principle and other constitutional guarantees.[22] In this context, the Penal Code of Greece, like many other criminal laws around the world, includes (along with the newly introduced provisions on 'crimes with racist elements')[23] 'traditional'

20 For more details, see Billis (n 16) 231–237 with further references.

21 On the historical roots and developments as well as on the international influences on the Greek criminal justice system, see Billis (n 16) 213–219, 265–284.

22 See also the Report from the Commission to the European Parliament and the Council on the implementation of Council Framework Decision 2008/913/JHA (COM/2014/027 of 27 January 2014). In the context of hate and expression crimes in Greece, see, for example (all in Greek), P Alikakos, *To Peristatiko Vias I Misous Os Aksiopoini Praksi* [Το περιστατικό βίας ή μίσους ως αξιόποινη πράξη] (Poiniki Dikaiosyni 2016) 36; Maria Kaiafa-Gbandi, *I Poiniki Katastoli Tis Ratsistikis Ritorias* [Η ποινική καταστολή της ρατσιστικής ρητορείας] (Poiniki Dikaiosyni 2016) 97; I Morozinis, *Apagoreusi Diakriseon Kai Eleutheria Tis Ekfrasis* [Απαγόρευση διακρίσεων και ελευθερία της έκφρασης] (Poinika Chronika 2010) 446; E Symeonidou-Kastanidou, *I Poiniki Antimetopisi Tou Ratsismou Kai Tis Ksenofovias Stin Ellada* [Η ποινική αντιμετώπιση του ρατσισμού και της ξενοφοβίας στην Ελλάδα] (Poinika Chronika 2015) 729; G Voulgaris, *Ta Egklimata Misous Kai I Poiniki Antimetopisi Tous Stin Ellada* [Τα εγκλήματα μίσους και η ποινική αντιμετώπισή τους στην Ελλάδα] (Poiniki Dikaiosyni 2015) 275.

23 According to article 81A PC: 'If the circumstances indicate that a criminal offence has been committed against a harmed person, the targeting of whom was due to characteristics related to race, skin colour, national or ethnic origin, genealogical descent, religion, disability, sexual orientation, gender, or gender identity, the punishment ranges shall be the following: α) In the case of a misdemeanour that is punished with imprisonment of up to one (1) year, the lower punishment limit shall be increased to six (6) months and the upper limit to two (2) years. In all other cases of misdemeanours, the lower punishment limit shall be increased by one (1) year. b) In the case of a felony, for which the stipulated punishment range is set at between five (5)

expression crimes, and, in particular, provisions on insulting behaviour,[24] discreditation,[25] defamation,[26] or the disparagement of the memory of a deceased person.[27] However, to initiate prosecution, all these cases require a criminal complaint by the person immediately harmed (Article 368 PC). Moreover, the Penal Code also provides a ground of justification, particularly with respect to cases involving scientific freedom, legal duties, or safeguarding rights and other justified interests.[28]

In addition, the Greek legislature decided to implement in 2014 the Framework Decision 2008/913/JHA of 28 November 2008 on combating certain forms and expressions of racism and xenophobia by means of criminal law. As a result, the criminalisation spectrum in terms of speech and expression crimes was expanded and, in particular, provisions criminalising the public expression of specific opinions regarding historical facts about mass atrocities were adopted in

and ten (10) years, the lower punishment limit shall be increased by two (2) years. In all other felony cases the lower punishment limit shall be increased by three (3) years.' Furthermore, according to article 361B PC: '1. Whoever supplies goods, offers services, or announces by means of public invitation the provision or supply of these, yet hereto excludes, on the grounds of abhorrence, persons due to their racial characteristics, colour, national or ethnic descendance, genealogy, religion, disability, sexual orientation, or gender identity or characteristics shall be punished with imprisonment of at least three (3) months and a pecuniary punishment of at least one thousand five hundred (1,500) euros. [...].'

24 Article 361 PC (Insulting behaviour): '1. Whoever, except in cases of discreditation and defamation (articles 362 and 363), insults the honour of another person with spoken words, through actions, or in any other way, shall be punished with imprisonment of up to one year or a pecuniary punishment. The pecuniary punishment may also be imposed along with imprisonment. 2. If the insult to the honour [of another person] is not particularly severe, taking into consideration the circumstances and the individual insulted, the responsible person shall be punished with detention or a fine. [...].'

25 Article 362 PC (Discreditation): 'Whoever in any way before a third party claims or disseminates with regard to another person a fact that can harm the honour or reputation of the latter, shall be punished with imprisonment of up to two years or a pecuniary punishment. The pecuniary punishment may also be imposed along with imprisonment.'

26 Article 363 PC (Defamation): 'If, in the case of article 362, the [claim about the] fact is false and the responsible person knew that it was false, he shall be punished with imprisonment of at least three months; along with the imprisonment, a pecuniary punishment may also be imposed. The deprivation of political rights in accordance with article 63 may also be imposed.'

27 Article 365 PC (Disparagement of the memory of a deceased person): 'Whoever disparages the memory of a deceased person with brutal or malicious insulting behaviour or through defamation (article 363) shall be punished with imprisonment of up to six months.'

28 Article 367 PC: '1. The following are not wrongful acts: a) unfavourable criticism of scientific, artistic, or professional projects; b) unfavourable statements contained in a document of a public authority regarding issues related to its service, as well as c) manifestations made in the execution of legal duties, the exercise of lawful power, or for the safeguarding (protection) of a right, or due to any other justified interest, or d) any similar cases. 2. The previous provision does not apply: a) where the aforementioned critiques and statements fulfil the constituent elements of the act of article 363, as well as b) when the manner of expression or the circumstances under which the act has been committed indicate the purpose of insult [according to article 361].'

Greece for the first time. The relevant current Greek provisions, entitled 'Public condonation or denial of crimes', are provided for in a special law.[29] According to this law,

> Whoever, intentionally and publicly, orally or through the press, via the internet, or in any other way or by any other means condones, trivialises, or maliciously denies the existence or the seriousness of crimes of genocide, war crimes, crimes against humanity, and of the holocaust or of Nazi crimes that have been recognised by a decision of an international court or by a decision of the Parliament of Greece, and that are directed against a group of persons or a member of such a group defined by reference to race, colour, religion, descent or national or ethnic origin, sexual orientation, gender identity, or disability, when the conduct is carried out in a manner likely to incite violence or hatred or which is threatening or insulting against such a group or a member of such a group, shall be punished with imprisonment of between 3 months and 3 years and a pecuniary punishment of between 5,000 and 20,000 euros [. . .].

In all cases, criminal prosecution shall be commenced *ex officio* (and not upon criminal complaint as in the case of traditional expression crimes). Moreover, as regards the particular act of public condonation or denial of crimes, the Greek legislature did not explicitly include any grounds of justification for the freedom of science or the preservation of similar justified interests.

The Richter case

In 2015, a few months after the provisions on 'Public condonation or denial of crimes' had come into force, the first criminal case under this new anti-racism legislation was commenced in Greece and, more specifically, in Crete. In fact, it was a high profile prosecution, with Heinz Richter, a German professor of history, as the defendant. The work of Richter, an extraordinary professor of modern history at the University of Mannheim, includes many books and international publications on Greek modern history.[30] In November 2014, the Faculty of Political Science of the University of Crete awarded Richter an honorary doctorate for his work on Greek history. The award provoked protests by historians, academics, and the Greek public. They claimed that Richter, in his work, had smeared the reputation of the Cretan resistance during the Second World War against the atrocities and mass executions committed by the Germans and, at the same time, had assigned noble motivations to the Nazi invaders.[31]

29 Article 2 of the Law 927/1979 as replaced by Article 2 of the Law 4285/2014.

30 See <www.geschichte.uni-mannheim.de/arbeitsbereiche/neuere_und_neueste_geschichte/team/apl_prof_dr_heinz_a_richter/>.

31 See, inter alia, the articles and reports published at <www.iefimerida.gr/news/238865/rethymno-dikasan-germano-kathigiti-istorias-giati-egrapse-gia-ti-mahi-tis-kritis>; <www.

More specifically, in his book on the Battle of Crete (*Operation Mercury: The Invasion of Crete*), published in 2011, the author describes Nazi paratroopers as 'brave knights' and 'idealistic', and characterises the practices of the Greek resistance – 'incited' by the British Special Operations Executive – against the German invaders as 'dirty' and 'brutal'.[32]

In the charges, the public prosecutor in Rethymno argued that these expressions and descriptions constitute a 'denial of the insulting nature of the Nazi crimes committed against the Cretan people' and are punishable under the new legislation on 'Public condonation or denial of crimes'. By contrast, many members of the Greek academic community came up with a petition in support of their German colleague underlining that 'it is extremely worrying that in the current 2015 criminal proceedings against historians have been initiated based on the positions they have taken in their scientific publications. Discussions on scientific matters should not be confined to the realm of populism'.[33]

The criminal trial started in December 2015 and concluded in February 2016 with the acquittal of Richter. In his concluding remarks, the trial prosecutor stated that while there may be historical mistakes in Richter's book, there are also doubts regarding the trivialisation or denial of war crimes committed by the Germans against the people of Crete, crimes against humanity, and of the Holocaust or of Nazi crimes. The prosecutor further stated that the descriptions in the book cannot incite hatred against the people of Crete and do not constitute insulting behaviour. In addition, Richter's defence stated that the law of 2014 is in violation of the constitutional freedom of expression and Article 10 ECHR, and that it would definitely be a violation of the principle of legality to apply this law to the case at hand (specifically, a violation of its *lex-praevia* element). This argument was based on the fact that the book was published in 2011, a time when the conduct described was in no way regulated by means of criminal law, and that the book had since been out of stock.[34]

patris.gr/articles/274051?PHPSESSID=s3a8m8qr6813e3c0r75akd8br5#.WH98n3pBfTY>; <http://goodnet.gr/rotator/articles/apofasi-pou-aifnidiase-ligo-prin-to-telos-tis-dikis-richter.html>; <http://tvxs.gr/news/ellada/athoos-o-rixter-alla-enoxi-i-boyli-poy-anagnorise-ta-nazistika-egklimata-stin-ellada>; <http://tvxs.gr/news/ellada/metaseismoi-pollon-rixter-gia-tis-times-ston-kathigiti-poy-eikrinei-tin-kritiki-antistas> (all in Greek).

32 See Heinz Richter, *Operation Merkur: Die Eroberung der Insel Kreta im Mai 1941* (Otto Harrassowitz 2011), 283–284, 285–286, 291 (in German). See also <http://tvxs.gr/news/apopseis/heinz-richter-epixeirisi-ermis-i-kataktisi-tis-kritis>.

33 See <www.grreporter.info/en/german_historian_trial_crete_his_research_world_war_ii/13688>.

34 For the respective news report on the trial hearings, see <www.28310.gr/rotator/articles/apallagi-tou-kathigiti-richter-proteine-o-eisaggeleas.html>. For an interview with Richter's defence counsel, see <www.lawspot.gr/nomika-nea/ypothesi-rihter-epistimoniki-ereyna-eleytheria-logoy-kai-ta-oria-toys>, and for an article written by the defence counsels, see <http://www.kathimerini.gr/849649/opinion/epikairothta/politikh/ypo8esh-rixter-mia-apotimhsh> (all in Greek).

Finally, the judgment of 10 February 2016 (Misdemeanour Court of Rethymno, Judgment No. 2383/2015) is particularly interesting in terms of the grounds given by the judge himself for acquitting Richter.[35] The judge did not examine in detail the facts of the case, specifically whether or not the expressions Richter had used in his book constitute a denial of an insulting nature of the Nazi crimes committed against the Cretan people. However, *inter alia* he did note that, in his opinion, the law of 2014 generally does not appear to contradict the fundamental rights and freedoms, insofar as the necessary condition for the punishment of the perpetrator is not only the public condonation or denial of crimes but also the probability that the conduct will incite violence or hatred, or be threatening or insulting.

Nevertheless, the judge thought there was another reason for declaring the provisions under consideration in violation of the Greek constitution. He noted that the crimes of the German invaders in Crete had been historically recognised not by an international criminal court but by specific legal acts of the Greek Parliament – a usual procedure in Greece in terms of genocide and mass atrocities. He then stated that the law of 2014 is contrary to the Greek constitution to the extent that such a parliamentary recognition of historical events suffices as a constitutive requirement for the crime of denial (although a similar condition is not included in the Framework Decision of 2008). The reason for this unconstitutionality is that the Greek Parliament is only authorised to symbolically or politically recognise the existence of mass atrocities and war crimes. In the opinion of the trial judge, however, such acts of recognition do not constitute rules of law in the narrow sense nor judicial decisions that can lead to the punishment of individuals. The judge argued that, in accordance with the principle of the separation of powers, it remains within the purview of the court to examine the existence as well as the legal characterisation of past conduct as crime. He further held that, in a democratic and pluralistic society, laws that recognise or 'create' historical facts cannot constitute a source of binding rules limiting the constitutional freedom of speech and academic freedom. Based on this finding of unconstitutionality, the Greek criminal court declared the defendant innocent.

Final thoughts

It is noteworthy that, in spite of the aforementioned judgment of acquittal, the University of Crete recently decided, also on the occasion of a provocative interview by Richter published in a Greek newspaper,[36] to revoke the honorary

35 For the (Greek) text of the Judgment no 2383/2015 (Misdemeanour Court of Rethymno), see <www.scribd.com/document/352791034/ΜονΠλημμΡεθ-2383-15>. See also <http://rethemnosnews.gr/2016/02/αθώος-ο-καθηγητής-ρίχτερ/> and <www.legalnews24.gr/2016/02/blog-post_95.html> (in Greek).

36 See below.

doctorate awarded to him.[37] With respect to this fact and the other issues highlighted above in the context of the judgment in the Richter case, a number of important overarching questions may be raised in terms of national, transnational, international, and transitional justice:

First, can history be recognised, protected, or 'created' by means of decisions, laws, and criminal laws made by parliament, especially considering that, in reality, even decisions of international criminal courts cannot always serve as accurate historical records? Is legalised history actually binding law with consequences for the individual? In other words, may parliamentary decisions and acts recognising the existence of historical atrocities assume the function of actual rules?

Second, do expressions and descriptions such as the ones used by Richter in his book actually constitute a denial of Nazi crimes? In this context, one should consider that the judicial task of deciding such questions may prove to be extremely difficult or even dangerous for legal certainty and legality, especially when it comes to beliefs and opinions having not always direct consequences in the outside world as well as to the preservation of fundamental principles such as the freedoms of speech and academic expression. That aside, should there be a ground of justification, at least regarding freedom-of-science cases?

Third, is the act of publishing a book that includes expressions and descriptions denying, for example, the Holocaust, a continuous crime? What about internet blog publications? This question is especially important with regard to the problems of the *lex-praevia* element of the principle of legality.

Finally, is it not preferable, also in terms of transitional justice, to settle problems and controversies about historical facts with the help of science and history, and outside of the courts, especially outside of the criminal courts, not least in order to avoid transnational political and diplomatic implications? The multiple layers of the *Richter* case might prove to be quite typical in this respect: Before his acquittal, Richter gave an interview to a Greek newspaper.[38] In this interview he spoke, among other things, about the destruction on Greek islands and in Greek villages caused by 'the Germans, the Italians, the communists and the nationalists'. He also noted that the Germans were in any case operating lawfully, i.e., in accordance with the rules of war. One could argue that this is moral relativism, an attempt to assign equal weight to the actions of the occupation forces and the local Greek guerrillas. In another interview after the trial against him, Professor Richter went on to say that, after his acquittal, he was called by a German Minister, in the context of the economic crisis, with the request to consult the German Government about the Greeks and their culture, specifically about the kind of

37 See <www.kathimerini.gr/861332/article/epikairothta/ellada/afaire8hke-apo-ton-xains-rixter-o-titlos-toy-epitimoy-didaktoros>.

38 Interview published at *ekathimerini-com* on 10 December 2015, see <www.ekathimerini.com/204196/article/ekathimerini/community/history-on-trial>.

people Greeks are.[39] On the topic of war reparations, Richter argued that they have already been paid to the Greek state and that, in the final analysis, it is the Greek state that owes Germany. Furthermore, in another remark the German professor claimed to be happy and honoured that his honorary doctorate was revoked by the Greek university, since, decades ago, the Nazis had also revoked Thomas Mann's honorary degree. However, Richter failed to acknowledge, at least in the interview at hand, that, while other national criminal justice systems might not hesitate to punish public (insulting or discrediting) expressions offhandedly comparing Nazis and contemporary universities or societies, Greece still has liberal judges who give priority to the constitutional freedoms of speech and scientific opinion over the undifferentiated application of an anti-hate and anti-racism criminal law.

39 Interview published in *Kathimerini* (newspaper) on 15 May 2016 (in Greek). For the whole interview in Greek, see <www.kathimerini.gr/859869/article/proswpa/geyma-me-thn-k/xains-rixter-oi-germanikes-apozhmiwseis-plhrw8hkan-kai-fagw8hkan>.

Part III

Comparative perspectives on corruption and financial crime

10 Relocating bribery

Facilitation payments as a crime against the market?

*Simon Bronitt**

Introduction

Peter Alldridge in his ground-breaking study of criminal law made the perceptive point that bribery can be defined

> [o]nly once it is established that arguments about bribery . . . are arguments about what sort of markets it is which are desired, rather than a matter of generalisation from some *a priori* moral truth about the behaviour of actors in markets.[1]

Alldridge's assessment formed part of a wider agenda of relocating criminal law, and in relation to bribery and other financial crimes such as insider trading, he proposed reconceiving the field as one of 'crimes against the market'.

Alldridge's relocation of anti-corruption law requires a more considered reflection on the purposes and effects of criminalisation, which in turn requires a wider 'no limits' interdisciplinary perspective that draws variously on history, regulatory theory, criminal justice and criminology. Responding to Alldridge's ambition for criminal law scholarship, this foray into anti-corruption law seeks to move beyond a law reform agenda fixated upon the promotion of criminalisation, codification and uniformity at the domestic and international level. Rather than the pursuit of legal formalism, with its inevitable 'obsession with definition',[2] this chapter promotes a regulatory reform agenda that bridges the traditional criminal/civil law divide, one that is neither hostile to legal hybridity nor pluralism in its evaluation of measures (both legal and non-legal) for combating corruption.

The first part of this chapter explores the multiple aims (or policy objectives) of contemporary anti-corruption law, tracing the significant impact of international

*I would like to thank Zoe Brereton for her excellent research assistance.

1 Peter Alldridge, *Relocating Criminal Law* (Ashgate 2000) 166.

2 As Lindsay Farmer points out, the dominance of this model of scholarship in the UK has meant that academic criminal law has rarely escaped from the task of rationalising its fundamental principles and definitions: 'The Obsession with Definition: The Nature of Crime and Critical Legal Theory' (1996) 5 *Social and Legal Studies* 57. An online version of this article can be accessed at <www.uk.sagepub.com/cross/files/Chapter1-Article2.pdf>.

treaties and conventions upon definitions (relating to key offences and defences), enforcement powers and legal remedies. A recurrent critique emerges concerning legal indeterminacy especially in relation to the fundamental definition of corruption.[3] The chapter explores the impact of legal indeterminacy through a case study on the legal status of facilitation payments in Australia, comparing relevant law, policy and practice in the United States and United Kingdom. Through an examination of the history, policies and practices relating to 'facilitation payments', the chapter evaluates the legitimacy of practices designed to 'grease' the wheels of international trade. Facilitation payments are not uncommon, though they continue to have hazy legal status globally, ranging from legally permissible or at least tolerated in some jurisdictions (United States and Australia), to potentially criminally corrupt in others (United Kingdom).

The second part then explores the impact of legal indeterminacy more generally on law enforcement policies and practices in relation to bribery. Legal scholars commonly claim that legal indeterminacy significantly hampers law enforcement action. As is the case within domestic legal systems, uncertainty about the scope and application of law at the transnational level is regularly resolved through negotiation (both informal and formal) between the parties. In transnational bribery cases, there are many 'pay-offs' for law enforcement agencies and corporations that pursue 'negotiated justice' outcomes. For both parties, out-of-court settlement agreements offer the 'pay-off' of avoiding the high costs and uncertainties associated with civil or criminal litigation. Another 'pay-off' is that such settlements contribute to national anti-corruption capacity building by creating significant revenue streams for the state, as well as law enforcement agencies, which will receive large sums from the payment of penalties, disgorgement of illegal profits/assets and reimbursement of costs related to the investigation.[4] There is, of course, the potential pitfall that settlements are seen by the wider community and civil society organisations as simply another corporate 'pay-off'; put crudely, a form of legalised 'bribe' offered to the state to defer or terminate enforcement action without the defendant admitting any liability.[5]

3 This aspect of the debate resonates with the controversy over the definition of terrorism that has hampered building international consensus in international criminal law.

4 While consistent with the user-pays principle, the corporation's offer to reimburse investigation costs incurred may place regulatory agencies under undue pressure to 'cut a deal' in cases where the evidence disclosed and public interest ordinarily would support prosecution rather than settlement. There is a risk that such settlements will undermine public confidence in the administration of justice, amounting to an abuse of process: see Simon Bronitt and Zoe Brereton, Submission to The Senate Legal and Constitutional Affairs Legislation Committee, *Crimes Legislation Amendment (Combatting Corporate Crime) Bill 2017*, 14 March 2018.

5 Negotiations may involve corporations striking a 'global settlement' involving multiple regulatory agencies across borders. The US Department of Justice brokered such a deal relating to allegations that Innospec, a firm with operations in the US and UK, had bribed officials in Indonesia. As part of the settlement, Innospec pleaded guilty to conspiracy to corrupt

Negotiating settlements is often beyond the reach of courts. Though less visible, settlements should not be viewed as 'exceptional' or 'deviant' aspects of our regulatory system. As this chapter concludes, processes of negotiated justice, as a form of self-regulation between the parties, may be unavoidable, though this does not mean that these practices should remain unregulated.[6]

The basic thrust of my argument is that the contemporary policy priority attached to criminalisation and legal formalism is misplaced: regulatory pluralism and legal hybridity (which innovatively melds civil and criminal law measures) does *not* impede law enforcement per se. Drawing on insights from the field of regulatory studies, the chapter challenges common regulatory assumptions that underpin much of the architecture of global anti-corruption law (both international and domestic), policies and practices (both corporate and government). The conclusion is that legal *form* is less important than legal *legitimacy*, which in our assessment, rests on the twin policy values of effectiveness (establishing what 'works') and respect for fundamental human rights (establishing what is 'fair').

Relocating anti-corruption law: crime against global markets

Laws proscribing corruption are not new. As Alldridge points out, offering and receiving bribes and misuse of public office are some of the earliest public wrongs known to the criminal law.[7] Like many common law crimes, its underlying rationale for criminalisation has imperceptibly shifted over time to accommodate changing social, political and economic conditions.[8] As earlier sociolegal studies

Indonesian officials in *R v Innospec Ltd* [2010] EW Misc 7 (EWCC). Thomas LJ trenchantly criticised the terms of the plea deal, where Innospec agreed to paying a penalty in the UK not exceeding US$12.7 million. In his sentencing remarks, Thomas LJ pointed out that under English law, judicial sentencing autonomy could not be fettered in this way, though 'reluctantly' sentenced in accordance with the agreement. Admonishing the Serious Fraud Office, he directed that no further agreements should be negotiated. Pre-trial negotiations have since been placed on a statutory basis, with judicial oversight of the process, with the introduction of a Deferred Prosecution Agreement scheme by the *Crime and Court Acts 2013* (UK).

6 Self-regulation itself may be subject to regulation, what some regulatory theorists call 'meta-regulation': Cary Coglianese and Evan Mendelson, 'Meta-Regulation and Self-Regulation' in Robert Baldwin, Martin Cave and Martin Lodge (eds), *The Oxford Handbook on Regulation* (Oxford University Press 2010). After reviewing the various definitions, Coglianese and Mendelson conclude that meta-regulation 'focuses very much on outside regulators but also incorporates the insight from self-regulation that targets themselves can be sources of their own constraint. Meta-regulation refers to ways that outside regulators deliberately – rather than unintentionally – seek to induce targets to develop their own internal, self-regulatory responses to public problems'.

7 Alldridge (n 1) 178, noting that the offences date back to the thirteenth and fourteenth centuries.

8 See Bruce Buchan and Lisa Hill, *An Intellectual History of Political Corruption* (Palgrave Macmillan 2014) 9.

have demonstrated, legal evolution often occurs without courts acknowledging explicitly major societal transformations.[9]

Early corruption offences were conceived as abuses of *public* office, with bribery viewed as a breach of the duties of fidelity owed by state officials to their sovereign. The criminal law thus focused on outlawing the corruption of judges, jurors and other officers of the Crown. Criminalising corruption within the private sector in the twentieth century extended the 'breach of duty' rationale to the 'private' relationship between corporations and their agents/employees. An alternative rationale for the criminalisation of corruption is 'market protection', from which Alldridge drew his concept of a 'criminal law of markets'. The harms of corruption are thus conceived as being economic rather than moral or political,[10] with bribery amounting to a 'fraud on the market'.[11] On this view, corruption offences have a financial integrity rationale that seeks to prevent and deter conduct that distorts economic competition within local and global markets. As explored below, the drivers of contemporary corruption law are increasingly linked with globalisation: the emergence of a global economy, mobility of people and capital, and the need to promote uniformity of legal standards across markets.[12] There are, of course, other rationales, such as the promotion of international development and respect for human rights.[13] In recent decades, this rationale, promoted by Transparency International and other non-governmental organisations, is driving global anti-corruption strategies.[14]

9 Jerome Hall, in his landmark study of the law of theft, traced the changing conception of property interests, extending tangible goods and chattels to include a wider range of frauds involving intangible property within the credit economy of the nineteenth century, see Jerome Hall, *Theft, Law and Society* (Little, Brown & Co 1935).

10 Cf Tom Campbell, 'The Normative Grounding of Corporate Social Responsibility: A Human Rights Approach' in Doreen McBarnet, Aurora Voiculescu and Tom Campbell (eds), *The New Corporate Accountability: Corporate Social Responsibility and the Law* (Cambridge University Press 2007) 537 who drew attention to the often 'overlooked … moral justification of the pursuit of profit in a market system'. Campbell proposed that 'the pursuit of profitability within market norms may itself be regarded as a socially beneficial activity, certainly in a market economy'.

11 Ibid. 181.

12 Stephen Bottomley and Simon Bronitt, *Law in Context* (4th edn, Federation Press 2012) Ch 15.

13 A number of scholars have sought to position anti-corruption efforts in the human rights sphere. For example, Maina Kiai and Anthony Kuria, 'The Human Rights Dimensions of Corruption: Linking the Human Rights Paradigm to Combat Corruption' (2008) 4 (3) *Journal of Global Ethics* 247, 247. For arguments in favour of enacting a right to live in a society free from 'official corruption', see Mathew Murray and Andrew Spalding, 'Freedom from Official Corruption as a Human Right' (2015) Governance Studies At Brookings 1, and David Kinley, A New Human Right to Freedom from Corruption (9 February 2014) Sydney Law School Research Paper No. 14/12. Available at SSRN: <https://ssrn.com/abstract=2393205> or <http://dx.doi.org/10.2139/ssrn.2393205>.

14 Indeed, in 2016, Transparency International identified that the nexus between corrupt practices and inequality has been of primary importance in recent national election campaigns: Finn Heinrich, *Corruption and Inequality: How Populists Mislead People* (25 January 2017)

The global anti-corruption movement has generated a plethora of international treaties and conventions that, in turn, have shaped domestic law and policy in many legal systems including Australia, Europe and the United States.[15] Australia provides a case study on how domestic law has responded to these international legal obligations. Over the past two decades, federal offences have been drafted specifically to implement Australia's international obligations in the field, including the following conventions: (1) United Nations Convention Against Corruption (UNCAC); (2) Organisation for Economic Co-operation and Development (OECD) Convention on Combating Bribery of Foreign Public Officials in International Business Transactions; and (3) United Nations Convention Against Transnational Organised Crime (UNCTOC).[16] For example, the Criminal Code Amendment (Bribery of Foreign Public Officials) Act 1999 (Cth) (BFPO), implemented Australia's obligations under the OECD Convention. The BFPO amended the federal Criminal Code, inserting a new offence of bribery of foreign public officials (s 70.2 Criminal Code).[17] In December 2017, the Crimes Legislation Amendment (Combatting Corporate Crime) Bill was introduced to Parliament including possible amendments to the foreign bribery offence. There are two specific defences that apply to the offences of foreign bribery: (1) the defence of lawful conduct under foreign law (also known as the 'foreign law defence'); and (2) the facilitation payment defence. An advantage of the federal offences, compared with the State level anti-corruption laws, is that they apply across all (nine) Australian jurisdictions, as well as extending to conduct beyond its territorial borders.

Regulating facilitation payments: towards a global consensus?

International legal efforts have largely focused on building consensus around model laws for corruption and associated conduct, encouraging the adoption of harmonised (or functionally equivalent) laws governing the investigation, criminalisation, prosecution and punishment. However, global consensus over the fundamental definitional

Transparency International <www.transparency.org/news/feature/corruption_and_inequality_how_populists_mislead_people>.

15 See Adam Graycar and Russell G Smith (eds), *Handbook of Global Research and Practice in Corruption* (Edward Elgar 2011).

16 Under the Australian Constitution, the federal Parliament does not have a plenary power to enact criminal law. That said, federal Parliament, relying upon its foreign affairs power in the Constitution, may enact criminal laws to implement the terms of binding international treaties: see generally, Simon Bronitt, 'The Criminal Law of Australia' in Kevin Jon Heller and Markus D Dubber (eds), *The Handbook of Comparative Criminal Law* (Stanford University Press 2010).

17 Under s 70.2(1) of the Criminal Code (Cth) a person is guilty of the offence if that person 'provides', 'causes', 'offers to provide, or promises to provide' or 'causes an offer of the provision of a benefit, or a promise of the provision of a benefit' that 'is not legitimately due to the other person', and 'with the intention of influencing a foreign public official (who may be the other person) in the exercise of the official's duties as a foreign public official', to 'obtain or retain business' or 'obtain or retain a business advantage that is not legitimately due to the recipient, or intended recipient, of the business advantage'.

question – what is and is *not* corruption – has proved elusive.[18] A significant area of divergence in national legal approaches to transnational corruption relates to the law and policies governing facilitation payments made to foreign public officials.

Facilitation payments have been defined as 'unofficial payments made to public officials in order to secure or expedite the performance of a routine or necessary action'.[19] They are known colloquially as 'speed money', 'grease payments' or 'oiling the wheels'.[20] In Australia, facilitation payments may be exempted from prosecution by the defence contained in section 70.4 of the federal *Criminal Code* (Cth). The defence only applies where the value of the payment made to a foreign public official was of a 'minor nature'[21] and 'the conduct was engaged in for the sole or dominant purpose of expediting or securing the performance of a routine government action of a minor nature'.[22] Additionally, the defence requires that the person making or receiving the payment must make a record of the conduct as soon as practicable after the conduct occurred.[23]

The facilitation payment defence is controversial since it legitimises practices that would otherwise be corrupt. There have been calls for its abolition in Australia and the United States as a matter of sound public policy and best practice in international commercial dealings.[24] The key argument favouring abolition is that it would communicate an unambiguous policy stance on the criminality of making or receiving such payments, irrespective of the size, frequency or effect of these payments.[25]

The Australian inclusion of the facilitation payment defence was influenced by the United States' Foreign Corrupt Practices Act of 1977 (FCPA). The defence was inserted in order to prevent American corporations being placed at an economic disadvantage compared to competitors in jurisdictions that were not legally restrained from making such payments. Although at the time the FCPA placed the United States at the forefront of the global movement to stamp out foreign bribery,[26] the preservation of the exception for small and routine facilitation payments has been viewed as a serious weakness. As one commentator

18 As Graycar and Smith note, 'in many respects corruption is like an elephant – it's easier to identify than it is to describe!': (n 15) 6.

19 *Bribery Act 2010: Joint Prosecution Guidance of the Director of the Serious Fraud Office and the Director of Public Prosecutions* (Serious Fraud Office 2010) 8.

20 Ross P Buckley and Mark Danielson, 'Facilitation Payments in International Business: A Proposal to Make Criminal Code, s 70.4, Workable' (2008) 82 *Australian Law Journal* 92, 95.

21 See s 70.4(1)(a), Criminal Code (Cth).

22 See s 70.4(1)(b), Criminal Code (Cth).

23 See ss 70.4(1)(c) and 70.4(3), Criminal Code (Cth).

24 In the US context, see Chad Bonstead, 'Removing the FCPA Facilitation Payments Exception: Enforcement Tools for a Cleaner Business as Usual' (2014) 36 *Houston Journal of International Law* 503, 506.

25 In the Australian context, see Simon Bronitt, 'Policing Corruption and Corporations in Australia: Towards a New National Agenda' (2013) 37 *Criminal Law Journal* 283.

26 Bonstead argues that the FCPA was a 'clear statement of leadership for the United States in the international fight against corrupt payments to government officials': Bonstead (n 24) 505.

recently noted, '[t]he United States has lost some of its global anti-corruption leadership status because of this exception, and it is time for an amendment to the FCPA removing it'.[27]

In the Australian context, there is no official guidance on what constitutes a facilitation payment of a 'minor nature'.[28] Unlike the FCPA, the Australian regulatory model does not prospectively 'vet' the legality of facilitation payments.[29] The effect is that corporations subject to the jurisdiction of the federal Criminal Code must make their own assessment as to whether any proposed payment satisfies the two limbs of the defence, namely, that (a) the payment is of a 'minor nature', and (b) serves the sole or dominant purpose of facilitating 'routine government action'. There is a risk that, in the absence of judicial consideration of the defence, some corporations and their advisors may adopt a self-serving approach, assessing the 'significance' of the proposed payment relative to the overall value of the international transaction. In our view, this approach fails to acknowledge that even low value payments can have significant distorting effects on the decision-making of foreign officials, especially from developing countries where officials are often very poorly paid.[30]

There is a further risk that corporations will engage in what criminologists have called 'creative adaptation' where potential offenders constantly restructure their activities in order to lawfully circumvent or avoid the application of new regulations.[31] Thus, corporations may attempt to disguise larger facilitation payments by 're-packaging' them as series of smaller payments of a 'minor nature'. Overly stringent regulation may produce, in the words of leading criminologist Peter Grabosky, a class of 'avoidance entrepreneurs', in which sadly '[s]ome of the nation's best minds are thus mobilized to defeat the ends of public policy'.[32]

The United Kingdom, unlike Australia and the United States, has not recognised a facilitation payment defence.[33] That said, prosecutors in England and Wales have not pursued a strict law enforcement approach against facilitation

27 Ibid. 506.

28 Buckley and Danielson (n 20) 92.

29 See US Department of Justice and US Securities and Exchange Commission, *A Resource Guide to the U.S. Foreign Corrupt Practices Act* (2012) 25–26, which provides explicit guidance and examples of when transactions fall within the 'facilitating or expediting payments' exception.

30 The legislation does, however, include detailed guidance on what constitutes routine government activity with a lengthy (non-exhaustive) list of examples: s 70.4(1), Criminal Code (Cth). In the US context, 'routine services are generally regarded as "ministerial", or those for which the government official has no discretion': Bonstead (n 24) 507.

31 Peter Grabosky, 'Counterproductive Regulation' (1995) 23 *International Journal of the Sociology of Law* 347, 349.

32 Ibid.

33 'There is no exemption in respect of facilitation payments. They were illegal under the previous legislation and the common law and remain so under the Act': *Bribery Act 2010: Joint Prosecution Guidance* (n 19) 9.

payments, preferring to promote voluntary disclosure of facilitation payments by corporations, and to invoke the Crown Prosecutors' discretion not to proceed with a prosecution in the public interest.[34] To that end, the law enforcement and prosecution authorities have issued joint guidelines governing the Bribery Act 2010 (UK) that set the range of public interest factors that may be considered specifically in relation to the decision to prosecute foreign bribery. These factors are cross-referenced with the general public interest considerations contained in the Code for Crown Prosecution: see Appendix. In the next section, I explore how legal indeterminacy impacts regulation. Drawing insights from criminology, I examine the range of administrative practices that have developed to structure negotiations between corporations and regulatory authorities over allegations of transnational corporate corruption.

Socio-legal perspectives on legal indeterminacy, regulation and administrative justice

Legal certainty is regarded as a fundamental legal right and value in most legal systems, a vital aspect of the Rule of Law. Uncertainty is viewed as an anathema to the predictability of legal outcomes. Legal certainty, in this traditional view, is essential to curbing the exercise of arbitrary state power,[35] and in some jurisdictions, like the United States, the principle has been elevated to a constitutional principle that voids legislation for vagueness.[36] Criminological research, however, suggests that legal uncertainty or indeterminacy does not necessarily hamper either law enforcement action or the stability of legal orders generally. Empirical studies reveal that both rule-making and interpretation is not exclusively in the hands of the legislature and judiciary.[37] Across many fields, *administrative* rule-making and interpretation by regulatory authorities and public officials operate as curatives for legal uncertainty. Administrative guidance can be found in delegated legislation, as well as in guidelines and codes of practice. In relation to the latter, research has revealed that administrative interpretations may be highly novel, suggesting that legal

34 Ibid.

35 An influential proponent of this view was AV Dicey, the nineteenth-century English constitutional law scholar, who sought to distinguish between the rule of law, which is 'the absolute supremacy or predominance of regular law as opposed to the influence of arbitrary power, and excludes the existence of arbitrariness, of prerogative, or even of wide discretionary authority on the part of the government. Englishmen are ruled by the law, and by the law alone': AV Dicey, *An Introduction to the Study of the Law of the Constitution* (10th edn, Palgrave Macmillan 1965) 202, cited in Daniel Kalderimis, Chris Nixon and Tim Smith, *Certainty and Discretion in New Zealand Regulation* <www.regulatorytoolkit.ac.nz/topics-of-regulatory-interest/reducing-uncertainty-consumers>.

36 See for example, *Morales v Chicago* 527 US 41 (1999) per Stevens J at 56: 'Vagueness may invalidate a criminal law for either of two independent reasons. First, it may fail to provide the kind of notice that will enable ordinary people to understand what conduct it prohibits; second, it may authorize and even encourage arbitrary and discriminatory enforcement.'

37 For a review of the leading studies see Bottomley and Bronitt (n 12) Ch 10.

rules can be operationalised in ways (and for purposes) unintended by the legislature and courts.[38] The existence of administrative interpretation is not simply an echo of the 'gap' between the 'law in the books' and the 'law in action' earlier identified by legal realist scholars. Rather, the 'gap' is better viewed as being *constitutive* of the law and its processes. David Dixon, in his study of Australian and English policing, concluded that the law was not conceived by the police as a 'rule book' to be either followed or ignored, but rather as a 'tool' or normative resource used to advance public order, crime prevention and detection.[39] In relation to corruption, this 'gap' constitutes the legal spaces within which state officials conduct negotiations with potential offenders, in this case transnational corporations and their legal advisors. As research on domestic plea-bargaining reveals, legal uncertainties relating to procedural, substantive, and sentencing law provide significant incentives and resources for engaging the parties in charging and plea negotiations.[40] Indeed, the trend toward negotiated outcomes in the criminal law has intensified in the late twentieth century; the 'punitive turn' in criminal justice sought to curb judicial discretion through mandatory sentencing, a trend that 'has shifted power away from the judge to the prosecutor, as the charge prosecuted determines the sentence that must be passed'.[41] This has been further exacerbated by the increased use of aggravated offences and mandatory minimum sentences under which the prosecutor's choice of offence significantly limits the range of sentencing options for the court.[42]

As noted above, in cases of transnational corporate corruption, there is a wide scope for negotiation between state officials, prosecution authorities and potential corporate offenders over jurisdiction, legal liability and outcomes. As studies of the domestic criminal justice system above reveal, practices of negotiated justice pose a range of ethical and regulatory hazards. In the next section, I examine the extent to which the role of discretion (whether exercised by law enforcement or prosecution authorities) in negotiating settlements has itself been 'corrupted', and what safeguards, if any, operate to guard against misuses of public power. As noted above, one method for minimising such risks is to develop guidelines and policies, such as those which constrain prosecution discretion in relation to the Bribery Act 2010 (UK).[43]

38 David Dixon, *Law in Policing: Legal Regulation and Police Practices* (Oxford University Press 1997).

39 Ibid.

40 The classic UK study is John Baldwin and Michael McConville, *Negotiated Justice: Pressures to Plead Guilty* (Martin Robertson 1977).

41 Jacqueline Hodgson and Andrew Roberts, 'Criminal Process and Prosecution' in Peter Cane and Herbert Kritzer (eds), *The Oxford Handbook of Empirical Legal Research* (Oxford University Press 2010) 64, 81. As the authors notes the research suggests that 'plea bargaining makes the prosecutor, not the court, responsible for case disposition to a large extent': ibid. 89.

42 The High Court in *Magaming v The Queen* [2013] HCA 40 held, by majority, that the decision of a prosecutor to charge an aggravated offence of people smuggling (20 years maximum imprisonment), rather than the basic offence (5 years mandatory minimum), was 'neither incompatible with the separation of judicial and prosecutorial functions nor incompatible with the institutional integrity of the courts': per French CJ at [40].

43 *Bribery Act 2010: Joint Prosecution Guidance* (n 19).

Public officials are not the only actors participating in this negotiation process. An army of in-house lawyers and professional advisors also play a role in managing 'legal risk' for corporations. Like law enforcement officials, these corporate advisors act as 'gatekeepers' through the way that they 'translate' their clients' instructions into legal claims and defences. In this sense, lawyers acting as corporate advisors retain discretion in how they approach their professional role: on the one hand, they may adopt a highly ethical stance on corporate compliance with anti-corruption law (consistent with corporate social responsibility); on the other hand, they may become 'avoidance entrepreneurs' who devise legal risk management strategies that exploit legal gaps and regulatory loopholes. In light of the relative rarity of enforcement action, there is a risk that adverse legal outcomes (investigation, prosecution or conviction) may be viewed by corporations as another 'transaction cost' associated with engaging in global business – just another cost of doing business.

To sum up, adopting a sociolegal perspective reveals that there is more to an effective system of regulation than simply promoting legal certainty and uniformity. Legal compliance is rarely the outcome of simple rational actor calculations that balance the 'costs' of being caught against the 'benefits' flowing from non-compliance. It is well known that deterrence models typically over-estimate the regulatory power of enforcement, prosecution, conviction and sentencing on actor behaviour.[44] Research on compliance shows that many other factors come into play, including social and cultural mores, concern about reputation and maintaining legitimacy 'in the eyes of government, industry peers, and the public'.[45] Indeed, a systematic review of available research concluded that, contrary to the claims of regulators, prosecutors, judges, economists and legal scholars, the evidence did not conclusively establish that legal sanctions have significant deterrent effects on corporations.[46] Clearly then, depending on the particular legal setting, higher levels of compliance may be achieved through the voluntary use of agreements,[47] and

44 Bottomley and Bronitt (n 12).

45 Christine Parker and John Braithwaite, 'Regulation' in Mark Tushnet and Peter Cane (eds), *The Oxford Handbook of Legal Studies* (Oxford University Press 2003) 119, 131.

46 The systematic review reported that the deterrent effects upon corporations were 'mixed': Sally S. Simpson, Melissa Rorie, Mariel Alper, Natalie Schell-Busey, *Corporate Crime Deterrence: A Systematic Review* (Campbell Systematic Review 2014).

47 In Australia, in the 1980s, such corporate regulators favoured compliance through informal negotiations, rather than using court processes: Roman Tomasic and Stephen Bottomley, *Directing the Top 500: Corporate Governance and Accountability in Australian Companies* (Allen and Unwin 1993) 129. Undertakings are now enforceable before the courts through provisions inserted into the *Australian Securities and Investments Commission Act 2001* and the *Trade Practices Act 1974*. On the latter, see Christine Parker, 'Restorative Justice in Business Regulation? The Australian Competition and Consumer Commission's Use of Enforceable Undertakings' (2004) 67 *Modern Law Review* 209.

audits.[48] Other fields of corruption provide some salutary lessons in this respect: James Jacobs and Kerry Cooperman in their study of organised crime within the American labor movement concluded that civil actions and settlements under the Racketeer Influenced and Corrupt Organizations Act (RICO) 'achieved in just three years what decades of criminal prosecutions had failed to achieve'.[49]

Negotiating bribery and corruption in the 'shadow of the law': payoffs and pitfalls

Prosecutions of transnational bribery and corruption are a costly and relatively rare occurrence. Indeed, there is a strong trend towards negotiating out-of-court settlements, where multinational corporations offer a large 'without prejudice' payment in exchange for the prosecution deferring or discontinuing legal action against the corporation and its employees. A Bill, currently before the Australian Federal Parliament, proposes the adoption of a Deferred Prosecution Agreement (DPA) scheme as part of a broader policy encouraging self-reporting of criminal conduct.[50] It would, however, be wrong to assume that out-of-court settlements are extra-legal processes – as noted above, such negotiations about legal liability – both civil and criminal – occur 'in the shadow of the law'.[51] Legal norms (both domestic and international) are used as 'bargaining chips' in negotiations over civil and criminal liability, and determining the appropriate amount agreed to be paid in settlement of the matter.

The precise legal status of these settlements varies across jurisdictions, and depending on the jurisdiction the terms may not be disclosed to the public. Two notable examples reported in the media include:

- the US$100 million settlement between Mr Bernie Ecclestone and German authorities in 2014.[52] Mr Ecclestone, who allegedly made significant bribes to secure Formula 1 contracts, made the payment in exchange for the prosecution dropping pending corruption charges. The agreement, though

48 See e.g. Christine Parker, 'Regulator-Required Corporate Compliance Program Audits' (2003) 25 *Law and Policy* 221.

49 James B Jacobs and Kerry T Cooperman, *Breaking the Devil's Pact: the Battle to Free the Teamsters from the Mob* (NYU Press 2011) 213. See also James B Jacobs, *Mobsters, Unions, and Feds: The Mafia and the American Labor Movement* (NYU Press 2006).

50 See Crimes Legislation Amendment (Combatting Corporate Crime) Bill 2017 (Cth), introduced 6 December 2017.

51 This phrase was first coined in the context of family law settlements: see Robert Mnookin and Lewis Kornhauser, 'Bargaining in the Shadow of the Law: The Case of Divorce' (1979) 88 *Yale Law Journal* 950.

52 Reports of the size of the settlement varied: Reuters reported a settlement of £74.7 million (US $100 million), while the *Daily Mail* reported only £60 million: Jörn Poltz, Ecclestone Trial Halted After F1 Boss Agrees to $100 Million Settlement *Daily Mail* (online) 4 August 2014<http://uk.reuters.com/article/2014/08/05/uk-germany-ecclestone-trial-idUKKBN0G50N120140805>.

lawful in Germany, attracted significant criticism from non-government organisations.[53]

- the US$46 million settlement between Siemens and the Nigerian Government, concluded on 22 November 2010, in relation to alleged illegal payments by Siemens to Nigerian public officials between 2002 and 2005.[54]

What safeguards, if any, exist to prevent misuse of settlement processes? As noted above, there is a wide margin of discretion in how regulatory authorities and corporations negotiate liability and legal outcomes more generally.-[55] While settlements offer clear advantages to the parties – avoiding lengthy litigation – there is a danger that they send inconsistent messages (to both offenders and the general public) about the wrongfulness and gravity of corruption. Indeed, examined closely, the DPAs or settlements with corporations in the US and UK, though often revealing high levels of culpability, often relate to lesser charges linked to regulatory lapses, such as breaching 'books and records' and 'false accounting' offences, or in the UK, the broad strict liability offence of 'failure to prevent foreign bribery'.

A recent example of this type of global settlement for transnational corporate crime is the agreement entered into by Takata Corporation with the US Department of Justice (DOJ) in late 2017. The Takata Corporation had falsified safety tests of defective airbags, which had been linked to 12 consumer deaths and over 100 injuries.[56] According to the company's admissions, it knew that certain inflators were not meeting the specifications required and were rupturing during testing:

> Takata induced its customers to purchase these airbag systems by submitting false and fraudulent reports and other information that concealed the true condition of the inflators... Takata employees – including a number of key executives – routinely discussed the falsification of test

53 News of the Ecclestone settlement attracted the stern criticism from Transparency International: 'We need the law itself as a disincentive to bribery and corruption, and such settlements are a worrying trend, because we could see that more and more companies and individuals look for this way out': Simon Tomlinson, 'Bernie Ecclestone Pays £60 Million to Get Bribery Charge Dropped: F1 Boss Had Faced 10 Years in a German Jail' *Daily Mail* (online) 5 August 2014 quoting Robin Hodess <www.dailymail.co.uk/news/article-2716392/Prosecutors-agree-drop-Bernie-Ecclestone-bribery-charges-pays-60million-Deal-table-F1-boss-offered-20m-settle-corruption-trial.html>.

54 See Stolen Asset Recovery Initiative, 'Asset Recovery Watch' <http://star.worldbank.org/corruption-cases/node/18447>.

55 See Simon Bronitt and Philip Stenning, 'Understanding Discretion in Modern Policing' (2011) 35(6) *Criminal Law Journal* 319 reviewing the scope and limits governing police decision-making relating to investigation and prosecution.

56 Takata fined $1bn in US over exploding airbag scandal' *BBC News* (online) 13 January 2017 <www.bbc.com/news/business-38613030>.

> reports being provided to [their] customers in email and in verbal communications.[57]

The settlement and Takata's guilty plea was represented in the media release as a 'major win' for the DOJ, noting the serious nature of the conduct 'including the approximate 15-year duration of the fraud, the pervasiveness of the scheme into the executive level of management and the potential risk the fraud posed to drivers and passengers'.[58] Yet the seriousness of the dishonesty and risks to public safety sit uneasily with the charge of the offence of conspiring to commit wire-fraud – a lesser ancillary offence that criminalises transmissions by means of a wire, radio or television, communications about a fraudulent scheme,[59] and that does not differentiate between different degrees of corporate culpability.

Falling back on strict or no-fault liability ancillary offences as 'bargaining chips' in the negotiating process undermines a fundamental tenet of criminalisation that requires distinctions to be drawn between types of crime and penalties based on different levels of culpability (known as the 'representative' or 'fair labelling principle').[60] As a normative ideal, this principle aims to ensure that 'widely felt distinctions between kinds of offences and degrees of wrongdoing are respected and signalled by the law, and that offences are subdivided and labelled so as to represent fairly the nature and magnitude of the law-breaking'.[61] This differentiation performs a symbolic function: 'it can symbolise the degree of condemnation that should be attributed to the offender and signals to society how that particular offender should be regarded'.[62]

The increasing regulatory reliance upon charges that are light in both moral stigma and particulars as to the extent of company wrongdoing has been exposed by Jesse Eisinger's recent bestseller, where he paints a damning profile of regulatory culture within the Security Exchange Commission (SEC) and DOJ. In Eisinger's assessment, there is a professional caste of young lawyers working in these agencies who have become risk averse to prosecution, resorting to plea bargains, settlements and DPAs as the default

57 US Department of Justice, 'Takata Corporation Agrees to Plead Guilty and Pay $1 Billion in Criminal Penalties for Airbag Scheme: Three Takata Executives Charged with Wire Fraud and Conspiracy' (13 January 2017).

58 Ibid.

59 USC s 1343.

60 Andrew Ashworth, *Principles of Criminal Law* (OUP 2006) 88–90; James Chalmers and Fiona Leverick, 'Fair Labelling in Criminal Law' (2008) 71(2) *Modern Law Review* 217.

61 Ibid.

62 Ibid. For a discussion of how the strict liability element of the proposed offence of 'failure to prevent foreign bribery' included in the new Bill violates the 'representative' or 'fair labelling' principle, see Bronitt and Brereton (n 3).

regulatory response. Their fear that prosecutions might fail, tarnishing otherwise unblemished conviction records, produces a culture of regulatory timidity, or in Eisinger's colourful terms, the 'Chickenshit Club'.[63] It is this regulatory culture that explains the waning public confidence in corporate regulation in the US, where white-collar crime prosecutions are at a 20 year low, and the view that the DPA is a 'progressive legal instrument… [that] has been repurposed as a vehicle for facilitating corporate impunity'.[64]

The effectiveness of settlements in cross-jurisdictional cases is also problematic. A recent study commissioned by the World Bank and United Nations Office of Drugs and Crime (UNODC) analysed 395 settlements between 1999 and 2012.[65] The study found that settlements in foreign bribery cases, though increasingly common across both civil and common law jurisdictions, have not led to any significant repatriation of illicit assets/funds to those jurisdictions most affected by the alleged bribery. Although the total settlement values amounted to US$6.9 billion imposed against companies and individuals, nearly US$6 billion comprised settlements that had been concluded in a jurisdiction *different* from that of the allegedly bribed foreign public officials. The study found that a very small (3%) percentage of those settlements – worth only US$197 million – were returned to the jurisdiction whose officials were accused of accepting bribes.

Conclusion: facilitation payments as a crime against global markets

The lack of a global legal consensus surrounding facilitation payments spawned a profession of specialist legal advisors and intermediaries employed to 'push the limits' of transnational corruption law. On a cynical view, this caste of 'avoidance entrepreneurs' merely assist corporations to maintain outwardly a public commitment to combating foreign corruption, while privately facilitating corporate illegality by exploiting gaps and loopholes in the law. In the event that enforcement action looms, these entrepreneurs stand ready to negotiate 'without prejudice' settlements with state regulatory authorities. Attempting to ban settlements, however, is impractical bearing in mind its prevalence generally across legal systems, as well as the significant 'payoffs' for

63 Jesse Eisinger, *The Chickenshit Club: Why the Justice Department Fails to Prosecute Executives* (Simon and Schuster, 2017).

64 Patrick Radden Keefe, 'Why Corrupt Bankers Avoid Jail: Prosecution of White-Collar Crime is at a Twenty-Year Low' *The New Yorker* (online) 31 July 2017 <www.newyorker.com/magazine/2017/07/31/why-corrupt-bankers-avoid-jail>.

65 Jacinta Anyango Oduor, Francisca M. U. Fernando, Agustin Flah, Dorothee Gottwald, Jeanne M. Hauch, Marianne Mathias, Ji Won Park and Oliver Stolpe, *Left out of the Bargain: Settlements in Foreign Bribery Cases and Implications for Asset Recovery* (World Bank Publications 2014) <http://star.worldbank.org/star/publication/left-out-bargain-settlements-foreign-bribery-cases-and-implications-asset-recovery>.

the parties. There are, of course, 'pitfalls', some of which we have identified above. I have argued elsewhere that the negotiation and settlement process at present is not adequately regulated – its objectives are not defined, and the discretion exercised by the regulatory and law enforcement bodies is subject to either no meaningful control or review by the courts (as in the US), or in schemes where judges have some administrative review (as in the UK), these models risk infringing the separation of powers doctrine.[66] This legitimacy lacuna must be rectified as a matter of priority.

My core message in this chapter is that hybrid forms of regulation (such as settlements and DPAs) should not be viewed as deficient simply because they fail to conform to the criminal law trial-based paradigm of prosecution, conviction and punishment. As in other areas of the legal system, hybrid laws are here to stay, and in our view, such laws should be judged from the perspective of legitimacy, which, in our assessment, rests on the twin policy values of effectiveness (establishing what 'works') and respect for fundamental human rights (establishing what is 'fair'). As this case study revealed, contemporary scholarly debate to date has largely missed the point, trapped within a paradigm of legal formalism that proselytises uniformity and codification of universal legal norms. This paradigm is unlikely to be successful, not only because of the inherent pluralism of domestic legal orders, but also because it distracts the policy community from the following, more fundamental, questions: namely, what are the (multiple) aims of anti-corruption laws, and which measures are most likely to be effective and legitimate in changing the behaviour of states, corporations, private individuals and public officials engaged in corruption? In relation to legitimacy, the significance of symbolism should not be understated – and in this respect, the continued development of international treaties and global policing cooperation to combat corruption will play a significant role. As leading criminal law theorist, Nicola Lacey perceptively notes, since the instrumental effects of criminalisation are often uncertain, the distinctive regulatory contribution of the criminal law lies not in its standard-setting function, but rather in its conferral of legitimacy, 'one of the key symbolic resources of any regulatory system'. Future research agendas in relation to 'crimes against the market' must be relocated to address these broader questions.

66 For an overview of the DPA, and the differences between the US administrative model and UK judicial model, see Simon Bronitt, 'Regulatory Bargaining in the Shadows of Preventive Justice: Deferred Prosecution Agreements' in Tamara Tulich, Rebecca Ananian-Welsh, Simon Bronitt and Sarah Murray (eds), *Regulating Preventive Justice: Principle, Policy and Paradox* (Routledge 2017) 211–226. The proposed Australian model, discussed above at n 47, avoids infringing separation of powers, which is constitutionally entrenched, by vesting the independent oversight role in a retired judicial officer.

Appendix

Extracts from *Bribery Act 2010: Joint Prosecution Guidance of the Director of the Serious Fraud Office and the Director of Public Prosecutions* (Serious Fraud Office 2010) 9.

Public interest considerations:

Prevention of bribery of foreign public officials is a significant policy aspect of the Act. In the context of facilitation payments, the following public interest factors tending in favour of and against prosecution may be relevant. A prosecution will usually take place unless the prosecutor is sure that there are public interest factors tending against prosecution which outweigh those tending in favour.

Factors tending in favour of prosecution:

- Large or repeated payments are more likely to attract a significant sentence (Code 4.16a);
- Facilitation payments that are planned for or accepted as part of a standard way of conducting business may indicate the offence was premeditated (Code 4.16e);
- Payments may indicate an element of active corruption of the official in the way the offence was committed (Code 4.16k);
- Where a commercial organisation has a clear and appropriate policy setting out procedures an individual should follow if facilitation payments are requested and these have not been correctly followed.

Factors tending against prosecution:

- A single small payment likely to result in only a nominal penalty (Code 4.17a);
- The payment(s) came to light as a result of a genuinely proactive approach involving self-reporting and remedial action (additional factor (a) in the Guidance on Corporate Prosecutions);
- Where a commercial organisation has a clear and appropriate policy setting out procedures an individual should follow if facilitation payments are requested and these have been correctly followed;
- The payer was in a vulnerable position arising from the circumstances in which the payment was demanded.

11 Credit card fraud in Chinese criminal law

Liu Mingxiang

Legislative overview[1]

The first credit card was introduced to Mainland China in 1985, which occurred much later than the enactment of the first Criminal Law of the People's Republic of China (PRC) in 1979.[2] As a result, there are no specialised provisions in Chinese Criminal Law to regulate fraud crime committed by means of credit card. As credit card interactions became more common and widespread in Chinese social and economic activities, there was also a growing number of criminal cases relating to credit card fraud that have come to the attention of authorities. In response, the Supreme People's Court (SPC) and the Supreme People's Procuratorate (SPP) established relevant judicial interpretation[3] that clearly stated that this type of fraud case should be punished as general fraud. However, unlike traditional fraud, credit card fraud has specific characteristics which require specialisation.

1 Three points need to be made. First, this article only focuses on the problems of Mainland China since Taiwan, Hong Kong and Macao have their own criminal law systems. Second, the Chinese Legislator has enacted a unified Criminal Law in 1979 that includes nearly all the crime. Some crimes have been proscribed in other regulations including 'one-way criminal laws'. A one-way criminal law includes several provisions that focus on regulating a certain kind of crime. The Theft Act 1978 in England and Wales can be regarded as a one-way criminal law. The legislator revised the Criminal Law in 1997, which is still in force today. Third, the meaning of fraud in Chinese criminal law is much narrower than that in English law. Fraud only refers to the behaviour of defrauding which is punishable under Article 266 (fraud). The crime of fraud is also known as 'general fraud' or 'traditional fraud' since there are several specific types of fraud. For instance, the crime of credit card fraud, proscribed in Article 196, regulates the behaviour of defrauding by means of credit card.

2 See Yuqiong Deng and Chenglei Xu, *Judicial Application of Crimes of Endangering the Security, Benefits and Management Order of Financial Sector* (Law Press 2005) 331.

3 Supreme People's Court (SPC) is the highest court and the Supreme People's Procuratorate (SPP) is the highest procuratorate in China. Both of them have the right to make the interpretation of the provisions in Criminal Law, which should be complied with by all the judicial departments. This kind of interpretation has been called judicial interpretation in China. The judicial interpretation includes different forms including the Interpretation, Reply, etc.

Currently there are various new types of fraud that have sprung up in the financial sector. Hence, the legislator began to realise the necessity of setting up several specialised provisions to combat crime happening in the financial sector including credit card fraud. The Standing Committee of the National People's Congress[4] promulgated the Decision on Punishment of Crimes of Disrupting Financial Order in June 1995, which resulted in the establishment of new crimes, including that of credit card fraud, to regulate the order of the financial sector. The existing criminal law, revised in 1997, has absorbed all the crimes that were formerly proscribed in one-way criminal laws. Indeed, it distinguishes the crimes of financial fraud, including credit card fraud, from traditional fraud. These laws have been included in Article 5, within crimes of financial fraud, of Chapter III (crimes of disrupting the order of the socialist market economy) of the code.

The four types of *actus reus* listed in Article 196 (crime of credit card fraud), which were revised for the first time in 1997, are as follows: 'using a forged credit card; using an invalidated credit card; illegally using another person's credit card; and overdrawing with ill intentions'. Nonetheless there have been many cases where crimes were carried out by using credit cards obtained with false identity certification, which infringed upon the property interest of victims. Nonetheless, this type of behaviour cannot be punished by Article 196 since it has not been included in the four statutory types. However, many opinions contended that it should be punishable under Article 196 as its essence is analogous to the behaviour proscribed by the statute. It is for that reason that Amendment V to the Criminal Law[5] (Amendment V), adopted on 28 February 2005, covers this type of behaviour.

Incidentally, other relevant conduct including forging credit cards, applying for credit cards using false identity certification, and illegally holding another person's credit card, etc. has also been punished under Article 177 and Article 177a. Forging a credit card has been known to be one of the four types of behaviour listed in Article 177 (crime of forged or altered financial ticket) in 1997. With the rapid development of the use of credit cards in China, other acts that hamper the use of credit cards urgently needed to be criminalised. As a result, Amendment V established two crimes in Article 177a: impairing credit card administration and stealing, buying or illegally providing information materials about other persons' credit cards. The content of the crime of impairing credit card administration is

4 The Standing Committee of the National People's Congress is an important permanent branch of the National People's Congress. The National People's Congress enjoys the highest power including the legislative power. Some basic law (such as criminal law) can only be enacted or amended by the National People's Congress. The Standing Committee of the National People's Congress enjoys part of the power of the National People's Congress and can make partial revisions to the law as well as publish its interpretation.

5 The Amendment to the Criminal Law is the most important form of revision of the Criminal Law, which is made by the Standing Committee of the National People's Congress. There are nine amendments so far.

> (1) knowingly holding or transporting forged credit cards, or knowingly holding or transporting forged blank credit cards in relatively large quantities; (2) illegally holding other persons' credit card in relatively large quantities; (3) obtaining credit cards by using false identity certification; and (4) selling, buying, or providing other persons with, forged credit cards or credit cards obtained by using false identity certification.

The provision on stealing, buying or illegally providing information materials about other persons' credit cards states that 'whoever steals, buys or illegally provides information and materials about other persons' credit cards shall be punished for the crime of stealing, buying or illegally providing information materials about other persons' credit cards', and, 'any employee of a bank or of any other financial institution who, taking advantage of his position, commits the act of stealing, buying or illegally providing information materials about other persons' credit cards shall face aggravated punishment.'

Definition of credit card

Interpretation by the Standing Committee of the National People's Congress Regarding the Credit Card Proscribed in the Criminal Law adopted on 29 December 2004 (the 2004 Interpretation) states

> The 'credit card' proscribed in the Criminal Law refers to the electronic payment card that is issued by commercial banks or other financial institutions and that performs in full or in part the functions of payment for consumption, credit loan, transference and settlement, cash deposit and withdrawal, etc.

Accordingly, the scope of 'credit card' in Chinese criminal law includes not only traditional credit cards that have the overdraft function, but also debit cards that have the function of payment for consumption, cash deposit and withdrawal, etc. Moreover, fraud by means of using debit cards accounts for the vast majority of credit card fraud cases for the reason that debit cards are more widespread in China.

Incidentally, the purpose of the 2004 Interpretation is to resolve the dispute on how to qualify the use of a forged debit card and the use of another person's debit card. Some argued that they should be punished as crimes of financial certificate fraud (proscribed in Article 194) and credit card fraud, while others were in favour of applying the rules on general fraud. One of the reasons for this dispute lies in a conflict of the law and regulation relating to the credit card. At first, financial institutions had not differentiated between credit cards and debit cards; indeed, credit cards traditionally included debit cards in China. But a Notice of the People's Bank of China on the Measures for the Administration of Bank Card Business, adopted on 1 January 1999 (the 1999 Notice), stated that bank cards include credit cards and debit cards, which means debit cards do not belong to the scope of credit cards since 1999.[6] However, the existing Criminal Law was adopted in 1997. In addition, Article 3 of the Notice of the People's Bank of China on Issuing the Measures for the Administration of Credit Card Business adopted on 1 April 1996 (the 1996 Notice) stated that credit cards include different bank cards that have the function of payment for consumption, credit loan, transference and settlement, cash deposit and withdrawal, etc. Accordingly, credit cards had the same meaning as bank cards when the criminal law was enacted. Hence, from the perspective of legislative evolution, the definition of credit cards should be interpreted broadly, including the debit card. This interpretation is consistent with the 1996 Notice rather than the 1999 Notice.

As mentioned above, the 1999 Notice states credit card should be interpreted narrowly. Consequently, some scholars advocated that the meaning of credit card in criminal law should also be interpreted narrowly to maintain the unity of the legal order with the 1999 Notice. However, Professor Zhang Mingkai stated that,

> the unity of legal order calls for the harmony among different areas of law rather than the complete consistency of the legal concepts. Moreover, the requirement of the unity between the terms in criminal law and other areas of law will not only result in disharmonies in criminal law, but also inconsistencies between criminal law and other laws.[7]

Nevertheless, this author argues that the concepts should be interpreted, as far as possible, in the same way in different areas of law. For now, the terms of criminal law should be interpreted in the original way despite the meaning of the same term in other laws having changed. But the meaning of the terms proscribed in different laws should be unified in future legislation. As regards the meaning of credit card in criminal law, it is unwise for the legislator to stick to the original meaning as bank regulation has already clearly stated that credit cards are not equal to bank cards. In fact, we can see that the definition of credit cards in China is not limited to bank cards, but covers other electronic payment cards including traditional bank cards. Apparently, the scope of electronic payment cards is much broader than the scope of credit cards proscribed in both the 1996 Notice and the 1999 Notice. Therefore, the author advises that it is necessary to change the name of the crime of credit card fraud to electronic payment card fraud in future legislation.

6 Xinjiu Qu, 'Defrauding by Means of Debit Card Shall Be Punished by Credit Card Fraud' *Procuratorial Daily* (Beijing, 19 July 2004).

7 See Mingkai Zhang, *Study on Fraud and Financial Fraud* (Tsinghua University Press 2006) 642.

'Using credit cards' and 'illegally using another person's credit card'

Acts punishable under Article 196 are

> using a forged credit card, using a credit card obtained by using false identity certification, using an invalidated credit card, or obtaining the large amount property of others by using their own or others' credit card for the purpose of illegal possession.

It is generally said that the term 'using' mentioned above means taking advantage of the credit cards by common methods including payment for consumption, credit loan, transference and settlement, cash deposit and withdrawal, etc.[8] The offender who has not used the credit cards in a common manner, such as using the credit cards to pick locks to conduct a burglary, will be sentenced under Article 264 (Theft)[9] rather than Article 196.

It is irrelevant whether the cards used belong to the offenders themselves, to others or whether the cards used are obtained by legal means. What is clear is that whoever conducts the kind of behaviour mentioned above should be punished under Article 196. But it should be noted that the defrauders would have also violated Article 177a if they were the ones to forge the credit cards used. It is generally acknowledged that the method (such as forging the credit card) and purposeful behaviour (such as deceiving) have an implicated relationship, which should attract a more severe punishment on the basis of the penalty prescribed for the most serious of the crimes committed.[10]

But credit cards in the case of 'illegally using another person's credit card' can only be other persons' real and effective cards. What is more, they should not be obtained by means of stealing for the reason that the third paragraph of Article196 states that 'Whoever steals a credit card and uses it shall be convicted and punished in accordance with the provisions in Article 264 of this law.' Those who use the cards obtained by other legal or illegal means to carry out fraud should be sentenced in accordance with Article 196.

Violating the willingness of the cardholder is central to the crime of illegally using another person's credit card, especially as there is no need to hold the

8 See Mingkai Zhang, *Criminal Law* (4th edition, Law Press 2011) 712.

9 The meaning of theft is also much narrower than the meaning in British criminal law. It only regulates the behaviour of secretly taking possession of the object that is in the victim's possession without the victim's consent in China. It can be equated to simple larceny in England and Wales.

10 Implicated relationship and implicated offence are the conceptions of the theory in the continental law system. Implicated relationship means that the defendant has carried out several acts including method and purposeful behaviours. Both the method and purposeful behaviour has violated the criminal law. Taking the case mentioned above, for example, the defendant has violated Article 177a and Article 196. But the defendant is only to be sentenced for the heavier crime.

cards. The interpretation of several issues concerning the specific application of law in the handling of cases of crimes disturbing the administration of credit cards adopted in 2009 (the 2009 Interpretation) by SPC and SPP states that cases of 'obtaining the credit card information of another person by theft, purchase, fraud or any other illicit means and using it via an Internet or communication terminal, etc.' are covered by 'illegally using another person's credit card'. Such conduct constitutes credit card fraud.

There is no doubt among Chinese criminal scholars and judicial practice that whoever uses another person's credit card to go shopping will be sentenced in accordance with Article 196. Nevertheless, the real question is how to identify cases where defrauders use credit cards in automated teller machine (ATM). To resolve this dispute, the reply on how to determine the nature of the act of finding another person's lost credit card and using it on an automated teller machine was drafted in 2008 (the 2008 Reply) by SPP. This made sure that picking up another person's lost credit card and using it on an ATM should be identified as 'illegally using another person's credit card' proscribed in Article 196.

However, the dispute among the Chinese scholars has not settled down after the 2008 Reply. The bone of contention lies in the rule that machine cannot be cheated. Scholars hold different opinions on whether this rule should be applicable to the case of credit card fraud. The scholars who are in favour of its application argue that the crime of credit card fraud is a special form of general fraud which requires that the victim be a natural person rather than machine. Hence, illegally using the credit card at the ATM can be punished in accordance with Article 264 (theft) rather than Article 196.[11] On the contrary, the scholars who deny the application of the rule maintain that illegally using the credit card at the ATM can be punished under Article 196 since withdrawing through ATM is one of the most common functions of credit card.[12] The author agrees with the latter opinion for the reasons that follow.

First, it must be noted that this rule cannot be used as an argument. Indeed, the rule can definitely be applicable to the crime of general fraud since the Constitution requires the victim to be a natural person. However, fraud crimes committed by means of computers, including ATM, have their own distinctive features. To settle the contradiction between the rule and the constructive requirement of computer frauds properly so called, some countries, including Germany and Japan, have introduced a new crime knows as Computer Fraud since the 1980s. Countries that do not have a specialised computer fraud crime punish these cases as general fraud. An example is the second paragraph of Article 1 in Chapter 9 of Swedish Criminal Law, which states 'whoever inputs an incorrect or incomplete order, modifies a procedure or record, or influences the data processing illegally, if losses are caused to the others, or if gains are brought to the offenders, will be sentenced for fraud.' In

11 See Mingkai Zhang, 'Also on the Nature of Withdrawing Cash from an ATM with a Picked-up Credit Card: Discussion with Professor Mingxiang Liu' (2008) 1 *Tsinghua Law Journal* 91.

12 See Xianquan Liu, 'Judicial Holding of the Crime of Swindling Credit Cards' (2003) 3 *Tribune of Political Science and Law*.

short, computer fraud, which includes illegally withdrawing through ATM, is in essence equivalent to fraud rather than burglary.

Some scholars put forward that the rule should also be applicable to Article 196 since it is one of the special forms of Article 266.[13] The author argues, however, that some types of behaviour (such as overdrawing with ill intentions) proscribed in Article 196 cannot be fully covered by general fraud. In fact, not all the basic element of the constructive requirement of general fraud can be applicable to the crime of credit card fraud. There are two terms in its name both of which should not be ignored. It is different from fraud since 'credit card' acts as a qualifier to its name. It is evident that the ATM is a type of computer and computer fraud that is different from traditional fraud since it does not require someone has been deceived. In addition, opinions in Germany, Japan and other states on specialized crime of computer fraud will not argue that computer fraud need to possess all the requirement of the general fraud simply due to the name of the crime including the word (fraud). The legislation on the crime of computer fraud confirms its distinctiveness. Similarly, Chinese legislators also set up Article 196 in consideration of its uniqueness (such as illegally withdrawing through ATM). All in all, the rule cannot be applied to Article 196.

Secondly, withdrawing through an ATM is one of the common usages of credit cards. 'Using credit cards' and 'illegally using another person's credit card' is proscribed in Article 196. Therefore, illegally withdrawing through an ATM can also be punishable under Article 196. One scholar argues that we should interpret the article narrowly although there is no statutory limitation to the situation which happened in the ATM. In his opinions, 'using credit cards' and 'illegally using another person's credit card' implies the object of the fraud can only a natural person rather than ATM. He also argues that this limitation need not be defined in Article 196.[14] The author cannot agree with this argument for the following reasons.

First, from the common interpretation of the terms such 'using credit cards' and 'illegally using another person's credit card', it would not be possible to exclude the situation that happened in the ATM. There is therefore no basis for excluding fraud that involves an ATM.

Second, the narrow interpretation has no merit since there are no differences between withdrawing through ATM and withdrawing at the bank counter. Both of them have infringed the interest of the bank and share the same constitutive requirements. The only difference is that in the first instance the bank assistant would hand over the money to the offender at the bank counter while in the latter the electronic bank assistant would do the job through an ATM. The argument above has obviously violated the basic principle of a criminal conviction. In addition, it will lead to obvious imbalance in punishment. For example, suppose a person who picks up another person's credit card and knows the PIN

13 See Zhang (n 11).
14 See Zhang (n 11).

withdraws 100,000 yuan through an ATM, and is subsequently convicted of theft. According to the Article 264, the amount of 100,000 yuan is especially large, and will be punished by a fixed-term of imprisonment of no less than ten years or life imprisonment. Conversely, a person who withdraws the same amount of money through a bank counter would be punished under Article 196 and sentenced to a fixed-term imprisonment of no less than five years but not more than ten years. This disparity of the punishment is imbalanced and unacceptable.

Third, the narrow interpretation has violated the principle of legality, which requires the interpretation to strictly abide by the statutory provisions. It is acknowledged that, however, for the sake of the defendants it allows the judicial practice to broaden or narrow the interpretation. The principle in China prohibits any interpretation against the defendants. Only well-grounded reasons in line with the legislative spirit can allow the court to break this rule. The argument mentioned above, which aggravates the penalty, has obviously violated this principle.

The argument above has conformed to the theory of differentiating property crimes. It is widely accepted in China that theft means the offender steals the property without the knowledge of the owner, while fraud involves the owner handing over the property mistakenly to the offender or the third party by the means of deceit. In brief, the former requires stealing property while the latter requires swindling the person. And

> the behaviour of handing over defines the boundary between theft and fraud. If the victim freely handed over the property, the defenders will be sentenced under fraud rather than theft. If the victim has not handed over the property, the defenders will be sentenced under theft rather than fraud.[15]

Hence, the crime of fraud has been regarded as 'delivery crime'.[16] When it comes back to the relationship between computer fraud (including part of the credit card fraud) and traditional fraud, there are some differences. Traditional fraud means the offender lets the owner hand over the property mistakenly to the offender or a third party by means of deception. In contrast, computer fraud punishes the following conducts including: inputting the incorrect or incomplete data, illegally using the data, illegally influencing others' computer programme, making the computers hand over the property. In cases of 'using credit cards' and 'illegally using another person's credit card', the offender inputs the data of the credit card directly into the ATM, which is then followed by the ATM spitting out the money. As the ATM takes the place of a bank assistant to complete the work, 'from the perspective of the legal nature of ATM, it can be regarded as an electronic assistant which bears the same essence

15 See Hirano Ryuichi, *Several Issues on Criminal Theory (II)* (Yuhikaku Publishing 1982) 330. Quoted in Zhang (n 11).

16 See Atsushi Yamaguchi, *Strafrecht Besonderer Teil* (Yuhikaku Publishing 2003) 240.

of the natural person'.[17] From a legal point of view, there is therefore no difference between a delivery done by the ATM or by the bank assistant. Illegally withdrawing through an ATM has the characteristics of a 'delivery crime' rather than theft. It should therefore be punishable in accordance with Article 196.

'Overdrawing with ill intentions'

'Overdrawing with ill intentions' is one of the forms of conduct proscribed in Article 196. The second paragraph of Article 196 states that:

> Overdrawing with ill intentions means that a credit card holder who, for the purpose of illegal possession, overdraws beyond the norm set or beyond the time limit and refuses to repay the overdrawn amount after the bank that issues the card urges him to do so.

It is generally acknowledged that the concept of 'urge' includes written as well as oral requests. A common situation in which a person realises that the issuing bank has urged the cardholders to repay the money can be identified as 'refuses to repay the overdrawn amount after the bank that issues the card urges him to do so'. It does not matter whether the cardholder has received the notice. Article 6 of the Interpretation 2009 states that

> A credit card holder who, for the purpose of illegal possession, makes an overdraft beyond the prescribed limit or beyond the prescribed time limit and fails to repay the overdraft within three months after the card issuing bank demands repayment twice shall be deemed to have committed a 'malicious overdraft' as mentioned in Article 196 of the Criminal Law. A credit card holder who falls under any of the following circumstances shall be deemed to have 'the purpose of illegal possession' as mentioned in paragraph 2 of Article 196 of the Criminal Law: (1) making an overdraft in a large amount whiling knowing his inability to repay it and failing to repay it; (2) extravagantly spending the overdraft and failing to repay it; (3) fleeing or changing his contact information after making an overdraft to avoid repayment demand from the bank; (4) illegally withdrawing or transferring funds or hiding property to evade repayment; (5) committing illegal or criminal activities with an overdraft; or (6) any other conduct of illegally possessing and refusing to return funds.

'Overdrawing with ill intentions' also requires the amount involved to be relatively large, which is the same as with the other three forms of behaviours of

17 See Bingzhi Zhao, 'Jurisprudential Thinking after the Xuting Case' *Legal Daily* (Beijing, 1 June 2008).

deemed to constitute credit card fraud. But the required amount (10,000 yuan) for 'overdrawing with ill intentions' is larger than that applicable to the other three forms of criminalised behaviour (5,000 yuan). It implies that 'overdrawing with ill intentions' poses less societal danger. The author argues that the difference may reflect the behavioural nature of 'overdrawing with ill intentions'.

Whoever overdraws with ill intentions would have been punished for fraud before the enactment of Article 196. Dating back to January 1985, the SPP published the Conversion of the Comments on Disposing the Fraudulent Activity by Means of Credit Cards by Shanghai Municipal People's Procuratorate,[18] which emphasised that the fraudulent activity by means of credit cards should be punished as fraud. An interpretation of several issues concerning the specific application of law in the handling of cases of credit card crimes by the SPC and SPP in April 1995 stated that whoever overdraws with ill intentions, for an amount larger than 5,000 yuan and does not pay back at the expiration of three months after being urged by the bank, shall be punished as fraud. The revision of the criminal law in 1997 has put this behaviour (overdrawing with ill intentions) into Article 196. In short, the legislative body and courts have always affirmed this kind of behaviour is in essence fraudulent – a notion that has also been supported by scholars in China.[19]

It appears there is a dispute among other nations on whether this behaviour has the nature of fraud. In Germany and Japan, for example, scholars hold the opinion that 'overdrawing through an ATM with ill intentions' does not constitute fraud. But the judicial practice and general theory of Japanese criminal law consider the behaviour of 'overdrawing during shopping with ill intentions' to be fraudulent, which runs against the opinion of German scholars.[20] A verdict made by the German Federal Supreme Court in 1985 states that a person who is unable or unwilling to pay and still goes shopping with the merchants by means of a credit card, cannot be punished for fraud. This is due to the fact that the merchant has not been cheated, nor has the crime of abuse of trust been perpetrated,[21] as the offender has no obligation towards the issuing bank. This verdict prompted the legislator to enact a new crime in order to punish this kind of behaviour ('overdrawing during shopping with ill intentions'). This helped promote the development of legislation to some extent. As a result the

18 Conversion of the Comments on Disposing the Fraudulent Activity by Means of Credit Cards by Shanghai Municipal People's Procuratorate is a kind of judicial interpretation made by SPP. The SPP will convert the judicial practice or interpretation made by lower level procuratorate as a nationwide judicial interpretation that has binding force.

19 Zhang (n 11).

20 Ōya Minoru and Masahide Maeda, *Dialogue in the Criminal Law* (Yuhikaku Publishing 2000) 154.

21 Abuse of trust refers to a crime proscribed in many continental law systems (such as Germany). It is totally different from the provisions in the Sexual Offences Act 2003 of England and Wales. It is to some extent analogous to ss 1 and 4 of the Fraud Act 2006 in England and Wales.

German legislator had added a new crime of credit card abuse into the second law for the suppression of economic crime. This was then added to Article 266b of the criminal law in Germany which states 'whoever abuses the credit card to induce the issuer (issuing bank) to pay the money and loss is caused to the issuer, shall be sentenced to fix-term imprisonment of less than 3 years, or be fined'.[22] The existing German criminal law has incorporated the crime of credit card abuse, although it already contained provisions on general fraud and computer fraud. The penalty for credit card abuse is much lighter than that for the other two crimes discussed since there are differences in the nature and level of social harmfulness amongst them. Some perceptive scholars in Japan have also realised that the essence of 'overdrawing with ill intentions' should instead mean abuse of the trust between issuer and cardholder rather than fraud. They argued that the crime of abuse of credit card should also be enacted in future legislation in Japan.[23]

Similarly, the author agrees that the essence of 'overdrawing with ill intentions' should belong to 'abuse of the trust' rather than 'fraud'. This behaviour infringes upon the relationship between the card issuer and cardholder which will upset the whole credit card system and hinder the trading activity. That is why German criminal law has been revised to include a new crime of credit card abuse. There is no doubt that punishing this behaviour as credit card fraud rather than fraud after 1997 is an improvement in legislation. However, it is an instance of undeserved reputation since 'overdrawing with ill intentions' is not fraud by nature. Furthermore, the crime of credit card fraud is regarded as 'a pocket crime'[24] by scholars.[25] Hence the author suggests that future legislation should separate 'overdrawing with ill intentions' from credit card fraud and enact a new crime named overdrawing with ill intentions or abuse of credit card whose statutory punishment should be lighter than that of credit card fraud.

'Stealing a credit card and using it'

The behaviour of 'stealing a credit card and using it' is proscribed in the third paragraph of Article 196, which states that 'Whoever steals a credit card and uses it shall be convicted and punished in accordance with the provisions in Article 264 of this law'. Generally speaking, 'stealing a credit card and using it' belongs to the situation of 'illegally using another person's credit card', which is

22 Kamiyama Toshio, 'Economy Crime in Japan' *Japan Society Comments* (Japan 1996) 143–144.

23 See Munenobu Hirakawa, *Specific Provisions of the Criminal Law* (Yuhikaku Publishing 1995) 422.

24 'A pocket crime' refers to a crime that can include many types of behaviour. Its vagueness has occasioned considerable academic criticism.

25 See Mingxiang Liu, *Comparative Study on Property Crime* (China University of Politic Science and Law Press 2001) 265.

one of the four typical forms of crime known as credit card fraud. Thus, it is an absolute legislative exception that 'stealing a credit card and using it' is punished under Article 264 rather than Article 196. The evaluation of this legislation by Chinese scholars varies. Some argue it is rational[26] while others argue against it,[27] nonetheless, according to the principle of legality they should comply with it. It appears that the only thing that can be done is minimising the harmful effect of this legislation by proper interpretation and conviction.

Interpretation of the 'credit card' of 'stealing a credit card and using it'

The 'credit card' proscribed in the third paragraph of Article 196 should also be identified according to Interpretation 2004, which states that the scope of 'credit cards' includes not only the credit cards that have the overdraft function, but also debit cards. There is a wide dispute among Chinese scholars on whether invalid credit cards including forged and abandoned ones belong to the scope of 'credit cards'. Some argue that it includes not only the real and effective ones, but also the void, forged, altered and transformed ones.[28] However, the majority of the scholars hold the opinion that only the real and effective ones belong to the scope.[29] The author is in favour of the latter interpretation because the behavioural objects prescribed in criminal law are limited to real and effective ones if there are no specialised provisions suggesting including the false, void or forged ones. For example, the 'official documents, certificates or seals of a State organ', prescribed in Article 280 (crime of stealing, forcibly seizing or destroying the official documents, certificates or seals of a state organ) can only be real if effective. Stealing forged official documents, certificates or seals of a State organ cannot be criminalised. Moreover, stealing a forged or invalid credit card and using it with intention is definitely part of the situation of 'using forged or invalid credit card' proscribed in the first paragraph of Article 196.

Interpretation of 'using' of 'stealing a credit card and using it'

Only 'stealing a relatively large amount of property' can be punished under Article 264 according to the criminal law. A person who only steals a credit card cannot be convicted and punished in accordance with theft since the credit card itself is worthless. This behaviour cannot be punished as credit card fraud since it has not met the constitutive requirements of the crime.

26 See Zhang, *Study on Fraud and Financial Fraud* (n 7) 694.
27 See Wenyan Li (ed.), *Study on Financial Fraud* (Chinese People's Public Security University Press 2002) 304.
28 See Zhihui Zhang and Yuan Liu (ed.), *New Discussion on Financial Crime and Financial Criminal Law* (Shandong University Press 2006) 341.
29 See Zhang, *Study on Fraud and Financial Fraud* (n 7) 694.

The word 'using', as mentioned above, has been used in Article 196 several times, such as 'using forged or invalid credit cards', 'illegally using another person's credit card' and 'stealing a credit card and using it', etc. The word 'using' proscribed in Article 196 means taking advantage of the credit card by means of common methods such as payment for consumption. It is worth studying whether selling the credit card that was stolen can be identified as 'using' or not. Some scholars argue that 'selling' can be identified as 'using' since 'selling' also is fraudulent in nature.[30] Other scholars hold the viewpoint that there are pronounced differences between 'using' and 'selling'. Selling a stolen credit card cannot be punishable as in accordance with Article 264 'using' cannot include 'selling'.[31] The word 'using' means taking advantage of the object's function, while 'selling' means offering the object in exchange for money. The meaning of 'using' cannot include 'selling' because of their differences. However, if a burglar sells the stolen credit card to the acquirer and the acquirer commits the conduct proscribed in Article 196, the card-holder will suffer a loss of property. There is no doubt that, to combat the crime and safeguard the property, both burglar and acquirer should take responsibility for the loss of the cardholder. For example, suppose A steals his colleague's credit card which has 50,000 yuan on it and knows its PIN code, and then sells it to B at the cost of 45,000 yuan claiming he is selling his own card for urgent need. B then withdraws the 50,000 yuan after buying the card at the cost of 45,000 yuan. B cannot be punished as he just bought the card out of greed rather than with a requisite *mens rea*. B has also been cheated to believe that A is the owner of the card, who in turn cannot be punished considering that 'selling' does not equate to 'using'. It is evidently irrational. The key question of this idea lies at the notion that a third party (B), who has bought the credit card, replaces the burglar (A) to take advantage of the credit card by means of its common use (withdrawing) and therefore causes loss to the cardholder.

Therefore, 'stealing a credit card and using it' should include the circumstances in which the card was being used by the third party rather than by the burglar himself. Thus the burglar will be convicted as indirect principal if he let the incapacitated person use the credit card, or the third party withdraws the money without any criminal intent. Furthermore, if the burglar tells all the details to the third party and lets the third party use the credit card, both of them shall be punished as for a joint offence.[32] Coming back to the case mentioned above, A's activity of selling the stolen card which has got the 45,000 yuan is just a

30 See Xianquan Liu (n 12).

31 See Changsheng Ma and Ke Wang, 'Qualitative Analysis on Stealing a Credit Card and Using It' in Zhang Zhihui and Liu Yuan (eds), *New Discussion on Financial Crime and Financial Criminal Law* (Shandong University Press 2006) 370–371.

32 The third Party and the burglar shall be punished as for a joint offense of Theft rather than Credit Card Fraud since the third party is the successive joint crime.

superficial phenomenon. In essence, A has taken advantage of B's ignorant activity to get the money deposited in the card. Obviously, A is an indirect principal. Nevertheless, there are different situations in the cases of stealing a credit card and selling it. In some cases, the burglar has given all the details to the buyer and the buyer still uses the credit card, and therefore shall be sentenced as an accomplice. In other cases, the burglar deceives the buyer by representing he owns the card or accidently picked up the card, meaning the buyer can use it without any criminal intent. In such cases the burglar shall be punished as an indirect principal. It is noted that the behaviour of using the credit cards with intent by the buyer belongs to the circumstance of 'illegally using another person's credit card', which shall be punished in accordance with the first paragraph of Article 196 (Credit Card Fraud).

The real problem in China remains in what happens if the burglar steals a credit card and gives it to a third party for free (including the situation of allowing the third party to take it away), and the third party than uses it to withdraw a large amount of money. Can the burglar then be punished for the crime of theft? The author argues that the answer to this question depends on different situations: (1) Suppose the burglar steals a credit card and gets the PIN code. Then the burglar gives it to the third party for nothing and allows him to use it to get a large amount of money. The burglar shall be sentenced for theft even if he has not benefited from what he has done. (2) Suppose the burglar steals a credit card (the card has no PIN code) and gives it to the third party for free (including the situation of allowing the third party to take it away) and the third party then withdraws a large amount of money. Whether the burglar should be responsible for the activity of the third party depends on whether the burglar knew the stolen card had a PIN code or not. (3) Suppose the burglar steals a credit card and gives it to the third party for free (including the situation that allowing the third party to take it away). The third party then gets the card's PIN code and withdraws a huge amount of money. When it comes to this case, the burglar is only guilty of theft if he has the intention of helping the third party use the card, if he fails to do so he will not be found guilty.

Interpretation of the 'stealing' of 'stealing a credit card and using it'

'Stealing a credit card' means that the defendant secretly takes possession of a credit card that is in the possession of victim without the victim's consent. The behavioural object must be the credit card with the legal and valid information material of the cardholder rather than the blank credit card without any data. The defendant who steals a blank card and forges it by adding the magnetic information cannot be punished for the crime of theft. Similarly, the defendant cannot be sentenced for theft if he just steals the information material and forges a new credit card.

There are many cases in judicial practice where the defendant steals information material by means of peeking at the card number and PIN code, or by taking photos of the card's information with a mini-camera, data collector or any other technical equipment. The defendant then forges a new card with such data and uses it to steal a large amount of money.[33] Some scholars argue that the card itself is just a carrier to hold the information material, including the card number and PIN code, which is the flesh and blood of the credit card. The behaviour of stealing the information is not only the pre-step of forging a new credit card, but also plays a key role in deception. That is to say stealing a card's information is equal to physically stealing a credit card. Hence, they hold the opinion that this behaviour shall be punishable in accordance with the third paragraph of Article 196.[34] But this author argues that the behavioural object of 'stealing a credit card' can only be the credit card with the legal and valid information material, rather than the mere information material of the credit card.

> Because the behaviour of stealing means the transfer of possession and theft accomplished means the defendant has already taken the possession of the property which is in the possession of victim. … Peeking at the information cannot lead to the loss of the possession of credit card.[35]

In addition, to obtain the money, the defendant needs to forge a credit card after stealing the information. In terms of using the forged card, it is the typical case of 'using forged credit card' proscribed in the first paragraph of Article 196. In contrast, 'stealing a credit card and using it' means using the stolen card directly. In conclusion, stealing the information cannot be punished as theft.

In everyday life there is a possibility that the cardholder has not turned off the ATM and taken back his card after he has withdrawn the money allowing for another person to take the opportunity to withdraw a huge amount of money with his card. This case can be blamed on various factors such as simply forgetting to turn off the ATM, the breakdown of the ATM itself, and the defendant's deception. In such cases, the question of whether the judge can punish the conduct in accordance with the third paragraph of Article 196 arises. The author's opinion is as follows: first, in the case of the cardholder's fault, the defendant has not stolen anything although he has withdrawn the cardholder's money, since there has been no transfer of possession on the card in this specific situation. Second, cases where the defendant failed to remind the cardholder to take back the card by deception, cannot be punished as theft either. For example, V was making an inventory of his withdrawn money when his card was still inside the ATM. Defendant A touched V's left leg and V turned left to figure out what happened to him. At this moment, defendant B rushed to the ATM to put his card to the card port. Then V turned back and saw the card is outside of the card

33 See Tailing Zhang, 'Seven Persons Who Forged Credit Cards and Withdrew 900,000 Yuan Have Been Sentenced' *Beijing News* (Beijing, 25 August 2009).

34 See Lihua Wang, 'How to Convict the Behaviour of Peeking at Card Account and Pin code and Forging Debit Card' *Procuratorial Daily* (Beijing, 24 March 2003).

35 See Zhang, *Study on Fraud and Financial Fraud* (n 7) 707.

port. He thought the card had been dropped out by ATM and left. But what actually happened was that, his real card was still inside and in working order as the defendant withdrew the money through the ATM. There is still no larceny in this case, although some scholars argue the trick conducted by A and B is a kind of larceny.[36] In my view, the defendant's behaviour demonstrates that he let the cardholder forget to take back the card rather than transfer the possession of the card. In such cases the defendant cannot be sentenced for the crime of theft since larceny requires the transfer of possession of the property. Some may hold the opinion that defendant A and B have let the cardholder lose control of the card and taken the possession of the card inside the card port. They claim that what the defendants have done already meets the constitutive requirement of theft, as there is no doubt that the cardholder has lost the control of the card. But it does not mean that the defendants have taken control since the bank that installs the ATM has taken control of everything inside the ATM including the forgotten card. In other words, the owner of the ATM has taken the possession of the card immediately after V left. Hence, the defendants have not taken the possession of the card. But the defendants can still commit the crime although they have not taken control of the card.

To conclude, the question of how such behaviour can be identified arises. Some scholars hold the opinion that it shall be punishable as embezzlement since the defendants have 'unlawfully taken possession of an object which another person has forgotten about'.[37] The author does not agree with this idea, although there is no doubt that the card should be regarded as 'the object that the victim has forgotten'. The deposit of the cardholder, however, was still inside the cardholder's account rather than being forgotten. Hence, the deposit inside the account cannot be regarded as 'the object that the victim has forgotten'. The conduct therefore cannot be punished as embezzlement as the defendant has taken out the money from the account rather than the forgotten card. Moreover, even though the deposit inside the account can be treated as 'the object which the victim has forgotten' prescribed in Article 270, it was only forgotten inside the ATM. As previously mentioned, the money forgotten inside the ATM should be regarded as being in the possession of the bank who installed the ATM. Therefore, the defendants mentioned above should be punished for theft rather than embezzlement. In fact, the defendants have taken advantage of the working status of the ATM to withdraw the money. Only the cardholder can use the credit card to withdraw through the ATM according to the credit card regulations. Any other person without authorisation is not allowed to do so. This behaviour, in essence, is equal to 'illegally using another person's credit card', which shall be punished as credit card fraud.

36 See Feihong Wei and Shan Ye, 'A Discussion Concerning the Judicial Confirmation of Stealing the Credit Card and Using it at ATM' (2009) 3 *Journal of Henan Police College* 43.

37 See Wenhua Peng, 'Determine the Nature of the Behaviour of Using the Forgotten Bank Card in ATM' (2009) 6 *Political Science and Law* 48.

12 China's legal framework and challenges of the freezing, seizure and confiscation of financial crime proceeds

Cheng Lei

China, like most other countries across the world, is facing a huge challenge from various financial crimes, from credit card fraud to the embezzlement of public deposits, from internet fraud to telecommunication fraud with a number of victims. Those rising crimes have created huge headaches for China's criminal justice system, although China's Criminal Law has continued its efforts to curb those financial crimes in the past ten years.[1] This reaction is natural for a high-speed economic developing country, however, China's Criminal Procedure Law ignored the problem and legislators have not realised the importance of effective criminal justice institutions for fighting financial crimes. Imbalance between substantive law and procedure law leaves many legal loopholes for financial crime offenders.

Although penalties for financial crimes are more and more severe in Criminal Law, offenders continue their illegal acts as they realised it is very easy for them to make profits safely and the investigators find it very difficult to locate and confiscate their illegal earnings.

A framework that allows effective and timely freezing, seizure and confiscation is essential for combating financial crimes. The author will introduce China's framework in this aspect and show the challenges for law enforcement when they freeze, seize or confiscate illegal earnings of financial crimes.

Forgotten corner: property protection in the criminal procedure law

China's Criminal Procedure Law (CPL) was drafted and enacted in 1979 when China ended the ten-year disaster of the Cultural Revolution. At that time, the legislators rethought the lessons of the Cultural Revolution, which included torture and miscarriage of justice. Physical freedom was the focus of the 1979 CPL. Although China's CPL has been revised twice in 1996 and 2012, property was not the subject of the revision. A good example is that only seven articles

1 Since 1999, China's legislature has made eight amendments to the Criminal Law, six of which are related to the fight against financial crimes.

mentioned the word 'property' in the CPL before the latest revision of the law in 2012.[2] This situation resulted in an incomplete protection of property rights of both victims and defendants. More importantly, ignorance of the procedures for handling property cannot provide enough support for high-speed economy developments in China.

CPL's framework for freezing, seizure and confiscation

Article 64 of Criminal Law provides:

> All articles of property illegally obtained by the criminal element shall be recovered or he shall be ordered to make restitution or pay compensation for them. Contraband and articles of the criminal's own property used for committing the crime shall be confiscated. Articles of confiscated property and fines shall be handed over to the national treasury and shall not be diverted or otherwise disposed of.

According to this article, law enforcement should freeze, seize or confiscate three categories of property of defendants: property illegally obtained by crime, contraband and criminal's own property used for committing crime. In addition, most property is good evidence for proving crimes including financial crime, so law enforcement should search and seize them for evidence purpose.[3]

Search, seizure and freezing measures in CPL

CPL regards search, seize and freeze as investigatory measures provided for in the Chapter of Investigation Procedure.[4] The legal purpose and object of search, freezing or seizure should be evidence related to the guilt or innocence of suspects or defendants.[5] No judicial order or approval procedures exist, which means police officers or other investigators can decide to carry out a search or seizure on their own. The conditions for search or seizure are very broad. Law enforcement officials need not have reasonable doubt or other sufficient suspicion before they conduct a search or seizure. The only thing they need to show is that they can find evidence of guilt or innocence.

2 The CPL had 164 articles when it was drafted in 1979 and 225 articles in 1996. The latest revision of the CPL has 290 articles.

3 CPL 2012, Article 134.

4 CPL 2012, Articles 134–138 for search and Articles 139–143 for freezing and seizure.

5 CPL 2012, Article 134: 'In order to collect criminal evidence and track down an offender, investigators may search the person, belongings and residence of the criminal suspect and anyone who might be hiding a criminal or criminal evidence, as well as other relevant places.' Article 139: 'Assets or documents discovered during an investigation that may be used to prove the guilt or innocence of a criminal suspect should be sealed or seized; assets or documents irrelevant to a case may not be sealed or seized.'

Although the CPL requires investigators to show a search warrant or freezing or seizure warrant that they themselves issue, the law does not make clear contents of the warrant. In practice, the warrants only include when, where and against whom the search or seizure takes place. In addition, no time limit exists for searches, freezing or seizures.

When concluding a search or seizure, investigators should make a list of seized property before holders of property or other witness at the search or seizure scene. If the property seized or sealed is proved to be irrelevant to prove the case, it should be released within three days and returned.[6]

According to the above articles of the CPL, searches, freezing and seizures are focused on evidence. Some proceeds or illegal earnings do not directly prove cases, which are often neglected by law enforcement especially considering investigators are generally busy and turn a blind eye to crimes.

Confiscation

Criminal Law of PRC provides for two kinds of confiscation: Article 59 provides for the confiscation of all personal property of criminals that are not related to crime and are legal property; confiscation under Article 64 is related to property illegally obtained by crime, contraband or property used for crime. The former type of confiscation is a kind of sentence or supplementary punishment and the latter type of confiscation is a preventive measure, not penalty. The CPL doesn't provide procedures for the first category of confiscation and treats it as the sentence execution. For the second category of confiscation, the 2012 revision to the CPL creates a special procedure entitled Procedures for the Confiscation of Illegal Earnings in Cases Where the Suspect or Defendant Has Absconded or Died.

As I mentioned above, China's traditional criminal procedure ignored property rights to some extent. In addition, China does not permit trial in absentia, which means the court can only open a trial when the defendants are brought to a hearing. If suspects or defendants flee from justice or die before trial, all procedures of the case would be stopped, including the seizure or confiscation of property. The legal loophole was used by many financial crime offenders, especially corrupt officials. They flee from China or kill themselves at an early stage of the investigation. In this way, they or their families can keep huge illegal gains.[7]

6 CPL 2012, Article 143.

7 For example, according to China's domestic media reports, there were about 4000 corrupt officials who fled mainland China taking away about 400 billion RMB in total in past 30 years, see <www.qlwb.com.cn/2014/0929/216611.shtml>; China's media also report that from August 2003 to April 2014, there were 112 officials who killed themselves and the number in 2013 is 48, twice that of 2012, see <http://sh.sina.com.cn/news/b/2014-06-06/084197548_2.html>.

Legislators realised that the objective of corruption crimes or other financial crimes is illegal earnings. To fight this type of crime, China needed a new procedure for property confiscation. In the 2012 revision of the CPL, a new special procedure was created with four entirely new articles.[8]

Article 280 provides as follows:

> In cases of crimes of corruption and bribery, terrorism and other serious crimes, where the suspect or defendant has absconded and fails to appear before court one year after an arrest warrant has been issued, or where the suspect or defendant is dead, and the illegal earnings or other assets of the suspect or the defendant related to the case should be recovered pursuant to the provisions of the criminal law, the people's prosecutor's office may apply to a people's court for confiscation of such illegal earnings.

The scope of the procedure is limited as the legislators think it is a new procedure and at the beginning, they should apply it in few cases. There are two conditions for the procedure to apply: first, the suspect or defendant has fled from criminal investigation or trial for more than one year; secondly, only bribery, terrorism and other serious crimes can meet the legal preconditions. Serious crime is interpreted by the Supreme Court as crime that deserves life sentence or death penalty. However, what categories of crimes can be applied to the new procedure are not clear.

For property confiscation proceedings, the court opens a special trial based on an application of confiscation filed by the prosecutors. The prosecutors must prove that the property they seek to confiscate is illegal earnings. CPL does not say what the standard of proof is, but the Supreme Court suggests it should be the same as the standard of proof for conviction.[9] During the trial, the family members of suspects or defendants or other property rights advocates can attend the trial and argue their cases against the prosecutors. After the judge's decision on confiscation, the parties of the property confiscation procedure can appeal to a second instance court.

During the proceedings, if absconded suspects or defendants come back or are caught by law enforcement, the special procedure should be stopped. The prosecutor and the judge will transfer the case to the normal criminal procedure where property will be handled along the criminal case against the defendant.

8 CPL 2012, Articles 280–283.

9 CPL 2012, Article 53. CPL provides standard of proof for verdict as reliable and sufficient evidence, in which one sub-condition is beyond reasonable doubt. Article 516 of Supreme People's Court interpretation on CPL provides the same standard of proof for confiscation procedure for illegal earnings.

Challenges and future improvements

The current legal provisions and institutions in the CPL are scattered and messy, which is not enough to meet the challenges of financial crimes. As a result, China's law enforcement cannot control property or illegal gains of financial offenders. Consequently, financial crimes have been rising year by year because offenders can make profits easily from such crimes. Some challenges relate to legal provisions and some relate to low-level social governance mechanism.

Confiscation procedure

The new procedure established by the 2012 CPL cannot meet the challenges of financial crimes. Its main purpose is to crack down on corruption and terrorism crimes. Most financial crimes cannot reach the serious result with life imprisonment, so the court will not permit to initiate a property confiscation process. One exception is that when the suspects or defendants of financial crimes died before trial, whether or not his or her cases is serious, the property confiscation procedure can be launched independently from criminal cases. In reality, most offenders of financial crimes flee from justice, rather than die, so in most cases, the newly created confiscation procedure does nothing with the profits of financial crimes.

Weak investigation measures related to illegal earnings

Although the CPL gave law enforcement a lot of investigatory powers to search, freeze or seize, such powers don't work very well when financial crimes are becoming more and more invisible. Most financial crimes take place in the internet world, not in real life,so traditional investigatory measures are outdated to control new-style financial crimes.

In the new 2012 CPL, legislators gave the power of covert investigation to police officers and other investigators, with database mining and checking being one of the important special investigatory powers.[10] However, the barrier is that investigation departments cannot access the databases of banks or other financial management departments. Investigators can only check with banks about bank account information or bank transaction records of a designated person. All these investigation acts take place after the financial crimes are committed and with very low efficiency.

The solution is not very complicated as the CPL has provided investigation departments with special powers of covert surveillance including internet investigation, database mining and wire tapping etc. Article 150 of the CPL provides that all relevant units or departments should provide cooperation to police

10 CPL 2012, Article 148; Ministry of Public Security Regulations on Handling Criminal Cases 2012, Article 255.

officers that carry out such investigatory measures. Certainly, the legislators should clarify the rules on legal responsibility for declining cooperation.

Illegal earning tracking

The CPL treats illegal earnings along with the criminal responsibility and criminal cases. For example, investigation of cases means finding out by whom, where and how the criminal offence was committed and catching suspects. However, it is not clear from the law whether or not the investigator should track all illegal earnings. Investigators only took illegal earnings as an evidence issue. In fact, they need only collect records of related transactions, witness or confessions and it is not compulsory for investigators to track illegal earnings, which generally is more complex and takes a longer time than a criminal investigation. The process of tracking illegal earnings often needs international judicial cooperation, but a criminal trial in China has a clear time limit, which is six months for a first instance trial and four months for a second instance trial. Thus, judges cannot postpone giving their verdict on criminal cases until all illegal earnings are tracked and recovered. The end of criminal cases cannot solve the disputes between defendants and victims, although defendants are sentenced to imprisonments. Mass victims show a lot of dissatisfaction and distrust towards law enforcement and judiciary.

As a solution to this challenge, China's policy-makers should designate the court as responsible for tracking illegal funds. The judge's order should be executed by competent law enforcement authorities even after the end of the criminal trial.

Part IV
Environmental crime

13 Targeting transnational environmental crime through a multifaceted approach

Towards an inclusive governance of serious threats to sustainable development

Grazia Maria Vagliasindi

Introduction

The lack of reliable and comparable data on the actual number of environmental crimes detected, investigated, prosecuted and sentenced is commonly deemed to be a major challenge in the domain of environmental protection, affecting inter alia the correct assessment of the seriousness of environmental crime as a criminal phenomenon and, as a consequence, the legitimacy and effectiveness of related criminal policy responses.[1]

Nevertheless, a growing consensus exists among prominent international public bodies, such as the United Nations Environment Programme (UN Environment) and Interpol, that environmental crime is one of the fastest growing areas of criminality. Based, inter alia, on estimates from intelligence activities and performed seizures, the many crimes related to the exploitation of the environment are currently estimated to be the fourth largest criminal activity in the world, following immediately after drug smuggling, counterfeiting and human trafficking.[2]

Evidence has also mounted that environmental crime is often transnational,[3] i.e. that it often involves more than one jurisdiction in terms of its perpetrators, the

1 See Grazia Maria Vagliasindi, 'The Fight against Environmental Crime in the European Union and its Member States: A Perspective on the Enforcement System' (2016) 87 *Revue International de Droit Pénal* 151, 166–167 and 179–180.

2 See Christian Nellemann, Rune Henriksen, Arnold Kreilhuber, Dawyth Stewart, Maria Kotsovou, Patricia Raxter, Elizabeth Mrema and Sam Barrat (eds), 'The Rise of Environmental Crime – A Growing Threat To Natural Resources, Peace, Development And Security' (A UNEP-Interpol Rapid Response Assessment, United Nations Environment Programme and RHIPTO Rapid Response–Norwegian Center for Global Analyses, 2016) 7 <www.unep.org> and <www.rhipto.org>; Interpol–UN Environment, 'Strategic Report: Environment, Peace and Security – A Convergence of Threats' (December 2016) 1 <www.interpol.int> and <www.unep.org>.

3 See Christian Nellemann, Rune Henriksen, Patricia Raxter, Neville Ash and Elizabeth Mrema (eds), 'The Environmental Crime Crisis: Threats to Sustainable Development from Illegal Exploitation and Trade in Wildlife and Forest Resources' (A UNEP Rapid Response Assessment, UN Environment and GRID-Arendal, 2014) <www.grida.no>.

preparation, planning, direction, control, execution, objects and effects of the unlawful conduct or, finally, the movement or investment of the proceeds of the crime.

Environmental crime of a cross-border or transnational character (often referred to as transnational environmental crime, TEC) has steadily increased over the last decade.[4] In general terms, the rapid expansion of TEC black markets can be explained as an unwanted consequence of globalisation, which provides perpetrators with relevant opportunities in terms of free trade, commodity shipments, fewer border controls and easier transfers and laundering of funds.[5] It is worth adding that the same growth of environmental governance is deemed to have played a role in the expansion of TEC,[6] since the enactment and enforcement of environmental legislation and related control mechanisms, from a criminological point of view, significantly contributed to the parallel rise of lucrative activities carried out in violation of the applicable restrictions or bans.

Given that this is the general framework within which TEC has expanded, the response to this challenging criminal phenomenon clearly requires a deep understanding of its specific causes, characteristics and impacts.

This paper focuses on the complex dynamics underpinning the drivers, perpetrators, manifestations and impacts of TEC and how these dynamics affect (or should affect) the regulation and governance of this criminal phenomenon. The hypothesis is that, as a consequence of such dynamics, crime prevention and control policies require a multifaceted armamentarium, where targeted command and control mechanisms interact with consensual instruments. At the same time, intra-agency and inter-agency cooperation between all the public authorities concerned, as well as cooperation between the latter and citizens and stakeholders, should be fostered, as should public awareness of the phenomenon.

This chapter is structured as follows. First, the drivers, perpetrators, manifestations and impacts of TEC are summarised. Based on these, targeted command and control mechanisms are identified and analysed. Then, consensual instruments are discussed. Finally, innovative, inclusive cooperation tools and awareness-raising initiatives are addressed. Considerations on the way forward will make up the conclusion.

4 See Nellemann et al., 'The Rise of Environmental Crime' (n 2) 7–8.

5 See Lorraine Elliot and William H Schaedla, 'Transnational Environmental Cime: Excavating the Complexities – An Introduction' in Lorraine Elliot and William H Schaedla (eds), *Handbook of Transnational Environmental Crime* (Edward Elgar 2016) 4. With regard to environmental crime of transnational relevance in the specific context of the European Union, see Grazia Maria Vagliasindi, 'La direttiva 2008/99/CE e il Trattato di Lisbona: verso un nuovo volto del diritto penale ambientale italiano' (2010) 24 *Diritto del Commercio Internazionale* 449, 457–463.

6 Elliot and Schaedla, 'Transnational Environmental Crime' (n 5) 4; however, the authors note that this is somehow paradoxical. In fact, the lack of international global agreements covering a certain area of polluting or otherwise environment-affecting economic activities is a first and major facilitating factor for TEC; see, for instance, David Humphreys, 'Forest Crimes and the International Trade in Illegally Logged Timber' in Lorraine Elliot and William H Schaedla (eds), *Handbook of Transnational Environmental Crime* (Edward Elgar 2016) 168–189.

Drivers, perpetrators, manifestations and impacts of TEC

Five areas of environmental criminality are especially salient in TEC:

1. Illegal trade in endangered, threatened and protected wildlife (animal and plants) species or products and derivatives thereof (also referred to as illegal wildlife trade or wildlife trafficking);
2. Illegal shipment and illegal transboundary disposal of hazardous waste (also referred to as waste trafficking);
3. Illegal trade in (illegally logged) timber (also referred to as timber smuggling);
4. Illegal trade in controlled chemicals (including ozone-depleting substances, ODS); and
5. Illegal, unreported and unregulated (IUU) fishing (lately also referred to as fisheries crimes).

Some key features of these areas of criminality should be highlighted here.[7]

Significant opportunities for large profits are associated with this non-exhaustive list of TEC black markets, making TEC a high-profit criminal activity. Such opportunities arise from the fact that TEC black markets, which usually have a corresponding legal market, can offer activities and services at a lower cost than the corresponding legal market. In other cases, they offer the production or distribution of goods that are scarce in the legal market due to restrictions on access to resources or trade restrictions, or goods and services that are otherwise illegal by their classification. Thus, TEC is characterised by a profitable 'supply and demand' dynamic.

As Hayman and Brack note, 'criminal activities are structured around multilateral exchanges involving producers, processors, retailers and final consumers where supply and demand for services interact in a free-market

7 For a more detailed analysis of the features of TEC highlighted in this section, see, for instance, Gavin Hayman and Duncan Brack, 'International Environmental Crime: The Nature and Control of Environmental Black Markets' (The Royal Institute of International Affairs 2002) 1–42; Vagliasindi, 'La direttiva 2008/99/CE' (n 5); Glen Wright, 'Conceptualising and Combating Transnational Environmental Crime' (2011) 14(4) *Trends in Organized Crime* 332; Rob White, *Transnational Environmental Crime. Toward an Eco-global Criminology* (Routledge 2011); Lorraine Elliot and William H Schaedla (eds), *Handbook of Transnational Environmental Crime* (Edward Elgar 2016); Toine Saipens, Rob White and Wim Huisman (eds), *Environmental Crime in Transnational Context* (Routledge 2016); Eurojust, 'Strategic Project on Environmental Crime Report' (November 2014) <www.eurojust.europa.eu/doclibrary/Eurojust-framework/Casework/Strategic%20project%20on%20environmental%20crime%20(November%202014)/environmental-crime-report_2014-11–21-EN.pdf>; European Commission, 'Analysis and Evidence in Support of the EU Action Plan against Wildlife Trafficking' (Staff Working Document) SWD (2016) 38 final <http://eur-lex.europa.eu/legal-content/EN/TXT/PDF/?uri=CELEX:52016SC0038&from=EN>; Nellemann et al., 'The Rise of Environmental Crime' (n 2) *passim*; Interpol-UN Environment, 'Strategic Report: Environment, Peace and Security' (n 2) *passim*.

relationship'.[8] The factors that fuel this supply and demand dynamic vary depending on the criminal activity at issue. While some conduct may be driven by poverty, particularly at the low level of the supply chain (e.g. in the case of poaching),[9] TEC is usually profit-motivated. Profit is relevant as a driver in terms of positive patrimonial increase (e.g. with regard to a 'professional' dealer in endangered species or a shipment company engaging in illegal waste shipment) as well as cost-savings of environmental compliance (e.g. with regard to the producer of waste which is illegally shipped and dumped or the end-user of ODS who saves the cost of alternative, more expensive chemical products) and even tax evasion. In some cases, the so-called 'uncritical markets' fuel the supply and demand dynamic in that buyers do not take into account the way a certain good has been obtained, processed or transported.[10]

TEC usually consists of a criminal supply chain through which environmental commodities are trafficked with the contribution of various actors who intervene at different stages. Since the source of the commodity is typically located in a country (or continent) different from its final destination, perpetrators use a variety of commodity shipments methods and circulation routes as well as complex concealment and smuggling techniques to perform the displacement of the environmental commodities.[11] As it has been noted, '[c]omplicated networks of interaction exist that link raw materials and producers to customers through a web of supplier relationships with the involvement of ancillary specialist services and other key actors such as legitimate business, government officials and consumers'.[12] With the exception of low-volume, low-value cases (e.g. those concerning tourists who occasionally extract or buy protected wildlife species or derivatives thereof), TEC is often committed by loosely organised networks of individuals with some specialist knowledge in the concerned regulated area. In those cases, reference to the notion of 'organisation' has to be interpreted as referring to informal unity and reciprocity rather than to a hierarchical

8 Hayman and Brack (n 7) 6.

9 On inequalities associated with a generalised criminalisation of TEC-related illegal activities as far as poverty-driven crimes are concerned, see Peter Andreas, 'Transnational Crime and Economic Globalization' in Mats Berdal and Mónica Serrano (eds), *Transnational Organized Crime and International Security: Business as Usual?* (Lynne Rienner 2002) 37–38. It is worth recalling that poaching – a ring of the illegal wildlife trade chain – refers to a variety of offences that criminalise the unlawful taking of wild animals (for instance, poaching may involve the hunting of animals that belong to a protected species or illegal hunting outside designated areas).

10 On uncritical markets, see Christian Nellemann, Ian Redmond and Johannes Refisch (eds), 'The Last Stand of the Gorilla: Environmental Crime and Conflict in the Congo Basin (A Rapid Response Assessment, UN Environment and GRID-Arendal, 2010) 34 <www.grida.no>; see also Elliot and Schaedla, 'Transnational Environmental Crime' (n 5) 5.

11 For more details, see Interpol-UN Environment, 'Strategic Report: Environment, Peace and Security' (n 2) *passim*.

12 Hayman and Brack (n 7) 7.

structure.[13] However, evidence also exists of the involvement of more traditional hierarchically structured organised crime that has adapted its area of action to lucrative environmental crimes[14] (with the hypothesis that such involvement is directly proportional to the level of complexity of legislative regulation of a certain area and extent and depth of control mechanisms). These criminal groups take advantage of territorial divisions in terms of controls and enforcement of existing regulation.

Several forms of links between TEC and other crimes have been reported. Environmental crime can be a source of capital for more traditional crimes such as drug trafficking, and the two types of crimes may (although rarely) even be combined (e.g. wildlife species used to traffic narcotics). Environmental crime appears to be reliant on, or otherwise linked to, corruption, which offenders use as an instrument to evade national regulations (e.g. in the allocation of licenses to exploit resources or granting of certificates to trade in endangered species) and related controls (e.g. customs controls), to the extent that corruption has been regarded as an externality of some legislative and enforcement regimes in environmental matters. It is worth adding that a distinctive concept of 'illegal laundering' is also associated with TEC as a means to commit the crime, often in combination with corruption, fraud and forgery. For instance, endangered wildlife species are laundered as captive-bred ones through false certifications; illegal timber harvesting is laundered through seemingly legitimate *ex post* concessions; and hazardous waste is laundered as non-hazardous waste through false analysis and related official documentation. Lately, relevant links between environmental crime and money laundering have been reported, as well as cases of environmental crime being used to finance terrorist organisations. In sum, as UN Environment and Interpol posit, a 'convergence of crimes' exists as TEC is facilitated by and, at the same time, fuels other crimes.[15]

While every individual (as well as local community) can be affected by environmental crime in general and TEC in particular, thus being the potential or long-term victim of this criminal offence (an issue that is increasingly addressed by criminologists and public and private bodies), TEC is still considered technically a victimless crime since it mainly consists of an economic crime based on the consensual exchange of goods and services, with the consequence that there are rarely victims to complain of offences.

Multiple negative impacts arise from TEC. In addition to adverse impacts on environmental quality (air, land and water), biodiversity (endangered species) and natural resources (timber, fish stocks and other extracted or harvested resources),

13 On criminal networks and organisations with specific regard to environmental crime, see Hayman and Brack (n 7) 7; more recently, Lorraine Elliot, 'Criminal Networks and Illicit Chains of Custody in Transnational Environmental Crime' in Lorraine Elliot and William H Schaedla (eds), *Handbook of Transnational Environmental crime* (Edward Elgar 2016) 24–44, and literature therein.

14 Vagliasindi, 'La direttiva 2008/99/CE' (n 5) 458–460.

15 Interpol–UN Environment, 'Strategic Report: Environment, Peace and Security' (n 2) 1.

relevant direct and indirect economic and socio-political consequences are associated with TEC. Direct negative economic impacts, as well as significant hidden costs to society, arise from TEC. For instance, severe health consequences arise from the abovementioned environmental impacts, which result in significant costs in terms of healthcare and lost incomes. The loss of biodiversity (habitats and iconic protected species) as a consequence of environmental crimes, such as poaching, has a negative impact on wildlife-based tourism development and the sustainable utilisation and legal trade of wildlife, which often provide a significant contribution to local livelihoods and national economic development.[16] It is worth noting that this usually occurs in less-developed countries that offer some of the world's most well-known wildlife watching destinations. Losses of government revenue should also be mentioned. This is the case, for instance, with illegally harvested natural resources, which deprives states of related tax revenues. This type of TEC black market also contributes to depressing the prices of the resources and reducing the resources available for legitimate exports; both outcomes that have negative economic impacts on legitimate business. This also leads to notice that TEC has indirect negative impacts on fair competition as a result of the fact that an economic operator (e.g. the waste producer), through the commission of TEC, saves the cost of environmental compliance. Due to its links with other crimes, and with corruption in particular, TEC may undermine good governance and, especially where 'states of fragility' exist,[17] may significantly contribute to compromising the rule of law.

TEC as a serious threat to sustainable development and the need for a multifaceted response

As demonstrated by the above, the drivers, perpetrators, manifestations and impacts associated with TEC go beyond an environmental dimension. This criminal phenomenon can overall be best described in terms of a serious threat to sustainable development. In fact, the United Nations recognises that 'violations of environmental law undermine the achievement of all dimensions of sustainable development and environmental sustainability'.[18]

16 See DEFRA, DfID, FCO and Home Office, 'London Conference on Illegal Wildlife Trade. Declaration' (13 February 2014) <www.gov.uk/government/publications/declaration-london-conference-on-the-illegal-wildlife-trade>.

17 It is worth noting that over the years the Organisation for Economic Co-operation and Development (OECD) has switched its focus from 'Fragile States' to 'States of Fragility', in doing so stressing fragility as a heightened exposure to risk combined with a low capacity to mitigate or absorb these risks, that is to say a situation of vulnerability which can lead to violence, conflict, chronic underdevelopment and protracted political crisis and undermines the achievement of a just, peaceful and inclusive society. On the issue, see OECD, 'States of Fragility 2016: Understanding Violence' (OECD, 30 November 2016) <www.oecd.org/dac/states-of-fragility-2016-9789264267213-en.htm>.

18 UN, 'Environmental Law' <www.un.org/ruleoflaw/thematic-areas/land-property-environment/environmental-law/>.

In this respect, it is worth recalling that, on 25 September 2015, the UN General Assembly adopted the 2030 Agenda for Sustainable Development.[19] The agenda is composed of 17 Sustainable Development Goals and 169 associated targets aimed at achieving sustainable development.

The analysis of these Goals and targets shows that, given the overall characteristics of TEC highlighted above, a conspicuous number of these targets are directly or indirectly relevant in terms of a commitment of the international community to eradicate social, economic and environmental weaknesses which represent opportunities, causes, manifestations or impacts of the areas of criminality associated with TEC.[20]

This is the case, for instance, for Goal 12 ('Ensure sustainable consumption and production patterns'), whose targets encompass inter alia 'By 2030, achieve the sustainable management and efficient use of natural resources' as well as

> By 2020, achieve the environmentally sound management of chemicals and all wastes throughout their life cycle, in accordance with agreed international frameworks, and significantly reduce their release to air, water and soil in order to minimize their adverse impacts on human health and the environment.

The same holds true for Goal 14 ('Conserve and sustainably use the oceans, seas and marine resources'), whose targets encompass inter alia: 'By 2025, prevent and significantly reduce marine pollution of all kinds, in particular from land-based activities, including marine debris and nutrient pollution' as well as:

> By 2020, effectively regulate harvesting and end overfishing, illegal, unreported and unregulated fishing and destructive fishing practices and implement science-based management plans, in order to restore fish stocks in the shortest time feasible, at least to levels that can produce maximum sustainable yield as determined by their biological characteristics.

The targets of Goal 14 also include: 'Enhance the conservation and sustainable use of oceans and their resources by implementing international law as reflected in UNCLOS, which provides the legal framework for the conservation and sustainable use of oceans and their resources …'.

19 UN General Assembly, 'Transforming our World: The 2030 Agenda for Sustainable Development' UN Doc A/RES/70/1 <www.un.org/ga/search/view_doc.asp?symbol=A/RES/70/1&Lang=E>.

20 The Sustainable Development Goals are available at <www.un.org/sustainabledevelopment/sustainable-development-goals/>.

Moreover, targets of Goal 15 ('Sustainably manage forests, combat desertification, halt and reverse land degradation, halt biodiversity loss') concern inter alia 'Take urgent action to end poaching and trafficking of protected species of flora and fauna and address both demand and supply of illegal wildlife products' as well as 'Enhance global support for efforts to combat poaching and trafficking of protected species, including by increasing the capacity of local communities to pursue sustainable livelihood opportunities'.

Furthermore, Goal 16 ('Promote just, peaceful and inclusive societies') encompasses within its targets inter alia: 'By 2030, significantly reduce illicit financial and arms flows, strengthen the recovery and return of stolen assets and combat all forms of organized crime'; 'Substantially reduce corruption and bribery in all their forms'; 'Strengthen relevant national institutions, including through international cooperation, for building capacity at all levels, in particular in developing countries, to prevent violence and combat terrorism and crime'; and 'Promote the rule of law at the national and international levels and ensure equal access to justice for all'.

Finally, it is worth mentioning Goal 1 ('End poverty in all its forms everywhere'). This is an overarching objective of the Agenda, whose ambitious targets may well contribute to address what is also a driver of certain illicit conduct in the supply chain of TEC.

More generally, it should be stressed that all the Goals and associated targets set out in the Agenda, which are, by express statement, 'integrated and indivisible',[21] can be deemed extremely significant in terms of providing an overall context that minimises opportunities for and impacts of the commission of TEC. It is also worth adding that the Agenda acknowledges 'the role of the diverse private sector, ranging from micro-enterprises to cooperatives to multinationals, and that of civil society organizations and philanthropic organizations' in the implementation of the same Agenda.[22]

At the regional level, the Communication on the European Union (EU) Action Plan against Wildlife Trafficking, adopted by the European Commission on 26 February 2016, should be mentioned.[23] The Action Plan is a major contribution to the 2030 Agenda for Sustainable Development, and particularly to its Goal 15 as far as ending poaching and trafficking of protected species and addressing both demand and supply of illegal wildlife

21 UN General Assembly (n 19) 1/35.

22 Ibid.

23 Commission, 'EU Action Plan against Wildlife Trafficking' (Communication) COM (2016) 87 final <http://eur-lex.europa.eu/legal-content/EN/TXT/PDF/?uri=CELEX:52016DC0087&from=EN>.

products are concerned.[24] To this end, the Action Plan sets out a comprehensive pattern for joined-up efforts to fight wildlife crime inside the EU, and for strengthening the EU's role in the global fight against these illegal activities. In particular, the Action Plan – which is to be implemented until 2020 – comprises a series of measures that are based on three priorities: preventing wildlife trafficking and addressing its root causes; implementing and enforcing existing rules and combating organised wildlife crime more effectively; and strengthening the global partnership of source, consumer and transit countries against wildlife trafficking.[25] Thus, as explicitly stated, these measures 'are designed to address a complex problem holistically by involving all relevant organisations'.[26] Importantly, the Action Plan stresses that, in its implementation, 'it will be essential to work together closely with stakeholders, including civil society organisations and relevant business sectors, on many specific measures to make maximum use of the available expertise and knowledge and ensure maximum impact'.[27]

These considerations lead us to conclude that targeting the complex dynamics underpinning TEC requires a holistic approach. This implies a shift from a mere public regulation and correlative enforcement-based approach to a multifaceted governance paradigm, where the former coexists and interacts with the inclusive active involvement and contribution of non-state actors, legitimate business and citizens in tackling the deep roots, the complex manifestations and the pervasive impacts of TEC.

A targeted legal framework and effective related enforcement tools

The first component of a comprehensive and effective response to TEC is a tailored legal framework and sufficient related enforcement capacities, resources and training, with the aim of targeting the specificities of perpetrators and manifestations of TEC outlined above.

Since no global or regional agreement addresses TEC as such and as a whole, the legal framework indirectly or directly relevant to TEC is a very complex and articulated one. International, regional and domestic legislation is relevant to the phenomenon.[28] In particular, the legal framework relevant to TEC consists inter alia of:

- the environmental provisions agreed in international or regional Multilateral Environmental Agreements (MEAs) that States should transfer into domestic environmental administrative law;

24 Ibid. 4.
25 Ibid. 5.
26 Ibid.
27 Ibid.
28 For a more detailed analysis of the legal framework and related issues outlined in this subsection, see Grazia Maria Vagliasindi, 'The Transnational Dimension of Environmental Crime: A Legal Analysis' in Valsamis Mitsilegas, Saskia Hufnagel and Anton Moiseienko (eds), *Research Handbook on Transnational Crime* (Edward Elgar, forthcoming).

- the (rare) obligations contained in international or regional MEAs concerning the criminal consequences of the violations of the rules set out in the treaties, which States should transfer into their domestic criminal law;
- the provisions contained in international or regional agreements concerning issues of relevance to TEC as a criminal phenomenon, e.g. those on organised crime, corruption, money laundering, terrorism, confiscation and forfeiture of proceeds of crime;
- bilateral agreements on police and judicial cooperation;
- all the corresponding domestic/national administrative and criminal provisions.

Several characteristics of the current legal framework result in weaknesses in the prevention and repression of TEC. This consideration concerns both the environmental law and the criminal law apparatus.

An uneven design and implementation of environmental law at international, regional and domestic level is regarded as a contributing cause to the expansion of environmental crime. The lack of global MEAs in certain areas of relevance to TEC (e.g. as far as timber trade is concerned), unclear definitions in existing MEAs (e.g. that of 'hazardous waste' under the Basel Convention)[29] as well as uneven compliance by Parties with the obligations under existing MEAs, are facilitating factors for the commission of TEC. In addition, with a few exceptions MEAs do not address the punitive side of violations of the regulatory frameworks that are in place to comply with their international obligations; thus, responses to violations vary significantly among states, including cases where a given unlawful conduct is not sanctioned within a given jurisdiction.

This leads to the criminal law perspective, where weak (or non-existent) applicable criminal legislation and penalties, under-specialisation of police forces and lack of resources available to enforcement authorities are usually regarded as key factors unintendedly enabling perpetrators to undertake their illegal activities. These factors are coupled with the lack of globally agreed definitions on the constitutive elements of environmental crimes and the lack of harmonised or approximated sanctions: a situation that contributes to hamper customs, police and judicial cooperation whenever environmental crime, as is often the case, has a cross-border or transnational dimension. In fact, serious control, enforcement and judicial cooperation issues are generated by environmental crimes of a transnational character and several extraterritorial issues are associated with these crimes.[30] This is the case, for example, for extraterritorial companies that own 'flags of convenience' vessels engaged in IUU fishing. More generally, it is worth

29 Basel Convention on the Control of Transboundary Movements of Hazardous Wastes and Their Disposal (adopted 22 March 1989, entered into force 5 May 1992) 1673 UNTS 57.

30 See Hayman and Brack (n 7) 29. It is worth recalling that, according to Article 92(1) of the UN Convention on the Law of the Sea (adopted 10 December 1982, entered into force 16 November 1994) 1833–1835 UNTS 3 (UNCLOS), ships shall sail under the flag of one state only and shall be subject to its exclusive jurisdiction on the high seas.

recalling that a widespread model of development implemented in many countries promotes foreign investment in various sectors of their economies, and that foreign investment is often designed to finance activities related to the extraction of natural resources and/or large-scale industrial processes – activities that generate, in most cases, serious environmental impacts.[31]

These weaknesses in the regulatory framework and related enforcement mechanisms, coupled with the opportunities of high profits arising from the supply and demand dynamic underpinning TEC black markets (see above), contribute to making environmental crime and, in particular, environmental crime with a transnational dimension, a high-profit, widespread criminal activity with a low risk of detection.

Clearly, enacting and enforcing laws against an illegal form of trade, such as TEC, in a context where legal cross-border economic flows are greatly encouraged, is not an easy task.[32] However, a more systematic understanding of TEC as a criminal phenomenon is needed by legislators and policy makers, including its driving forces, modus operandi, impacts and gaps in applicable legislation which result in facilitating factors for the actors of TEC.[33] Indeed, a comprehensive and balanced approach is necessary at the legislative level, which adequately addresses both the individual and corporate offenders and the overall criminal market in which they operate. The result of such efforts should constitute the basis for national and international strategies, which include tailored legislative instruments and enforcement tools.

The adoption of a global international suppression treaty on TEC as such and as a whole is an appealing solution, as is the inclusion in MEAs of obligations of criminalisation including common thresholds of criminal penalties for the violation of the treaty's provisions. However, these solutions are also difficult to achieve, not least because criminal law is a core element of national sovereignty that states are reluctant to renounce.

This consideration is without prejudice to the important role that prominent international institutions may and actually do play in urging member states, through soft law instruments, to tailor their national legal instruments and

31 In this regard, it is interesting to note that as far back as 1994, the General Assembly of IUCN – The World Conservation Union, at its 19th Session in Buenos Aires, Argentina, on 17–26 January 1994, recommended that all States 'develop environmental policies which require foreign investors to apply measures aimed at minimizing negative environmental impact, as well as at restoring environments which have been altered by the effects of their operations' and called upon transnational corporations 'to implement, within their operations, measures aimed at minimizing their environmental impact, even in countries which do not have regulations governing this situation'; see <https://portals.iucn.org/library/sites/library/files/resrecfiles/GA_19_REC_034_Environmental_Impact_of_Transitional.pdf>.

32 See Elliot and Schaedla, 'Transnational environmental crime' (n 5) 4, who stress that: 'The expansion of TEC black markets is a consequence, albeit an unintended one, of a globalized liberal political economy'; with regard to the trafficking in illegal waste within the borders of the EU, facilitated by the free movements of goods and people, see Eurojust (n 7) 16.

33 Hayman and Brack (n 7) 6.

related enforcement tools to the seriousness of environmental crime, its transnational dimension and interconnectedness with upstream and downstream crimes. For instance, relevant resolutions in this sense, with a particular emphasis on wildlife crime, have been adopted by the UN Economic and Social Council (ECOSOC), such as resolutions 1994/15, 2001/12, 2008/25, 2011/36 and 2012/19; also worth mentioning are resolutions 16/1 and 20/5 of the Commission on Crime Prevention and Criminal Justice (CCPCJ) of the United Nations Office on Drugs and Crime (UNODC).

At a national level, appropriate administrative environmental legislation, which fully complies with international obligations set out in MEAs, should be put in place. Definitions in MEAs and domestic implementing legislation should be clear in order to orientate economic actors and facilitate controls and law enforcement.

As concerns criminal law, an important requirement is that serious violations of domestic legislation that was enacted to implement global and regional MEAs should constitute a criminal offence. Obviously, criminal law should not be used in a merely symbolic way and the level of penalties should be proportionate to the seriousness of the offence and consistent with the levels of sanctions provided for other crimes in the same jurisdiction. This said, the issue of non-existent or low penalties for environmental crimes should be addressed at the national level as it concerns deliberate violations of environmental law perpetrated in an organised manner in pursuing profit. It is worth noting that the level of criminal penalties also has an indirect effect in terms of prioritisation of environmental crimes in the law enforcement chain. Thus, national criminal legislation should include dissuasive penalties for serious environmental crimes, corporate responsibility and confiscation of proceeds of crime.

Penalties for TEC should be approximated to the maximum extent possible in order to avoid exploitation by offenders (often corporations and often variably organised) of discrepancies among national legislation. In addition, this approximation, together with the introduction of higher penalties for serious environmental crimes, would allow environmental crimes to fall under the umbrella of existing relevant international and regional legal instruments or otherwise 'activate' existing substantive and cooperation legal instruments whose application is currently blocked by an insufficient level of penalties for environmental crimes. This is the case, for instance, with the 2000 United Nations Convention on Transnational Organized Crime (the Palermo Convention) and, at the EU level, the Framework Decision 2008/841/JHA on the fight against organised crime or the EU provisions on the European Arrest Warrant. As mentioned above, a top-down approach (i.e. setting obligations of criminalisation and common ranges of penalties in a global suppression convention on TEC or in every MEA) would be very difficult to implement at least in the short run. However, the positive influence of existing international efforts through soft law instruments may realistically contribute to activate a spontaneous bottom-up approximation; this influence may also lead to the possible adoption of a Protocol to the Palermo Convention that would most likely deal with, given the current stage of development of international soft law instruments, transnational organised wildlife crime.

Given the highly technical nature of environmental crime in general and the cross-jurisdictional challenges posed by its transnational character, sufficient capacity, resources and specialisation of the enforcement authorities are essential, as is intra-agency and inter-agency cooperation. As to the latter, information sharing and illegal trade trends monitoring tools can be very effective in ensuring cooperation between enforcement authorities; this is the case, for instance, with the European Union-Trade in Wildlife Information eXchange (EU-TWIX).[34] It is also worth mentioning the benefits of cooperation through environmental enforcement networks,[35] which represent a relatively low-cost avenue towards the establishment and intensification of contacts between professionals and practitioners on the strategic, technical and operational level, on operational aspects and the sharing of best practices. Moreover, given the complexity of drivers, manifestations and impacts of TEC, agreements aiming to improve coordination and capacity of the various regulatory and enforcement intergovernmental agencies concerned are important. The International Consortium on Combating Wildlife Crime (ICCWC)[36] – composed of Interpol, UNODC, the Convention on International Trade in Endangered Species of Wild Fauna and Flora (CITES) Secretariat, the World Customs Organization and the World Bank – is a prominent example of such efforts.

The complex cross-jurisdictional issues associated with TEC – both concurring jurisdictions and extraterritorial jurisdictions – should be taken into consideration also at the legislative level, particularly as far as corporate crime is concerned. In this respect, regional enforcement cooperation agreements may help to overcome challenges related to multiple jurisdictions.[37] Moreover, a legislative basis for a so-called 'long-arm enforcement' should be provided to allow extraterritorial actions to enforce controls, prosecution and sanctioning also outside national boundaries,[38] including with regard to money laundering and confiscation of proceeds of crime.

34 See <http://eu-twix.org/>.

35 For example, the International Network for Environmental Compliance and Enforcement (INECE) or, at the EU level, the European Network for the Implementation and Enforcement of Environmental Law (IMPEL), the European Network for Environmental Crime (EnviCrimeNet), the European Network of Prosecutors for the Environment (ENPE) and the European Union Forum of Judges for the Environment (EUFJE).

36 See <https://cites.org/eng/prog/iccwc.php>.

37 Hayman and Brack (n 7) 26; the authors note that (at that time) the most innovative model was the 1996 Lusaka Agreement on Cooperative Enforcement Operations Directed at Illegal Trade in Wild Fauna and Flora, which makes extensive provision for shared, cross-border investigations into transnational wildlife poaching gangs in central and eastern Africa. At the EU level, Europol, Eurojust and, in a *de iure condendo perspective*, the European Public Prosecutor may assume a leading role in the region.

38 Hayman and Brack (n 7) 32–33.

It is clear that putting in place, implementing and enforcing a legal framework that is targeted at a relatively new but complex, pervasive, fast-growing and self-adapting criminal phenomenon is an extremely challenging operation, particularly in times of low public resources and concurring serious global threats like terrorism, which are very resource-demanding in terms of countering actions. This consideration, coupled with the specific features of environmental crime of a transnational character (demand and supply dynamics, involvement of corporations, links to corruption, fraud and money laundering, and a criminal supply chain that takes advantage of transport facilities to traffic environmental commodities), leads to the realisation that fostering consensual instruments and innovative forms of cooperation between state and non-state actors, legitimate business and the public are significant and relatively low-cost complementary tools to enhance the fight against environmental crime.

Non-binding mechanisms and corporate social responsibility

The potential role of voluntary mechanisms as an indirect tool in fighting environmental crimes should be explored, particularly in times of limited public resources. Rather than to international standards, such as those of the International Organization for Standardization (ISO),[39] the main reference here is to the Eco-Management and Audit Scheme (EMAS) provided for at the EU level.[40]

EMAS is a management instrument developed by the European Commission for companies and other organisations to evaluate, report and improve their environmental performance. In order to obtain and maintain the EMAS registration, this voluntary mechanism, among other requirements, demands full compliance with environmental legislation. It is worth noting that such an important requirement does not exist under established international standards, such as the ISO norms. In addition to the improvement of the organisation's environmental performance (which produces advantages in terms of a more efficient use of resources, resulting in cost-savings) and the enhanced reputation of the registered organisation (which is relevant as far as critical consumers are concerned), the EMAS registration provides competitive advantages to the adopting organisation (for example, preference in public tenders and reduction of the financial guarantees requested to obtain an environmental permit) under national legislations.

Incentives to adopt non-binding mechanisms like EMAS, which require full compliance with environmental legislation, should be further enhanced, and this should be done not as an alternative to command and control mechanisms. The voluntary adhesion to such mechanisms by a given organisation, in implying

39 See <www.iso.org/home.html>.

40 Regulation (EC) No 1221/2009 of the European Parliament and of the Council of 25 November 2009 on the voluntary participation by organisations in a Community eco-management and audit scheme (EMAS), repealing Regulation (EC) No 761/2001 and Commission Decisions 2001/681/EC and 2006/193/EC [2009] OJ L342/1.

compliance with environmental legislation, should indirectly contribute to reducing the risk of the commission of environmental crimes within the adopting organisation.

This might also lead to increased effectiveness of those mechanisms that aim to prevent the commission of crimes within corporations, i.e. the compliance programmes. It should be noted that certain national legislations on corporate responsibility for environmental crimes (for example, in Italy and Spain) refer and give relevance (in terms of exclusion of responsibility or reduction of the punishment) to the adoption and effective implementation by corporations and collective entities of 'organisational models' (similar to the compliance programmes) that set out procedures, responsibilities and control mechanisms that aim at preventing the commission of crimes within the corporation. Although not identical in terms of requirements and content, the environmental management system under the EMAS scheme has similarities to the abovementioned 'organisational models'. Indeed, both instruments are based on a strong preventive approach.[41] This appears to be of extreme relevance in terms of preventing environmental crimes as well as associated crimes like corruption, which experience has shown are often a tool for or otherwise connected to the commission of environmental crimes.

As such, a shift from a mere criminal responsibility-based approach to a more comprehensive one, which combines the former with the conscious involvement of corporations and organisations in general in the prevention of environmental crime, is, from the perspective of an enhanced corporate social responsibility, a crucial step towards a more inclusive and therefore effective governance of the criminal phenomenon. This might represent a very important tool to address those sometimes unavoidable incentives that, as mentioned above (section 1), a globalised economy unintendedly provides to the commission of TEC.

Awareness raising, stakeholders involvement and public–private partnerships

As well as stressing the potential role of enhancing voluntary mechanisms, a further question should be asked about the potential role of private actors in the fight against environmental crime.

In particular, the complexity of TEC as a criminal phenomenon gives rise to the need to explore the potential of new systems of governance of TEC and the role that state actors, non-state actors, legitimate business and citizens can play therein. The main reference here is to public–private partnerships, i.e. those partnerships where customs, police and other law enforcement authorities, on the one side, and legitimate business and other involved stakeholders, on the other, join forces to tackle illegal trade.

41 Vagliasindi, 'La direttiva 2008/99/CE' (n 5) 484–485.

Recently, relevant examples of such partnerships can be found with regard to illegal wildlife trade, a criminal phenomenon that is often organised and mainly transnational in nature. In fact, illegal wildlife species, and products thereof, typically travel long distances from source-field to market. This transport-intensive activity involves air, land and sea ports, passenger and cargo airlines, shipping companies, express couriers, freight forwarders and customs brokers. As mentioned above, wildlife traffickers exploit the increasing connectivity of global transportation, online markets, and gaps in law enforcement to minimise the risk of detection during operations.

Thus, since illegal trade in wild animals and plants and derived products features such a global dimension, removing vulnerabilities in transportation and customs administrations in terms of the detection of illegal wildlife trade and legitimately enhancing cooperation and networking between the transport sector, customs administrations and enforcement authorities is essential in order to address this crucial stage of the wildlife trafficking chain.

In this respect, the Reducing Opportunities for Unlawful Transport of Endangered Species (ROUTES) Partnership should be mentioned.[42] Funded by the United States Agency for International Development and led by the non-governmental organisation TRAFFIC, ROUTES was established in 2015 with a five-year mandate. It is an innovative partnership that brings together international conservation organisations, donors, governments, and the transportation and logistics industry in pursuing the goal of disrupting wildlife trafficking by reducing the use of legal transportation supply chains.

The United for Wildlife Transport Taskforce Buckingham Palace Declaration of 15 March 2016 should also be mentioned.[43] This Declaration is another example of those horizontal arrangements that combine public financial and technical support with private sector initiatives. This public–private partnership, signed by high-level leaders of airlines, shipping firms, port operators, customs agencies, intergovernmental organisations and conservation charities, aims at raising standards across the transport industry and enhancing the industry's responsible role in combating illegal wildlife trade, as well as fostering cooperation between the transport sectors, customs administrations and law enforcement authorities.

Signatories to the Declaration commit themselves to improve staff training and increase passenger, customer, client and staff awareness of the nature, scale and consequences of illegal wildlife trade.

42 See <http://routespartnership.org/>. It is worth mentioning a report, recently released within the projects of the ROUTES Partnership, which examines the trends, transit routes, and modus operandi used by wildlife smugglers exploiting the aviation industry with regard to the trafficking of ivory, rhino horn, reptiles, and birds by air from 2009 to August 2016 and presents data-based recommendations for preventing wildlife trafficking through the air transport industry; see Mary Utermohlen and Patrick Baine, 'Flying Under the Radar. Wildlife Trafficking in the Air Transport Sector' (22 May 2017) <http://routespartnership.org/industry-resources/publications/flying-under-the-radar-summary-final.pdf/view>.

43 See <www.unitedforwildlife.org/#!/>.

This means that the transport industry commits itself to provide staff with training to detect certain anomalies (e.g. weight or smell) in passenger baggage and cargo shipments, with the aim of identifying and reporting suspected illegal wildlife. Reportedly, such increased staff training resulted, for instance, in a cargo employee detecting ivory blocks wrapped up in chocolate bar wrappers in an unusually heavy box of chocolates.[44]

In terms of actions directed at passenger, customer and client awareness, one example is that, given the widespread diffusion in the use of international airlines, the simple distribution of a flyer synthesising the unlawfulness of illegal wildlife trade and related criminal consequences, as well as the devastating impact of this criminal market on biodiversity, economies and development, would represent a relatively low-cost action with extremely far-reaching effects as far as ignorant-of-the-law potential actors of illegal wildlife trade on the demand side are concerned. At the same time, such awareness-raising initiatives would be extremely effective in targeting the abovementioned 'uncritical markets' (see above), which are a driver of TEC in that buyers do not take into account the way that a certain good has been obtained, processed or transported. Thus, such a commitment, if implemented, may have relevant positive effects in terms of raising the awareness of the public. Actual examples of passenger awareness campaigns include an airline painting two of its aircrafts with pictures of endangered animals and the United for Wildlife logo, and another airline partnering with a foundation to show conservation videos on its in-flight entertainment system.[45]

In addition to these objectives, the system outlined in the Declaration is based inter alia on adopting practical measures to enhance information sharing and detection and stopping the transportation of illegal wildlife products, such as, for example, by enhancing data systems or improving information-passing from the transport sector to relevant customs and law enforcement authorities, where permitted by law. The Declaration also aims to support the development of mechanisms by the World Customs Organization and national customs authorities to aid the detection and prevention of trade in illegal wildlife and their products; one of these mechanisms could be to build up data-based risk profiles for wildlife trafficking.[46]

The implementation of the commitments set out in the Declaration would significantly contribute to increasing prevention, detection and reporting of wildlife trade when such trade is illegal under international and national laws.

44 See Aircargonews, 'Focus: Illegal wildlife trafficking – Killing by numbers' (*Aircargonews*, 13 April 2017) <www.aircargonews.net/news/forwarders/single-view/news/focus-illegal-wildlife-trafficking-killing-by-numbers.html>.

45 See Kerry Reals, 'Eels on a Plane: How the Aviation Industry is Tackling Wildlife Trafficking' (*The Guardian*, 18 July 2017) <www.theguardian.com/heathrow-sustainable-mobility-zone/2017/jul/18/eels-on-a-plane-how-the-aviation-industry-is-tackling-wildlife-trafficking>.

46 See Aircargonews (n 44).

It has been reported that the implementation of such commitments has resulted in 'several instances of companies taking action against suspect shipments and working directly with relevant customs and law enforcement services, which have resulted in the detection and seizure of illegal wildlife shipments'.[47]

The Declaration, which meets some of the priorities set out in the UN Sustainable Development Goals as well as in the EU Action Plan against Wildlife Trafficking, fosters a role for the involved business sector and may effectively contribute to achieving a greater public awareness of illegal wildlife trade and preventing traffickers exploiting legal transportation facilities, thus having a positive impact on prevention, deterrence and repression of illegal wildlife trade.

Innovative initiatives like the ROUTES Partnership and the Buckingham Palace Declaration show that transport industry leaders are now aware of the global impact of illegal wildlife trafficking as well as of the exploitation of the transport sector by the offenders.[48] The commitments made and actions taken to build awareness, capacity and strategic and cohesive responses to tackle wildlife trafficking show a corporate social responsibility approach by those transport industry leaders who consider it to be a corporate priority of theirs to tackle illegal wildlife trade. Thus, these initiatives are a key element of a multi-actor concerted international response against illegal wildlife trade. In addition, the public–private partnerships against wildlife trafficking may represent a model to enhance cooperation and networking between legitimate business, customs administrations and enforcement authorities in the fight against other forms of illegal trade, as well as for similar awareness-raising initiatives.

Conclusion

The dynamics underpinning TEC and its drivers, perpetrators, manifestations and impacts are very complex. While these dynamics vary among the various areas of criminality relevant to TEC, a common nucleus can be identified in that TEC black markets usually have a corresponding legal market and they flourish because of the demand for illegal goods and services. Thus, a supply and demand dynamic characterises TEC which, with a few exceptions, is a profit-motivated crime, with profit taking the form of both a patrimonial increase (usually on the side of the supply) and cost-savings of environmental compliance (usually on the side of the demand). As to perpetrators and

47 See Reals (n 45).

48 It is also worth recalling that in 2015 the International Air Transport Association (IATA) signed a Memorandum of Understanding with the Secretariat of the Convention on International Trade in Endangered Species of Wild Fauna and Flora (CITES) to cooperate on reducing illegal wildlife trafficking.

manifestations of the crime, TEC is characterised by a criminal supply chain in which multiple actors intervene. These actors are individuals and corporations or corporate-like entities, usually acting in an organised manner, within which the concept of organisation ranges from loosely-organised criminal networks to more hierarchically-structured criminal groups. This criminal supply chain takes advantage of legal commodities, like shipment cargos and other transport means, to perform its criminal activity. Corruption and forgery are often means to commit TEC; tax evasion and money laundering are examples of downstream crimes associated with TEC. Impacts of TEC transcend environmental conservation and protection to encompass economic, social and political long-lasting consequences to the extent that TEC can be regarded as a threat to sustainable development.

Targeting this complex criminal phenomenon requires a multifaceted approach. Obviously, an appropriate legal framework should be in place that targets the specific features of TEC. In addition to harmonised definitions in relevant environmental administrative law, this should encompass an approximation of definitions of the criminal offences and related sanctions at least at the regional level, together with a level of criminal sanctions, which recognises environmental crime of a transnational character as a serious crime, also for the purposes of international instruments on transnational crime. Legal (criminal or administrative) responsibility of corporations for environmental crime should be in place, as well as forfeiture and confiscation measures to target the proceeds of crime. The convergence between TEC and other crimes, in particular corruption and money laundering, should be reflected at the legislative level. Sufficient capacity, resources and specialisation should be guaranteed for security forces in order to enforce the legal framework, including through intra-agency and inter-agency cooperation.

However, the complex dynamics underpinning TEC require a shift from mere public regulation and a related enforcement-based approach to a multifaceted governance paradigm where the public action (legislation, control and enforcement) coexists and interacts with the inclusive contribution of non-state actors, legitimate business and citizens.

This implies, for instance, that further incentives should be provided for the adoption by corporations and organisations of voluntary mechanisms, such as EMAS at the EU level, which aim to improve the environmental performances of the adopting organisation through a process that inter alia requires compliance with environmental legislation. This would indirectly contribute to minimising the risk of the commission of environmental crime by individuals within the organisation, in a perspective that combines criminal liability with corporate social responsibility.

Moreover, cooperation between state actors and non-state actors appears to be a formidable tool to eradicate the possibility of taking advantage of commodities commonly exploited by TEC perpetrators as well as to contribute to raising awareness of the devastating consequences of TEC and, in doing so, to eradicate the deep roots of TEC as far as demand and supply dynamics are concerned.

Currently, initiatives along these lines have been adopted mainly with regard to wildlife trafficking. The ROUTES Partnership and the Buckingham Palace Declaration are relevant examples of a mutual effort between international public bodies, customs administrations, law enforcement agencies and legitimate business towards detection and prevention of TEC and awareness-raising. Moreover, they represent a model for similar initiatives in other areas of relevance to TEC, which would benefit from the interaction of public and private actors for the purpose of depriving criminals of commodities, detecting crimes and, above all, preventing environmental crime of a transnational character, also by increasing the awareness of the public about the challenging and interconnected economic, social and environmental consequences of this criminal phenomenon.

Further enhancing the multifaceted governance approach outlined so far would contribute to increasing the rates of detection and punishment of TEC as well as to eradicating the roots of TEC and ensuring sustainable livelihoods of local communities and economic development, thus meeting the ambitious objectives of the international community as far as sustainable development is concerned.

14 Preventing illicit waste-exports from the Netherlands to China

Toine Spapens, Shanna Mehlbaum and Rudie Neve

Introduction

Recyclable waste is big business. Large amounts are exported from Europe to other parts of the world, for example to be treated and re-used as raw materials. This concerns paper waste, scrap metal, electronic wastes, mixed plastics, waste tyres and end of life vehicles. Destinations are countries in Asia and Africa, but more recently also in South America.[1] Low shipping costs have made it economically attractive to move low-value waste across the globe, and China's industry is a major destination.

'Waste-relations' between China and the Netherlands are particularly interesting, because the majority of waste shipments leaving the European Union (EU) are shipped through the Dutch port of Rotterdam. The harbour is the biggest in the EU, handling some 50 per cent of all cargo exported from the Union on sea-going vessels.[2] In 2009 this amounted to almost 10 million 20-foot equivalent unit (TEU) containers, of which 15 per cent was estimated to contain waste. The Netherlands and Germany mostly contribute metal waste, cables and electronic waste. Ireland and the United Kingdom are important sources of household waste, which is first shipped to the Netherlands where recyclable materials such as plastic, paper and metal are sorted out and sent on to destinations outside the EU. Smaller amounts of waste originating from a variety of other Member States are also transhipped via Rotterdam.[3]

Although the market for trans-frontier shipments of waste is carefully regulated, it is assumed that large amounts of waste are unlawfully exported.[4] General estimates range from 10 to 20 per cent.[5] Annual estimated value of the illegal

1 IMPEL, 'Third Country Collaboration Project: Final report' (February 2014).

2 UNEP, 'Waste Crime – Waste Risks Gaps in Meeting the Global Waste Challenge: A Rapid Response Assessment' (2015).

3 Shanna Mehlbaum and Toine Spapens, 'Enforcing the EU-WSR: Challenges of Cross-border Cooperation' (Project BlockWaste, 2017).

4 Björn Appelqvist and Jeff Cooper, 'Waste Trafficking, Challenges and Actions to be Taken' (ISWA Task Force on Globalisation and Waste Management, 2013).

5 UNEP, 'Basel Convention: Instruction Manual on the Prosecution of Illegal Traffic of Hazardous Wastes or Other Wastes' (2012); Jim Baird, Robin Curry and Paulo Cruz, 'An Overview of Waste Crime, its Characteristics, and the Vulnerability of the EU Waste Sector' (2014) 32(2) *Waste Management & Research* 97.

waste trade lies between US$10 and 12 billion and the activity thus generates very high revenues to the criminal actors involved in the trade.[6] How many shipments exported from the Netherlands are in violation of regulations is unknown. However, Dutch enforcement agencies investigate tens of substantial cases each year, far more than other EU Member States.[7] How many cases involve waste shipments destined for China is unknown.

The aim of this chapter is to explore the *modi operandi* of operators who ship waste illegally to China and how to better prevent these practices. This chapter is organised as follows. To begin with, the second section describes the regulatory framework for waste shipments from the EU to third countries and China in particular, as well as the different agencies involved. The third section presents an overview of the cases and the fourth section describes the *modi operandi* of waste traffickers. In the fifth section we present an overview of the problems enforcement agencies experience in tackling waste trafficking and address initiatives that have been taken to improve enforcement and cross-border cooperation. Finally, the last section offers some conclusions.

The regulatory framework

As mentioned above, transfrontier shipment of waste is carefully regulated to prevent unwanted effects to the environment, to human health and to non-human species. The main instruments at the international level are the Basel Convention on the Control of Transboundary Movements of Hazardous Wastes and their Disposal (the 'Basel Convention') and the OECD Council Decision on the Control of Transfrontier Movements of Waste Destined for Recovery Operations. Within the EU these were transposed into the Regulation on the Supervision and Control of Shipments of Waste within, into and out of the European Community, also known as the Waste Shipment Regulation (WSR) (259/93/EEC, amended by Regulations 1013/2006 and 660/2014).

The main purpose of the WSR is to prevent the shipment of environmentally harmful waste to countries that do not have the provisions to cope with these wastes. Another aim is to ensure environmentally sound processing of the waste.[8] The WSR and the Basel Convention include the following important general obligations: to begin with, it is prohibited to export or import hazardous wastes or other wastes to or from a non-party State. Second, no waste may be exported if the State of import has not given its consent in writing to the specific import. Third, information about proposed transboundary movements must be

6 Françoise Comte, 'Environmental Crime and the Police in Europe: A Panorama and Possible Paths for Future Action' (2006) 15(7) *European Energy and Environmental Law Review* 190.

7 UNEP, 'Instruction Manual on the Prosecution of Illegal Traffic of Hazardous Wastes or Other Wastes' (n 6).

8 ECRAN, 'Workshop Report: Trans Frontier Shipment of Waste (Joint Workshop Wg Waste, Wg Ied/Chemicals And Wg Ecena)' (25–26 May 2016).

communicated to the States concerned, by means of a notification form, so that they may evaluate the effects of the proposed movements on human health and the environment. Fourth, transboundary movements of wastes must only be authorised where there is no danger attaching to their movement and disposal.

The WSR categorises waste in two lists: green and amber. Green (Annex III, Annex IIIa and Annex IIIb) refers to non-hazardous waste, whereas amber concerns hazardous waste (Annex IV and Annex IVa). In addition, export or import prohibitions may apply to specific countries (Annex V). With regard to third countries, export of waste intended for disposal is prohibited unless to European Free Trade Association (EFTA) countries that are also party to the Basel Convention. Export of hazardous waste to non-OECD countries is prohibited. Export of non-hazardous waste is allowed to OECD countries and to non-OECD countries depending on the response of the importing country.

The WSR requires either notification of shipments or a so-called Annex VII document. Notification is usually necessary in cases of hazardous or non-listed waste and for any type of waste shipped for disposal. If green-listed waste is shipped to a non-OECD country for recovery, notification is necessary when the importing country requires this. It may allow a so called Annex VII procedure, which is more lightweight. It requires the shipment to be accompanied by an Annex VII document and the person arranging the shipment and the consignee must have established a contract in accordance with Article 18 of the WSR. The procedure is also applicable when waste listed in Annex III or IIIA is shipped for recovery to a non-OECD country that has approved the lighter procedure for that particular type of waste and has communicated this to the EU.[9]

Although individual States differ widely when it comes to the authorities responsible for enforcement of trans-frontier shipments of waste and their respective competences, three types of agencies are generally involved: environmental inspectorates, Customs and police, as well as public prosecution services.[10] In some countries competences to enforce environmental regulations are shared between administrative authorities, Customs and police, whereas in others a single authority, for example the Environmental Protection Agency, is responsible. Cases in which humans are injured as a result of environmental violations will be handled by criminal enforcement agencies (usually in joint teams with administrative enforcement agencies).

Administrative bodies are usually competent for inspections in harbours and processing facilities and they may impose sanctions, such as warnings and fines, and are entitled to revoke licenses. Competence of Customs is in some countries limited to inspection, but in others Customs may conduct independent criminal investigations as well. In the EU, Customs are competent for shipments coming in or going out to countries outside the Union.

9 Emma Nurmi, Dorte Skjøtt Jakobsen, Beate Langset, Margareta Eriksson, Pär Kollberg and Kaija Rainio, 'Shipments of Green-listed Waste: A Nordic Survey' (Nordic Council of Ministers 2017).

10 IMPEL, 'Is What You See, What You Get? Project Report' (2006).

In the Netherlands, violations of WSR regulations may be dealt with administratively or through criminal procedure depending on the severity of the case. Less severe violations are dealt with administratively. Cases in which societal and environmental impact is substantial will be handled by one of the 11 specialised environmental police investigation teams, comprising about 400 detectives and the public prosecution service, usually with the aid of environmental experts from administrative bodies. Inspection agencies may transfer a case to law enforcement, if administrative penalties would not have the intended effect. The public prosecutor may start a criminal investigation independently, if he or she is of the opinion that the administrative bodies fail to take adequate measures. However, where possible, multi-agency cooperation and coordinated efforts are preferred.[11]

As explained above, this chapter focuses on trans-frontier shipments of waste from the Netherlands to China. Because it is a third country and not a member of the OECD, China may receive from the EU only recyclable non-hazardous waste. Although China allows shipments under Annex VII, the country does require extra guarantees. First, China demands that the composition of the green listed waste complies with its national procedures (Annex III, column D). Second, exporting companies must have a Chinese licence and only a limited number of permits are available. Importing companies must also be licensed by the Ministry of Environmental Protection of China and prior to shipment foreign exporters are expected to check this. Third, every single shipment must be checked and authorised by the China Certification and Inspection Group (CCIC), which is part of the General Administration of Quality Supervision, Inspection and Quarantine (AQSIQ). A trader must send photos to CCIC inspectors to allow determination of the composition of the waste. The CCIC performs its own inspections of planned shipments in European harbours, including Rotterdam.

In addition, Dutch administrative authorities and Customs may also carry out physical inspections of containers or run these through scanners. However, given the vast number of containers shipped through the Rotterdam harbour, such inspections must be based on risk analysis and only a very small percentage of waste shipments is checked. Emphasis is on shipments entering the country (and the EU) and less on export.

Waste-trafficking from the Netherlands to China: cases

Empirical data was mainly derived from the court files of 13 major criminal investigations of illegal shipments of waste from the Netherlands to China. Each case required an investigation that took several months up to more than a year to complete. In the Netherlands, files of police investigations are available for academic research under specific conditions. Important restrictions are that the cases must have been brought before the court of first instance (the case may still be pending in the court of appeal) and that persons and entities must be anonymised.

11 Toine Spapens, *Handboek Milieucriminaliteit* (Reed Business 2016).

Case files may range from several hundred to several thousand pages and contain evidence gathered by means of regular investigative methods (e.g. interrogation of suspects; hearing of witnesses; searches of premises); special investigative methods (e.g. interception of communication, covert observation); and financial investigation as well as information on how the investigation was conducted.

The case files were collected in the context of an ongoing PhD study by Shanna Mehlbaum on waste-related environmental crimes. She collected 110 cases in total on waste dumping, asbestos, contaminated soil and waste trafficking covering the period of 2000–2012.[12] China was involved in 13 cases, all related to illegal waste shipments originating from the Netherlands. The same cases were analysed by Rudi Neve in a study of waste shipments from the Netherlands to Asia and Africa carried out for the National police.[13] Table 14.1 gives a brief overview of the empirical data.

The table shows that in most cases the waste destined for China had been sorted, at least to some extent, before shipment. This is also visible in the fact that in a majority of the cases recycling and waste collecting companies were organising the shipments. In the remaining cases, trading companies and shipping agents were the main suspects. Investigations were carried out mostly by the Human Environment and Transport Inspectorate (ILT) and the police. The ILT is the national administrative authority competent for inspection of waste shipments but it also has a small intelligence and investigation department (IOD), to carry out criminal investigations. However, special environmental investigation teams of the police usually carry out large-scale criminal investigations with the support of a small number of experts from other agencies, commonly staff of the ILT and Customs. Other agencies involved were the Fiscal Intelligence and Investigation Service (FIOD), which is competent for tax-related offenses, and provincial authorities who are responsible for licensing and inspection of treatment facilities, for example.[14] Cooperation with foreign enforcement agencies mostly concerns Belgium. Although shipments were destined for

12 It usually takes several years before cases are handled by the court – cases are not considered urgent because suspects are seldom kept in pre-trial detention and often the main suspect is a legal entity – which explains why more recent cases could not be used.

13 Rudie Neve, *Geglobaliseerde afvalcriminaliteit: Illegale praktijken in de afvalstromen naar Afrika en China* (Dienst Landelijke Informatieorganisatie 2012). The criminal business processes of four cases have been analysed earlier in the context of a EU research project entitled Blockwaste (Iina Sahramäki, Serena Favarin, Shanna Mehlbaum, Ernesto Ugo Savona, Antonius Spapens and Terhi Kankaanranta, *Crime Script Analysis of Illicit Cross-Border Waste Trafficking, Key Findings* (Police University College/Transcrime 2016), and one case was described in detail in an instruction manual on the prosecution of waste trafficking: UNEP, 'Instruction Manual on the Prosecution of Illegal Traffic of Hazardous Wastes or Other Wastes' (n 6).

14 In 2013, environmental licensing and inspection of fixed installations (e.g. production facilities) and works (e.g. infrastructural and building activities) was transferred from the provinces and municipalities to 28 Environmental service agencies, because small municipalities in particular were unable to handle complex inspections and because licensing and inspection was often the responsibility of the same person which was considered an integrity risk: Henk Ruessink and Toine Spapens, 'Politie en milieuhandhaving' in Erwin Muller, Edward van der Torre, Bob Hoogenboom, Nicolien Kop (eds), *Politie: Studies over haar werking en organisatie* (Kluwer 2014).

Table 14.1 Criminal investigations of waste trafficking from the Netherlands to China

No.	*Period*	*Type of waste*	*Suspects*	*Enforcement agencies NL*
1	2001–2003	PVC paste	Trading companies	Administrative authorities (licensing), police, ILT (inspection)
2	2003	Metal waste	Recycling company	ILT, Belgian police
3	2003–2004	Cable and transformer waste	Recycling companies; shipping agent	ILT, Customs, police
4	2005	Household waste	Recycling companies	ILT, Customs, Fiscal Investigation Unit
5	2005	Shredded refrigerators (containing CFKs and polyurethane insulation)	Waste collecting company	Police
6	2005–2006	Metal waste and cables	Import and export company	Police, ILT
7	2005–2006	Metal waste (aluminium, motor parts) polluted with chemicals	Waste collecting company; shipping agent	Police, ILT, Customs
8	2006–2008	Plastic waste	Waste collecting company	ILT
9	2007	Plastic waste	Recycling company	ILT
10	2008	Used toner cartridges	Recycling companies	ILT
11	2009	Metal waste	Recycling company; shipping agent	Police, ILT, Administrative authorities
12	2009	Plastic waste	Paper recycling company	Police, ILT, Inspectie leefomgeving Belgium (environmental inspection)
13	2009–2010	Plastic waste (toner cartridges, wires, PCB's, plastics contaminated with glass and sand)	Waste collecting company; shipping agent	Police, ILT, Inspectie leefomgeving Belgium (environmental inspection)

China (in some cases via detours), Chinese authorities were not involved in the investigations.

Modi operandi

General analysis of waste shipments that were found to be in violation shows that in 52 per cent of cases non-compliance was related to missing or incomplete

Table 14.2 Overview of *modi operandi*

No.	*Not properly notifying shipments*	*Not notifying shipments*	*Company collects or exports waste without an operating license*	*Concealing the shipment's destination*	*Contamination of recyclable waste/ Mixing of recyclable and hazardous waste*
1	x	x		x	
2	x	x		x	
3	x	x	x		
4	x	x			
5	x	x	x	x	x
6	x	x			
7	x	x			x
8	x	x			x
9		x		x	x
10		x		x	x
11	x		x		x
12	x	x		x	x
13	x		x	x	

documentation or to shipments of non-hazardous waste contaminated with (small) residues of hazardous waste. The remaining 48 per cent could be regarded as more serious illegal exports that were either not declared at all, or consisted of a mix of hazardous and non-hazardous waste or were destined for countries to where export was explicitly prohibited.[15] Whether such figures also apply to shipments leaving the Netherlands for China is unknown. The types of violations are, however, comparable.

As explained above, only recyclable waste may be exported from the Netherlands to China. Problems may first occur when recyclable waste is contaminated with hazardous waste. If contamination is not detected, this may result in products (partly) manufactured from polluted materials and this may cause health risks. It may also result in economic damage for instance when countries refuse to let the goods enter their markets. Second, criminals may export hazardous waste under the pretext that it is recyclable waste. When this is discovered at the destination, it may not be possible to return the shipment or dispose of the waste in an environmentally sound manner. Table 14.2 gives a brief overview of the main *modi operandi*.

The table shows that companies involved in illegal waste shipments from the Netherlands to China use a range of methods to prevent detection, most importantly by avoiding the regulatory system altogether by not

15 Baird, Curry and Cruz (n 5).

declaring[16] shipments, or collecting and exporting waste through companies that do not have a permit for that type of business activity and by concealing the shipments' final destinations. Failing to disclose the true composition of the waste, or declaring it as second-hand goods and exporting recyclable waste contaminated with other pollutants or intentionally mixing it with hazardous waste, can be observed in five cases. If shipments were declared, the authorities received false or incomplete information in seven cases.

Hiding the true nature of the waste and non-declaration

Falsifying transport documents to hide the true nature of the waste shipped, is an important method to circumvent WSR and is found in all cases (n = 13). One way of doing this is by declaring the goods as 'second-hand' instead of waste. Waste may also be classified in a wrong category, for example to mask that it is hazardous waste, but sometimes also to avoid taxes. Legal definitions are complex and sometimes unclear as well as ambiguous, and even in the EU the Member States have implemented general provisions, such as the WSR, differently.[17] Non-compliant operators may exploit such ambiguities and gaps in regulations.

Within the WSR and the Basel Convention, waste is defined as 'any substance or object which the holder discards or intends or is required to discard'. A waste holder is responsible for classifying the waste. Despite this definition there are various interpretations of the term 'waste' and which goods it exactly covers. The problem is further compounded by a lack of harmonisation between the codes of different countries, or by different requirements between countries with respect to the conditions under which a substance or object must be disposed of and thus considered a waste.[18] For example, in Germany, second-hand goods such as electronics and vehicles are required to function upon export. If a computer is plugged in and does not work or if a car fails to start, it is considered to be waste. In the Netherlands, however, inspections are usually limited to face value checks of whether the goods are carefully packed to avoid damage during transportation or simply crammed into a container.

Although uncertainties and gaps in regulation may be put forward by defence lawyers afterwards, the perpetrators start with concealing the true nature of the shipment. A common way of doing this is by putting neatly packed and clean recyclable waste in the front of the container and other types of (hazardous) waste in the back. Inspectors can only detect this by unloading a container or by

16 Note that the Waste Shipment Regulation uses the term 'notification' rather than declaration.

17 Serena Favarin, Margaux Morganti, Ernesto Ugo Savona, Iina Sahramäki, Terhi Kankaanranta, Leila Suvantola, Shanna Mehlbaum and Antonius Spapens, *Crime Proofing Analysis of the Waste Regulation: A Special Focus on the European Union, Finland, Italy and the Netherlands, Key Findings* (Police University College/Transcrime 2017).

18 UNEP, 'Waste Crime' (n 2).

running it through a scanner, which is time-consuming. The cases analysed here show that waste exporters count on a low probability of getting caught.

The CCIC inspection method based on photographs is also vulnerable to fraud, because exporters can submit pictures on which everything seems to be in order and add other types of waste afterwards. They may also send photographs of completely different shipments.[19] In one of the cases examined the police investigation proved that pictures sent to the CCIC were taken at entirely different locations. Even if CCIC inspectors perform a physical check, exporters are able to add other waste later on because CCIC is not an enforcement agency and cannot seal containers.

Detection of suspicious shipments is further complicated by the fact that (both in the Netherlands and internationally) environmental inspectorates and Customs use different code systems: the WSR/Basel system on the one hand and the international tariff codes on the other.[20] As a result, a shipment that is classified as waste under the WSR system may be documented as goods by Customs and thus not inspected. The issue is further complicated by the fact that shipments often contain waste collected from different sources, which is sorted and repackaged before it is sent on to Asia. In one example, a shipment of waste cables contained ground cable with and without bitumen as well as other types, such as household cable. In this case, ground cable with bitumen is a different category of waste.[21] Although the EU has worked on a transposition table of the WSR/Basel and customs codes, harmonisation is still an ongoing process.

Apart from declaring waste, while hiding its true nature, exporters may also choose not to notify the authorities about the shipment at all. They usually claim that this is not necessary because it is a shipment of second hand goods, to which the WSR does not apply, whereas in reality the shipment contains (hazardous) waste. Because administrative enforcement agencies and Customs primarily focus on checking declared shipments, perpetrators assume that the risk of getting caught if they avoid the regulatory system may be even lower. Of course, they must also calculate the risk of interception when the containers enter China, but this too is viewed as an acceptable risk.[22]

Port hopping and taking detours to avoid inspection

Port hopping refers to non-compliant waste exporters trying to avoid detection and declaration procedures by shipping waste through European ports with more lenient scrutiny regimes. Exporters may also deliberately send shipments destined

19 Neve, *Geglobaliseerde afvalcriminaliteit* (n 13).

20 Algemene Rekenkamer, *Coordinated Audit on the Enforcement of the European Waste Shipment Regulation: Joint Report Based on Eight National Audits* (2013).

21 Angela van Heeswijk, Amy Oerlemans and Charles Nijssen, *IMPEL-TFS Seaport Project. 'Illegal Waste Shipments to Developing Countries, Common Practice': Project Report, June 2003 – May 2004* (Arcadis 2004).

22 Neve, *Geglobaliseerde afvalcriminaliteit* (n 13).

for mainland China via other destinations in order to circumvent the CCIC procedure. Neve observed that exporters send shipments through the nearby Belgian port of Antwerp instead of Rotterdam because inspections there are considered less thorough.[23] In some of the cases studied here, offenders chose the port of Antwerp because their shipments were flagged by Dutch Customs because of earlier rule violations. Port-hopping is not easy to detect, as operators will give logistical reasons for switching ports, such as demurrage, handling, storage, lower transport costs, and a particular shipping line may sail only from a particular port. To some extent Antwerp and Rotterdam are indeed 'twinned' and many companies involved in waste export have offices in Belgium as well as the Netherlands.[24]

The case examples above show that the practice of sending waste to China via detours is a more serious problem, because it undermines the key requirement of the WSR that to ensure proper treatment the final recipient of the waste must be known. Administrative agencies must be able to check whether the recipient can indeed manage the waste adequately. However, when waste is destined for Asia and Africa this is often impossible. Competent bodies in the EU Member States often cannot check if a specific company even exists and if so, whether it is able to process specific types of waste without harming the environment. Furthermore, the customs regulation requires only disclosure of the next country in transit.[25] CCIC inspections only apply to shipments destined for mainland China and operators circumvent the procedure by sending waste via intermediate destinations, which may be changed when the cargo is still under way.[26]

Hong Kong is a popular stopover (on paper), but also Vietnam and the United Arab Emirates.[27] In five of the studied cases Hong Kong was the 'final' destination on paper and in two others, Malaysia. Neither of these territories have (major) facilities to treat or reuse waste. In one of the cases studied the recipient in Hong Kong was a small office located on the ninth floor of an office building. According to WSR the country from which the shipment originated must be informed when the final destination changes and agree with this, but in practice the requirement is unenforceable because it is impossible to keep track of the shipment after it has left the harbour. Although Dutch agencies may be suspicious when the aforementioned destinations appear in notification documents, they are usually unable to refuse an export permit. Stopping the shipment in China is also difficult. If it is sent via an intermediary destination – at which the waste may be sorted and repackaged again – it is often impossible to trace back

23 Ibid.
24 UNEP, 'Basel Convention: Instruction Manual' (n 5).
25 Algemene Rekenkamer, *Coordinated Audit on the Enforcement of the European Waste Shipment Regulation* (n 20).
26 Neve, *Geglobaliseerde afvalcriminaliteit* (n 13).
27 Ibid.

the shipment to the EU, whereas returning it to the previous port of origin will probably not result in proper treatment. Sending a shipment back to the country of origin is an expensive operation and can be complicated due to uncertainties about ownership, especially when documents have been falsified, and containers that were refused entry may well end up abandoned in the ports.

Unintentional contamination and intentional mixing of waste

Unintentional contamination of green-listed waste with hazardous waste is an important problem. Paper waste, inevitably contains some metal in the form of staples and plastic from binders. Recyclable waste such as paper and plastics is also sorted from household waste and may be polluted with hazardous waste such as oil and with other banned substances such as animal waste products (e.g. chicken feathers). Households in the UK and Ireland are not yet obliged to separate paper and plastics from other waste and much household waste is exported to the Netherlands (and Belgium) for sorting and re-export. If the waste is insufficiently cleaned (or not at all) there is a substantial risk of contamination. Another important source of waste plastics originating from the UK is agricultural plastics which often contain residues of pesticides.

Although requiring recyclable waste to be 100 per cent 'clean' is practically and economically unfeasible, there exists no EU regulation on how much contamination is acceptable. Authorities may be reluctant to set such standards because it would enable exporters to reduce their efforts to stay just within limits. Exact standards may lead to juridical bickering if these are not accompanied by procedures on forensic testing, and those procedures and their execution in the field may of course also be challenged in court.

Although some countries have set standards for certain types of waste, including China and the Netherlands, others have not and shipping agents are thus confronted with judgements of what is acceptable that may differ between jurisdictions.[28] According to a guideline of the Ministry of Infrastructure and the Environment, green-listed waste exported from the Netherlands may not be contaminated with hazardous waste and not contain over 2 per cent of other recyclable materials. The Chinese authorities, for example, require waste plastics to be crushed, colourless and odourless and to have been washed to remove any obvious contaminants. Remaining pollution of the total shipment may not exceed 0.01 per cent for chemicals and 0.1 per cent for metal or sand.[29] Recently, the Chinese authorities announced the introduction of a maximum

28 Algemene Rekenkamer, *Coordinated Audit on the Enforcement of the European Waste Shipment Regulation* (n 20).

29 Aya Yoshida, 'China: The World's Largest Recyclable Waste Importer' in Michikazu Kojima (ed.), *International Trade of Recyclable Resources in Asia* (Institute of Developing Economies 2005).

allowed contamination of 0.3 per cent for all imports of secondary materials by the end of 2017.[30]

Contamination may also be the result of intentional mixing of green listed waste and hazardous waste. In two cases studied here household waste was collected in the UK and sent directly to China. The Netherlands have seen several other recent examples. One concerned a paper and plastic recycling company that in 2016 handled 1.2 million tons of waste and shipped it to destinations all over the world, including to China. In 2013, this company was suspected of deliberately mixing paper and plastic with household waste, rendering a profit that was estimated at several million euros. The company did not notify these shipments.[31] In a similar case in 2011, a recycling company added residual waste and household waste it had imported from the UK and Ireland to waste paper shipments. Furthermore, employees drew up transport documents in which the weight of the waste was inflated to increase profits even further. After the start of a criminal investigation, the company went bankrupt in 2013. It took until January 2017 before the owners of the former company were convicted and sentenced to prison terms ranging from 6 to 12 months.[32] Even if the waste is recyclable as such, perpetrators may still cheat, for instance by mixing high quality metal scrap with inferior metal waste to make extra money. Metals recycled from cable and electrical appliances for example, are not suitable for the manufacture of high quality products, such as locks.[33]

Enforcement and cross-border cooperation

The previous section showed that perpetrators apply a variety of methods to traffic waste. In this section, we explore the difficulties experienced by enforcement agencies responsible for tackling illicit trans-frontier shipments of waste. To begin with, we will describe, focusing on the Netherlands, challenges at the national level. Next, we will address cooperation and information exchange within the EU, and finally between the EU and China.

Enforcement of waste trafficking in the EU Member States and the Netherlands in particular

A number of studies have been carried out to explore the main enforcement problems at the national levels in the Member States. These can be divided into three main categories.

30 Robin Latchem, 'China Spells Out Illegal Waste Strategy' (MRW, 9 March 2017).

31 RTL nieuws, 'Recyclingbedrijf verdacht van miljoenenfraude' (29 January 2013).

32 Pieter van Klinken, 'Celstraf voor directeuren Van Puijfelik Breda: 'Ordinaire milieucriminelen' (BN/De Stem, 24 January 2017).

33 Neve, *Geglobaliseerde afvalcriminaliteit* (n 13).

The first is a general lack of priority when it comes to tackling waste trafficking, which results in lack of staff, knowledge and means with enforcement agencies.[34] This may result in information and intelligence not being followed up, but also in problems of interpreting complex regulations. For enforcers, the main challenge is to detect illegal waste shipments before they leave port. The cases we studied often started after inspections, sometimes in the course of special enforcement operations aimed at waste transports. The large number of containers handled in the port of Rotterdam alone and the limited resources available renders it impossible to check every shipment and thus only small selections of waste shipments, either random or based on risk analysis, are inspected.

A second problem is that in most countries many organisations are involved in the enforcement of WSR.[35] This calls for cooperation and exchange of information within countries, but both agencies' priorities and their interpretation of specific legal provisions may differ. In some countries regulators have good cooperation based on official memoranda of understanding or other service-level agreements. This is not the case everywhere, and in some countries, there is no cooperation at all.[36] Lack of cooperation may lead to uncoordinated actions, but also to information gaps, and differences in how respective agencies carry out inspections.[37]

In the Netherlands, cooperation between inspection agencies, police and Customs is relatively well established. In most of the cases included in our study, waste trafficking is detected during inspections initiated by the ILT. Inspections are often executed jointly with Customs' environmental specialists, police and other agencies, such as the Traffic Inspectorate of the Ministry of Traffic and Waterworks. These agencies exchange information on a case-by-case basis as well as structurally. Staff involved in these inspections are usually trained in enforcement of Regulation 259/93.[38] Since 2013 the parties decide collectively in the so-called *Milieukamer* (Environmental Crime Decision Room) on how to follow-up detection of irregularities. These may be dealt with administratively but they may also be the starting point of a criminal or joint investigation. The Customs and the ILT also cooperate in drawing up risk profiles and in implementing enforcement priorities.[39] Although cooperation during inspections runs smoothly, joint investigation teams sometimes experience troubles because

34 Van Heeswijk et al. (n 21); Arcadis, *Impel-TFS Seaport Project II: International Cooperation in Enforcement Hitting Illegal Waste Shipments* (2006).

35 Algemene Rekenkamer, *Coordinated Audit on the Enforcement of the European Waste Shipment Regulation* (n 20).

36 Van Heeswijk et al. (n 21); UNEP, 'Waste Crime' (n 2).

37 Nancy Isarin, 'Overview of the Challenges and Needs of Parties and Various Stakeholders in Preventing and Combating Illegal Traffic in Line with the Requirements of the Basel Convention (Gap Analysis)' (2014).

38 Arcadis (n 34); JW van de Wardt, L van Loon and MJM van der Sanden, *Enforcement of European Waste Shipment Regulation* (Algemene Rekenkamer 2012).

39 Van de Wardt et al. (n 39).

of a knowledge difference between different agencies. Environmental police investigation teams have more experience with criminal investigation tactics and techniques, whereas employees of the ILT have far more knowledge of the technical aspects of waste trafficking and complex environmental regulations. While police officers often lack specific knowledge about waste, environmental specialists lack experience in writing verbatim reports in the context of a criminal case.

From a legal point of view, information exchange during (joint) investigations is usually not a problem, because provisions exist in the shape of covenants. A serious case may, for instance, be taken up in the context of a Regional Information and Expertise Centre (RIEC), which is a platform for information exchange between the public prosecution service, the police, administrative authorities, and the Tax authority. Relevant parties may use the RIEC to coordinate respective actions or work together in a joint team, depending on the types of interventions chosen. However, practical issues may still complicate information exchange, such as the fact that all agencies have their respective information systems, which are tailored to their needs but not so much with interchangeability in mind. One example is that databases differ in how company names are registered, meaning that all information has to be checked manually.

At a more general level, non-case based structural information exchange is less evident. To begin with, this is more complicated because of differences in orientation and sometimes a lack of trust, but also because data protection laws are far more restrictive when it comes to the provision of police information to other public agencies, than the other way around. To begin with, administrative authorities are future oriented and aim at halting non-compliant behaviour rather than punishing crimes already committed, whereas the police and the public prosecution service are predominantly rear-view oriented. As a result, the latter often judge administrative enforcers as being too lenient.[40] Furthermore, whilst criminal law enforcement is politically independent, this is different for administrative agencies. National, provincial and local authorities may sometimes intervene to soften measures against violators of environmental regulations, particularly when it concerns economically important corporations. Instructions to move cautiously may also lead to a certain reluctance to exchange information with the police, which detectives may in turn perceive as a sign of corruption.[41]

On their part, the police generally have a culture of secrecy, and when it comes to exchanging information outside the context of an actual investigation, administrative agencies often compare the police to a 'black hole': it gladly accepts every piece of information from others but little or nothing is returned. Police information is subject to strict data protection requirements, but administrative

40 Toine Spapens, *De complexiteit van milieucriminaliteit: De aard van het misdrijf, deopsporing en de samenwerkingsrelaties.* (Inaugural Lecture, Police Academy of the Netherlands, Boom Lemma uitgevers 2012).

41 Ibid.

agencies often view the police as not very flexible when privacy laws do leave an opening. From a psychological perspective good cooperation depends on reciprocity and if one party fails to return information, this will also reduce motivation with the others.

As explained above, WSR offences may be punished administratively as well as criminally. The ILT can issue warning letters and orders subject to a penalty payment, as well as impose financial penalties and revoke export and operating permits. The public prosecution service may bring cases to court and impose financial penalties and prison sentences, but it may also choose to settle the case out of court.[42] Although the maximum prison sentence for economic offenses is six years, almost no perpetrators are sent to jail. The ILT mostly issues warning letters and orders subject to penalty payments. Figures from the Rotterdam district of the public prosecution service compiled by the General Accounting Office (GAO), show that in 2008–2010, 64 per cent of the cases were settled out of court and 31 per cent were not prosecuted at all. The GAO judged the latter as particularly disturbing. The main reasons why prosecutors did not want to go to court were inadequate or unconvincing evidence; the fact that an administrative intervention was preferred; and long procedural delays which usually result in (strongly) reduced penalties. Of the cases that did go to court, 78 per cent resulted in a fine. With 10 per cent, the acquittal rate was also relatively high.[43] One could state that out-of-court settlements are unsatisfactory too, because a company can thus avoid a conviction and a criminal record. As a result, administrative authorities may also not be able to impose measures such as refusing future licenses.[44]

Cooperation within the EU

Waste shipments from the Netherlands to China often involve other EU Member States. In the cases studied the waste originated from other Member States (five cases), or shipments were sent to China via the Belgian port of Antwerp (five cases). In one case, the export licence held by a German company was fraudulently used for shipping waste from Dutch and Belgian ports. Thus, cooperation between the Member States is often crucial for tackling illegal waste trafficking.

The problems experienced at the national level are to some extent mirrored in challenges to cooperation within the Union. Although the EU-WSR sets a common standard, differences occur in its implementation in national legislation and enforcement guidelines.[45] Differences also occur in the availability of

42 Van de Wardt et al. (n 39).

43 Ibid.

44 Toine Spapens, Monique Bruinsma. Lonneke van Hout and Jessica de Jong (2013). *Vuile Olie: Onrechtmatig verwerken en mengen van olieproducten als vormen van milieucriminaliteit* (Boom Lemma uitgevers 2013).

45 Favarin et al. (n 17).

(trained) personnel and the means to carry out inspections and investigations. Maximum penalties vary substantially between countries, and low penalties may preclude application of more intrusive investigative methods.[46] Finally, each Member State organises enforcement differently. In the Netherlands, for example, administrative enforcement of the WSR is organised at the national level whereas in, for example, Belgium, Italy and Sweden, inspections are carried out by regional or even local authorities. All of this presents substantial barriers to cross-border cooperation. Next, we will focus primarily on information exchange.

As mentioned above an important difference is between case-based exchange of information and pro-active exchange aimed at detection. Similar problems occur as described above. In case-based situations, 'horizontal' information exchange is usually possible from a legal point of view. Of course, all sorts of practical hurdles may be encountered, such as finding the right person or department, slow responses, legal obstacles, and so on. Law enforcement agencies may exchange information via avenues such as Interpol, police liaison officers and Eurojust, and Customs may communicate via their Enforcement Network Communication Platform. Administrative enforcement agencies lack such provisions, but may find contact details of counterparts in the EU on the website of the European Union Network for the Implementation and Enforcement of Environmental Law (IMPEL).

'Diagonal' information exchange is problematic from criminal law enforcement to administrative enforcement agencies. Here, no explicit legal framework exists for the cross-border exchange of requests for mutual assistance.[47] The competent judicial authorities must weigh requests against national data protection laws and conventions, such as the European Convention on Human Rights. Lacking specific guidelines, individual magistrates come to different conclusions as to what is allowed and what is not. The problem of making available police and judicial information for administrative purposes in another Member State is on the agenda of the European Commission.[48] Belgium, Luxembourg and the Netherlands are currently discussing adaptation of the existing Benelux police cooperation treaty in this respect.

Information exchange is also required at a more general level, for instance to detect shipments or new *modi operandi*.[49] Here, the main challenge is to better ensure systemic exchange of intelligence. No obligations to exchange non-case based information exist, and the main problem is that enforcers perceive feeding information to a foreign counterpart 'spontaneously' as complicated 'extra work'. Enforcement agencies are usually understaffed and overburdened as it is;

46 Toine Spapens, 'Cross-border Police Cooperation in Tackling Environmental Crime' in Rob White (ed.), *Transnational Environmental Crime* (Ashgate 2011).

47 Toine Spapens, Maaike Peters and Dirk Van Daele (eds), *Administrative Measures to Prevent and Tackle Crime* (Eleven Publishing 2015); UNEP, 'Waste Crime' (n 2).

48 Spapens, Peters and Van Daele (n 48).

49 UNEP, 'Waste Crime' (n 2).

language barriers may occur; people may not know whom to contact abroad and do not have time to find out, and so on.

Initiatives to improve the situation are mainly undertaken by international cooperation networks. The World Customs Organisation (WCO) established Environet, a communication platform, and IMPEL organised a network of national contact points in each of the Member States. However, there exists no EU-database in which intercepted illegal waste shipments can be registered, comparable to EU-Twix for seizures of protected wildlife.

Cooperation networks primarily aim at capacity building, through activities such as exchanging best practices and setting up joint projects. The police set up EnviCrimeNet in 2011, as a follow-up to the Augias project that targeted waste trafficking in the EU.[50] In 2012, a network of public prosecutors working in the environmental field (ENPE) was established and now comprises 12 Member States and three other European countries. Finally, the Customs cooperate globally in the WCO and in the EU they participate in IMPEL. IMPEL is particularly active in the field of WSR and has organised numerous (joint) inspection actions, training activities and seminars to exchange experiences and best-practices. The network also initiated recommendations to the EU in order to improve the legal framework.

Cooperation with China

Cooperation with third countries is more challenging than cooperating within the Union and this is also visible in cases of illegal waste shipments from the Netherlands to China. In fact, even attempts at cooperation are hardly mentioned in the case files. Chinese recipients of waste and shipping agents are not included in Dutch investigations, even if there is evidence of active involvement, for instance because they falsified documents. In only one case did Dutch detectives go to China to interrogate a suspect who was a representative of a Chinese company that claimed to be the recipient of waste, whereas in reality shipments ended up at entirely different locations. However, the Chinese authorities only allowed to hear this person as a witness and this turned out to be a frustrating affair because he claimed to have little time for the interview and refused to sign his statement and to appear before the court if necessary.

Difficulties also occur in information exchange and little is known about Chinese recipients and how they process the waste, and about the harm inflicted on the environment when they fail to correctly treat it. Suspects in our case examples usually claim that the waste is sorted and recycled in a safe way, even if export was in violation of the WSR. An example is a case in which unstripped waste cables were shipped to China. Stripping is required before export because

50 Toine Spapens, 'Building Trust and More: The Importance of Police Cooperation Networks in the European Union' in Saskia Hufnagel and Carol McCartney (eds), *Trust in International Police and Justice Cooperation* (Hart Publishing 2017).

of the risk that cables will be burned to retrieve the metal, causing air and soil pollution. The Chinese recipient claimed the cables would be treated in an environmentally sound way, knowing that the Dutch authorities were unable to verify this. Communication with Chinese authorities is often perceived as difficult: if Dutch authorities request further information they almost never receive a reply. China and the Netherlands are different in almost every aspect of enforcement of transfrontier shipments of waste, such as the number of enforcement agencies involved and their competences; their ability to identify and analyse hazardous waste; procedures regarding waste shipments; and the severity of sanctions available.[51]

When it comes to improvement of cooperation, the Netherlands takes part in the initiatives taken by IMPEL and the WCO. The IMPEL working group on transfrontier shipments of waste (IMPEL-TFS) has suggested establishing a simple but robust contact regime with China through existing national contact points and to arrange exchange visits and participation in training and inspection projects. National laws and requirements of respective importing should be clarified and made available to all national contact points.[52] IMPEL also set up the Asian Network for Prevention of Illegal Transboundary Movement of Hazardous Wastes. At the global level, UNEP established the Regional Enforcement Network for Chemicals and Waste (REN) in 25 Asian countries. It focuses on the prevention and enforcement of illegal transboundary movements of harmful chemicals and hazardous waste.

An example of a project aimed at improving cooperation is Operation Demeter, which was initiated by the WCO in 2009. It focused specifically on waste shipments from Europe to Asia.[53] Demeter involved 65 countries including the Netherlands, China and Hong Kong. The operation led to 56 reported seizures of metal scrap, household waste and end-of-life vehicles, to non-functioning or 'used' electrical and electronic equipment, granite and silicon barrels. The Netherlands reported 17 seizures and Hong Kong reported eight. Mainland China reported over 8,927 tons of hazardous and other waste illegally imported from North America and Europe in 30 seizures, ranging from waste batteries and copy machines to waste engine oil and waste tyres. In addition, they detained more than 20 suspects and fined 31 operators for illegal shipments.[54] Operation 'Demeter' was repeated in 2012 and 2013.

A positive development is a growing awareness of the importance of compliance and enforcement in countries at the receiving end of the waste streams.[55]

51 Juan Wang, *Transboundary Shipment of E-Waste: Regulations, Systems, Stakeholders and Solutions* (Master's thesis, Delft University (the Netherlands), 2009); Isarin (n 37).

52 IMPEL, *EU–Asia Collaboration Project: Final Report* (20 February 2013).

53 WCO, 'Operation Demeter Executive Summary' (2010).

54 Ibid.

55 Henk Ruessink and Gerard Wolters, 'Combating Illegal Waste Shipments through International Seaports – A Call for Concerted Public and Private Approaches' (9th INECE Conference, Whistler, Canada, 18–24 June 2011).

The Chinese government for example launched Operation 'Green Fence' in 2013.[56] During the operation, China Customs supervised 45.5 million tonnes of imported solid waste, investigated 1,176 cases in different categories of smuggled waste, arrested 380 suspects and conducted an audit of over 2,608 enterprises.[57]

Legislation in China is in transition and the authorities are becoming increasingly strict in 'keeping the garbage out', according to a representative of the ILT we interviewed in the context of the BlockWaste project.[58] In March 2017 customs authorities launched Operation 'National Sword' (sometimes called Green Fence II). During an 11-month period Customs, police, the environmental protection agency and AQSIQ will join forces to seriously strengthen supervision of waste imports.[59] Furthermore, in July 2017, China informed the World Trade Organization (WTO) of its intentions to fully ban import of certain scrap materials by the end of 2017.[60] Furthermore, on 31 December 2017 China put a halt to the import of most types of plastic waste, which caused great turmoil amongst waste traders. Experts in the trade industry foresee great economic impact on their business, since the Chinese recycling industry is the world's largest.[61] The Chinese authorities stated that measures were necessary because the large amounts of recyclable waste contaminated with other waste or mixed with or hazardous waste, was seriously polluting China's environment.[62]

Conclusion

This chapter has highlighted the main methods of illicit waste trafficking from the Netherlands to China. Perpetrators apply tricks to avoid detection before a shipment leaves the EU as well as upon entry into China. Generally, enforcement agencies have limited resources to detect and inspect illegal waste shipments, particularly if these are not declared. Improved cooperation between the Netherlands and China as well as between the Member States of the EU is necessary but challenging. Consequently, investigations in the Netherlands often stop at the border. Although the cases studied all involved China, the Dutch police attempted only once to interrogate a Chinese recipient of the waste, with little result. For agencies in the EU it is almost impossible to check information provided by Chinese companies on their capabilities to treat or recycle waste, and attempts to communicate with the competent authorities to verify

56 UNEP, 'Waste Crime' (n 2).
57 WCO, *Illicit Trade Report 2013* (2014).
58 Mehlbaum and Spapens (n 3).
59 Latchem (n 30); Recycling International, 'China "Tightens Screws" on Scrap Imports' (16 March 2017).
60 Mark Carpenter, 'ISRI Statement on China's Intent to Ban Certain Scrap Imports' (ISRI, 18 July 2017).
61 Ibid.; Latchem (n 30); Recycling International (n 59).
62 Tom Miles, 'China Says It Won't Take Any More Foreign Garbage' (Reuters, 18 July 2017).

information are usually left without reply. The reasons are difficult to assess and would require further study.

Within the EU, structural information exchange outside the scope of investigation cases is also underdeveloped. Spontaneous notification of, for instance, intercepted shipments destined for or originating from another Member State, depends on motivated individual enforcers, but should be part of the organisational culture of the competent agencies.[63] Unfortunately, a registration system for intercepted shipments, comparable to the EU-TWIX for wildlife, is not in place. According to a police officer we interviewed in the context of the BlockWaste-project, feasibility of such a system was briefly studied in the context of the Augias-project, but at the time judged too complicated because of data protection laws.[64] Establishing such a system would, however, be advisable.

It is interesting to notice that China has recently been increasing its efforts to prevent hazardous waste from entering the country and China also played an important part in the Demeter-operations initiated by the WCO. However, stopping waste at the Chinese borders does raise the problem of what to do with these shipments, especially if the 'owner' cannot be identified or turns out to be a P.O. Box and containers cannot be shipped back. It is therefore essential to also prevent shipments from leaving port in the EU and the Netherlands in particular, but this requires systematic feedback allowing EU enforcement authorities to tighten inspection on or shutting down companies involved in the trafficking as well as to refuse to authorise shipments destined for 'treatment facilities' in China that only exist on paper. The ban on imports of specific types of recyclable waste recently imposed by China will radically change the waste market and it is difficult to predict how waste traders, and particularly illegal operators will respond. Careful monitoring of future developments remains.

63 Margaret Gay, 'Overcoming Barriers to Joint Working: Group Structures Required (B13)' (Life Smart Waste Project, 2017).
64 Mehlbaum and Spapens (n 3).

15 Motivators for IUU fishing in the Indo-Pacific

Erika J. Techera and Jade Lindley

Introduction

Maritime crimes are prevalent throughout the Indo-Pacific and include trafficking of people, weapons and drugs, piracy, armed robbery at sea and environmental and natural resource crimes.[1] Fisheries crimes are one example of these activities that plague the Indo-Pacific region negatively, affecting economies and marine environments as well as placing at risk human and food security.[2] Illegal, unreported and unregulated (IUU) fishing includes a range of offences:

- Contravention of domestic and regional fishery management organisation (RFMO) laws;
- Non-reporting, misreporting or under-reporting of catches and failure to report other relevant matters not strictly required by law but that are advisable;
- Undertaking activities that States have not regulated; and
- Activities of stateless vessels and non-parties to RFMOs.[3]

1 For a general discussion of maritime security issues in the region see David Michel and Ricky Passarelli (eds), *Sea Change: Evolving Maritime Geopolitics in the Indo-Pacific Region* (Stimson Center 2014). Other commentators also confirm an expansion of maritime crimes in the region: Joon Num Mak, 'NGOs, Piracy and Maritime Crime in South East Asia' (2013) 228 *Asia Pacific Bulletin* 1–2; Tim Lynch, 'Illegal, Unreported, Unregulated Fishing, and The Universal Fisherman', (May–June 2007) *Maritime Studies* 20–23.

2 Agnew et al. demonstrate an expansion of IUU fishing in the Eastern Indian and NorthWest Pacific areas: David J Agnew, J Pearce, G Pramod, T Peatman, R Watson, JR Beddington and T J Pitcher, 'Estimating the Worldwide Extend of Illegal Fishing' (2009) 4(2) *PLoS ONE* e4570. doi:10.1371/ journal.pone.0004570, 2. They also confirm the significant damage that IUU fishing can do to species as well as collateral damage to ecosystems: ibid. 4, 5.

3 FAO, *State of the World's Fishers and Aquaculture: Contributing to Food Security and Nutrition for All* (FAO 2016), 97. For a detailed definition see FAO, *International Plan of Action to Prevent, Deter and Eliminate Illegal, Unreported and Unregulated Fishing (IPOA-IUU)*, adopted 23 June 2001 at the 120th Session of the FAO Council, para 3.

IUU fishing predominantly operates out of sight and is therefore difficult to quantify, but research estimates that up to 26 million tonnes of fish are caught illicitly each year, equating to more than 15 per cent of the world's capture fisheries.[4] Other reports estimate total economic losses between US$10 and US $23.5 billion per year.[5] In 2015, the World Wildlife Fund reported that over 85 per cent of global fish stocks are at significant risk of IUU fishing.[6] Beyond the financial loss, the marine environments, and fish stocks within them, are at serious risk of permanent damage. Calculating maximum sustainable yields and safe catch limits of highly mobile species, such as fish, is challenging in any regulatory environment. Where some actors are operating outside the law, and illicit catches are not included in catch data, stock estimates are likely to be exaggerated and overfishing, as well as the collapse of fisheries, becomes a very real possibility. Therefore, enhanced law, policy and management responses are needed to prevent those risks being realised. This is critical in the Indo-Pacific region where people and economies are dependent upon fisheries and as noted above, maritime crimes are prevalent.[7] Although the international and regional communities have regulated to address IUU fishing, existing research indicates that the region is facing ongoing fishing-based crimes potentially exposing it to other more serious crimes.[8] Therefore, enhanced regulatory responses must be developed, but before doing so the underlying drivers for this behaviour need to be explored. This research exposes critical motivators for the criminal activities which in turn can inform regulatory responses.

The specific regional context is also relevant in addressing the challenge of IUU fishing. The Indo-Pacific region is vast, encompassing continental countries and island states dotted within wide expanses of ocean. Each nation differs from the next in size, population, development status, socio-cultural and politico-legal environments, as well as the size of the maritime zones over which each have jurisdiction.[9] Given this lack of homogeneity, motivations to respond to IUU

4 Ibid. iii.

5 Agnew et al. (n 2), 4.

6 World Wildlife Fund, 'Illegal Fishing: Which Fish Species Are at Highest Risk from Illegal and Unreported Fishing?' (WWF October 2015). <http://assets.worldwildlife.org/publications/834/files/original/Fish_Species_at_Highest_Risk_from_IUU_Fishing_WWF_FINAL.pdf?1446130921>.

7 United Nations Office on Drugs and Crime, *Transnational Organized Crime in the Pacific: A Threat Assessment* (UNODC 2016). <www.unodc.org/documents/southeastasiaandpacific/Publications/2016/2016.09.16_TOCTA_Pacific_web.pdf>, 10.

8 See, for example, Judy Putt and Katherine Anderson, *A National Study of Crime in the Australian Fishing Industry* (Australian Institute of Criminology 2007).

9 For example, India and China are vast countries with large populations and economies in transition. Australia is a developed nation but given its large Exclusive Economic Zone (EEZ), is still challenged in monitoring its waters. Many other nations are Small Islands Developing States (SIDS) such as Fiji, Samoa, the Maldives and Seychelles, with countries such as Vanuatu being amongst the least developed in the world. Many such States have much larger EEZs than land-based territory. Under the UN Convention Law of the Sea the coastal State has sovereignty

fishing, and commit often scarce resources, also vary widely. Drivers such as the desire to protect against broader maritime security threats and to facilitate the blue economy agenda play an important role in encouraging responses, though disproportionately. Greater understanding of what motivates governments and regulators can be valuable in devising better solutions and maximising uptake at the national level.

This paper applies crime opportunity theory to the complex challenge of IUU fishing. In doing so the purpose is not to de-value existing law and policy responses, nor to identify replacements for them. The aim is to shed light on why these responses have failed to have optimal effect. A further goal is to show that the application of criminological theory, rather than legal doctrinal or regulatory theory, has value and thus the significance of inter-disciplinary approaches to natural resource challenges is demonstrated. Furthermore, this paper explores drivers for State responses to IUU fishing, the analysis of which remains important if greater support is to be obtained for existing international and regional law and uptake at the national level.

Background

Legal responses to maritime crimes have largely been in the form of reactive laws[10] that address 'symptoms rather than the root causes' of the problem.[11] The foundation for such responses is the law of the sea. Oceans governance has at its core the United Nations Convention on the Law of the Sea (UNCLOS), which establishes maritime zones, codifies prohibitions on piracy and enforcement options, such as hot pursuit, as well as creating general obligations to protect and preserve the marine environment.[12] UNCLOS introduced concepts such as 'maximum sustainable yield' and 'total allowable catch' in an effort to prevent overfishing, but detailed fisheries management was encouraged at the sub-global level through regional fisheries management organisations (RFMOs), combined with some specific instruments such as the Fish Stocks Agreement[13] in relation to straddling and highly migratory stocks. The role of RFMOs varies depending on their establishing instrument, but may involve setting catch and fishing limits,

over the first 12 nautical miles of ocean, called the territorial sea. From 12 to 200 nautical miles is the EEZ over which the coastal State has sovereign rights to explore and exploit living resources including fish stocks.

10 Joe McNulty, 'Western and Central Pacific Ocean Fisheries and the Opportunities for Transnational Organised Crime: Monitoring, Control and Surveillance (MCS) Operation Kurukuru' (2013) 5(4) *Australian Journal of Maritime and Ocean Affairs* 145–152, 146.

11 Mak (n 1) 1.

12 United Nations Convention on the Law of the Sea, 10 December 1982, 1833 UNTS 3, 21 ILM 1261 (1982), entered into force 16 November 1994.

13 UN, *Agreement for the Implementation of the Provisions of the United Nations Convention on the Law of the Sea of 10 December 1982 Relating to the Conservation and Management of Straddling Fish Stocks and Highly Migratory Fish Stocks,* New York, 24 July 1995 (A/CONF.164/37).

adopting technical and conservation measures, as well as facilitating cooperative and governance arrangements between Member States to enable effective control and management of fisheries within that region.[14] Measures adopted by RFMOs are usually binding on Member States, but these countries do not always align with those fishing in the region. Other cooperative arrangements exist outside RFMOs and are sometimes focused on specific issues such as cooperation, monitoring and enforcement.[15] Together, these legal frameworks, and the national laws that implement them, address both species-based and area-based measures: licensing of fishing vessels, establishment of catch limits, protection of endangered species and closure of certain seasons and waters. Fisheries crimes are not normally a significant part of such regimes.

UNCLOS does not mention IUU fishing specifically. At the global level the FAO has taken the lead in addressing the problem under its mandate of eliminating food insecurity. The legal responses adopted by the FAO include 'soft law' at the international level with binding regulation mostly left to national governments to adopt at the domestic level; but again there has been little focus on criminal activities.[16] The most specific instrument is the FAO International Plan of Action to Prevent, Deter and Eliminate Illegal, Unreported and Unregulated Fishing (IPOA-IUU). It takes into account the special situation of developing countries (a matter of significant relevance to the Indo-Pacific) and includes principles such as the underlying goal of conservation and sustainable use of living natural resources, the necessity for comprehensive and integrated approaches, the use of phased implementation, as well as principles of transparency, non-discrimination, participation and coordination. It encourages flag, coastal, port and market states to adopt national plans of action that implement the IPOA-IUU and to work through appropriate RFMOs to prevent, deter and eliminate the problem.[17] Beyond its aim of eliminating illegal fishing, the IPOA-IUU does not address fisheries crime in a comprehensive way. Reference is made

14 Organisation for Economic Co-operation and Development, *Fishing For Development – Background Paper For Session 5: The Role Of Regional Fisheries Management Organisations (RFMOs)*, (TAD/FI(2014)11), (OECD 2014) <www.oecd.org/tad/events/fishing-for-development-2014-session-5-RFMOs.pdf>, para 25.

15 *Niue Treaty on Cooperation in Fisheries Surveillance and Law Enforcement in the South Pacific Region*, 9 July 1992, 32 ILM 1238 (1993), entered into force 20 May 1993.

16 For example, FAO 'Code of Conduct for Responsible Fisheries', adopted at the 28th Session of the FAO Conference, Rome, 31 October 1995. See also FAO, 'Agreement to Promote Compliance with International Conservation and Management Measure by Fishing Vessels on the High Seas', adopted at the 27th Session of the FAO Conference, 24 November 1993.

17 FAO, 'International Plan of Action to Prevent, Deter and Eliminate Illegal, Unreported and Unregulated Fishing (IPOA-IUU)', adopted 23 June 2001 at the 120th Session of the FAO Council. For a critique of the IPOA-IUU and its implementation see May Ann Palma 'Combatting IUU Fishing: International Legal Developments' in Quentin Hanich and Martin Tsamenyi (eds) *Navigating Pacific Fisheries: Legal and Policy Trends in the Implementation of International Fisheries Instruments in the Western Central Pacific Region* (ANCORS 2009) 71–103.

to the adoption of legislation that makes it a 'violation' to conduct a business or trade in IUU fishing products and that States should adopt measures to prohibit landings and transhipments of IUU fishing catches, but no recommended suite of criminal law options is included. Approaches at the international level are largely restricted to market- and trade-related measures.

IUU fishing is an issue significant enough to warrant global concern but the responses to date including those outlined above have not resulted in its elimination. When coupled with increasing involvement of transnational organised crime, and taking into account the environmental degradation and socio-economic harm it can cause, the need for enhanced and more effective responses is magnified. It is in this context that new perspectives and approaches must be explored.

Crime opportunity theory

There is little doubt that some IUU fishing is undertaken by otherwise legitimate fishers, but given that it is a low risk and high gain activity, increasingly it attracts transnational organised criminals as well.[18] IUU fishing is enabled by other criminal activities such as corruption, document fraud and money laundering and occurs alongside tax crimes, drug and people trafficking, forced labour and wildlife crime.[19] As McNulty has noted, this context provides a 'rich smorgasbord of opportunities for transnational organised crime to thrive and prosper'.[20] Every Indo-Pacific nation is a regional stakeholder and must play a role in keeping ocean areas free from criminal activity. Yet, existing laws, regulatory approaches and policing strategies have not been successful in reducing the scale of the problem. Therefore, ways must be identified to overcome obstacles that hinder the achievement of more positive outcomes and criminological theory is applied here with this aim.

Crime opportunity theory provides a valuable lens through which to explore the most effective methods and coordinated responses to control IUU fishing within the Indo-Pacific because it exposes underlying drivers. Crime opportunity theory provides that when there is a low risk of apprehension and opportunity for high gain, combined with a motivated offender and suitable environment, the likelihood of offending increases.[21] As with any criminological theory, the usefulness of crime opportunity theory may be challenged in the context of certain crimes or types of offending. Commonly, crime opportunity theory is

18 United Nations Office on Drugs and Crime, *Transnational Organized Crime In The Fishing Industry Focus on: Trafficking in Persons Smuggling of Migrants Illicit Drugs Trafficking* (UNODC 2011).

19 United Nations Office on Drugs and Crime, *Fisheries Crime* (UNODC 2016) <www.unodc.org/documents/about-unodc/Campaigns/Fisheries/Fisheries_Leaflet_PRINT.pdf>, 3–4.

20 McNulty (n 10) 146.

21 Ronald V Clarke 'Opportunity Makes the Thief. Really? And So What?' (2012) 1 *Crime Science: An Interdisciplinary Journal* 3.

tested against property crime, however, it has been used to explain various others, such as agricultural crime, organised crime, white collar crime and domestic violence.[22] Crime opportunity theory is well placed to explain IUU fishing, as it is useful in deconstructing elements that contribute to the reasons why offending occurs in a certain setting.

The rationale for the use of crime opportunity theory within this paper is to explain how the motivations of offenders, combined with other situational factors, expose the Indo-Pacific to maritime crimes and inform enhanced responses to IUU fishing. Environmental criminologists seek to understand why wrongdoing occurs in certain spaces by critically analysing crimes against relevant theory.[23] Although academic and government attention has been paid to legal and regulatory frameworks, little inter-disciplinary analyses have been undertaken that apply criminological theory to enhance the effectiveness of responses to IUU fishing. Explaining IUU fishing through crime opportunity theory and adopting responses to address gaps may therefore have a collateral effect on other crimes in the region.[24] For example, addressing the intentional and deceptive failure to adequately license vessels and to fish in restricted areas and for protected species, as well as the use of outlawed fishing gear and equipment, could have the effect of reducing unrelated maritime crimes that cause environmental harms and/or help weaken criminal networks engaged in the trade of other illicit products.

Crime opportunity theory pioneer, Ronald Clarke determined that

> [p]eople without pre-existing dispositions [to crime] can be drawn into criminal behaviour by a proliferation of criminal opportunities, and generally law-abiding people can be drawn into committing specific forms of crime if they regularly encounter easy opportunities for these crimes, especially in their occupations.[25]

22 See, for example, Daniel P Mears, Michelle L Scott and Avinash S Bhati, 'Opportunity Theory and Agricultural Crime Victimization' (2007) 72(2) *Rural Sociology* 151–184; Edward R Kleemans and Christianne J de Poot, 'Criminal Careers in Organized Crime and Social Opportunity Structure' (2008) 5(1) *European Journal of Criminology* 69–98; Michael L Benson, Tamara D Madensen and John E Eck 'White-Collar Crime from an Opportunity Perspective' in Sally S Simpson and David Weisburd (eds) *The Criminology of White-Collar Crime* (Springer 2009) 175–193; Rob T Guerette and Shannon A. Santana 'Explaining Victim Self-Protective Behavior Effects on Crime Incident Outcomes A Test of Opportunity Theory' (2010) 56(2) *Crime and Delinquency* 198–226.

23 See, for example, Gohar A Petrossian, 'Preventing Illegal, Unreported and Unregulated (IUU) Fishing: A Situational Approach', (2015) 189 *Biological Conservation* 39–48; Richard Wortley, Lorraine Mazerolle and Sacha Rombouts (eds) *Environmental Criminology and Crime Analysis* (Taylor & Francis 2008).

24 Marcus Felson and Ronald V Clarke, *Opportunity Makes the Thief: Practical Theory for Crime Prevention*, Police Research Series Paper 98, (Home Office Policing and Reducing Crime Unit 1998) 30.

25 Ronald V Clarke, 'Opportunity Makes the Thief. Really? And So What?' (2012) 1 *Crime Science: An Interdisciplinary Journal* 3.

Whilst this might explain some IUU fishing, evidence has emerged of the link between transnational organised crime and illegal fisheries; the scale and organisation of some of these enterprises is significant.[26] Criminal syndicates may have different motivations from opportunistic fishers. For example, with reducing supply and increasing demand and therefore higher prices for fish and seafood, criminals are motivated to engage in IUU fishing alongside other maritime criminal activities.[27] Again, by unpacking the motivators, better informed decisions can be made about legal responses.

The challenges of IUU fishing

As outlined above, IUU fishing encompasses illicit activities and those that are poorly managed, as well as activities and/or areas that are not regulated. Clearly, enhanced responses are needed and in some areas further regulation: for example, where there are gaps and unregulated areas and activities to be addressed. This chapter, however, focuses on fishing that violates, or at least disregards, existing international, regional and local fishing laws and regulations.

Applying crime opportunity theory, it can be seen that IUU fishing takes advantage of the vastness of the oceans and the hidden nature of activities which creates an environment where there is low risk of capture. Combined with this is the high market value of certain species. Although there is little solid data about which species are caught and in what proportions, analyses point to high value stocks, which may include lobster, shrimps, prawns, shark fin and blue fin tuna,[28] including low-volume resources such as abalone.[29] The high value of incidentally caught species, as well as the absence of guardianship at sea, and therefore the ability to yield additional catch without fear of sanction, may encourage IUU fishing. The difficulties of monitoring ocean activities and the market demand for certain species are not factors that law- and policy-makers can easily influence. Furthermore, even the best monitoring and enforcement focuses on the end result of IUU fishing, not its causes. Therefore, other elements articulated in crime opportunity theory, including factors that motivate offenders, must be explored.

Understanding the complex and many drivers for participation in IUU fishing is essential to developing a suitable response. The Pew Charitable Trusts note, '[i]llegal fishing is an economic crime driven by a growing world demand for fish and other seafood, and the globalization of the market'.[30] Criminals engage in IUU fishing for myriad reasons, but undoubtedly economic aims

26 United Nations Office on Drugs and Crime (n 18).
27 United Nations Office on Drugs and Crime (n 19), 3–4.
28 Agnew et al. (n 2) 3; McNulty (n 10) 147.
29 United Nations Office on Drugs and Crime (n 18) 3.
30 Pew Charitable Trusts, FAQ: Illegal, Unreported, and Unregulated Fishing' <www.pewtrusts.org/~/media/legacy/uploadedfiles/peg/publications/fact_sheet/iuufaqwebpdf.pdf> accessed 24 July 2018.

dominate.[31] Much like other crimes, greed, ease and profitability, weak governance, poor monitoring and enforcement all reportedly contribute to IUU fishing.[32]

A 2002 Australian Government report identified the following types of IUU fishers: the habitual or repeat offenders, the opportunists, and the ignorant.[33] While the majority of IUU fishers are organised criminals, some 'ignorant' or 'opportunistic' IUU fishers disregard the law to yield a larger catch or take advantage of regulatory gaps and poor law enforcement. Some IUU fishers are driven to do so as their livelihoods are under threat and they have few other economic opportunities.[34] Worst affected are destitute fishers and subsistence fishing communities heavily dependent on fishing for their livelihoods and as an important food source.[35] Historically, particularly for ignorant or opportunistic IUU fishers, when fish stocks were in abundance, illegal fishing was a low-risk, high-return activity. Even if caught, prosecution has been unlikely with low fines, compared to potential profits for selling illegally caught fish.[36] As fish stocks are coming under increasing pressure, greater attention has turned towards addressing these activities. In order to remove the motivation to offend it is therefore critical to improve weak governance, eradicate poverty, and provide sound economic policies including sustainable livelihood options.

Turning to the other group, it is most likely that 'habitual or repeat offenders' are highly organised.[37] Organised IUU fishers are more likely to deliberately target the vulnerable and most valuable species, and engage in other offences including 'environmental offences, theft, fraud, quarantine violation, tax evasion, and serious crime against people'.[38] Again, the solution must involve improved governance, as well as the eradication of corruption and underground economies.[39] International legal responses have sought to establish strong regulation, leading to sustainable and responsible fisheries. For example, flag, coastal, port and market state measures have been adopted in response to

31 Agnew et al. (n 2) 4; McNulty (n 10).

32 Teale N Phelps Bondaroff, Tuesday Reitano and Wietse van der Werf, *The Illegal Fishing and Organized Crime Nexus: Illegal Fishing as Transnational Organized Crime* (The Global Initiative Against Transnational Organized Crime and The Black Fish 2015) 22. Agnew et al. found a particularly strong link between IUU fishing and poor governance: Agnew et al. (n 2) 4.

33 Victorian Parliament Environment and Natural Resources Committee, *Inquiry into Fisheries Management: Second Report* (Parliament of Victoria 2002) <www.parliament.vic.gov.au/images/stories/Reports/VPARL1999-2002No166.pdf>, 244.

34 Mak (n 1) 2; Phelps Bondaroff et al. (n 32) 62.

35 United Nations Office on Drugs and Crime (n 18).

36 Pew Charitable Trusts, 'FAQ: Illegal, Unreported, and Unregulated Fishing' <www.pewtrusts.org/en/research-and-analysis/fact-sheets/2013/08/27/faq-illegal-unreported-and-unregulated-fishing> accessed 24 July 2018.

37 Victorian Parliament Environment and Natural Resources Committee (n 33) 243–245.

38 Phelps Bondaroff et al. (n 32) 37.

39 Mak (n 1) 2.

declining fish stocks in many regions of the world.[40] But IUU fishing involves disregard for existing laws, regulations, boundaries and marine life, and as such it is reasonable to assume that highly organised offenders also have a disregard for other seafaring rules and international laws. For example, they may operate under open registries, often referred to as flags of convenience. Open registries often operate out of developing countries seeking to gain market share of foreign investment by offering advantages for their shipping services. By flagging a vessel to an open registry, a shipowner minimises its fees payable to charter the vessel, making it cheaper with fewer formalities than registering a vessel to a developed nation.[41] Unscrupulous owners benefit from the anonymity provided by the open registry.[42]

Regardless of whether the fishers have alternative options, the lack of consequences due to weak monitoring and enforcement coupled with high profits renders IUU fishing an appealing option for those who otherwise do not have employment or engage in even higher risk activities, such as maritime piracy.[43] In recent years, despite an escalation in global awareness and effort to control IUU fishing, transnational organised criminals take advantage of weak governance and poor law enforcement at port and sea borders to engage in these activities alongside other maritime crimes.[44]

IUU fishing and transnational organised crime

It is clear that IUU fishing in the Indo-Pacific is a complex issue. While some illicit activities may be engaged in by otherwise legitimate fishers, the majority of IUU fishers are part of large transnational organised crime syndicates. Organised crime involves groups or syndicates acting in unison to commit serious crimes or offences for a material or financial benefit.[45] IUU fishing is a profitable, clandestine industry, with conditions that attract organised criminal syndicates. It is facilitated by the globalised nature of the fishing industry and freedom of the seas, which allows transnational mobility of vessels.[46] IUU fishing occurs alongside legitimate fisheries but relies on its organised illegitimate activities to enhance profitability and facilitate further criminal offending. IUU fishing 'entrepreneurs' take advantage of regions that lack effective governance, and where weak legal systems and few available resources exist to protect marine life or

40 FAO, 'Code of Conduct for Responsible Fisheries' (n 16); FAO 'Agreement on Port State Measures to Prevent, Deter and Eliminate Illegal, Unreported and Unregulated Fishing' (n 16).

41 Jade Lindley, *Somali Piracy: A Criminological Perspective* (Routledge 2016).

42 ITF Seafarers, '*Inside the Issues: Fisheries*' <www.itfseafarers.org/ITI-fisheries.cfm> accessed 7 September 2016.

43 Phelps Bondaroff et al. (n 32) 24.

44 United Nations Office on Drugs and Crime (n 18).

45 McNulty (n 10) 145.

46 Ibid.

borders; they target species with high market value, resulting in low risk of law enforcement and very high rewards.[47]

Transnational organised crime syndicates have 'structures, systems, communications, hierarchy and financial controls' around their operations.[48] Marine resources may be caught in the waters of one State, offloaded in another State or on the high seas, often for processing, exported to the market State and profits laundered to recipients in another State.[49] Furthermore, IUU fishing is often a cover for other illicit activities, frequently using the same routes, ports and corrupt border officials to evade interception.[50] Research suggests that frozen illegally caught fish may provide an effective cover to traffic other contraband, including wildlife and drugs.[51] There is global awareness of these interconnections, but despite the United Nations General Assembly committee on fisheries management and conservation meeting semi-annually since 1991, they only articulated their concern about the link between IUU fishing and organised crime in 2008.[52] Specifically, it noted:

> [C]oncerns about possible connections between international organized crime and illegal fishing in certain regions of the world, and encourages States, including through the appropriate international forums and organizations, to study the causes and methods of and contributing factors to illegal fishing to increase knowledge and understanding of those possible connections, and to make the findings publicly available, bearing in mind the distinct legal regimes and remedies under international law applicable to illegal fishing and international organized crime.[53]

This United Nations General Assembly Resolution clearly refers to the need to address the low risk of apprehension, but also recognises the importance of understanding underlying drivers. For example, reiterated in subsequent resolutions is the directive for 'States, in accordance with international law, to strengthen implementation of or, where they do not exist, adopt comprehensive monitoring, control and surveillance measures and compliance and enforcement schemes' to enhance the response to IUU fishing and related crimes.[54] Endorsed

47 Ibid. 146.
48 Ibid. 145.
49 United Nations Office on Drugs and Crime (n 18).
50 Ibid. 3.
51 UNODC (n 19), 11; Phelps Bondaroff et al. (n 32) 62.
52 United Nations General Assembly, 'Sustainable fisheries, including through the 1995 Agreement for the Implementation of the Provisions of the United Nations Convention on the Law of the Sea of 10 December 1982 Relating to the Conservation and Management of Straddling Fish Stocks and Highly Migratory Fish Stocks, and Related Instruments', A/RES/63/112 (5 December 2008), para 59.
53 Ibid. para 59.
54 Ibid. para 60.

by the United Nations General Assembly as an issue of great concern, Member States are charged with the responsibility to act and explore all motivators including those beyond poor governance, surveillance and enforcement.

The coexistence of IUU fishing and forced labour

Declining catches and therefore reduced profits means fishers and fishing companies seek out cost-cutting methods. A transnational organised crime requires a string of accomplices to facilitate it. In the first instance, IUU fishing requires a crew willing to fish for illegal catches. Invariably, the organised criminals do not undertake these activities themselves, but rather others, often trafficked onto the vessel, are forced to work for little or no money. Forced labour involves coercion to work through violence or intimidation, accumulated debt, retention of identity papers or threats to inform immigration authorities[55] and often involves desperate people facing poverty being sold, smuggled or trafficked into working for long periods at sea. Because fishing vessels operate offshore, the slave labour aboard these vessels is difficult to monitor, just as IUU fishing is hidden.

This factor has emerged as a growing concern in IUU fishing over the last decade. Although abolished in the nineteenth century, slavery is still present in developing and developed countries in various forms.[56] Estimates reveal that 20 million people work in conditions involving coercion with around 68 per cent in forced labour.[57] Modern-day slavery involves restricted movement, control of personal belongings and lack of fully informed consent. Forced labour at sea involves workers who have no choices, no means of escape and must work under extreme conditions for little or no pay; this essentially amounts to slavery.[58]

Forced and unpaid labour is often found alongside IUU fishing and therefore facilitates its existence. Fishers, generally migrants, may willingly agree to work aboard the vessel, however, the conditions they are exposed to daily defy international labour and human rights standards. In the Asia Pacific, the fishing sector accounts for 53 per cent of all forced labour in that region.[59] Extensive

55 International Labour Organization, 'The meanings of forced labour', March 2014 <www.ilo.org/global/topics/forced-labour/news/WCMS_237569/lang–en/index.htm>.

56 The Walk Free Foundation, 'Global Slavery Index 2014', (Hope for Children Organization Australia Ltd 2015) <www.walkfreefoundation.org/news/resource/the-global-slavery-index-2014/> acccessed 24 July 2018

57 MBA Central 'The Business of Modern Day Slavery', <www.mbacentral.org/business-modern-day-slavery/> accessed 13 March 2016.

58 International Labour Organization, 'Forced Labour in Fishing: How Big is the Problem?' (International Labour Organization 2015) http://www.ilo.org/global/about-the-ilo/newsroom/features/WCMS_429031/lang–en/index.htm; International Labour Organization 'Fishing and Aquaculture', (International Labour Organization 2012) http://www.ilo.org/ipec/areas/Agriculture/WCMS_172419/lang–en/index.htm.

59 Walk Free (n 56) 53.

global research provides countless examples of poor conditions.[60] The 2016 Global Slavery Index noted the

> abuse of migrant workers on fishing vessels, often young men and boys, who have endured brutal treatment including physical abuse, excessive and inhumane working hours, sleep and food deprivation, forced use of methamphetamines, and face being thrown overboard if they become ill or injured.[61]

Workers kept at sea for years at a time support South East Asia's US$7 billion annual exports fishing trade.[62] Using low or unpaid workers ensure organised criminal leaders pocket greater profits, but it can also be a motivator in itself.

Again the international community has responded with the International Labour Organization adopting the Maritime Labour Convention in 2006. Although this treaty came into force in 2013 only 80 States have signed it and Indonesia, for example, is not amongst them.[63] The 2007 ILO Convention Concerning Work in the Fishing Sector (Work in Fishing Convention) sets standards for commercial fishing industry workers, but only attracted enough signatories to enter into force on 16 November 2017. Legal responses to IUU fishing can only be successful if a sufficient number of States adopt and implement them. This leads to the issue of what drives governments to respond to the enablers that facilitate IUU fishing.

Motivations of states in controlling IUU fishing

Whilst most States have adopted some form of fisheries regulation, responses to IUU fishing are more piecemeal, with fisheries crimes being particularly poorly legislated and enforced. Logistically, policing the Indo-Pacific is a monumental challenge for any one nation. Under UNCLOS, each littoral State is required to control activities in its territorial waters (up to 12 nautical miles from land) and exclusive economic zone (EEZ) (between 12 and 200 nautical miles).[64] Beyond these areas no one State has policing authority, in line with the freedom of the

60 Ibid.; Environmental Justice Foundation, 'Seafood not slavefood' <http://ejfoundation.org/campaigns/oceans/item/seafood-not-slavefood>.

61 Erika Techera and Jade Lindley, 'Curtailing Maritime Crime: Countries should look at multinational approaches to regulating and limiting illegal fishing, trafficking, smuggling and other sea crimes' (Indo-Asia-Pacific Defense Forum 5 December 2016) <http://apdf-magazine.com/curtailing-maritime-crime/>; Walk Free (n 56).

62 Esther Htusan and Margie Mason 'More than 2,000 Enslaved Fishermen Rescued in Six Months' (Associated Press, 17 September 2015) <http://bigstory.ap.org/article/ceecf8df237e49bf8fe59d47fa3515b0/more-2000-enslaved-fishermen-rescued-6-months> accessed 24 July 2018.

63 International Labour Organization, 'Ratifications of Maritime Labour Convention 2006' <www.ilo.org/dyn/normlex/en/f?p=NORMLEXPUB:11300:0::NO::p11300_instrument_id:312331> 24 July 2018.

64 UNCLOS, Articles 3 and 57.

high seas doctrine.[65] However, flag States are encouraged to work within RFMOs and cooperate through them in managing fisheries on the high seas.

As noted above, international efforts have largely been developed under the auspices of the FAO. The motivator in that regard is addressing food security with the FAO empowered to collect data and provide assistance to States to that end. The IPOA-IUU is a targeted instrument focused on addressing this specific problem. Its adoption and widespread endorsement demonstrates that States are motivated, but the translation into national plans of action and binding domestic legislation has been much poorer. At the domestic level each State within the Indo-Pacific has its own legal system and regulatory frameworks and these may or may not align with neighbouring states, making harmonised responses to the IPOA-IUU challenging. Again the international community has responded in an effort to provide more coordination. The FAO Port State Measures Agreement, which permits port States to monitor and seek compliance with fisheries regulations within national waters and on the high seas, has recently come into force having attracted sufficient signatories.-[66] The endorsement of this document does indicate further support for harmonised regulatory measures, but by themselves these measures can only prevent landings of excess catch or prohibited species and do not identify where a species has been caught and therefore they can only ever address part of the problem.

In terms of regional fisheries management, a number of multilateral RFMOs operate in the Indo-Pacific. Despite some efforts to create a level of cohesion across the region, fragmentation between the States prevents seamless compliance with, for example, vessel registrations, tracking equipment, monitoring and enforcement. Each State in the region has varying political will, and motivations and levels of participation in counter-IUU fishing efforts.

Outside RFMOs there have been other collaborative responses to IUU fishing. For example, several Eastern Africa states bordering the Western Indian Ocean have developed a multilateral collaborative response, FISH-i Africa.[67] The marine resources in this region provide a vital source food and jobs, supporting local economies. Unsustainable activities motivated the collaborative response to protect the marine environment and economies destroyed by criminals who undermine legitimate industry.[68] The joint operation between the eight participating nations – Comoros, Kenya, Madagascar, Mauritius, Mozambique, Seychelles, Somalia and Tanzania – increases capability unachievable by each individual nation.[69] The FISH-i Africa task force progresses the goals of the collective, including information sharing. Task Force countries share information and

65 UNCLOS, Article 87.

66 As at 14 November 2016, the FAO Port State Measures Agreement had 47 signatories: FAO, 'Agreement on Port State Measures to Prevent, Deter and Eliminate Illegal, Unreported and Unregulated Fishing, Adopted 22 November 2009 at the 36th Session (12/2009)' <www.fao.org/fileadmin/user_upload/legal/docs/037s-e.pdf>.

67 FISH-i Africa, *Why FISH-i Africa?* <www.fish-i-africa.org/about/why-fish-i-africa/>.

68 Ibid.

69 Ibid.

intelligence on flagged and licensed fishing vessels operating in their fishing zones and ports to help identify and intercept illegal operators.[70] The potential expansion of the program to include other Indo-Pacific nations is dependent on political will, effective working relations and territorial disputes between potential participants like Japan, China, Taiwan and Vietnam.[71]

The success in developing positive and effective working relationships is the first step to controlling IUU fishing. Some other bi- and multilateral relationships exist in the Indo-Pacific, in particular, between the United States and several small Pacific Islands.[72] These collaborations are mutually beneficial to States involved, strengthening trading and security partnerships.[73] Once a regional platform is harnessed, options to trial innovative solutions to IUU fishing are possible. Further research is necessary to explore the viability and legal boundaries of using autonomous and remote unmanned technologies to monitor activities and gather data across thousands of square kilometres of high seas.

Motivators to respond to IUU fishing may depend on the perceived benefit for a participating State. As explored above, food security appears to be one such driver and opportunities provided by the blue economy is another significant motivator to participate. The blue economy concept involves balancing wealth that can be obtained from the oceans with protection and sustainable management of resources. Both consumptive and non-consumptive utilisation is envisaged combined with conservation. It has been said that '[t]he blue economy concept has the potential to act as a key driver of sustainable development and political stability through the Indo-Pacific region'[74] and indeed it has been incorporated into a number of politico-economic agenda. The Seychelles and Mauritius, for example, have both implemented marine policies based on the blue economy concept, which demonstrates its ability to potentially play a harmonising role and perhaps drive renewed efforts to address IUU fishing upon which it depends.[75]

70 Ibid.

71 Natasha Howells, 'Can Seychelles Anti-Illegal Fishing Initiatives be Replicated Elsewhere?' (*Future Directions International*, 2 July 2014) <www.futuredirections.org.au/publication/can-seychelles-anti-illegal-fishing-initiatives-be-replicated-elsewhere/>.

72 United States Department of State, 'U.S. Relations with Fiji' (*Bureau of East Asian and Pacific Affairs*, 9 February 2015) <www.state.gov/r/pa/ei/bgn/1834.htm>; James Hurndell, 'The Value of Ship Rider Agreements in the Pacific' (*Center for Strategic and International Studies*, 10 December 2014) <http://cogitasia.com/the-value-of-ship-rider-agreements-in-the-pacific/>; United States Department of State, 'U.S. Policy in the Pacific Islands' (29 September 2010) <https://2009-2017.state.gov/p/eap/rls/rm/2010/09/148318.htm>.

73 Ibid.

74 Anthony Bergin, 'Australia–Japan Cooperation in the Indian Ocean Blue Economy' paper presented at the National Security College Indo-Pacific Maritime Security Conference: Challenges & Cooperation <http://docplayer.net/40121779-Australia-japan-cooperation-in-the-indian-ocean-blue-economy.html>.

75 Ibid.

Analysis

Fisheries regulation operates to provide a foundation of rules and processes for legitimate fishers. It has been used as the predominant tool to address IUU fishing but has had a sub-optimal effect because it does not adequately address the high value of fish stocks (although some trade-based measures are in place), low risk (monitoring and criminal enforcement) or motivated offenders (what causes the person to engage in criminal activity). Increasing this type of regulation is unlikely to solve the problem and can have unintended consequences on subsistence and traditional fishing by introducing greater regulatory burdens. Furthermore, too much regulation can disincentivise compliance and therefore other levers must be found to address the issues.

Crime opportunity theory requires a motivated offender combined with high likelihood of reward and low risk of apprehension. An offender may be motivated primarily by economic gain, but also availability of other elements that support IUU fishing, in particular corruption and lax regulatory enforcement at several points along the supply chain. The ability to engage with corrupt officials may be a facilitating motivator for criminals. Most commonly, IUU fishing is enabled by vessels flagged to open registries, using the opportunity of transhipment, or mixing illegal with legal catches at sea, using ports of convenience, and tax havens.[76] Each of these methods intends to disregard or in some way evade controls in place that protect marine resources, promote fair market share and provide the relevant State with revenue. Not only must direct motivators be addressed but also facilitators of IUU fishing including forced labour and other issues explored in this chapter. It is clear though that there are other relevant enablers that have not yet been explored; for example, maritime insurers are not addressing IUU fishing and research indicates 'some IUU vessels are covered by marine insurance'.[77]

The issue of low risk of apprehension is a very real one. This chapter identifies a number of challenges in achieving effective oceans monitoring, control, and surveillance, to ensure human and food security in the region including the vastness of the Indo-Pacific region. Furthermore, reliance on regional neighbours to coordinate responses can be difficult, given the different political contexts and relationships, economic drivers, presence of corruption, and weaknesses in governance including the rule of law.

Lucrative fishing grounds are accessible illegally and strengthened government efforts will provide protection for them. Improved and enhanced policing capabilities can be achieved by combining technology and regional cooperative arrangements to remotely monitor the vast region and reduce opportunities for clandestine offending. Further research is needed into these technologies. In

76 Bondaroff et al. (n 32) 3.

77 Dana Miller, U Rashid Sumaila, Duncan Copeland, Dirk Zeller, Baris Soyer, Theodora Nikaki, George Leloudas, Stig T Fjellberg, Rebecca Singleton and Daniel Pauly, 'Cutting a Lifeline to Maritime Crime: Marine Insurance and IUU fishing' (2016) 14(7) *Frontiers in Ecology and the Environment* 357–362.

addition, bi- and multilateral patrol arrangements, such as shiprider agreements, can also supplement capacity.

The high value that can be achieved for some protected stocks can be addressed in part by the Port State Measures Agreement that seeks to harmonise approaches to landings at different port facilities. Labelling and consumer awareness initiatives can also place pressure on illegitimate fisheries. Therefore, increasing transparency about maritime crimes among consumers, in particular IUU fishing, is essential to encourage informed choices and sustainable purchases.

Whilst some otherwise legitimate fishers may be engaged in IUU fishing and criminals engaging in fishing-based crimes are opportunistic, increasingly they are organised. What drives these people into fishery crimes? In part, it is the availability of other assets that enhance profitability including the availability of flags of convenience, and free and low cost labour. In particular, consideration should be given to peripheral risk factors on land and at sea that increase the likelihood of trafficking in persons and forced and low cost labour. Finally, further work is needed to better understand how transnational organised criminal syndicates facilitate IUU fishing and other enabling crimes (such as trafficking in persons) and what motivates them to do so.

Conclusion

IUU fishing occurs throughout the world but is particularly prevalent in the Indo-Pacific region where vast ocean areas, weak governance and lack of capacity hamper monitoring and enforcement. Fishing-based crime increases the vulnerability of species, placing pressure on the natural environment and ultimately food and economic security. Analysing IUU fishing from a theoretical viewpoint facilitates richer insights into ways in which it may be controlled. Crime opportunity theory has provided a useful lens through which to deconstruct motivators that encourage organised criminals to engage in IUU fishing.

This chapter has exposed drivers leading offenders to commit IUU fishing in the Indo-Pacific and peripheral issues that enable its continuation. Applying crime opportunity theory to bring a theoretical understanding to the causes can be useful in devising more effective responses adoptable across the region. In the long term though, developing specific regional solutions to the Indo-Pacific issues is likely to have the greatest permanent and sustainable benefit. Framing IUU fishing as a national security issue has gone some way in encouraging States to commit resources to the problem. However, as Rahman points out, there are limits to maritime cooperation in certain contexts.[78] He points to physical geography of the region being a challenge and although there are examples of

78 Chris Rahman, 'The Limits to Maritime Security Collaboration in the Indo-Pacific Region' paper presented at the National Security College Indo-Pacific Maritime Security Conference: Challenges & Cooperation <http://ro.uow.edu.au/lhapapers/2887/>.

collaborative initiatives[79] maritime boundary disputes hamper joint enforcement arrangements.

The solutions appear to lie in multi-faceted responses.[80] It is clear that multiple legal frameworks address different aspects of IUU fishing across a number of subfields.[81] The above analysis demonstrates that by applying crime opportunity theory it can be seen that there are an equal number of motivators to engage in IUU fishing, and in order to ensure the root causes are addressed, it is necessary to 'frame maritime crimes in a wider perspective'.[82] Therefore, responses must be multi-faceted including improving governance, increasing cooperation and reducing economic incentives as well as removing enablers such as forced labour.

79 For example, the Southeast Asia Maritime Security Initiative: ibid. 42.
80 Ibid. 43, who points to the need for maritime security cooperation to be pursued on multiple paths.
81 For example, law of the sea, fisheries regulation, labour law, maritime and shipping regulation and environmental and natural resources law.
82 Mak (n 1) 2.

Index

Page numbers in *italics* denote an illustration, **bold** a table, n indicates an endnote

For Product Safety Concerns and Information please contact our EU representative GPSR@taylorandfrancis.com Taylor & Francis Verlag GmbH, Kaufingerstraße 24, 80331 München, Germany